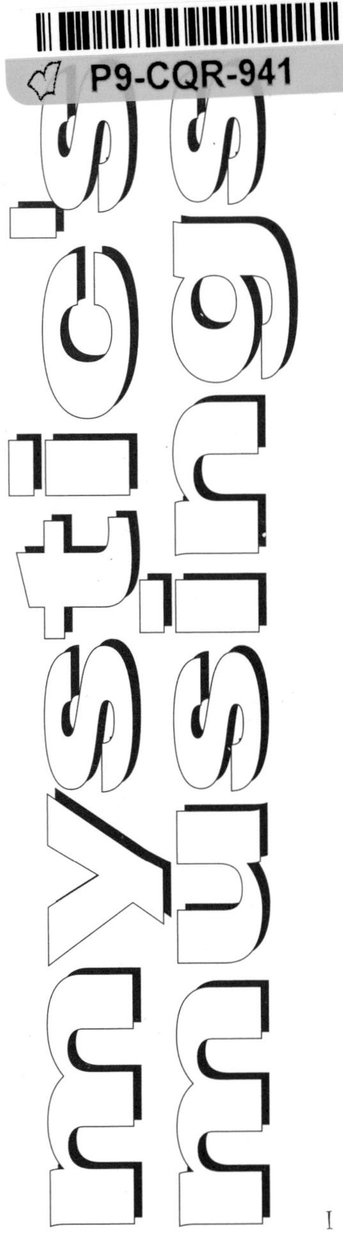
P9-CQR-941
mystic's
musings

The ascending snake denotes the human aspiration for the Divine. The downward pointing triangle denotes the facilitation of the descent of the Divine. The sun and the moon on either sides of the triangle represent that which is beyond duality. Sadhguru used powerful means to facilitate the descent of the Divine to fulfill the consecration of the Dhyanalinga - a glorious process of descendance of the Divine.

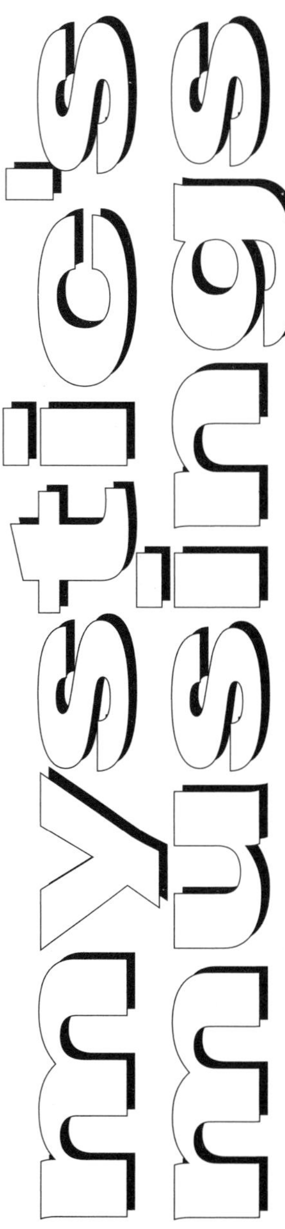

a Profound Mystic of our times

Mystic's Musings

ISBN 81-86685-59-6

First Edition: July 2003
First Reprint: June 2004
21st Reprint : October 2015

Cover design, photographs, typesetting, book layout and compilation done by: The Archives of IshaYoga Center

Published by :

Isha Foundation
15,Govindasamy Naidu Layout
Singanallur, Coimbatore - 641005 INDIA

Phone: +91-422-2515345
E-Mail:info@ishafoundation.org

₹ 295.00

Introduction

Even at a time when there is great versatility in people's understanding of the word *spiritual*, it is hard to fit Sadhguru into the category of a Spiritual Master in an established sense of the word. If you think he is someone who walks on water, who materializes things out of thin air, reads people's minds, looks into a crystal ball and tells people what they did and what they ought to do, you are in for a surprise. And if you think not, you are in for a bigger surprise!

For those of us who have had the good fortune of being a witness to all the contradictions, paradoxes, compassion and Grace - sparks and thunders apart - from a million other things that he is, attempting to describe him is certainly not an enviable task. Yet, the possibilities and promises for the layman and the world, in this most blessed phenomenon of our time are so rich and plenty that it would indeed be criminal to not make an attempt, however clumsy.

I first met Sadhguru sixteen years ago, when I had just finished my schooling and was in college. A particular teacher in my school had enthralled us to seek a spiritual master - actually the more sacred version of it - a *Guru* - and be initiated by him, like he himself was. My imagination, fired by books like The *Autobiography of a Yogi* and other similar works led me to yearn for a similar esoteric opportunity. For a couple of years, the picture of a sagely being with a long, flowing, grey beard sitting under a banyan tree and teleporting a handful of disciples into the other worlds was deeply imprinted in me.

So, when I first met this clean-shaven, blue jeans and T-shirt clad man speaking flawless English and riding a motorcycle, as Sadhguru was in those days, I did not in the least think that I had met the Guru. However, the forty minutes that I spent in his introductory talk temporarily distracted me from the sage under the tree and made me look forward to his teachings and practices with the hope that it would help my near-sightedness and my studies - my most pressing problems then.

As years passed, and I got to spend a little more time with this person, unknown to me, bit by bit, little things in me began to align and orient themselves to seek the higher realms of knowing and living and to not settle for the mundane and the mediocre. Ever since then, in scarcely detectable ways, undeterred by my own undoings, Sadhguru's Grace and unseen hands continue to transform my life, taking me beyond my limitations to a destination unknown and undreamt of.

To find a real Guru, a true Guru, or the best Guru, is the most common Quest of the seeker. Especially in this culture, where the spectrum of spirituality spans from the devout to the atheist, from the pious to the *aghoras* - the gory and the unsightly, from the ascetic to the emperor, from the selfless, industrious karma yogis to the academic Vedantins; obviously, getting one's prescription right is of paramount importance.

Sadhguru's response to the predicament has been, "You cannot choose a Guru. Deepen your longing and the Guru will choose you," - a reality from his own life.

Sadhguru's ways are very unorthodox, if not wild, totally devoid of conformity and other tell-tale marks of one who has been through the *garadi*[1] of a Guru. So it was only natural to assume that Sadhguru evolved by himself, an example that one wished to emulate. Sadhguru takes utmost care as to how he deals with each person he encounters. Somewhat like the famous saint who threw a volley of stones at the visitors to his ashram taking care that not one stone ever hit anybody, Sadhguru's abrasive ways have always fostered growth. Yet being with such a person meant there was no knowing what could happen next. This always kept us on tenterhooks.

So one morning, at a sathsang in the ashram when Sadhguru spoke for the first time about his Guru who graced him three lifetimes ago and the Dhyanalinga, the reactions were mixed. For many, it was reaffirmation of their secret belief and wish of Sadhguru being connected to a sacred and ancient lineage of Masters, but for clumsy novices like myself who were bumped and bounced often on this roller coaster ride with him, it was like an insurance policy. "Despite his wild ways," I distinctly remember thinking, "this man is actually accountable ..."

Of all the wonderful traits of Sadhguru, the one that endears him to one and all is that of being a friend. As one who abhors the seriousness that people on the spiritual path often get into, Sadhguru often imparts the most profound teaching with utmost nonchalance. His uncanny sense of humor not only delivers the message, but also gives the seeker the much-needed break from the monotony that often sets in.

---

1 *garadi*: a traditional school of physical culture. The ever watchful Guru of the *garadi* carefuly molds the character of the disciple before imparting the training that will empower him with untold physical powers.

To a disciple who lamented in a poem that he sought to become an eagle in the sky, but only managed to become a hen looking up to the eagle, pat came the reply:

'The hen that you are, how will you know what deceptive ways Grace will descend.
It is Grace that br ought you here and it is Grace that will deliver:

I prefer the hen that looks up to the sky than an eagle that flies but always looking down.

How high is not the question, but how intense is your longing for the sky .

May you always be in Grace.

- Sadhguru

To print in the form of a book the Master's words about the sacred, spoken to carefully prepared disciples and to make it available to the uninitiated and the indifferent alike is definitely a sacrilege at Isha, where 'live transmission of the experience' is the mantra.

However, this book is not to create another mirage in the harsh deserts of life, but to spread the sacred fragrance of bounty and abundance of the presence of an Oasis of a Living Master and an invitation for one and all to come, drink, dive and dissolve into it. Those of us who have been blessed by being involved in making this book happen bow down in gratitude to Sadhguru for enabling us to make this priceless offering to the world.

In the history and the lore we have heard of many Blessed beings who strive to enlighten the world in their own ways. Some from the solitude of the mountains, some from their palaces, some from their hermitages, some in the battlefields and some in the marketplace. Sadhguru, whose abode once was the peaks of the Velliangiri Mountains, in a symbolism that is true of His own life and work, now has descended to the foothills to inspire and infuse the seeking into the beings of the plains.

At a time when we are overwhelmed by the innumerable calls all around by leaders of sorts exhorting the masses to follow them, these verses from a poem by Sadhguru summarize what is typical of Him:

. . . I was born like you, I eat like you,
sleep like you and I will die like you
but the limited has not limited me
life's bondages have not bound me
as the dance of life progresses
this space, this unboundedness has become
unbearably sweet

become love and reach out
become me!

- Swami Nisarga

Note to the Reader

This work is a collection of the words of wisdom of the Master spoken to close disciples over a period of ten years at various occasions and settings. Covering the topics that he seldom addresses otherwise in the public, these words were spoken to foster the growth of those few who had the good fortune of being with him for a long time.

To the casual reader, it can shock, provoke, amuse. intrigue and entertain, but when approached with the openness and innocence of the one who seeks, it can start a powerful process within - a journey and a pilgrimage into the very core of Existence.

In an effort to reproduce the words of the Master in their original form, words and expressions from Sanskrit and other Indian languages used extensivey by the Master are retained as such and described in the glossary at the end of the book.

Short poems by Sadhguru adorn each chapter of the book and Swami Nisarga writes the brief introductions that follow, as well as the afterword. In presenting this priceless work we hope you will be able to be one with the Master and His Grace.

Namasthe.

Contents

Chapter - 1

Seeker's Predicament

Seeker's Predicament

From muses and mystics you did hear
Seeming to be the sounds of phantom lands

In ignorance's bind, life like phantom seems
Oh, creatures of surface, the depths of life will you ever seek.

– Sadhguru

Sadhguru. In His presence, even the uninitiated go into explosive states of meditation.

The adventurous one. *Sadhguru, ever willing for adventure has had a hand in every form of sport that one can think of; from motorcycling to hang gliding, rafting to skydiving.*

Knowing not where he comes from, knowing not where he is bound, the seeker's predicament is indeed pathetic. Trapped in layers of ignorance that bind more tightly than any cement or concrete, the seeker's pain is known only to those who have lived it.

Starting his journey from an obscure point in evolution, where life chooses to bestow awareness and conscious seeking in him, the seeker is confronted with a plethora of choices and uncertainties on the path. Without proper guidance and the necessary Grace, like a rudderless boat, the seeker goes in endless circles in a boundless ocean, alternately chasing some glimmer of light on the horizon and plugging those self-destructive leaks his ignorance keeps punching into himself.

Like a solitary shepherd in the mountains, lovingly resting his flock under the moonlit skies between two hard days of a long journey, whose course and outcome are known only to him, these interactions with the Master reflect a rare kind of intimacy, understanding and compassion that spring from the Master's deep urge to share and deliver.

He knows that the kindness, the insights and the wisdom, which he so generously shares, soothe the bruises and the wounds of the day and firm up the resolve of the flock to walk with him one more day. Thus, day after day, the Master charms his flock, infusing an ethereal lightness into those he can, while numbing the pain and biding his time with those he cannot.

Seeker: Sadhguru, as I walk this path, I am becoming aware of the many fears and insecurities I have within me. How do I leave these behind and move ahead?

Sadhguru: You don't have to leave your fears and insecurities because they don't really exist. You keep creating them unconsciously. If you don't create them, they don't really exist. Why you create them and how to stop creating them, that's your question. The fundamental reason why fear has arisen in you is – one way of looking at it is – in this vast existence of which you don't know the beginning or the end, you're just a little human being. Being the small entity that you are right now, naturally fear is there. It's overwhelming; there is fear and insecurity about what will happen to you.

As long as you're identified as a physical body, as long as your experience of life is limited to your physical and mental faculties, fear and insecurity are inevitable. It's just that different people may be at different levels of fear and insecurity. Today, if your life is happening well, you might have forgotten your insecurity. Tomorrow, if your life is turned upside down, you will be reminded because it's always within you. Only when a person begins to experience himself beyond the limitations of his physical body and mind, then this person can become free from insecurity and fear.

Experiencing yourself beyond the physical is what we're referring to as spiritual. When I say spiritual, don't think it is about going to a temple. Don't think it is about praying for this or that. If you look at your prayers, ninety-five percent of the prayers in the world are all about either asking for something, fundamentally asking for protection, or for being taken care of. There's nothing spiritual about it; it is plain basic survival. In most people, the very basis of prayer is fear and insecurity. If prayer exists in your life as an act only, it is obscene, being reverential towards one aspect and not being so to everything else. If you become prayerful, that's wonderful, and if you're using an act of prayer towards becoming that quality, that's fine. Now if you're routing your survival through the heavens, that's very stupid; even worms and insects take care of their own survival. So when I say spiritual, I am talking about you beginning to experience that which is not physical. Once this spiritual dimension is alive, once you start experiencing yourself beyond the limitations of the physical and the mental, only then there's no such thing as fear. Fear is just the creation of an overactive and out-of-control mind.

Seeker: But Sadhguru, isn't it very natural and human to become anxious when things don't go the way we expect them to?

Sadhguru: Why are you making all your incapabilities natural and human? Now if a few things aren't going smoothly in my life and if I don't become anxious about them, if I retain my sense of balance and continue to do what I have to do, would you call me inhuman? Is that what you're saying? When things aren't going the way you want them to go, that's when your capability is most needed. When you become anxious, do you become more capable or less capable? Less capable, isn't it? When you most need your capability, you're forsaking it; would you call that an intelligent way to act? So what you're saying is to live unintelligently is human; that's a very wrong idea. To live intelligently is what being human is all about.

Seeker: Much of the anxiety I experience comes through my relationships. Isn't it reasonable to expect some understanding from other people?

Sadhguru: When you live in this world, there are various types of complex interactions happening. As your field of play increases, the complexity of interaction also goes on increasing. If you're just sitting in a cubicle, working on your computer with only one other person, you need only a little understanding; but if you're managing a thousand people, you need a vast understanding of everybody. Now suppose you're managing a thousand people and you want all these people to understand you, then you're not going to manage anything. You need to understand the limitations and the capabilities of these thousand people and do what you can; only then will you have the power to move the situation the way you want it to go. If you're waiting for these thousand people to understand you and act, it is only a pipe dream; it's never going to happen.

The Silent Revolution of Self Realization. An evening sathsang with Sadhguru, in South India, draws over 100,000 people from all walks of life.

Seeker: Suppose somebody is in a close relationship with me and is very important to me. Shouldn't I expect better understanding from them?

Sadhguru: That's the point; the closer the relationship is, the more effort you should make to understand them, but that's not what's happening in your case, Ram. It so happened, once there was a man who had been slipping in and out of a coma for several months, with his wife staying at his bedside night and day. When he came to, in those few moments of consciousness, he motioned for her to come closer. As she sat beside him, he said, "I've been thinking…you have been with me through all the bad times in my life. When I got fired, you were there to support me. When my business went down the tubes, you were there working overtime and doing night shifts. When I got shot you were by my side. When we lost the house in that legal clash, you were right there beside me. Now my health is failing, and you're still by my side.

Of the Mountains. *With a vision of the mountains in His eyes ever since His childhood, a trek to the mountains is an essential part of His life and sharing.*

Now when I consider all this, I think you only bring me bad luck!" This is exactly what you're doing to yourself and to your relationships. Somebody becomes closer and dearer to you only as you understand them better. If they understand you, they enjoy the closeness of the relationship. If you understand them better, then you enjoy the closeness.

Seeker: This is easier said than done. It is difficult to always be there...

Sadhguru: See, it's not that the other person is totally bereft of understanding. With your understanding you can create situations where the other person would be able to understand you better. If you're expecting the other to understand and comply with you all the time while you don't understand the limitations, the possibilities, the needs and the capabilities of that person, then conflict is all that will happen; it is bound to happen. Unfortunately, the closest relationships in the world have more conflict going on than there is between India and Pakistan. India and Pakistan have fought only three battles.

In your relationships, you have fought many more battles than this and are still fighting; isn't it so? This is because your line of understanding and theirs is different. If you cross this L.O.C., this Line of Control, they will get mad. If they cross it, you will get mad. If you move your understanding beyond theirs, their understanding also becomes a part of your understanding. You will be able to embrace their limitations and capabilities. In everyone, there are some positive things and some negative things. If you embrace all this in your understanding, you can make the relationship the way you want it. If you leave it to their understanding, it will become accidental. If they are very magnanimous, things will happen well for you; if not, the relationship will break up.

All I am asking is: do you want to be the one who decides what happens to your life? Whether they are close relationships, professional, political, global or whatever, don't you want to be the person who decides what happens in your life? If you do, you better include everything and everybody into your understanding. You should enhance your understanding to such a point that you can look beyond people's madness also. There are very wonderful people around you, but once in a while they like to go crazy for a few minutes. If you don't understand that, you will lose them. If you don't understand their madness, you will definitely lose them. If you do, then you know how to handle them. Life is not always a straight line; you have to do many things to keep it going. If you forsake your understanding, your capability will be lost. Whether it's a question of personal relationships or professional management, in both places you need understanding; otherwise, you won't have fruitful relationships.

Seeker: Talking specifically about the work situation, there's a company we have been approaching for business and they're taking their own sweet time in letting us know if we've got the deal. It's extremely frustrating and de-motivating. I'm tempted to just curse the client and move on. Now if our understanding encompasses the client's difficulties, we may be more at peace, but wouldn't that dull the edge we need to pursue and close the deal?

Sadhguru: If you really want the best deals in life, don't try to make deals. You must be in such a way that your client should fall in love with you in every way. This is not a trick. The deal will happen if it's necessary; it won't happen if it's not. The deal is for both people's well-being, so it must be needed by both of you. Once we live in the world, there are transactions. Some are of a personal nature, others are different.

All of them affect your life. Whether you talk to a taxi driver for a minute, or you talk to your boss, or speak to your client, husband, wife or child; every transaction is affecting your life. Now the problem with you is that you hold one transaction above the other. You involve yourself more with one and less with the other. It won't work like that. All these things are needed for you to have a fruitful life. Why don't you just fall in love with the whole situation? As long as you wish to be in that situation, make it happen like a huge love affair. Why not? That's how it should be. Only then work becomes effortless. What is it you're calling a love affair? It's unconditional involvement and doing whatever is needed. If you don't have that sense of involvement, you will always try to get the best deal out of somebody. That means you must meet the dumbest people in the world. Intelligent people will never bite your dumb deals. There once was this almost confirmed bachelor who for months had been pursuing an attractive lady and became her most devoted admirer. At long last he collected sufficient courage to ask her the most momentous of all questions. "There are quite a lot of advantages to being a bachelor," he began, "but there comes a time when one longs for the companionship of another being. A being who will regard one as perfect, as an idol to be worshiped and treated as one's absolute own, who will be kind and faithful when times are tough and hard, who will share one's joys and sorrows." To his delight he saw a sympathetic gleam in her eyes. She nodded in agreement and then said, "I think it's a great idea! Can I help you choose which puppy to buy?"

So do you see that for you to make a deal, you should only meet people who are more stupid than you? If you meet people who are more intelligent than you, there's no way to get the deal to your advantage. If you just give yourself and see how both of you can be benefited from the deal, then whenever it is possible, it will happen. Of course, deals are subject to many other conditions such as market situations, economic conditions or the world situation, but if you establish your inner way of being and are doing the best you can do, then what has to happen, according to your capability, will happen. What you can't do won't happen anyway. Even if you break your head it won't happen, but that's okay. You need not be a super human being capable of doing everything. If you don't do what you're capable of doing, that's when it's not okay, that's when you have failed. So don't worry about always pulling off deals, deals and more deals. Just learn to offer yourself, which is the best possible thing that you can offer to the whole situation. Then naturally people will take it if it's what they need.

God didn't intend this. You have become a disciple of the devil if your whole life is about making deals. The devil is always making a deal with somebody. God never made a deal with anybody. Once it so happened that a priest was walking on the street and he saw a man who had just been stabbed. The man was lying face down on the street, struggling for breath and writhing in pain. The priest had always been taught that compassion was the highest thing, love is the way, and all that stuff. Naturally, he ran to the man. He turned him over and saw that it was the devil himself. He was shocked and horrified and quickly backed away. The devil begged him, "Please take me to the hospital! Do something!" The priest hesitated and thought, "Why should I save you, the devil? You're against God. Why should I save you? You should die. The whole priesthood is about somehow banishing the devil, and it looks like somebody has almost done a good job of it. I'll just let you die." The devil said, "Don't do this. Jesus told you to love thine enemy, and you know I am your enemy. You must love me." Then the priest said, "I know the devil always quotes the scriptures. I'm not going to fall for that." So the devil said, "Don't be a fool. If I die, who will come to church? Who will seek God? Then what will happen to you? Okay, you won't listen to the scriptures, but now I am talking business; you better listen." The priest understood that this was true. With no devil, who would come to church? This made business sense. He immediately put the devil on his shoulders and took him to the hospital.

So don't go about making deals for selfish reasons. Maybe you haven't attained to your full Divine nature, but at least in this case let us imitate God for a while. God doesn't make deals. Deals will be offered to you in so many ways. In a way, everybody is just a businessman. Everybody is trying to pull off some deal: some in the market place, another maybe at home, another maybe in the temple, and a few maybe even with their spiritual process, but everybody is trying to pull off some kind of a deal. When you get a good deal, you are all very civilized and nice but if a deal goes bad, you will yell and scream. All priorities in life will change. Deals may sometimes boomerang in your face. One day Shankaran Pillai's barn burned down. Shankaran Pillai, feeling dejected and deflated, refused his lunch and set off for the bar to drown his misery. His wife, taking things into her own hands, called the insurance company and boomed into the phone, "We had that barn insured for five lakh rupees and I want my money NOW! My husband is so upset he's missed his meals!" The agent replied, "Hey, Mrs. Pillai, hold on a minute. Insurance doesn't work quite like that. We will need to ascertain the value of what was in the barn and provide you with objects of comparable worth." There was a long pause before Mrs. Pillai very gravely replied, "Then I'd like to cancel my husband's life insurance."

Seeker: Oh my God...

Sadhguru: Who wants something of comparable worth, especially a husband of all things! (Laughs). Wouldn't you agree Joyce? There's something called *vasanas.* Do you know what vasana means? They are certain old qualities and flavors within you. However much you may try to pretend that you're a very nice and loving person, when deals are offered, suddenly old vasanas will take control of you. There's an urge to bite the deal. That's why on the spiritual path we talk about setting a goal. If you set a goal for yourself, you don't bite any deals on the side and you don't go off the path. The goal itself doesn't take you anywhere. In fact, it's a barrier. It has to be dropped somewhere in the process of growth. The goal is only there to ensure that you don't make any more deals. It's not there to get you bound. It's there to release you from the temptation of deals.

Seeker: Sadhguru, how does yoga help me perform better in this environment?

Sadhguru: When we say 'yoga', probably for many of you it means some physical postures, twisting yourself into some impossible postures. That's not what we're referring to as yoga. Yoga means to be in perfect tune. Your body, mind and spirit and the existence are in absolute harmony. When you fine-tune yourself to such a point where everything functions so beautifully within you, naturally the best of your abilities will just flow out of you. When you're happy, your energies always function better. Do you see that when you're happy you have endless energy? Even if you don't eat, if you don't sleep, it doesn't matter; you can go on and on. Have you noticed this? So just knowing a little happiness is liberating you from your normal limitations of energy and capability.

Now yoga is the science of activating your inner energies in such a way that your body, mind and emotions function at their highest peak. If I don't sleep for two days, you won't notice any difference in me. I can still have a full day of activity. When your body and mind function in a completely different state of relaxation and a certain level of blissfulness, you can be released from so many things that most people are suffering from. Right now, you come and sit in your office, and you have a nagging headache. Your headache isn't a major disease, but it takes away your whole capability for that day. Just that throbbing takes away everything. With the practice of yoga, your body and mind will be kept at their highest possible peak.

There are also other dimensions to it. When you activate your energies, you can function in a different way. As you're sitting here right now, you consider yourself to be a person. You're identified with many things, but what you call as 'myself' is just a certain amount of energy. Do you know, modern science is telling you that the whole existence is just energy manifesting itself in different ways? If this is so, then you're also just a little bit of energy functioning in a particular way. As far as science is concerned, this same energy which you call as 'myself' can be here as a rock, lie there as mud, stand up as a tree, bark as a dog, or sit here as you. Everything is the same energy, but functioning at different levels of capability.

Similarly among human beings, though we're all made of the same energy, we still don't function at the same level of capability. What you call capability or talent, what you call your ability to do things in the world, your creativity, is just a certain way your energy functions. This energy, in one plant it functions to create rose flowers, in another plant it functions to create jasmine; but it's all the same energy manifesting itself. If you gain a little bit of mastery over your own energies, you will see, things that you never imagined possible, you will do simply and naturally. This is the experience of any number of people who have started doing these practices. It's the inner technology of creating situations the way you want them. With the same mud that we build such huge buildings, initially people were building little huts. They thought that's all they could do with it. With the same earth, haven't we built computers? What you call a computer is dug out of the earth. Do you understand what I am saying? We thought we could only dig mud and make pots or bricks out of it. Now we dig the earth and make computers, cars, and even spacecrafts out of it. It's the same energy; we have just started using it for higher and higher possibilities. Similarly, our inner energies are like that. There is a whole technology as to how to use this energy for higher possibilities. Every human being must explore and know this. Otherwise, life becomes very limited and accidental; you get to do only what you're exposed to. Once you start activating your inner energies, your capabilities happen in a different sphere altogether.

Seeker: Master, there are so many different kinds of yoga. How do I know which type of yoga is best for me?

Sadhguru: Right now, the only things which are in your experience are your body, your mind, and your emotions. You know them to some extent, and you can infer that if these three things have to happen the way they are happening, there must be an energy that makes them happen. Isn't it? Without energy all this can't be happening. Some of you might have experienced it; others can easily infer that for these three things to function, there must be an energy behind them. For example, this microphone is amplifying the sound of my voice. Even if you don't know anything about the microphone, you can infer that there's a source that powers it. So these are the only four realities in your life: body, mind, emotion, and energy. These are the only four realities. So whatever you wish to do with yourself, it must be on these four levels. Whatever you wish to do you can only do it with your body, your mind, your emotions or your energy. If you use your emotions and try to reach the ultimate, we call this *bhakthi* yoga; that means the path of devotion. If you use your intelligence and try to reach the ultimate, we call this *gnana* yoga; that means the path of intelligence. If you use your body, or physical action to reach the ultimate, we call this *karma* yoga; that means the path of action. Now if you transform your energies and try to reach the ultimate, we call this *kriya yoga*; that means internal action.

These are the only four ways you can get somewhere: either through karma, gnana, bhakthi or kriya – body, mind, emotion, or energy. These are the only four ways you can work with yourself. "No, no, no, I am on the path of faith. I don't need to do anything else." Is there anybody here who is only head - no heart, hands and energy? Is there anybody here who is only heart - not the other things? You're a combination of these four things, isn't it? It's just that in one person the heart may be dominant, in another person the head may be dominant, in yet another person the hands may be dominant; but everybody is a combination of these four. So you need a combination of these four. It's just that, only if it's mixed in the right way for you, it works best for you. What we give for one person, if it's given to you, may not work well for you because that person is *so much* heart and *this much* head. Only when it's mixed in the right proportion it works for you. That's why on the spiritual path there's so much stress on a live Guru; he mixes the cocktail right for you, otherwise there's no punch.

There is a wonderful story in the yogic lore. One day, one gnana yogi, one bhakthi yogi, one karma yogi, and one kriya yogi were walking together. Usually these four people can never be together, because gnana yogi has total disdain for every other yoga; it is the yoga of intelligence. Normally, an intellectual person, a thinking person has complete disdain for everybody else. A bhakthi yogi, full of emotion and love, thinks all this gnana, karma and kriya yoga is just a waste of time. Just love God and it will happen. The karma yogi thinks that everybody is lazy and that they have all kinds of fancy philosophies; what needs to be done is work. One must work and work and work. The kriya yogi just laughs at everything. The whole existence is energy. If you don't transform your energy, whether you long for God or you long for anything, nothing is going to happen. So they can't be together, but today they were walking together. Then it started to rain. They were in the forest and it started raining. They started running, looking for shelter, and there they found an ancient temple which just had a roof, no walls on the sides. In the center, there was a Linga. So these people went inside the temple for shelter. The storm became more and more furious and it started blowing in torrents. The fury of the storm was getting into the temple so they went closer and closer and closer to the Linga. There was no other way to be because it was just blasting them from all sides. Then it became very furious. There was no other place; the only way they could get some protection was for all four to hug the Linga. Suddenly they felt something enormous happening. A huge presence, a fifth presence was there. Then all of them said, "Why now? For so many years we have pursued You and nothing happened; why now?" Then Shiva said, "At last the four of you got together. I have been waiting for this to happen for a long time."

Seeker: How does one always remain young in spirit, Master? Life somehow seems to be catching up with me.

Sadhguru: A seeker is always young. Whatever the physical age of the body, it doesn't matter. You have to be eternally young. The day you become old, it's over. Anyway, how can you become old in spirit? Only by carrying the past, isn't it? If you carry sixty years of burden with you, you're sixty years old. If you don't carry anything, you're like a newborn. The physical body may develop limitations, but the way you are has no limitations. It simply has no limitations. You are this many years old or that many years old simply because you carry that many years of garbage with you; and this whole thing about celebrating birthdays and remembering that you're that old is making sure that you fix milestones. I used to have a farmhand working for me, a very simple chap. His innocence was most touching. He was nearly fifty years old. If you would ask him his age, he would say, "Maybe I am twenty – twenty five." He had no sense of years. He didn't know. When the rain came, he would plough, then he would throw the seeds. When food came, he would eat. Life went on like this for him and he didn't know his age. Maybe he was unintelligent, but when an intelligent person lives like this, he becomes a sage. He was a saint, not knowing, not carrying the burden of the past. Moment to moment, just see the weight of the load you're carrying. Your face has become squeezed up. The burden is evident. It's there and it shows.

Seeker: Sadhguru, all of human life on this planet is always revolving around good and bad. The very basis of right and wrong is good and bad, but I have heard you say many times that there's no such thing as 'good' and 'bad'. Can you speak more about this, Sadhguru?

Sadhguru: People always believe that they are good and somebody else is bad, isn't it? That's the only way they can carry on their missions in the world. Right now, we're on this part of the Himalayan road, from Pipal Koti – actually, from Rudraprayag to Badrinath[1]– they are making it into a two-lane highway. Every year, so many people die here because of landslides and vehicles going off the road. Driving here on these curves, one mistake and you've had it. When you travel here, you give an enormous responsibility to the driver. Just one mistake of his and you're finished. Every year, so many people make those mistakes. If you don't know this, when you see a small heap of scrap metal on the side of the road, it's usually a salvaged vehicle. I can tell you this now since we are at the end of the trip (laughs).

So they are laying a two-lane highway. Is it good or bad? It's good, because people like you can travel in more comfort, with less risk; so that's good. Today, a lot of people may tell you to stop building roads, disfiguring the mountain, and disturbing the creatures on this planet. So for them, this is bad.

1 Badrinath : a place of pilgrimage in the Himalayas.

Just because those in power, or the majority, think something is good, it won't become good. Maybe it would be better to take a person as an example. Now whatever a terrorist is doing, is it good or bad? You tell me.

Seeker: It's bad.

Sadhguru: Why? What is he doing?

Seeker: He's the source of suffering for many people.

Sadhguru: You can look at it that way. In the same situation, who is good and who is bad all depends on which side of the border you're on. Is India good or is Pakistan good? You're on this side of the border, so obviously Indians are good; Pakistanis are evil. If you were on the other side of the border, you would be arguing for the other side. It all depends on what you're identified with. Accordingly, you have your 'goods' and 'bads'. You can't think beyond that. Your thinking itself is limited to your identifications. Your identifications are always limited, so your thinking is also limited. With this limitedness, why do you get into this nonsense about deciding what's good or bad? The moment you say something is bad, you can't stop disliking it, can you? Can you say, "This is a bad person, but that's okay with me"? On the surface you may say it, but if he gets closer to you, though initially it is just dislike, later it will turn to hate. The moment you identify something as good or bad, you're just dividing the world.

Now somebody comes and says they want to walk the spiritual path. So I tell them, "Okay, stay here for a week. Let us see what we can do." Then he says, "No, no, Saturday is my cousin's birthday; I have to go. I can be here only for three days." So I ask, "All right, but how far would you like to go with this?" He says, "All the way." Then I say, "So in three days, all the way? Anyway, you do these few things when you're here, then let's see what to do next." He will say, "No, I don't like this." Then I tell him, "Okay you give me a list of things that you like. We will do only that." He sits there, thinks seriously for a while and writes down half a dozen things. So I ask, "What? In this vast existence, you like just about half a dozen things, and with that, you want to be spiritual?" Where is the possibility?

The moment you create good and bad, you're dividing the world. Once you divide it, where is the question of inclusion? Where is the question of yoga? Where is the question of becoming one with everything? Where is the question of knowing truth? Your division is because of your stupidity; it has got nothing to do with reality. Good and bad are always according to your ego requirements. If you go by this, you enslave yourself to the dualities of life; you divide the existence. So the question of turning spiritual never arises.

Seeker: Sadhguru, most of the time, in any given moment, I don't seem to know what's required of me. I am clueless in thought, emotion and action. How does someone truly know what's needed in any given moment?

Sadhguru: If you are sitting here as a bundle of thoughts, opinions, and emotions, you will never know what's needed. Most people are like this. What you call a human being is not really a being; it is just a bundle of thoughts, emotions, and opinions that were gathered from elsewhere. If you're in this condition, you will never know. If you simply sit here as life, you always know. You will always know what's needed. You don't need to think about it. You don't have to educate yourself to know. Any human being who is able to sit here as life will simply know what the other beings around him need; but if he's sitting here as a bundle of thoughts, emotions, and opinions, his whole perception will be distorted and he will never know. He will always come to the wrong conclusions about life. When you don't know what's happening with life, you will only drive your life with your thoughts, opinions and emotions. This can lead to a whole calamity within yourself and, if you're a powerful person, to the whole world. This is happening right now. People are highly opinionated, isn't it?

Seeker: Master, there seems to be a correlation between being open to possibilities and being educated. Being educated seems to impose a kind of logic which prevents openness. There also seems to be an inverse correlation between economic prosperity and being open to spiritual possibilities. Is this so?

Sadhguru: Let me put this question the other way around. The question that's being asked is: "Do uneducated people have better possibilities of spiritual Realization, or do poor people have more possibilities of being spiritually Realized?" Am I right? Fundamentally, the word 'education' means to cultivate your mind, to constantly imbibe new possibilities; that's what education means. Now can education become a barrier for these new possibilities? Yes, it can. Anything can become a barrier, for that matter. You already mentioned yours, education and wealth. Not just education and wealth - power, fame, position - anything can become a barrier, but anything can also become an access. It's not education or wealth which can open or close you; it's just how you relate to them. If you have seen education itself as a possibility, which it is - in certain dimensions of life education is a possibility which opens up many vistas – it's the same for wealth. If you have money or wealth it can open up many possibilities in the world around you and also within you. Let's say one day you want to stay at home to meditate, so you don't go to work. You can do that. If your condition is such that you have to work for every meal, then that possibility is closed. Even if you wish to meditate, your hunger will take you to work. Now you have money, so if you wish, you can sit; that possibility is open.

So are education and wealth, in some way, working as a barrier for spiritual growth? It could be, and it is so for a lot of people, unfortunately. This is not because there's something wrong with money or with education; it's just the way you relate to them. If you have seen them as a means, then there's no problem; but if your whole sense of who you are has come to you only from your qualifications, or from your bank balance, then yes, education and money are barriers, not only for your spiritual growth, but also for your physical and mental well-being. If you're seeing them only as a means, only as tools for access, then they are in no way barriers. In fact, they can be very useful because they bring you so much understanding and so many possibilities and in many ways your life is more free. So by themselves they aren't barriers, but you can make them into barriers if you wish.

Seeker: It has happened that they have become barriers, if you look around the world. Why have they become barriers? That seems to be a statistical observation today.

Sadhguru: If you go by statistical comparison between cultures, between the East and the West, the distinction isn't just in terms of education and wealth. There are a whole lot of cultural differences. For example, if you take India and the United States, India is considered to have a strong spiritual tradition and the U.S. is seen as an economic culture. Everything is fundamentally economics in that culture.

So the difference is cultural. Individually, if you look at them, there isn't much difference. Here, there's a whole spiritual tradition, so people have taken to that possibility because it has always been available. There, when a young person grows up – let's say when he's twelve or thirteen years old – all that he knows is what's available to him in that culture. So that's how he goes. It takes a little extra intelligence for a person to look beyond what's available in his culture.

In India, whether you like it or not – even if you have an allergy for it – spirituality gets lobbed into you one way or the other. In your families, in the society, wherever you go, some of it will touch you. It didn't happen because you were longing for it. Naturally, it touches you because it was everywhere. So if you look at the statistics, it's not fair to just take economic well-being and educational background as the basis; there's a whole cultural equation. The reason why there's so much spirituality in this land and has always been is because it has always been a very stable culture. It has remained steadily in one place for thousands of years. If any culture remains steadily in one place for many years, then definitely spirituality will become a huge force in that land; but when the cultures are new, naturally economics will be the most important aspect of that culture.

Wherever the culture is very old, the mystical will be very active. Wherever the culture is new, economics and social well-being will be most active because those are the first things that you will attend to in your life. Only when your economic and social needs are well taken care of, then – as an individual or as a culture – you start looking beyond for other dimensions. Until this is taken care of, you will only be thinking of settling these things. You can't talk spirituality to a man who is hungry on the street; it won't mean anything to him. There are many spiritual aspirants, *sadhus* and *sanyasis* who have chosen to be hungry, they're different. But you can't talk mysticism to somebody who is hungry due to life situations. In many ways, a culture which is new is hungry, hungry for life and well-being, because the people still remember the difficulties that their forefathers had gone through to build it.

A culture that has matured for thousands of years has developed an understanding of renunciation, giving up well-being and taken up walking on the street in pursuit of Realization. Nowhere else in the world will you see this, but in India we know it. So many kings and emperors have dropped their kingdoms – their wealth, their comforts, their pleasures – and walked the streets as beggars. Nowhere else in the world has such a thing happened. It can only happen in a culture that has been steady for a long period of time, where slowly other dimensions of life have become more important than physical survival. So your psyche is going beyond survival instincts. When survival is still important, all you seek is well-being.

Just now, Doug was mentioning this: it seems that in India people aren't bothered by danger. It's not that they aren't bothered about danger. It's definitely true that the longing to survive, the need to survive and the conscious urge to survive are stronger in the West than here. Here, if death comes, people take it so much more easily than people there do. Since Western cultures are young, the survival instinct there is strong. After ten thousand years, they will also be this way, because by then physical well-being and social well-being won't mean as much to them; they will be looking for other dimensions. It's unfortunate that cultures have to take so long to realize this. Generally cultures may take a long time, but individuals need not take that long. Out of your intelligence you can see it right now, and the spiritual process is always individual.

Seeker: Master, will the teachings and practices you've given to me help me break my rigidity and flower?

Sadhguru: I am glad you understand that it is your rigidity which has prevented your flowering. You can become rigid in many dimensions. During the practice of *yoga asanas* you realize how rigid you are physically. It takes a little more awareness for you to know the rigidity in your mind and emotions. Somebody who's very rigid in his thoughts and emotions believes that he's perfect because he doesn't allow room for any other way of looking, thinking, or feeling. When you meet this man, you think he's pig-headed, but he thinks he's perfect. Similarly, there can be rigidity in your energy. For someone whose energy is very fluid, the very first day of the simplest *yoga kriya*, and the energy will start moving and transforming, whereas for another person, even after practicing it for a long time, nothing seems to happen. This simply depends on how malleable the energies are. The rigidity in all these dimensions isn't really separate, they're all interconnected. The rigidity in one dimension manifests itself into the others.

On Patanjali's[1] path, yoga is a system where it doesn't matter what kind of a fool you are, what level of unawareness you're in, what kind of karmic bondages you have; there's still a way for you. If you're willing to at least bend your body, you have already broken one *karma*[2]. If your forehead touches your knee, then you have broken a physical karma. This is not a joke; it's quite an achievement for a person who has never done it before. This simple limitation would have increased with the passage of time. Even the little flexibility that's there in you today will become less as time goes by. A day will come when you're totally rigid, both physically and mentally. This is happening to everybody. Look at your own life; see how flexible you were at the age of ten or twelve, both physically and mentally. At the age of twenty, the flexibility is considerably less and at the age of thirty, most of it has gone. Not only physically; mental rigidity has also set in very severely as you progress on this path; it's not progression, rather it is regression. Life is just a regression for most people. They are not growing; they are going backwards. Even what little assets they have come with, they don't grow; they just go backwards, unfortunately. Whatever advantage you were born with, you haven't enhanced it; you have only taken it backwards.

Every advantage that comes to most people only ends up as a curse. Money, influence, comfort, intelligence become only curses to most people. They actually come as blessings but you turn them into curses. You're not using your intelligence to reach the peak of your consciousness, to become peaceful and loving. You're using your intelligence to drive yourself crazy. For example, you think it would be very nice to be a peasant. They seem to be very simple. It looks romantic to you, but if suddenly you become a peasant, you would curse the whole world. If you were sent to earn your living for three days, everyday you would curse the whole world. When you have that, you dream of this and when you have this, you dream of that. Maybe you call it romantic, but it's just plain stupidity. It destroys life.

Anybody who goes against life, anybody who goes against that which is the source of life is plain stupid. He's an utter fool, and all I am asking of you is to watch, just watch whether you are for the Creator or against the Creator, every moment in your life. If you see this, everything will be settled. If you can't

---

1 Patanjali : considered the father of yogic sciences.

2 *karma* : referring to past action, the cause of all bondage.

think of your Creator, just think of me. Every action that you do, just see whether you're for me or against me. If you do this, things will be settled. Your mind will be settled if you just do this *sadhana.*[1] It needs diligence. Otherwise, it's not going to happen. With every moment and with every breath, just see. If you have the diligence to see, this sadhana is enough for you. It will clear up your mind totally. Tomorrow you will be ready for *samadhi.*[2]

Seeker: It sounds so easy, so close, but is it really that simple, Sadhguru?

Sadhguru: It is actually very simple, but because of you it has become extremely complicated, because of your personality. The path by itself is not complicated. The complexities that one encounters on the spiritual path aren't because of the path. The complexities are only there because of the mess that is your mind. The path is very simple, but because you're there, it becomes extremely complicated. Nothing moves within you. You become rigid, as if rigor mortis has set in. You need the Master's Grace to quell the madness of your mind. If you allow this, then the path is too simple, as the path is the destination. If you simply sit here now, everything will pulsate with the existence. If you just sit here, your whole being will pulsate with the existence. There's no other way to be, unless you make an effort to be some other way. How can you be away from the existence in which you live? How is it possible? It envelops you in every way, inside and out. Nobody can ever be away from it. It's just that you're doing everything to stay away, maybe unconsciously. Just stop doing that and everything will be okay. Now just to get you to stop doing all that nonsense, we have started you on these kriyas.

In one way if you look at it, all of this isn't necessary. If you ask J.K.[3] how long to hold *kumbhaka*[4] to get *Enlightened,*[5] he will just throw you out of the place, because it is not so. It is true that this is not so, but unfortunately it's needed right now. You have kept your energies suppressed to such an extent,

---

1 *sadhana* : a device, a spiritual practice.

2 *samadhi* : of equanimity, a merging of the subject and the object.

3 Jiddu Krishnamurti : twentieth century spiritual master of great repute.

4 *kumbhaka* : breath retention during yogic practice.

5 Enlightened : though used loosely in contemporary jargon, the term enlightenment here and elsewhere in this book refers to an advanced stage of the spiritual evolution of a being usually resulting in a deep experience of oneness with the existence.

the mind has become so oppressive that it suppresses life to the point where nothing moves except what's needed to support the ego. Your energies are moving only to the extent that is convenient for your ego; a little more energy and the ego will burst. The moment energy rises within you, everything is dissolved. The ego knows it very well. That's why it has kept it suppressed. If you don't have any energy, then again the ego will become very weak. When all energy is cut off, the ego will feel very weak and it doesn't like that. So it just allows the amount of energy which supports and feeds it well. If the energy becomes too much, the ego will be shattered. If *Kundalini* [1] begins to rise, everything will be shattered and nothing will be left. You will be just a force merging with everything around you. You won't have a will of your own anymore. Since you're not willing to surrender your will, we're prodding you through this sadhana to provoke your energies.

That's why the path of asana and kriya. Since you're not able to do it by yourself, just activate creation itself in a certain way. If it begins to move, it settles everything. It's like a flood. Have you ever visited a place just after a flood? If you have seen the place before and after, the change is incredible. People think it is sad; people generally think it is a tragedy. Yes, naturally it is a tragedy if you see what it leaves behind or what it takes away – your homes, your crops or your centuries-old world are wiped away in only a few hours of fury. So your sadhana isn't about getting somewhere. It's just a way, a method to unleash a flood so enormous that it wipes away your petty creations and leaves you as the Creator intended you to be.

Seeker: Master, can anybody get Enlightened by practicing simple yogic practices? Are there other means towards Enlightenment? How will I know if I become Enlightened? How does one identify an Enlightened being?

Sadhguru: Senthil, what do you mean, can anybody get Enlightened? The question is whether every human being is capable of Enlightenment. If you're capable of ignorance, you're also capable of Enlightenment, isn't it? An animal isn't capable of ignorance, please see that. An animal is never ignorant,

---

1 *Kundalini* : Cosmic energy which is depicted as a snake coiled at the base of the spine.

nor is it Enlightened, but a human being is capable of being ignorant. You are, aren't you? If you're capable of ignorance, you're also capable of Enlightenment. The question is, when will it happen to you?

Now you ask me, "How will I recognize it? If I get Enlightened, how will I recognize it?" When it happens, there will be no question about it, because it will pervade every dimension of who you are in such a glorious way that there will be no question about it. There will never be the question, "Am I really Enlightened or not?" There will be no such thing; it won't give room for any such doubt. It depends on what your idea of Enlightenment is. There are many Enlightened beings, but you will never know who they are or where they are, because they never declare it. They have no need to do that. Only when a person has to do a certain type of work, he goes through the shameful process of declaring his Enlightenment, because people can't see it. He has to declare it and by doing so, many people will question and probe it. Many people will say it is false. It's quite a shameful thing to declare I am Enlightened.

Most Enlightened beings will never declare it, and you will never know. You need not know whether somebody is Enlightened or not. What's your problem? If it happens to you, it's wonderful. Whether somebody is Enlightened or not, what difference does it make to you? So, "If it happens to me, how will I know?" You don't worry about that. If you're capable of missing such an event, Senthil, don't worry, I will tell you.

Seeker: Sadhguru, I can accept you as my Guru, but to become one with all the participants here...

Sadhguru: The ego is always like this; it is not seeing how to be in tune with what's surrounding it. It's always trying to stick out. Among people, you want to stick out like a sore thumb, and a sore thumb always hurts. Maybe it sticks out, but it hurts. Sticking out always hurts. Once, after returning from London, Shankaran Pillai – who was decked out in new tight denim pants, body-hugging satin shirt and was sporting a new hairdo – went to the nearest park to show off his new look. He approached an old man who was sitting on a bench and sat down next to him. The old man stared at Shankaran Pillai, looking him up and down. His stare finally focused in on the six inch multicolored spikes coming out of his head

The spikes were all flashy colors – orange, purple, green, yellow, blue and pink. Shankaran Pillai looked over at the old man and said sarcastically, "What's the matter, old timer? Never done anything wild in your life?" Without batting an eye the old man replied, "Well, I got drunk once and had a date with a parrot and I was just wondering if you were my son." These days, you're making a whole culture of trying to stick out. The more exclusive you try to be, the more excluded you're getting from life and existence, hence the hurt.

The more you try to be special, the more you get hurt. Just be, just melt and become part of the wind around you, the earth around you, become a part of everything. You're here only for a while. At least when you're in a place like this, where nobody is going to trample on you, let your defenses down. Let it be. Forget your comforts, your sensibilities, your likes and dislikes. Leave all that nonsense and be with me. Live like the snakes. Just crawl around, eat and if you feel like curling up under a tree, do it; at least for a few days, it's worthwhile. I am telling you, a lot of barriers can be removed by going out and living in nature. That's the reason why, when one begins a spiritual journey, they go to the Himalayas or to some other mountain. By merging with nature and living there, the ego will be destroyed, just by doing that. That itself is half the sadhana.

I met some *Naga Babas* [1] in a place just above *Kedar,* [2] in the Himalayas, and stayed with them for two days. They had run out of money; they were hungry and cold. For two days I took care of their food and spent time with them. I only had on a little woolen in-shirt and a T-shirt. Fortunately, somebody had given me a shawl which was a big blessing. If the shawl hadn't been there, I would have frozen. It was so cold that even my insides were shivering. I could literally feel the stomach bag shiver. These Babas are naked sadhus who aren't supposed to wear anything that is stitched. They wrapped something like a shawl over themselves, because it was too cold. They weren't even wearing footwear and they didn't even have money for tea. They were saving the little they had to go to the *Kumbha Mela.* [3]

---

1 *Naga Babas* : people belonging to a certain spiritual sect in North India, who wander naked with vibhuthi smeared on the body even during the coldest winter seasons of the Himalayas.

2 *Kedar* : short for Kedarnath - a spiritually powerful place in the Himalayas.

3 *Kumbha Mela* a major spiritual and religious festival. A nexus of cosmic energy every twelve years which finds confluence. Every one hundred forty-four years is referred to as Mahakumbha Mela. A gathering of sages and mystics.

That was more important for them than having something to eat. When I asked them what their sadhana was, they said they were doing nothing. They just roam about like the nagas, the snakes. Their Guru had told them to spend twelve years in the Himalayas and then he would initiate them. When one is so uni-directional that he can wait twelve years, being oblivious to harsh weather and difficult living conditions and just wait for his initiation, reaching the highest can't be denied to him.

There's not much for the Guru to do; whether he has something to give or not, these guys will get it anyway because of the very way they have made themselves. They don't need a Guru. If a man has that much patience and stamina that he can stay twelve years, not knowing when or if the next meal is going to come, just waiting in that terrifying cold in a queue to be initiated, he will get it anyway. That itself is a sadhana. The Guru knows that if he initiates someone the same day the person comes to him, it will be wasted on the man. He will waste the whole opportunity. So he sends hundreds of people to the mountains like this every year. Maybe only some of them make it – many run away because it's a very difficult path. It's very tough to stay in such conditions. When a person is willing to do this, whether he does it or not, that's not the point. If he's willing to go to any length, that man gets it. It is that simple.

When people are calculating how much to give, and how much to hold back – like Jesus said, "You can't serve me and Mammon at the same time." When Jesus used the word 'Mammon', he used it to be almost synonymous with pleasure. So Jesus said, "You can't serve me and Mammon at the same time. If you want to be my disciple, you have to leave Mammon." If you're seeking comfort – it's not that you shouldn't be comfortable; it's not about having comfort or not, but if you're seeking comfort, forget it. This path is definitely not yours. What he said is very true.

The very purpose of putting a group of people together like this is to help you understand your likes and dislikes, which are the basis of all the limitations you have set for yourself as a person. Take a careful look at your personality; you will see it is just a bundle of likes and dislikes. These likes and dislikes have risen from your enslavement to the duality of life, which is the bedrock of ignorance. The very word 'yoga' means to transcend this duality and know the oneness of existence. Various devices have been used to help people go beyond this enslaving duality. You like or dislike something simply because somewhere deep down you have identified it as either good or bad. Whatever you identify as good you can't help liking and whatever you identify as bad you can't help disliking.

This is why the Hindus created the personality of Shiva as a complex amalgamation of all that's beautiful, ugly, terrible, pleasant, good and bad. They made him the highest so that in accepting him, you accept everything. You transcend the limitations of your likes and dislikes and in turn, your dualities. Here you see all the varieties of human beings. If you can accept the likes of a few of those who are here, who are going about like self-appointed messengers of the Divine, you have transcended. Do you see the weirdest of the weird? (Laughs, pointing toward a few participants).

Seeker: If I am on the spiritual path, how do I deal with family members or friends who are making it very difficult? There seems to be a fine line between comforting them and telling them to grow up, or just to open their eyes, or even to just bang them on the head. How can I deal with a situation like this? They're not in total acceptance even though they say they are, and they continue to demand too much out of me.

Sadhguru: Everyone has to handle the reality according to their choices. For whatever you may choose, there is a consequence. Don't be in a fool's paradise and believe that you can get away without paying a price. For everything there's a price. The spiritual path is never in anybody's way. It's just your choices about where you go, what you do, how much time you spend here or there that cause the conflict or the disturbance. This is not new; it has always been so, whether you're going to a party or the cinema. Someone in your family wants to go to the mountain; you want to go to the beach. The same problem will be there. Isn't it? So it's not about your spiritual path, it's just incompatibility with where you want to go, and where you don't want to go. Your spiritual path isn't in conflict with anybody. The conflict is in your choice about doing things in your life. These need to be handled as usual; you see how much of what is most important to you and act accordingly so that life goes on.

If your spiritual longings are taking you completely away from the situations in which you live, then there will be a certain amount of disturbance and conflict. Not really conflict, because conflict happens between two people; there will be some disturbance. It is always bound to be there, unless people around us are so mature that they're willing to accept things they can't understand, which is rare. Now, the question comes from a certain sense of guilt and discomfort. "What am I doing to the other members of the family?" These kinds of thoughts may come, but enshrining one's limitations isn't a great thing to do, either for you or for the other person. It may be painful to break your limitations. However painful it is, it's worth breaking them. How do you do it? If you can administer it gently, it's wonderful. Sometimes it can't be done so. It's not that it can't be done gently, but the other people refuse to make it gentle. They feel that if it happens gently you will escape the guilt of doing it. Somewhere there is an intention that, if you get to do what you want to do in your life, you must suffer. So they will do everything to see that you feel guilty about it. On the day Gautama, the Buddha, who was just seeking – not even knowing what, but just seeking – left his kingdom, his wife and an infant child, and like a thief, walked away in the night, probably his family saw him as the most terrible man, but how glad we are that he did those terrible things, aren't we? If he hadn't done those terrible things, the world would have been poorer, and those people who lived with him wouldn't have been any better. Anyway, maybe they would have found some other misery after some time.

Seeker: So when you're in a relationship, that's a commitment too. The family and children come first. You have spoken about commitment, and how people should be committed. So why doesn't this hold true on the path of spirituality? When it comes to spirituality, doesn't it seem like you're abandoning your family and walking away from social structures just to pursue your spiritual interest?

Sadhguru: For your spiritual path, there is no need to walk out of anything. It's just that, when the family structure is made in such a way that it doesn't allow for any other possibility except for breeding and brooding, then it becomes a breaking point; not otherwise. In what way is spirituality breaking up any family? The family breaks up because of its own intolerance, because of its own immaturity, because of its own limitations that people are trying to set upon each other; not for any other reason, not because of spirituality.

Seeker: Sadhguru, how do I deal with being so obsessed with the spiritual path?

Sadhguru: Once you are on a spiritual path, if you're genuinely on the path, you're not just obsessed; you are possessed. If you want to hit the peak of your consciousness, all the energy that you have has to be focused in one direction. If you're throwing it in ten different directions, it's obvious you're not going to get anywhere, isn't it? Even if you throw all the energy that you have in one direction, still it may not be sufficient. That's why the Master fills in that space of lifting you up when it's needed; but if you want to distribute your energy in ten different directions, then definitely it will be futile. So don't be obsessed; be possessed by the path. There's nothing else for you; everything else is just to get you there. Only when it becomes like this, your spiritual path means something.

If it's not so, if it's a side interest in your life, that you like spiritual entertainment – different people seek different types of entertainment and some people dabble with spirituality – that's up to you. I have nothing to say for such people, but if you're really seeking to know, then your whole being should be focused in one direction. You're completely possessed by it. This doesn't mean you will become unreasonable. This doesn't mean you can't run a family. This doesn't mean you can't fulfill your social responsibilities. Just use them as a spiritual process for yourself. Every breath, every step, every act that you perform in your life becomes a spiritual process. Only then there's no conflict. When you say, "This is my spiritual path, this is my family, this is my profession, this is my club, these are my drinking friends," then you have a conflict. If you eat, you eat only because you want to know. If you drink, you drink only because you want to know. If you work, you work only because you want to know. Then there is no conflict.

Seeker: Sadhguru, sometimes I feel dull and sluggish. Can you tell me how to become more energetic and more alive?

Sadhguru: There are many ways to look at this and understand it. One level of energy that you know is the food that you eat, the water that you drink, the air that you breathe, the sunlight that you receive.

These things are becoming energy in your system, the day-to-day energy that you experience, to some extent – in different people to different extents. Another way of looking at it is that what you call 'life' or what you call 'yourself' is energy. How alive you are, how wakeful you are, is how energetic you are. So your ability to convert the food that you eat, the water that you drink, the air that you breathe, whatever else you consume, whatever inputs go into the system; to convert them into active, productive energy in you – is different in different people.

It's not just about digestion and assimilation. The conversion of energy happens in different states, depending on how alive or how awake your own energies are. You might have seen, once you start certain spiritual practices, your level of energy is totally different. Your ability to stay awake, your ability not to be tired, your ability to just go on with life, is so much better once you start these practices. If you practice these kriyas daily, you can see that if you don't do them for one day, there's a distinct difference. In a way, all spiritual practices – when I say 'spiritual', I am talking about the kriyas or even *dhyana*[1]– are fundamentally to make your energies more awake than what they are now.

Whether we're talking about Kundalini or simple plain energy as in the English language, it's basically about raising ourselves to a higher level of energy. What you call 'life' itself is energy. So if you want to function on a higher plane of life, you need a higher level, a higher quality of energy. There are many methods to do it, and most of you have already started with some simple methods. There are other ways to energize a person which can be more dramatic; but dramatic methods of energizing need proper preparation, balance and control over life. That requires much more awareness from a person, to know what he's doing and not doing with himself. Most people, even the so-called spiritual people, ninety-eight percent of the time don't know what's happening within themselves. When it comes to their body or their energy, they don't know at all. Even when it comes to their mind and emotions, most of the time they don't know until it becomes acute.

Right now you're sitting here and a certain emotion may be building up within you in a very small way and you're not aware of it. If somebody comes and calls you an idiot, you explode. Now you think you're angry.

---

1 *dhyana* : meditation.

This has been building up, probably for days, weeks, or months, but it's not in your consciousness or awareness because of your state of energy or the way you are. Many factors are involved. So what's happening within you isn't in your awareness. When what's happening within you isn't in your awareness, the whole process of life is accidental, your energy is accidental. When it is accidental, you see one day you're energetic, the next day you're not. It's like this.

You definitely would have noticed, on a certain day you're very happy; you seem to be very energetic on that day. Another day you're not so happy; you have no energy. So one reason we're always talking about being peaceful and happy is not for the sake of being peaceful and happy, but because only if a person is peaceful and happy, his energies begin to become alive in a certain way. Otherwise the system is simply blocked up. Only if these energies are alive, you can activate them towards a higher possibility. So when you talk about being energetic - for different people being energetic means different things. In a sense, for a school kid, being energetic means being able to go to school, play games, come back home and fall asleep. For a laborer on the street, it means to be able to perform his activity all day. Maybe for an executive it means to sleep less, to travel more, to be more productive. For a yogi, he doesn't want to sleep or eat. He wants to be that way for many days - just being alive by his own contact with existence, not by putting something into him.

Being energetic means different things to different people in different areas and different perspectives of life. Right now, when you say 'energetic', if it's just about being a little more energetic in performing your day-to-day activities in the world, the practices that you're doing will definitely take care of it. If that's not enough, there are ways to upgrade that a little bit so that it can be taken care of. For me, being truly energetic means that when you sit here, the physical body is no more a limitation for you. If your energies are really active, the physical body is no more a limitation. Energy becomes the main contact. Right now, your body, mind and emotions are the main contact that you have with the rest of the world. That's how you communicate, that's how you reach out. You can touch somebody either physically or mentally. With your thoughts, you can communicate or emotionally you can convey something. This is how you are.

Once you're truly energetic, you can communicate with everything in the existence energy-wise. When you start communicating energy-wise, there's no distinction between this and that. Once the barrier is broken, that's ultimate nature. When you start a spiritual process, being energetic means going beyond all limitations, because in energy there is oneness. In the physical body there can never be oneness. In mental thought there can never be oneness. We may talk about oneness, but it's never going to happen. With our emotions we may think we're one, but we're still separate. No two people can feel exactly the same way. You may believe so, but if you have any sense, within a short time you will realize that it's not so. Some people may take years to realize; a few people will realize quickly, but everybody will realize. No two people are exactly alike physically, mentally, emotionally; it's not possible. When you become truly energetic, oneness is just natural. That's the way it is.

Seeker: Sadhguru, at your gatherings or sathsangs people are transported to states of extreme ecstasy. Are these people specially blessed? Am I condemned to a state of rock-like yoga?

Sadhguru: You first decide what's important to you. Now that you refer to me as 'Sadhguru', is being with your Guru more important, or having what somebody else has in their pocket more important to you? "No, no, no, I don't want what they have in their pocket. I want what they are having in their heart, or their head, or wherever." It's not any different. You aspiring to be as rich, as beautiful or as ecstatic as somebody isn't any different. When you sit with your Guru, you just sit with him. Don't worry about what's happening to somebody or what's not happening to you. Your whole life will be wasted. First of all, why did you look at somebody else? You were supposed to be with me in the sathsang. Why are you even noticing somebody else? If you're totally with me, you shouldn't even notice what's happening to somebody.

There was a beautiful incident which occurred in Arjuna's[1] life. It's of a totally different nature, but it is relevant. The royal tutor, Dhronacharya, was teaching all those brothers – one hundred and five of them – the artistry of archery, how to shoot an arrow. He himself was a great archer; there are many

1 Arjuna : the hero of the great Indian epic, *Mahabharatha*.

legends about him. One day, Dhronacharya set a little toy parrot upon the topmost branch of a tree. Then he told his whole class, one hundred and five princes, "Now we will go out. There's a parrot on top of the tree and you're required to shoot this parrot. Let's go." He took them outside, pointed out where the parrot was and, one by one, asked them to set their arrow to the bow and aim. When they aimed he said, "Wait." He kept them in the position of aiming for a few minutes, and then asked them, "What do you see?" They said, "Oh, we see the leaves, the branches, the parrot," this and that, everything, including the whole sky. When it came to Arjuna, he aimed and Dhronacharya asked, "What do you see? What all do you see?" Arjuna said, "Just one point on the neck of the parrot. That's all I see." And that was all he saw. That's why Lord Krishna chose Arjuna to give the teaching to and nobody else, because the man was set. He sees only what he has to see and nothing else. This man will make it.

Now when you sit there, I ask you to close your eyes. If somebody makes a little noise, you want to open your eyes and see what's happening behind you, what's happening around you, what's happening everywhere. Sathsang is about you simply being with me. Don't worry about what's happening with somebody. It's not even your business to notice what's happening to somebody. You just be with me. Then there will be no problem.

Seeker: Sometimes I get the feeling that people create so much trouble in their lives, so much suffering, simply because they're not sensitive enough to see that what they sow is what they reap. For example, when they get angry, jealous or hateful... In such situations, what's possible for people to do? I wish people were more sensitive. I feel that if I somehow try to interfere, I will just create more trouble.

Sadhguru: You're asking about your ability to make somebody's life – it's actually about this that you're asking – to make his future and his liberation. If you have to make it, first of all you have to earn his trust, which doesn't come easy. It takes an enormous amount of work, responsibility, energy, wisdom and simple sense to earn that trust from people. Even if you can earn this trust, it's different for different people. There are a dozen people sitting here. I can't interfere with their life to the same extent. Isn't it?

There are some people, if they are going the wrong way, I can just hold them by their hair and turn them around and say, "This is the way." No problem, they will go that way. With somebody else I have to say, "Please, go this way," but they're not going to go this way, they're going to go that way, an in-between way. I have to just allow that to happen, even though I know it's not the best for them. So with each individual your ability to interfere with their life and do what's needed is different, depending upon how much trust you have earned from that person. To earn this trust you need time, you need energy, you need effort; so many things are involved. Otherwise, trust doesn't come. On the surface, everybody will bow down to you. Everybody will say this and that; that's not the point. When it really comes to the crunch, how far you can interfere is a wisdom and a simple sense that you need to have. You can't interfere to the same extent with everybody. Certainly that man who's going on the street, even if he's walking to his death, I can't stop him and say, "Don't go there. Go here." I can't say that. I will allow him to walk to his death because there's nothing else to do. Most of the time there's nothing else to do, because he wouldn't be available.

How much you can do and what you can do with a certain individual is always limited, depending on how open and how willing he has become. For ages, spiritual masters have always been talking about willingness, trust, surrender, these kinds of things, not because they want somebody to surrender to them, but because that's the only way they can truly interfere with somebody's life and set his life on a different track altogether. Otherwise, you have to always work within the limitations of the other person's understanding. If I do something which isn't within the realm of your understanding, immediately you will leave. So I am constantly working only within the limitations of your understanding, not in totality. If I interfere in totality, you will leave. That's why I said being a yogi is wonderful, fantastic, but being a Guru is frustrating.

Seeker: Master, the more I seek the spiritual path, the more confused I become. Yet at the same time there seems to be a kind of clarity – a confused clarity. Will a time come when there will be clarity without confusion, and if so, how do I create that?

Sadhguru: The more you seek the spiritual path, the more confused you're becoming. That's a good sign, because confusion is always a better state to be in than living in stupid conclusions. With the stupid conclusions that you had made in your life, there was comfort, there was solace, and there was convenience. There was a false sense of security in these.

Now you step onto a spiritual path and everything becomes turmoil. All the things that you were comfortable with look stupid now. Things that you valued and cherished suddenly look so insignificant and not worthwhile. Everything has turned upside down. There's a very beautiful Zen saying: "When you are ignorant, mountains are mountains, rivers are rivers, clouds are clouds, trees are trees. Once you enter the spiritual path, mountains are no more just mountains, rivers are no more just rivers, clouds aren't just clouds, trees aren't just trees. But once you arrive, once you are Enlightened, once again mountains are mountains, rivers are rivers, clouds are clouds, trees are trees." From ignorance to Enlightenment, it is a full circle back to the same place, but a huge difference, a world of difference, a difference which is indescribable.

Once you enter the spiritual path, everything is in turmoil, everything is in question. You don't know where you stand. You don't know anything. Before knowing anything about spirituality, you were at least comfortable, self-satisfied. You ate *pongal* in the morning, drank coffee, and you thought that was the ultimate. Whatever your breakfast was, you thought that was the ultimate pleasure. Now, nothing matters. You don't feel like eating, don't feel like sleeping, don't feel like doing anything, because nothing is really worthwhile anymore. It never was worthwhile. You just deceived yourself into believing that it was. If it was truly worthwhile, how could it go away? If you truly knew what's what, how could you get confused? The very fact that you're confused means you didn't know, isn't it? You had made wrong conclusions, just for the sake of comfort and security.

If comfort is all you're seeking, you must psych yourself up to believe you're perfect, that everything is okay with your life. "My house is good, my husband is wonderful, my life is great, my children are fantastic, even my dog is fabulous. This is it; this is life." You must tell yourself this every day, and go on with it. It will be quite good, nothing wrong with it. It's just that it is limited, and this being will never settle for anything limited. It doesn't matter in how many ways you try to fool yourself; somewhere there's a longing. Carefully look at all the happiness that you have known in your life. On the surface there's happiness, but somewhere deep inside, there's a certain suffering in everything. The suffering is just because the suppressed being is always longing. To even become conscious of this suffering, people take lifetimes.

Entering the spiritual path means you have become conscious of your suffering. You were suffering unconsciously; now you have become conscious of it. Conscious suffering is always deeper than unconscious suffering, but it is good, at least you're conscious about it. As long as you haven't become conscious, the suffering will always remain. Once you have become conscious, it need not remain forever. There's a possibility, isn't it? Entering the spiritual path is a possibility, being with a Guru is a possibility, that's all it is. If the possibility has to become a reality, the first thing is that you're willing to see everything the way it is. You're at least willing to recognize your limitations. If you want to hide your limitations, where's the question of liberation? Where is the possibility? You have destroyed it completely, isn't it?

If you're chained right now and if freedom has to come some day, the first and foremost thing to see is that you're chained. If you're refusing to see that you're chained, the question of liberating yourself never arises. So when you realize that you're chained, there will be pain, there will be suffering, there will be struggle, there will be confusion. Now old memories will say, "I was better off before." This is the way of your mind. When you were in high school, your mind told you, "Oh, kindergarten was so fantastic." You know how you went to kindergarten. When you went to college you said, "Oh, my high school days were so wonderful," but we know how you went through high school also. When you were done with your education, you said, "My university days were the most blissful days!" We know how you struggled to write your assessments, to find the book that you wanted in the library. We know how you suffered all those classes and those professors, but now that it's over, you claim it was fantastic.

So as a part of your survival technique, memory has a way of erasing certain unpleasant things and making the past always more pleasant than what's there right now. This is a trick of survival. Otherwise, psychologically, you will crack up. You always have something to fall back on and say, "Oh, it was wonderful." Now there's a confused clarity. Isn't that good? You're confused and still clear. On a certain day, a farmer with a truck full of animals is on his way to the market for auctioning. He comes upon a hitchhiker, and gives the man a lift. On the way to town, the farmer starts sipping on some home brew, swerves off the road and crashes in a big ditch. The hitchhiker is thrown out of the truck and into the ditch, with shattered ribs, a busted leg and a smashed arm – he's totally in pieces. The farm animals are also seriously messed up. The farmer is the only one with only a few cuts and bruises. He gets out of the truck and inspects his animals. The chickens have broken legs and wings, and can barely move. "These chickens are useless now," the farmer explodes. "Nobody will buy them!" He grabs his shotgun from the truck and shoots the chickens. Next, he sees that the pigs are all busted and bleeding. "These pigs are worthless too!" So he reloads the gun and shoots them, too. The farmer then looks at the sheep that are in the same state as the chickens and the pigs, and screams, "Worthless sheep!" He reloads his shotgun and blows away the sheep. The injured hitchhiker witnesses all this carnage in great horror. The farmer then moves over to the ditch, peers inside, and shouts, "Are you okay, down there?" Instantly the hitchhiker, crawling up really fast, says, "SURE, I'VE NEVER FELT BETTER IN MY WHOLE LIFE!"

That means even if we throw you into hell, it doesn't matter; you will be clear. Now I am not interested in sending people to heaven. I am interested in making people in such a way that, even if they go to hell, nobody can make them suffer. That's freedom, isn't it? "I want to go to heaven, I want to go to heaven," is a huge bondage. Suppose you land in the wrong place. Suppose someone hijacked your airplane on the way to heaven. He didn't crash it; he just landed it in the wrong place. You're finished, aren't you? You're always living with something that can be taken away from you by somebody or something. True liberation is when nobody can take away anything from you; and that which can't be taken away from you is your blissfulness, your inability to suffer. "I want to go to heaven", means you're still capable of suffering. That's why you want to go to a good place, isn't it? Gautama[1] repeatedly said, "I don't want to

---

1 Gautama : referring to Gautama the Buddha.

go to heaven. I want to go to hell." People thought he was crazy, but that's how a liberated man will be. "What's my problem with hell? Anyway they can't make me suffer, so I will go to hell." This man is free, isn't he? So if you're confused and clear, that's good. "When will all my confusions go away? When will absolute clarity come?" I don't want to fix a date, but I bless you, let it be today. Why tomorrow? It's twenty past ten; there is one hour and forty minutes left of today. That's a lot of time, you know? An hour and forty minutes is not little; it's an enormous amount of time. Let it be today.

Seeker: After a long time I have just learned to let go and let things happen. Then yesterday you told me that I had to work towards it. I am very confused, Sadhguru!

Sadhguru: Now Marie-Christine, now that you're confused, that's good. That's the intention, to keep you always confused. Confused means you're still looking. Confused means you still don't know. Please understand: there are only two ways for your mind to be right now. There's no such thing as 'let go' in your mind. Either it's confused or it has made some conclusion. I always prefer to have you confused rather than being in some stupid conclusion about what it is. So now talking about letting go – I know this 'let go, let go' thing has been talked about too much, written about everywhere – "You must let go." What is it that you want to let go of? You don't even know what you should let go of. So right now 'let go' is also another idea, another opinion of yours about life. As long as you are alive, you're not really able to let go. At the most, if you're fortunate, you may place your life in somebody else's hands with trust. That's the biggest thing you can do. Letting go is just a phrase that never happens. It's just that your mind has acquired a new formula: 'Let go, let go'.

I have never really asked anybody to let go, if you haven't noticed this. Though I know thousands of people misinterpret me as, "You asked us to let go," I never asked you to let go. I just asked you to look at life simply the way it is, not because it is my teaching, or my idea, or my opinion as to how to live well; it is simply because that's the way it is. All I am asking you is to get involved. This 'let go' has become a *mantra*[1] for all kinds of people, for drug addicts, for sex maniacs, for fatalists, and for people who are afraid of taking their life into their hands and creating what they should. For all these people, 'let go' has become a good formula. "Oh, we have let go." You have left your lives in the hands of the planets and stars. That's the 'let go' for you. This kind of 'let go' will let you down. Once a hypnotist bombastically said he would take everybody in the hall together into a 'let go' state of hypnosis all at once. "I want you each to keep your eyes on this antique watch. It's a very special watch. It has been in my family for six generations," he said. He slowly began to swing the watch gently back and forth, while quietly chanting, "Watch the watch, watch the watch, watch the watch..." The crowd became mesmerized as the watch swayed back and forth, back and forth, light gleaming off its polished surface. Hundreds of pairs of eyes followed the swaying watch. Suddenly, it slipped from the hypnotist's fingers and fell to the floor, breaking into a hundred pieces. "Shit," said the hypnotist. IT TOOK THREE WEEKS TO CLEAN UP THE THEATRE!

This is what will happen with your 'let go' philosophy. It's not a 'let go'; it is just a convenience that you have chosen. So don't bother about this 'let go' business. Not once did I ever tell you to let go. I noticed that you were getting into this frame of mind, into this frame of deception within yourself of letting go and believing that you had let go, but you still haven't gotten into that state. I know many people around me who are in 'let go' philosophy and doing irresponsible things. If somebody asks them, "Why are you doing this?" They will say, "It's all Sadhguru's will. Only Sadhguru makes me do everything," for all the idiotic things they do. See, the line between devotion and deception is very thin. Why I am constantly attacking devotion is not because I am against it. It is the most wonderful thing that can happen to you to become devoted, but I am always attacking it because the line between devotion and deception is so thin that most people will remain in deception for a lifetime, believing they are in devotion. If you really let go, if there's such a thing, devotion is a real 'let go.' If you're truly devoted, you are an absolute 'let go,' but you can't do it. You can't try to become devoted; it won't help. You can't practice devotion. When your experience of something becomes so overwhelming, helplessly you become devoted.

I have many devotees around me. When I say I have devotees around me, don't think that all the

---

[1] *mantra*: a syllable or a pure sound

people you see bowing down, clutching at my feet, are my devotees. No, they are different (laughs). Devotees are people – in many ways, they don't know why they are here, but they are helplessly with me; they are the true devotees. Devotion has entered them. Their mind rebels against it, their mind tells them, "This is stupid. Why are you doing everything that this man says? Leave him and go," but helplessly they are here. They can't go anywhere, not because they are held by somebody or hypnotized, but simply because they have been so overwhelmed by the experience of someone that they are in devotion. The mind doesn't agree with devotion, but they have become devoted. People bow down because they believe that if they bow down they will get something. That's not devotion. You have asked this question as if there was a contradiction between letting go or being devoted and working towards something. A devotee is somebody who can work twenty-four hours of the day without feeling that he has done anything. If you give him twenty-four hours of activity, still he doesn't feel that he has done anything. He's a devotee; that's a true 'let go'. If you think letting go means that you don't have to do anything, that somebody is going to take care of you all the time; that's not 'let go'.

That amounts to deception, because now you haven't completely given up your likes and dislikes, your personality, what you consider as 'myself'. It's not totally gone. Yes, there have been moments of experience, but it's not totally gone. At the same time, talking about letting go won't work. Right now, you're sort of preparing yourself with a 'let go' philosophy. You have been strengthening this philosophy for some time now, especially in the last six weeks, because the time to go home has come. New situations and old situations will confront you. You already know what those situations are. You already know how you will react to them, but you need an excuse as to how you will react to them. So 'let go' is a good excuse. That's why I told you, you must work towards it. If you don't work towards it, it won't happen.

Seeker: Master, is it true that on the path of liberation much effort has to be put in by the sadhaka, but finally it is Grace that takes you there?

Sadhguru: Your effort is to defeat all your efforts.

Seeker: After that, one becomes effortless and finally it is the Grace?

Sadhguru: The Grace is also you.

Seeker: How?

Sadhguru: All the effort is to demolish the structures that you have built. What's true can't happen with effort. The ultimate reality can never happen with effort because it is beyond all that. The effort is always to demolish what you have already built with effort. With your own effort you have built so many structures; so with your own effort you clean up your mess. Truth is not something that you do. It's in the lap of truth that you exist. There is no question of you doing it, and if you do it, it must be a lie. Isn't it? So the moment you use the word 'Grace', you will always start looking up, wanting to receive. Don't worry about that. Your business is to demolish the structures which you have built. Grace is not something that you ask for, that you crave. If you demolish the blocks that you have built up, Grace will happen.

Seeker: Are you talking about conditioning?

Sadhguru: Conditioning is only one part of the structure. You have built so many other structures. Okay, you can call it conditioning; we call it karma though. Karma is a more complete word. Conditioning tends to describe only certain aspects of life. Karma includes all of it.

Seeker: We're so helpless because we try and the trying is of no use. Things happen, but on the spiritual path there comes a point when you just have to let go, to stop trying.

Sadhguru: That's what most people have done in the world. See, most people have even stopped aspiring for anything. You can't let go. How can you let go? If you let go, it is still an effort, isn't it? Like yesterday somebody was trying to say, "You know we can't do anything. We just have to go with the flow of things; that's surrender." The moment I said it is succumbing, he got mad. Somebody who's talking about surrender, if you as much as say anything, he will flare up. If people have surrendered where's the question of anger? One who has surrendered has nothing of his own. That's what it means. So where can he have likes, dislikes, or anger? It is simply impossible.

Seeker: After coming to this yoga, my self-image has taken a beating. It is totally shattered.

Sadhguru: Every human being, either consciously or unconsciously, through the process of what we call life, creates a certain image of himself, a certain personality. This image that you have created within yourselves has nothing to do with reality. It has nothing to do with the Self, with your inner nature. It's a certain image that you have built, most of the time unconsciously. Very few human beings have built a conscious image for themselves. All others have built images according to whatever kind of patterns or external situations they fell into. The external influences – maybe your mother, father, teacher or some great man you looked up to, or with a mixture of all these influences you formed an image of yourself. Everybody has some image of what they are, isn't it? Okay, since you came to this yoga, this image has been taking some beating, but it's not totally broken. It doesn't break so easily. If it's broken completely, if you shatter it totally, you are a Realized being, but it doesn't break because the mind is still active. It just tries to modify the image a little bit, adjust the image to the new situation. You know, if the color doesn't go with the external situation, you repaint yourself a little bit. All kinds of adjustments are made, but there's no fundamental change in the image itself.

'Shattering' means living without the image. 'Shattering' means dropping the image altogether. Changing the image is different. See, when you were in school, you had a certain image of yourself, but when you moved into college your image went through a revolutionary change. Again, maybe from being unmarried to married, the image goes through a big change. Still, the underlying factor, the main aspect of your image, hasn't changed. Even in those cases something of the old has been retained. Maybe a lot of things changed, but still the fundamentals have been retained. The skeleton is still the same. Maybe you even changed the flesh, but the skeleton has remained the same. Wouldn't it be nice if you could change the skeleton and see? Wouldn't it be wonderful?

Seeker: How is this skeletal change possible, Sadhguru?

Sadhguru: When you take this – what you know as yourself – into a different dimension. See, what you know as yourself, you didn't choose consciously; it happened. You picked it up here and there, in bits. It's a rag doll. Now, if you are intelligent enough, if you are aware enough, you can recast your image to a totally new image, whichever way you want it, consciously. It is possible, but you should be willing to leave the rag doll. Can you? Are you willing?

Seeker: It sounds too daunting.

Sadhguru: If you have sufficient intelligence and awareness, it can be done. When you drop it totally, another image won't be needed. You can just pick up things and drop things as needed; they won't stick to you. Now with you, I am not talking about dropping your image. I am just talking about transforming your image. Transformation is always fundamental. I won't tell you how you should be. You decide how you want to be. If you want help, we will help you out, in between. For the skeleton, you decide. Flesh and blood we will fill up slowly.

Seeker: Sadhguru, after the Samyama[1] program, I started to feel that I have become more involved in life in a way and it is making me grow at a very fast pace. But at the same time, I feel that before, I had a certain innocence that was allowing me to at least see myself as walking a spiritual path. Now, I feel I am becoming a little more materialistic, selfish, and egoistic. Also, I'm not too sure, but I think

1 Samyama : an eight day meditation program offered by Sadhguru where one is transported to explosive states of meditativeness. Held at Isha Yoga Center.

I have become too confident and my ego has grown a little bigger and all I wanted to do earlier on was to just disappear. So I ask you, what's happening to me?

Sadhguru: Marwan, I think I told you that if you're seeking physical and mental well-being, the Isha Yoga program and Bhava Spandana [1] are more than enough. Only if you really want to know – not out of curiosity – when your longing burns you enough that you begin to think, not just in terms of life, but you want to know what are the very fundamentals of your creation, you want to know what this is all about, only if such a longing has come, you must go to Samyama. You have been there; you know it's a different world in itself. It's another world. Someone who hasn't been there won't believe that people can be like that for seven to eight days.

Whatever you call it, hell or heaven, whichever way, it is not of this world. Samyama hasn't made you more egoistic and more of all this that you say. It's just that it has taken away some of your pretensions and you're more bare. A man had a habit of grumbling at the food his wife placed before him at family meals. Then he would say the blessing. One day, after his usual combination complaint-prayer, his little girl asked, "Daddy, does God hear us when we pray?" "Why, of course," he said, "God hears us every time we pray." She thought for a moment and then asked, "Does he hear everything else we say the rest of the time?" "Yes dear, every word," he replied, encouraged that he had inspired his daughter to inquire about spiritual matters. Then she asked, "Then which does God believe, what we say during prayer or at other times?"

What you were hiding in many ways is now simply bare, both to you and the people around you. That's good, because if you deceive yourself about yourself, you're just wasting life, isn't it? If you deceive the world, there is a karma attached to it and it's up to you if you want to do that; but if you deceive yourself, you're lost forever, isn't it? These two things must be understood. This awareness and energy are very deeply connected. If one wants to move into higher states of awareness, the support of the energy is most essential. Without the necessary energy, nobody is going to be aware; awareness is going to be just a dream. People only talk about awareness. You being aware of who's walking next to

1 Bhava Spandana : a four day, high intensity residential program offered as a part of Isha Yoga programs.

you or what's happening around you is not it. That everyone has to have; even a dog has it better than you. Awareness means that you're becoming aware of dimensions which aren't in your normal experience of life. Initially, when this awareness comes, your system doesn't know how to handle it; your body doesn't know how to handle it. Your body will go crazy, your mind will go crazy. Your mind doesn't know how to handle it because awareness comes with furious energy, or because of furious energy, awareness comes. So these two things can't be separated. Higher dimensions of awareness mean higher dimensions of energy.

You trying to project yourself as a good man was very important to you at one point. Now suddenly, the deception has fallen off and who you are is simply there. It's good, even if it causes disturbances around you. Being straight with life is more important than being good. If you're not straight with life, then you will get entangled and entangled and more entangled. Those who aren't straight with life, as time passes, sadness overtakes them; they can't help it. Even if everything in their life is working out very well, you will see their faces hanging slowly. They don't even know why. Do you see many faces like this around the world, driving a Rolls-Royce but still their face is hanging, living in a palace but still their face is hanging? Don't you see this all around you? This is simply because of self-deception.

If you don't know how to be straight with life, over a period of time, it will take its toll. Slowly, once youth passes, you will see your face will hang. It's so much more important to be straight with life than to be polite, than to be good, than to be moralistic – to simply be straight with life, and especially with yourself. If you have intelligence, you will understand and come to terms with this. If you don't, you will get knocked around in your life; but that's an external situation. The world around you, you handle it to whatever extent you're capable of, but within yourself, if you don't know how to be straight and address all aspects of who you are properly, then slowly over a period of time, a cloud of unexplained misery will hang around you.

In a short-lived career as a policeman, Shankaran Pillai was assigned to traffic control. Towards the end of the month, in order to meet his quota of speeding vehicles, he stopped a farmer for speeding in his tractor, piled high with hay. Shankaran Pillai began to lecture the farmer about his excessive speed, and began to throw his weight around to make the farmer feel small and uncomfortable. Finally, Shankaran

Pillai got around to writing the ticket. As he was doing that, he kept swatting at some flies that were buzzing around his head. "Having some problems with circle flies there, are you?" the farmer asked. Shankaran Pillai stopped writing and said, "Well, yeah, if that's what they are. I had never heard of circle flies." The farmer said, "Well, circle flies are common on farms. See, they are called circle flies because they are almost always found circling around the back end of a mule." Shankaran Pillai says, "Oh," and goes back to writing the ticket. After a minute, he suddenly stops and says, "Hey wait a minute; are you trying to call me a mule's arse?" The farmer fearfully says, "Oh no! Pillai saar (sir)! I have too much respect for law enforcement and police officers to even think about calling you a mule's arse." Shankaran Pillai replies, "Well, that's a good thing," and goes back to writing the ticket. After along pause, the farmer says, "Hard to fool those flies though!" So instead of carrying a blissful *ojas*[1] around you, you will carry a cloud of misery around you. Now we can call you evil. You may not have any evil intentions, but you're spreading misery in the world. It's not because you're a criminal that we call you evil, but because you're spreading misery. Every moment of your life you're sowing seeds of misery around you. This is evil, isn't it? Unintentional evil. Most of the evil people in the world are unintentionally evil. They don't really have evil intentions, but slowly their energy becomes that way.

So what's happening to you is fine, because you're becoming aware of things that you weren't aware of for all these days. Some moments, you're not able to handle it; it's okay. See, if you're driving at twenty kilometers an hour, you never go out of control, isn't it? If you go slowly, at ten or twenty kilometers an hour, you won't go out of control. It's only when you're driving at a hundred and fifty kilometers per hour that there's a chance of going out of control, but then you're also covering an enormous distance. In an hour that man makes twenty kilometers; you make a hundred and fifty kilometers. That's an enormous difference, but the possibility of going a little out of control is there. For that, safety measures have always been fixed. These safety measures are like dampers. There are so many people around me who are capable. There are so many around me that, if I didn't have to take care of their safety, we could have dozens of Enlightened beings around us right now. Only because I don't want any one of them to crash, I put dampers along the way. Because of these safety measures, they are a little slow. It doesn't matter.

---

1 *ojas* : subtle energy.

They are driving very fast, but because of the safety rules and the corners they have to slow down. They're not allowed to go at the same speed. This slows down the process, but it's safe.

When you're on the straights, you must go full speed, isn't it? If even on the straights, you're going at twenty kilometers per hour, then it's a waste of life, because you're not going to be here for a million years. There's a certain span of time that you call life, within which something meaningful should happen. Otherwise, one will definitely die in regret, and your life doesn't end with death. If you're hoping that everything will end with death, you're a fool. That's all I can say. Your life doesn't end with death. It takes on so many other forms. It can take on very unpleasant forms. It's these unpleasant forms which we refer to as *naraka* or hell. Hell is not a place somewhere where all of you will go and suffer, and heaven doesn't mean the other place. If you take on an unpleasant form beyond this body, we say you're in hell. If you take on a pleasant form, then we say you're in heaven. If you go beyond the bondage of all form, then we say it is *mukthi* or liberation.

A spiritual seeker is not interested in going to heaven or hell. He wants to go beyond this duality of hell and heaven also. So as your energies mature, you may see qualities you never thought were part of you, not because some new quality is coming, simply because something you never dared to face is coming up and you are facing it. It's fine, it's perfectly okay. The only thing is that you shouldn't throw it on all the people around you. You handle it. Okay? You throw your tantrums on people and say, "Now I did Samyama, my karmas are coming out. You have to bear with me." Don't give them your karma, don't throw your circle flies on people around you. You handle them yourself (laughs).

Seeker: Master, in my experience on this path, it's not always such a joyride. I feel intense pain too, pain that's around me.

Sadhguru: Now, that which you call as 'me' or as 'you' are the same. Whatever you do, every action, every thought that you generate touches the world in some way. So whatever you do touches everything. As you become more and more sensitive, as you become more and more aware, as your consciousness expands, this becomes a life experience, not just somebody's teachings. If you're sensitive enough, if you're intense enough, if you're loving enough, whatever happens somewhere will happen to you also. You can actually feel it, maybe in a small way. Though it can happen only if you're open enough at that moment. Otherwise it won't; you will miss it. So your question will be, "Okay, if pain comes to you, why should it come to me?" I am telling you, that will be your growth.

Once, Shankaran Pillai happily agreed to take his wife to visit a holy place, hoping she would renounce some of her worldly desires. So he chose a monastery in Himachal Pradesh[1] and they set off on their pilgrimage. This monastery is perched high on a cliff. The only way to reach it is to sit in a basket and be pulled to the top by the monks up there. Shankaran Pillai, his wife – a big woman – and a monk, huddled together in the basket. The monks at the top were pulling and tugging with all their might. Obviously, the ride up this steep cliff became terrifying. With each tug, Shankaran Pillai was getting exceedingly nervous. Once they reached about half way up, he noticed that the rope was old and frayed. He gave a quick glance towards his wife, then to the rope and again to his wife. Then in a trembling voice he anxiously asked the monk in the basket, "How often do you guys change the rope on this thing, anyway?" The monk thought for a moment and answered brusquely, "Whenever it breaks." So, not everything in life comes as a joyride, Raja. Don't think that you will grow only in pleasure. Most people will grow only with pain, not with pleasure. It's unfortunate, but that's the truth. Generally people only go down with pleasure. They don't go up with pleasure. Please see, the quality of a human being is like this, when life offers more and more pleasures to a man, he doesn't grow. He goes down. In terms of the real quality of a human being, only when suffering comes, when pain comes, does a man stand up as a human being. You can see great human beings surface only when the society is really suffering. When India was under the oppression of British rulers, how many wonderful people stood up? Where are they now? They have just fallen back into their comforts, that's all. All those Gandhis, Patels, Tilaks are still there, but they're dormant. When pain came, they all became alive. They left everything behind and stood up as giants. Where are they now? This is the human misfortune that still there's not enough intelligence in the world that human beings will rise to their peaks when everything is well. They wait for calamities.

1 Himachal Pradesh : a North Indian state in the Himalayan region.

Seeker: Sadhguru, if the spiritual and the mystical realities are beyond that which is physical, beyond the five senses, is there ever a point where we are cognizant of spiritual experience or growth? How do we know if we're progressing or regressing spiritually?

Sadhguru: It is only the physical dimension which can grow and diminish. You're constantly going on trying to strengthen your limitations, and at the same time claiming that you want to become spiritual. Stop reinforcing your limitations. Limitations will wear out by themselves. If you just see them as limitations they will fall apart, but you're going on reinforcing your limitations. So don't try to progress or regress. You're talking about dimensions which aren't in your present level of experience. When you're approaching a dimension which isn't in your present level of experience, don't try to create a roadmap. Don't try to make a roadmap of unknown terrain; it will be a great mistake. Just see that you have no map. Right now, you don't have the necessary faculties to know anything which is beyond the physical. If you recognize this, if you understand this, if you accept this absolutely, only then the other dimension opens up.

In certain situations, with overwhelming energy and presence, we have broken the limitations of your five senses and made you experience dimensions beyond, but you're not able to sustain this. The idea of overwhelming you was that once you get a glimpse of something beyond, you will have the necessary intelligence not to attach too much importance to the limitations in which you exist. I want you to understand this clearly. Don't try to do anything about your sense organs. Going beyond your sense organs isn't in your hands. The only thing you can do is to stop attaching importance to your own ways of thinking and feeling, your thought patterns, your emotions, and your opinions. Don't attach any importance to them. Then your limitations will become weaker and weaker and one day collapse.

Seeker: I love God very much, but He doesn't seem to be responding.

Sadhguru: Somu, if you really love God, seeing Him would be the ultimate. Yes? If you love Him, you hold Him as the highest, you hold Him above creation, isn't it? He's the Creator. Seeing Him,

being with Him, would be the highest. If you have no trust in Him, then you talk in terms of existence, of no-mind, and all these things. The moment there's no trust, the whole issue becomes terribly complicated. Then you have to split hairs to do things, simply because love is missing. Trust means unconditional love. It's that kind of love where the other side need not respond. You simply love. You must have loved like this when you were in school and college. The other side wasn't responding, but you went on loving. Once it happened, a young boy in college went to his professor and said, "I need your help." The professor said, "Sure, I am here to help you." The boy said, "No, it is not academic, it is something else." So the professor said, "Tell me..." The boy named the college beauty and said, "I am in love with her and I am fifty percent successful. For the other fifty percent, you have to help." The professor asked, "What do you mean, fifty percent successful?" The boy replied, "Well, I am madly in love with her, but she hasn't responded!" In your college-day love, with every step you were expecting that she would at least turn around and look at you. This is not that kind of one-sided love. This has total trust.

When a person has that kind of love that he doesn't expect the other side to even respond, it's okay. If God doesn't respond, it's okay. You have firm faith that he's there. Now look at this and see, we always love those who are not here. With most people it is so; they always love the dead when they're not here any more. When they were living, you couldn't look them in the face, you weren't even on talking terms, but once they're dead you love them. You always love those who are not here, and it's the same thing with God. If he was here with you, if you had to share your food with him, if you had to share your life with him, then you would have had enormous problems with him, but because he's not here now, or at least not in your experience, it's easy to love him. One day, a mother and a little boy went to the cemetery. For the seven-year-old boy, it was his first visit to a cemetery. The mother sat down in one place as she was dedicated to one particular grave, but the boy was curious and went around the cemetery reading the inscriptions on every tombstone. After he was done with his rounds, he came to his mother and asked, "Mom, where do they bury all the horrible people?"

Love is not a joy; it is a deep wonderful pain. It is a very deep, tearing, wonderful pain. Something within you should tear; not just something, everything within you should tear. Only then you know what love is. If it feels pleasant, that's not love, it's just convenience. Maybe you felt a little affection. If you have ever loved, everything inside you tears apart, really tears apart. It's painful, but wonderful. That's how it is.

When you start feeling like this about everything and everybody, then going beyond your limitations – physical and mental – naturally happens by itself. It doesn't happen by trying. If you try to go beyond your physical limitations with effort, you only injure yourself; but when it happens like this, it simply happens, physical limitations are no more limitations.

This isn't about training your being. Nobody can ever train their being. It doesn't take any training from anybody. You can't train God. You think it's just like training the dog, Blackie, here. You throw a ball and say, "Go Blackie, go get it, get it Blackie!" It will run and bring back the ball for you. You're trying to train God like this, showing him dog biscuits and telling him, "Come on, get me this, get me that." When you still haven't come to a point in life where a gracefulness, or the Grace of your inner being, has permeated onto the outside, then it's very important that you at least develop some gracefulness on the level of your body and mind. This is not growth. This is like covering a naked man. Without this covering you would be naked and lost. So this is just clothing to protect you until you reach a point where you don't need it. Those who have no hope of being loved by anybody, they are always hoping God will love them. Those people who have no hope of ever being loved by anybody, yes, only God can love them (laughs). Some sage or saint might have talked about loving God, but now that you have a logical mind, a thinking mind, a doubting mind and a questioning mind, don't talk about loving God; it doesn't make

The mystical beat. An informal gathering brings out the charmer in Him.

any sense. The only reason you have started thinking about God or the Creator is because you have experienced the creation. Before you came, all that you call as creation was there, so you just assumed that somebody must have created it, and you started giving names and forms to that Creator. So your idea of the Creator has come to you only through the creation. Now you hate the creation, you hate the person sitting next to you, and say that you love God; it doesn't mean anything. It won't lead you anywhere, because if you hate the creation, what business do you have with the one who created all this? Only if you have fallen deeply in love with the creation, then you have something to do with the one who created this. It's very significant that Jesus said, "Love thy neighbor." He doesn't mean falling in love with the person next door, he means just loving the one who's next to you right now, this moment, whomever it may be. You don't know what evil could be happening in his mind; it doesn't matter whether he's good or bad, whether you like him or dislike him, just to love him the way he is. If you do this, then you merge with creation. Once you merge with creation, that's the only way to the Creator. Creation is the only way, or the only doorway to the Creator. If you reject creation, you can't know anything about the Creator. So don't worry about loving God. See if you can bring love into your breath, into your step, into every act that you do, not towards anybody or anything; if you can just bring the longing to merge with everything around you, then creation will lead you on to the Creator.

Seeker: How will I know when that's happening, when God is actually responding in my life?

Sadhguru: God never responds.

Seeker: How will I know exactly when he stepped into my life?

Sadhguru: Somu, you will know that God loves you when somebody manages to love you (laughs).

Seeker: I sometimes notice that some people seem to keep spirituality separate from life. Why is this? I find it very difficult to understand why this is the case, because awareness is not only when you're meditating. My second question is, if the purpose is 'Self'- Realization, why do we need a Guru?

Sadhguru: About the first part of the question – if your spirituality is time-bound, five to seven in the morning or six to eight in the morning, or whatever time, you're just trying to be spiritual; there's nothing spiritual about you. What conclusions have you made about being spiritual? If you have made the conclusion that being spiritual means speaking kindly to everybody, you're mistaken. If someone is communicating with different aspects of life in different ways, out of their understanding, out of their sensitivity, out of their own experience – they know how to communicate with a baby, a buffalo, a mountain, they know how to speak to the bus driver – they know it out of this awareness, then it's wonderful and fine. That's how life should be.

If someone, out of their so-called spirituality, is trying to speak with whatever they believe is kindness or goodness, to every aspect of life, they are just moralistic and stupid. Maybe they are good people, but they have no sense of life. There's no inner experience; it's just coming from their goodness and morality. They may make good citizens, but they won't know anything of the beyond. Now, if one is communicating in different ways with different aspects of life because of their unawareness, or because of their prejudices, that's a different aspect altogether. So how one talks to a bus driver may be a way of seeing where that person is, or may not be at all. It's best that you don't judge a person by the way they are speaking to a bus driver or to a man on the street at a certain moment. Now, if one has a pattern of addressing something kindly and another aspect of life rudely, then you know it is coming from ignorance. It has nothing to do with spirituality or anything. First of all let's understand that spirituality is not a moral code. Spirituality means you're beginning to experience that which is beyond the physical. It has got nothing to do with the way you communicate and handle the world around you. The way you do that is just a question of your capability, your intelligence, your exposure, your inclination, and what kind of objectives you have in your life. So how you communicate with the world is in no way an indication of your spiritual process. Swami Nityananda was a yogi, sitting in the forest, absolutely blissful, but if people came anywhere near him, he threw stones at them. He never hit anybody, but he madly threw stones at them. As far as people were concerned, he was a madman throwing stones. It was only much later, when people looked back they were able to see that not once did he hit anybody. He threw stones, always making sure that they didn't hit anybody. He just didn't want people around him. He knew that if people came, they would ask for things, and because of the way he was – his energy was in a certain state – naturally things would happen, miracles would happen. Then people would gather and mess up his whole life. So if people came anywhere near him, he would throw stones at them.

If you go by one's behavior, about what he's doing or what he's saying, then you will definitely come to a wrong conclusion, a wrong judgment. If you had known Sadhguru Shri Brahma, he would even kick people! If somebody came and said something stupid to him, he would just kick them, not out of arrogance, not out of hatred, and not out of anger; that's how he dealt with people. Now he doesn't (laughs). This is not because he has become more Realized or less Realized, it is simply because he has become a little smarter with the world. So how you operate is just a question of your inclination, your intelligence and your exposure, and things like that; it has got nothing to do with your spirituality. If someone is behaving senselessly in his life and always talking about spirituality, you know why. It's a fad; spirituality is a fad for him. Now you saying, "I'm open" – see, what openness you're talking about is in terms of, "I am willing to go anywhere." Willing to go anywhere is good; on one level, it is openness. Now wherever you go, you're willing to go all the way; that's real openness. If you become, "Wherever I go, I am willing to go all the way", that openness would reap more harvest than, "I am willing to go anywhere."

After all this, you demolish your own question: "If spirituality means seeking all the time, why do I need a Guru?" Let's say, all that you're seeking is to go to Kedarnath right now. Somebody is driving; the roads are laid out. If you came alone and there were no proper directions, definitely you would have wished, "I wish there was a map to tell me how to get there." On one level, a Guru is just a map. He's a live map. If you can read the map, you know the way, you can go. A Guru can also be your bus driver. You sit here and doze and he will take you to Kedarnath; but to sit in this bus and doze off, or to sit in this bus joyfully, you need to trust the bus driver. If every moment, with every curve in this road, you go on thinking, "Will this man kill me? Will this man go off the road? What intention does he have for my life?" then you will only go mad sitting here. We're talking about trust, not because a Guru needs your trust, it's just that if there's no trust you will drive yourself mad.

This is not just for sitting on a bus or going on a spiritual journey. To live on this planet, you need trust. Right now, you trust unconsciously. You're sitting on this bus, which is just a bundle of nuts and bolts and pieces of metal. Look at the way you're going through the mountains. Unknowingly, you trust this vehicle so much. Isn't it so? You have placed your life in the hands of this mechanical mess, which is just nuts and bolts, rubbers and wires, this and that. You have placed your life in it, but you trust the bus unconsciously. The same trust, if it arises consciously, would do miracles to you. When we say trust, we're not talking about anything new to life. To be here, to take every breath in and out, you need trust, isn't it? Your trust is unconscious. I am only asking you to bring a little consciousness to your trust. It's not something new. Life is trust, otherwise nobody can exist here.

So if you can draw your own map, if you can drive your own bus, that's wonderful. But on an uncharted path, if you go without a map, it may take lifetimes to find a certain place. It may take lifetimes to cross. If you go with a map you will cross easily. If you go with a good bus driver you will cross very easily; that's the difference. It's not that you can't do it yourself – you can. We don't know how long it will take. That's the question.

Chapter - 2

With the One Who Knows

*W*ith the One Who Knows

Life and death live in me at once
Never held one above the other

When one stands far, life I offer
In closeness, only death I deal

In death of the limited
Will the deathless be

How to tell the fools
Of my taintless evil.

– Sadhguru

Guru-shishya paramparya. *The explosive touch.*

Joyful romp. *Ever playful, Sadhguru brings out the child in everyone.*

After seeking enters a being, sooner or later, one arrives at a point where one desires the guidance and the grace of the One Who Knows, One who has been through this uncharted but inevitable metamorphosis. Blessed are those who seek One, more blessed are those who actually encounter One.

However, relationships repeatedly defiled by imposters and charlatans and one's own inner defilement stand in the way of simply sitting at the Master's feet, just receiving.

Sanctified in the tradition as the *Guru-shishya paramparya*, being with the One Who Knows is eternal and the most sacred of all relationships. Having been a forlorn seeker himself in a previous lifetime, refusing to bow down before any human form, Sadhguru, in his present lifetime plays the role of the One Who Knows.

Dispelling fears and misgivings of bondage and exploitation, Sadhguru answers questions paramount to the seeker – How do I choose my Guru? Is a Guru really necessary? How best do I make use of the Guru? And then, in case I don't make it in this lifetime, will he see me through in another lifetime?

Secure under the wings of the One Who Knows, the seeker has the luxury and space to explore within, and the entire Existence too, with the kind of reckless abandon that the Creator Himself would envy.

Seeker: Like many people around me, I am seeking the ultimate Truth and the right guidance to experience it. Sadhguru, can you tell us how a person finds his Guru?[1]

Sadhguru: If you are truly a seeker of Truth, Truth cannot hide from you. It is in the lap of Truth that you have happened. Most people who claim to be seekers are only seeking security, solace, or the fulfillment of their desires. Their life is just an expression of their greed and fear. Do you see, many people in the world shamelessly claim to be God-fearing? They are not God loving, they are God-fearing. Unless you have fallen in love with creation, how can you love the one who created it? Like Jesus said, "Love thy neighbor." Everyone can love God, as He does not demand anything from you, but to love the one next to you right now costs life. It is a challenge. It takes much courage to do this. 'Love thy neighbor' is a very good device for breaking your illusion of loving the one who is in the heavens.

A genuine seeker, a person who develops an urge within, will always find his Guru. He may find it in a man, in a woman, or he may find it even in a rock. He will definitely find it somewhere, there is no doubt about it. When any being calls or really yearns, the existence answers. If the thirst within you is strong enough, God always answers.

Seeker: Sadhguru, is spiritual transformation possible without the help of a Guru?

Sadhguru: The reason why there has always been so much importance and stress in this culture on a Guru is that without a Guru there can be no spiritual process. Without him you cannot transform yourself.

1 Guru : lit. *dispeller of darkness*. A spiritual Master.

How can you transform yourself into something that you don't know? You can only work towards what you know, isn't it? How to work towards that which you don't know? To do that, you have to be so aware as to be able to see the natural tendencies of every aspect of energy in the existence, which is moving or is tending to move in a certain direction. You need to understand this and start moving that way. Only a person who has that sense of awareness can walk without a Guru. Others, if they walk without a Guru, they will just flounder and flounder and flounder.

Through the Grace of the Guru, in a moment, with just a clap of his hands, things can happen. Sometimes certain situations or certain energies can also do things to people. In these situations, they are acting like a Guru – maybe not in the physical form, but that is what is happening. Transforming yourself into that which you don't know, or that which you have not tasted, is logically impossible. I am not ruling it out totally. It is possible, but only for very few people. For most people, it is remote. It is not impossible, but it is very remote.

Seeker: Is that why so many people seem to love you to the point of madness, since you are the one who can show us the path? But really, Jaggi, personally for me, Realization or no Realization, I just love you very much.

Sadhguru: I didn't know that. That is news to me…I am the most insensitive man in the world, aren't I? (Laughs). Most of the time, people's longing towards the Master is unconscious. Why such crazy longing is unconscious is because when the energy level deepens, it is neither mental nor emotional. It is just like a plant, not longing for water emotionally or mentally – it is a deep energy longing. If there is a drop of water there, the roots will find their way to it. There is no emotion in it. There is no mind in it. It is a different kind of intelligence. It knows where to go. It knows where its life is. Wherever you place it, it will just find its way. Not even by mistake will it go this way or that way. It will not go any other way because it has a deep longing. This longing is not thought, not emotion, it is just life's longing for itself. That is how it is.

Seeker: So, did we have an unconscious longing to find you? I mean, to find a live Guru? You know, unconsciously were we always searching for you and that's why we are here? I'm not sure how to ask this...

Sadhguru: If you have difficulty in forming the question itself, it must be a very difficult question! (Laughs). Yes, naturally, everything moves in that direction.

Seeker: Now that we are accompanying you on this trip to the Himalayas,[1] and some of us even have the privilege of riding on this bus with you, I am wondering, what is it within us that has created the opportunity to have access to you? What is the difference between people who have access to a Guru and people who don't?

Sadhguru: Now John, you would like to believe that you are the chosen few? Do you know chosen people have always been eternally in trouble? I must tell you a joke. Once, the leader of the Jewish community on planet Earth, Joshua Goldberg, had his annual dinner appointment with God. So he went to dinner, and God arrived and sat down at the table with him. A few breadcrumbs were served for dinner. God said Grace and started eating. Joshua just sat there. God looked at him and said, "Joshua, my son, why don't you eat?" Joshua said, "Father, can I ask you a question?" God answered, "Okay, my son." Joshua asked, "Dear Father, are we really the chosen people?" God replied, "Why, my son, why do you doubt? Yes, you are the chosen people." Joshua asked, "Father, are we really, really, the chosen people?" "Yes, Joshua. Why are you beginning to doubt? You are the chosen people." Then Joshua asked, "Dear Father, are we really, really, really the chosen people?" "Yes, yes, yes, you are the chosen people!" Then Joshua got up from the table, straightened his jacket and said, "Why don't you choose somebody else for a while?"

---

1 Himalayas : Every alternate year, Sadhguru takes Isha meditators to the Himalayas to allow them to experience the mystical dimensions of these sacred mountains.

So why are we here? Okay, if you're just talking about being on this bus, *yes*, you are the chosen people (laughs). Why does one person get access to certain possibilities? Let us look at it this way: I want you to look at me not as a person, but as a possibility. Why certain people get access to certain possibilities and others don't, that is the question. Now, this is not really true. It is not that only certain people get access to this possibility. Anybody who is truly longing, always has access to this, to this energy, which you right now refer to as me. Everybody may not have access to the person; that is obvious. It is always so.

Maybe I have to tell you this at this point; I have initiated more people I have not met than people I have met; that is the reality. When someone really longs, I initiate them, wherever they may be, when the longing is deep enough to receive me. When someone's heart cries out to know, I am always there. So as far as the possibility is concerned, this possibility has happened to a lot more people who have never seen my face, but if you're talking about the person, that is not of great significance. Maybe it is a pleasure, or, if you're too close around me, like Doug, it could be a torture putting up with me and my demands – like holding this microphone on this bumpy bus ride, finding my sunglasses or locating my favorite Frisbee (laughs). If you're sitting two seats away from me, it can be a pleasure. If you're right next to me, it can be a torture.

Being with a Master is never comfortable, because He will break all your limitations, all your ideologies. So knowing the person or having access to the person can be on many levels. Having access to the possibility is only because of the longing that one may have. There are many people who have close access to the person, but don't know anything about the possibility yet. Knowing the person is of no great significance. Probably it has been put forth by many people in many different ways. Gautama[1] put this forth very beautifully. When somebody asked about Ananda Tirtha, who was constantly with Gautama throughout his life and remained unenlightened until the end; when people asked, "This man is with you all the time. Why has nothing happened to him?" In answer, Gautama asks, "Can a spoon taste the soup?" So that says it all. You need sensitivity, to be life sensitive, not ego sensitive.

1 Gautama : referring to the Buddha.

Seeker: Sadhguru, a lot of Enlightened beings have a few people who are close to them. Is it because they are able to relate to these people better, or is it because of some past life connections?

Sadhguru: If a person is Enlightened, he can relate to anybody. There is really no problem about relating with whomever he is with at that moment. He can absolutely relate to any person, be totally with anyone. It is very possible for him. Even if the other person is not willing, he can still relate to him and his limitations as well, and still be okay with him; but he might choose, at certain times, to be with certain people. One reason is, he has a specific objective. He has a plan as to what he wants to do. For that he needs certain people.

For example, Ramakrishna Paramahamsa[1] was deeply attached, or at least it looked like he was deeply attached, to Naren, who was later known as Vivekananda. People around Ramakrishna resented this. Many other people who were always around him, hankered to be with him. Vivekananda was a truant disciple to begin with, overly logical and arrogant. The others were so much more dedicated than he was, but still Ramakrishna sought Vivekananda. Every other day Vivekananda would get angry with Ramakrishna and walk off saying, "I will go back to my college, I have got work," and Ramakrishna would go searching for him in the town. This man had never really been in town, but he would go with tears in his eyes, search for him, and then beg him to come back. All the other disciples of Ramakrishna would be deeply offended, "Where is the need for our Guru to run behind some hothead, begging him to come? All of us are here, he can teach us. Why does he go after this fool?" Not only his disciples, but also his wife Sharada was deeply offended. She would ask, "Why Naren all the time? So many people are here, waiting for you. Why do you go after this Naren?" But Ramakrishna knew, without Naren things would not happen. His message would not be taken to the masses. He knew, today these people could be on, tomorrow, they could drop off.

Once this comes up in the society, all sorts of rumors will go on. "Oh, maybe it is like this. Maybe he is his real son, his biological son. Maybe it was hidden from us. Maybe he is homosexual. Maybe he is

---

1 Ramakrishna Paramahamsa : an ecstatic saint of the mid-nineteenth century.

seeking this young boy in some other way." These kinds of things happened around Ramakrishna, but the reason why he was seeking Vivekananda like that was, he saw him as the ideal carrier for his message. He knew, if Vivekananda was not sufficiently prepared by the time he leaves, then his whole work, whatever he had to offer to the world, would die with him; he knew that. So he acted almost like Vivekananda's slave. Many people thought it was totally undignified for him to behave like that with Vivekananda, but he went about like this because he had a clear objective, and he had no problem as to how to do it. He just did what worked, that is all.

Another aspect of it is that there could have been energy bonds, not emotional bonds. It is not a question of being able to relate better. There could have been a certain energy bond, which people could not understand. That is, this Enlightened being may not have been able to operate as a physical person without the support of somebody else, maybe one, two, or even ten people. He may have been just using them to keep his physical body going, in many ways. Otherwise, he would have been incapable of sustaining his physical body by himself. There could have been energy bonds. Or it is just that people think that somebody else is closer, simply because for everything that has to happen, this person generally depends on one person, because he sees this person seems to have much more sense and a deeper understanding of everything that is said and done.

This was very beautifully demonstrated by Ashtavakra, an Enlightened being. Ashtavakra was the Master for Janaka Maharaj, who was a king. Janaka was a Realized being himself, who continued to be a king because Ashtavakra told him, "You must continue to be a king because people deserve an Enlightened king." Whenever Janaka found a break from his administrative and royal duties, he always came to Ashtavakra, who was in a hermitage in the forest, and spent time there, as any other disciple. He sat there with the other disciples. All the other disciples were monks. They were *bhramhacharis*, fully dedicated to Ashtavakra. Their Master's word was everything for them. Their life was for him to do anything he wanted with them. Janaka was a king; he was married with many wives, and as a king he had many social involvements. He had everything, and more, than any normal king.

So there was resentment with the other disciples who were monks. First of all, someone had taken this step of being a monk or a bhramhachari out of his own choice, because he sees it as a suitable path to walk upon.He sees that by going into a family situation, his spirituality or his spiritual urge could completely evaporate. Just to see that his spiritual thirst is not evaporated, he is willing to forgo certain things in his life and pursue his path in totality. He need not have any resentment towards someone who has all this and still pursues spirituality, but unfortunately he does, because somewhere, there is resentment that they are enjoying all the luxuries that life has to offer and spirituality as well. They are having the best of both worlds, so there is resentment.

Ashtavakra treated Janaka with utmost graciousness, so that too was bothering them. Though they have accepted him as their Guru, somewhere, the logical mind asks these questions: "Is it only because he is a rich man, a king, that he is being treated better than us?" This question was always there, and now, there are so many emotions that are involved in this, which is a daily affair for every Guru. This was not just for Janaka, but for Janaka it was dramatic because he was a king. I am sorry to say that this is not so just for Ashtavakra, but for every Guru, this is an issue in his life. For Ashtavakra, it was such a dramatic situation, because he was handling a king and monks together. The difference and the distinction between the two was too vast and too stark.

One day, they were all sitting in a *sathsang*,[1] and one of the disciples asked this question: "Why is it that you're always treating Janaka special and we are not being treated the same way?" Ashtavakra just smiled and said, "I will answer this, but not now." They felt even more hurt, because they thought he was avoiding this question because Janaka was there. Ashtavakra waited and at a certain time he engineered a situation where somebody came running and said, "The monks' clothes! The monkeys are taking them away!" These clothes were nothing except loincloths and maybe just a piece of cloth to wrap around their shoulders when it got cold. These clothes were hung outside to dry. When Ashtavakra was still speaking in the sathsang, the moment they heard the news, all the monks got up and ran to save their clothes. Then they came back and sat down. Ashtavakra just continued to speak and after some time, one of the king's messengers came and blurted out, without even asking the Guru's permission whether he can speak or not, he just blurted out that the king's palace was burning. Janaka just looked at him and asked him to get out of that place. He said, "How dare you enter this place without the Master's permission? Get out!"

---

1 *sathsang* : in communion with Truth, a congregration of seekers

Then Ashtavakra waited for a moment and said, "His palace is burning, and he got offended that his man interrupted my speech, but you people, just your stupid clothes, which are not worth anything to anybody, the kind of clothes that would be thrown away – for that, without even looking at me you ran after them. That is the difference! And that is why the difference."

Janaka's way of being was such that, though he was an Enlightened being and a king as well, a rare combination, sitting at his Master's feet was the highest Grace in his life. He was always aspiring for this opportunity and still sat there, which most people would not do. So such a man being treated special was very natural. You don't carry rocks in your hand the way you carry a flower. You carry a flower with a different sense of gentleness and give a different priority to it, isn't it? When you want to offer something to God, you don't offer a rock. I am not saying a rock is any less; it is just that a flower is more evolved. Accordingly it gets treated. This goes for people also. This does not mean you don't care for a rock. You care for it, and you do more work with it because it needs more work. That is different, but definitely the way you handle it is different. If you don't have this distinction, then you will be a fool with life. In the name of equality, you will destroy all the beauty of life.

Seeker: Sadhguru, can a relationship between the Master and disciple in previous births be carried on for lifetimes?

Sadhguru: Yes, definitely. Generally, this is the only relationship which can be carried for lifetimes. The work continues. There have been husbands, wives and lovers who have come together again for lifetimes because their love was so strong, but that is very rare. Generally, it is the Master-disciple relationship which gets carried for lifetimes. All the other relationships come together for convenience. Once it is over, it just breaks apart. To know this, first of all you need to come to an understanding as to what a relationship is, why there are human relationships. Now, you have formed various types of relationships in your life, some for your emotional needs, physical needs, financial needs, social needs, psychological needs, or a few just for comfort; in many ways you have formed relationships. Whatever kind of relationship you have formed, fundamentally it is concerned and based only with the body. When the relationship is based in the body, once the body drops, the relationship just evaporates. That is the end of it. Only if a relationship transcends physical limitations – when I say physical, I am referring to the mental structure and emotional structure also as physical – only when you in some way transcend the physical limitations, there is a possibility of this relationship extending beyond lifetimes or across lifetimes.

So generally, it is only the Master-disciple relationship which extends this way, though there could be a few examples of other relationships going beyond physical limitations. This is because the Master-disciple relationship continues always. Even if the disciple has no idea of the Master's being, the Master's business is only with the disciple's being. This relationship is always energy-based. It is not emotion-based, it is not mind-based, nor is it body-based. It is only energy-based. An energy-based relationship does not even realize whether the bodies have changed or not over lifetimes. It continues until the energy reaches dissolution. It just continues. For the energy there is no rebirth. It is only the body which is reborn. The energy just continues as one flow and accordingly carries the relationship. So definitely, this is one relationship which is carried on because it is purely an energy-based relationship.

Seeker: Sadhguru, are there people here with you now that were connected to you in your past life?

Sadhguru: Yes. Many people who were connected to me in some way over three hundred and seventy years ago, not only those who supported us, but even those who persecuted us, who tormented us, are somehow mostly in Coimbatore today. All of them are not our meditators, but they are with us. It is like that. That is the way life functions.

Why all these people land up in one place is – why is the breeze blowing in this direction and not the other way? Do you know why? See, the whole momentum of the wind in the world is just this: the sea is a place where the humidity is high, so the pressure and the density are also high. When the land gets heated up, the density is low. Wherever the density is low, there the wind rushes. Then it rains, and then that becomes high density. Then the wind moves backward, as the wind movement is always towards low density. Wherever there is emptiness, everything rushes there. So when the karmic bag is empty here (pointing to himself), all those other bags of karma[1] which have been one way or the other connected to that for so many lifetimes tend to slowly move towards that direction, knowingly or unknowingly. Mostly unknowingly, they slowly move in that direction, because for all of them there is a possibility now. When one bag empties, everybody has the opportunity to become empty.

Sometimes it also happens that a nearly empty bag comes in search of past karmic connections to empty itself. That could be an opportunity for both beings to dissolve that aspect of the karma, but if one is not alert to their inner situations, these opportunities could be completely missed. Someone here among you knows this firsthand. Let us ask Bharathi how she missed one such situation.

Bharathi: A few years ago, before the Dhyanalinga [2] consecration, Sadhguru specifically told me that my father of my Raigarh birth, who was in his final stage of spiritual evolution, would come and visit me. He described this person, his attire, and his demeanor, and said such a person would visit me in thirty days. Many times, I had seen such a person in certain states of meditative clarity. Sadhguru went on to say that he was within one hundred to two hundred kilometers away in the southerly direction, that he would find me within thirty days, and when he comes I should ask him in and serve him a meal. By doing this, I would be able to dissolve some of my unfinished karma which had been hanging on for a long time. About two weeks later, towards mid-morning, the security person at the gate sent word that there was a man asking to see me. When I asked what he wanted, I got a message that he just wanted to see me. Engrossed in my routine, I said that I was not willing to meet any strangers. After some time, I came to know that the man was still waiting at the gate, insisting on seeing me. In irritation and curiosity I stepped out of the house and saw this person standing with a certain dignity, obviously not expecting anything from me. He looked at me with an unusual sense of tenderness, which I ignored. I said, "I don't know who you are and I want nothing to do with you," and turned my back on him. Later, suddenly, in a moment of clarity, it dawned on me: this was the man of my vision and also of Sadhguru's description. I immediately contacted Sadhguru who was traveling, and the first thing he said was, "He came and went. He has emptied himself." Then I knew how, in my unawareness, I missed such an opportunity.

---

1 Karma : referring to past action, the cause of all bondage.

2 Dhyanalinga : a powerful energy form consecrated exclusively for the purpose of meditation, at Isha Yoga Center.

Sadhguru: Whatever the past karma, it is like this: let us say, until the age of thirty you earn ten million rupees. Now you can either squander it or make it grow. In the past, you might have created some riches within you. In this life you may either add to it or squander it, but definitely some quality of that will be there in your life, though in unconsciousness it may go to waste. So because of your spiritual practices, *sadhana,* those riches may manifest now in terms of material comfort, like a good house, the right kind of atmosphere, or maybe good people around you. In spite of all this, you may not make use of it and just become complacent. That is the whole cycle. Why I repeatedly say that the whole game is like the *Snake and Ladder* game is: you climb the ladder and there you're happy. The very comfort that comes out of it, that comes out of good karma, may make you complacent and that is it, down through the snake you go. Then once suffering comes, you start looking and grow. You may squander it and go down again. This is the way of the fool, wasting his energy; but someone who has sufficient intelligence in him should even take each breath as a step towards growth. It is very much possible. Like how she shared, the reminder comes. Even after reminding a person hundreds of times, if he still does not wake up, if he is still lying down in his comforts, what can we do? He will be lost. He has to suffer once again, and then maybe seek growth.

This whole spiritual process is not happening to even one percent of the population. For all others, when things are going well they are laughing, and when things go bad they are crying. There are very few people in the world who, whichever way it is, are okay and balanced. For them nothing is a great benediction, nothing is a problem. Everything is just another life situation through which they can become free. The rest of the people are all the type who will go the way the situation pushes them. They are like cattle. You have evolved into a human body, but otherwise there is no real difference. Between the way animals live and generally the way people live, is there any great difference qualitatively? Maybe quantitatively there is a lot of difference. There is more variety to your activity; you drive a car, you watch television. All that nonsense you do, but qualitatively, where is the difference?

If the difference has to come, it can only come with awareness; there is no other way. This awareness need not be just dry. When it is filled with love, this awareness just multiplies. Generally, mental alertness is mistaken for awareness, but awareness is a far deeper dimension than just mental alertness. When awareness arises within you, love and compassion will be the natural follow-up. When you're very loving, you are very aware; can you see that? Now, if you're not able to relate to things around you, to people around you, it is not because there is something wrong with you. You're either a little misplaced, or out of your own foolishness you got misplaced in this life.

Once you become aware, you have to make the little arrangements that are needed to put yourself in the right place. If you know you're a coconut, then you should have fallen here at the foothills, not on the mountaintop. It is of no use; you can't grow there. You have to roll down somehow. If you have to roll down, maybe you have to lose something. If the coconut has to reach the foothills, maybe a man has to pick it up and bring it down. Maybe he will peel it and take off the skin. You don't know what you will lose. Something will be lost. The man who carries it is bound to take off something. Life is like that. For whatever you do, you have to pay a price. Let me tell you a joke. A man sat in a train traveling from Bristol to London, with a baby in his arms. Halfway through the trip, another man with two big suitcases got on the train and sat down next to him. The first man said, "Those two suitcases look just like mine; are you a salesman too?" "No," the other man replied, "I'm on the way to the airport. I'm flying to Greece." Then he asked, "So what are you selling, anyway?" "Condoms," the first man replied. Shocked, the other man said, "Condoms? And you're taking your son with you while you sell condoms?" "Oh, this is not my son; it is a complaint from Bristol."

Without a price, you get nothing. You better know this. Whether you pay the price here or there, you can't escape it, you will always pay. That's the law of karma. There is a price for everything. What kind of physical situations you land up in have a very strong karmic basis. The very fact that you are here today proves that your physical situation has been conducive enough to allow you to be here. There are many who desire to be here, but for many reasons it has not happened for them. They are yet to earn it.

Seeker: Master, you have ignited a flame in me, and I am burning up now. Tell me how to take it to the world. I want the whole world to know you. I want the world to know this…

Sadhguru: The journey has begun. When you first came to Isha,[1] many of you simply came either out of curiosity, or maybe seeking some physical or psychological benefits. After some time, even after you finished the program, being around was still good entertainment. It was a place to come to meet people. But after a while, some of you were helplessly pulled towards yoga. Whether you wanted to come or not, somehow you were here. Until now, I would say most of you, more or less, have remained spectators – maybe involved a little, but still spectators. Are you willing to change and make this shift from being a spectator to being a real participant in this yoga?

Moving from being a spectator into actually becoming a part of the action are two very different things. When you are a spectator, if things go well for your team, you jump up with joy and clap. When things go bad, you look the other way. Now when you become a part of the action itself, both your involvement and your experience will change in a dramatic way. There is no real risk for a spectator. He may enjoy the game or he may feel a little depressed because the game didn't go well, but when you are a part of the action itself, everything is at stake in so many ways. It is like this: if there is a race going on, to sit and watch as a spectator is one thing. Mind you, a spectator is also involved, but the person who is actually racing is on a different level of involvement: he's the one who really takes the risk of racing. Now that you have decided to take the step of moving from spectator-hood into the real play, into the very core of the action, you had better know what the nature of this action is, and what it demands from you.

Now that many of you here have taken the step of being involved, let us see what is needed out of a person who's taking a step like this. Right now, whatever you call as 'yourself' is simply a certain formation of the mind you have collected. It is a certain type of information in your mind. When you say, "I'm a good person," "I'm a bad person," "I am haughty," "I am meek," or whatever you may say, all those things are simply certain formations of the mind, or in other words, it is just past accumulation. You simply live through your past. If the past is taken away, most people are just lost. Everything depends on the past.

---

1 Isha : name chosen by Sadhguru for the foundation created to offer a spiritual possibility to humankind.

It is the previous moment which rules everything. This moment is not important. As long as the personality is important, it simply means the previous moment is important. This present moment is not important, because the personality belongs to the past.

In this moment you really have no personality, do understand this. The personality that you carry is a dead thing. When you're carrying a dead body over your shoulders, you can't walk very far. With a dead body, which way can you head? Only to the burial ground, isn't it? If you carry a dead body for too long, you will have to bear with terrible smells. Your personality, the stronger it is, the more odoriferous it is. You can go far in life only when you can leave your past. This is like a snake shedding its skin. Do you know how a snake sheds its skin? One moment it is a part of its body, the next moment it sheds its skin and just goes on without turning back. If every moment one is like a snake leaving the skin behind, only then there is growth. When a person is living moment to moment like this and doesn't carry the burden of the past with him, he is a truly sinless person. He does not carry anything with him. Being sinless doesn't mean that he did not do anything with his life. That would be being a dead person. He did everything that a person could possibly do to know life, but his actions never left any residue, nor did he build a personality out of the actions he performed.

Have you heard of the Saint Suka? He wrote the *Shrimath Bhagavatham*. He was Saint Vyasa's son. Suka was a pure being, a truly sinless being. He had a certain flavor about him which could change at any time. This quality is like that of a flavor, which is not really a flavor. It is flavorlessness, but it is not bland either; it has its own quality. There was a particular incident which happened in his life. One day he was walking by himself in the forest, naked. As he was walking by, there was a lake where a few nymphs, *jala kanyas*, were bathing. As they were by themselves in the forest, all the women were bathing together and playing in the water, naked. Suka came upon the lake, looked at them, and just walked by. While looking at them he just kept walking. The women were not ashamed, nor did they try to hide themselves, they just continued their play. Suka walked off.

While looking for Suka, his father Vyasa came after him. He was over seventy years of age, an old man, and a great saint. Vyasa came and saw Suka passing by this lake where the nymphs were having a bath. He also came into the clearing near the lake while following Suka. When the women saw him, they immediately rushed for their clothes. Suka was a young man in the prime of his youth and naked. The ladies were not ashamed. They were also naked and they were not upset about it. Vyasa was an old man, completely dressed. When he came, they rushed for their clothes! So he went to them and asked, "What is this? I am an old person, and I am dressed properly, whereas my son is young and naked at that. When he came near you, you were not disturbed, but when I came, you're acting like this. Why?" They said, "He has no sense of sex about him. We did not feel anything. He carries no sexual identification. He's just like a child; but you, though seventy years old and finished with the physical aspect of sex, it is still very much there with you."

Only that person who does not carry the previous moment to this moment, only that person is free from everything, and that quality will be felt everywhere. Within a few moments of meeting you, people will trust you to the extent that they would not even trust their parents, or husbands, or wives, simply because you don't carry the burden of the past with you. If you carry the past with you, then you will also smell like anybody else. The whole world stinks with personalities. Everybody has his own strong smell or personality. These are the various stenches in the world, and they keep clashing all the time. When one does not carry this odor, one can cross over this existence. One not only passes through this world effortlessly, one will pass through the very process of life and death effortlessly. This person crosses the ocean of *samsara* without any effort. What looks like a great effort for somebody else will be happening for this person without any effort. Everything just simply happens. All your anger, hatred, jealousy, fear, everything is based in the past. The moment you carry the past and future, you become a donkey. You become a real ass, because the burden is such. Carrying that burden, there is no way anybody can live his life intelligently.

Much love and compassion is needed to carry this message. You may pretend, but when you are burdened, compassion can't come through. When you're so light that nothing matters, only then you can truly be compassionate. Love and compassion flow out of a person only when there is no sense of burden. Now, what you're normally calling as 'love' has become a great burden. It's not love; it is simply various needs, your own needs and your greed covered up with a pretense called love, which is not love at all. To fulfill many things you cover it up with a raiment called love. You can taste love and compassion in your life only when you are in this moment, fresh, absolutely without any burden. If you are carrying your personality with you, there is no way this is possible. There may have been some moments in your life when you felt true compassion towards something or somebody. In those moments, all your personality, who you are, what you are, everything would have melted. Nothing would have been there. You are simply there in that moment.

Seeker: Why is there so much stress on love and compassion on this path, Master?

Sadhguru: Of all emotions, compassion is the highest that man can experience. When someone lives in compassion, not just love, only then he is a real seeker, because very easily love becomes attachment and a bias. Love can become a great prejudice against you, somebody else, or anything.

In the Indian culture you never told your parents, your wife, your husband or your children, "I love you." This was not a part of this culture because the moment you say it, it's almost like it's not there. You're only trying to assert it. Love is not an assertion. Love is a supplication. An asserting mind can never be a loving mind. On the day of the big men's-only booze party, a gentle, quiet, and unassuming fellow who had missed a few of these kinds of parties was goaded by his chauvinistic friends to be more assertive with his wife. "You don't have to always do the things your wife asks you to do. Go home tonight and show her you're the boss." The man, after hearing these same words many times over, was finally set on fire with enthusiasm and couldn't wait to try the friends' advice. He rushed home, slammed the door, shook his fist in his wife's face, and growled, "From now on you're taking orders from me. I want my supper right now and after you put it on the table, go upstairs and lay out my best clothes. Tonight I'm going out with the boys and you're going to stay home where you belong. And another thing, do you know who is going to comb my hair, iron my pants, polish my shoes, and tie my tie?" "I certainly do," said the wife very calmly, "the undertaker."

Patanjali,[1] to differentiate between asserting and loving, called this 'the original mind'. What is this original mind? The mind that you carry right now is a collection, an accumulation. It is garbage that you

1 Pathanjali : considered the father of yogic sciences.

have piled up over a period of time. If you can leave it behind and walk away, then you are in your original mind. Others may call this 'no mind', this original mind. This is something that 'was', something that 'will be', always. When you are in your original mind – there might have been rare moments in your life when you tasted your original mind – true love or compassion just well up within you. Only if you can leave your garbage and walk away this moment, only then is this possible. Only then the seeker who carries my message becomes a Master, otherwise he just stagnates. Just carrying my message is itself an accumulation, some nonsense that you gathered somewhere. Maybe it is useful for a few people, but may never lead to any great transformation.

The few that carry my message to the outside world are teachers. A teacher is an eternal student. The moment he stops being a student, he is not a teacher anymore. That is the way it is. The day he thinks, "I am a teacher," he is finished. It is over. This is a constant process of learning. Once you are in this moment, there is no past. Everything is new; everything is seen fresh. If at any moment you think you know, and you teach, that means you're carrying the past burden. Maybe right now this is convenient, but the same convenience will become a tremendous torture after some time. It will. I have seen people systematically destroy themselves, step by step. Not carrying the past burden can be very easily done for the person who can simply be here.

The process of training people to carry my message is not to go out and do some nonsense to somebody else. That is not the point. This whole process is a way of growth. It is an effective tool for your growth. Teaching is for you to grow and during the process somebody else might be benefited. In the African lore there is a saying: "When the lion feeds, many animals eat." That's all it is. It's not a service that you're doing. It is just that you chose that kind of a path, that when you walk, many others benefit. When something is left unfulfilled within you, when a complete illumination has not happened within your own being, there is nothing one can really teach. There is nothing that can be transmitted. It is just that you're a driver, and you take the passengers along with you. Maybe you have the opportunity of handling the wheel for a while. That does not make you big in any way. It is just that you're also a passenger, but happen to be the one who is holding the wheel. If a person has to develop, he has to grow into humility and love. He has to evolve into a certain gracefulness; a gracefulness not of the body, not of the clothes, not of the exterior, but a certain gracefulness which can't be expressed in words. If a person has to grow into this, it can only come when moment-to-moment life becomes caring, the kind of caring which hurts. This can happen only out of deep love and compassion.

Seeker: Sadhguru, tradition always teaches us to be reverential towards God. How is this understood in relation to the way Mirabai or Akka Mahadevi or many other such saints have taken God as their lover?

Sadhguru: Where there is no love, how can there be reverence? When love reaches its peak, it naturally becomes reverence. People who are talking about reverence without love, know neither this nor that. All they know is fear. So probably you're referring to God-fearing people. These sages and saints, especially the seers that you mentioned, like Akka Mahadevi, Mirabai, or Anusuya and so many of them in the past, have taken to this form of worship because it was more suitable for them. They could emote much more easily than they could intellectualize things. They just used their emotions to reach their ultimate nature. Using emotion and reaching the ultimate nature is what is called as *bhakthi* yoga. It's a different form of worship.

Every culture has various forms of worship. Some people worship God as the Master, themselves as slaves. Sometimes they even take God as their servant, or as a partner in everything that they do. Yet others worship Him as a friend, as a lover, as their own child, the *Bala Krishna*. Generally, you become the feminine and you hold Him as the ultimate purusha – the masculine. So how you worship is not at all the point. How you communicate is not the point. The whole point is just how deeply you relate. These are the different attitudes; but whatever the attitude, the love affair is such that you're not expecting anything from the other side. Not even a response. You crave for it, but if He doesn't respond,you're not going to be angry, you're not going to be disappointed or anything. Your life is just about craving, and making something else tremendously more important than you. Whether it is existent or not, even that doesn't matter. That is the fundamental thing.

For the whole path of bhakthi, the important thing is, something else is far more important than you. So Akka, Mirabai and the others like them, their bhakthi was in that form, and they took this mode of worship. They took to worshipping God or mainly Shiva as their husband, because in India, when a woman reaches a certain age, marriage is almost like a must and it always happens. These women, these bhakthas, wanted to eliminate that dimension of being married once again to a man, because they have chosen the Lord Himself as their husband. They did not care for any other relationship in their lives.

The purpose of the path of devotion is just dissolution. In fact, the very word devotion comes from the word dissolve. The only objective of a devotee is to dissolve into his or her object of devotion. So how they relate to their object of devotion does not really matter. Whichever way they can relate best, that is how they do it. The reason you asked this question, in terms of reverence juxtaposed with love – being a lover or a husband – is because the word 'love', or being a lover, is always understood as physical. That is why this question. How can you be physical with somebody and still be reverential? This has been the tragedy of humanity that lovers have not known how to be reverential towards each other. When I say 'reverential', in fact the very objective of love is to dissolve into somebody else. The English expression of falling in love is really appropriate and very beautiful, in the sense that they always talked about 'falling' in love. Nobody ever talked about standing up in love, or climbing in love, or flying in love, but falling in love, because always, when what you consider as 'me' falls, a deep experience of love can happen within you.

If you look at love as an emotion, you can see that love is more like a vehicle to bring oneness. The very object of love is to become one. It is the longing to become one with the other which we are referring to as love. So when it is taken to its peak, becoming reverential to that which you consider worthwhile, to become one, is very natural. For whatever sake you are willing to dissolve yourself, it has to be reverential. Otherwise, how can you feel it is worthwhile to dissolve? If you think it is something that you can use, or something that you can just relate to, and benefit from, there can be no love because the object of love is always to dissolve. Whatever you consider as worth dissolving into, dissolving yourself into, is bound to be revered; there is no other way to be.

Seeker: Sadhguru, you have said at times, in a few sathsangs, that the problem with women in spirituality is that they go after the Buddha rather than the Buddha-hood, or in other words, after the Master rather than his teachings. How do you substantiate this?

Sadhguru: (Laughs) I didn't say this, Gautama said it.

Seeker: You also said this.

Sadhguru: I just repeated Gautama's words. I only reminded you about that, probably in some sathsang. When his disciple, Sangamitra, insisted that women should be allowed on the path of *Dhamma* that Gautama was offering to the world – when women were not yet a part of it – Gautama said, "My path will stay vibrantly alive for two thousand five hundred years, but if I allow women onto it, it will last only for five hundred years." When Sangamitra insisted and asked, "Why is it so?" Gautama said, "If a woman comes and sits with me, for her, more than my Buddha-hood, I will become more attractive because of her emotions and the very duality of man and woman." It is in this context that he said that women prefer to go after the Buddha rather than the Buddha-hood. Of course, a Buddha is the embodiment of the Buddha-hood, but she would miss the point. In other words he meant that she would be attracted to the man who embodies this quality more than the quality itself, because there is a natural attraction within her towards the opposite.

So it was said in that context, but it need not always be true. At a certain point in her life, a woman will look beyond that and seek. History and the present situation also prove that. Definitely, there is a tendency for a woman to get more attracted to the embodiment of the quality than to the quality itself, because generally for a woman, her fundamental way of seeking would be through emotions, and emotions always need an embodiment. Without embodiment, emotions can't flow. It is because of the path of bhakthi that we have embodied every quality in this culture as different gods. They are just different qualities in nature, but we have identified them or embodied them with different forms, because the people who were seeking were doing so through their emotions; and without embodiment, they would not be able to seek. It is in that context that Gautama said what he said.

Seeker: Sadhguru, to make it more personal, how has it been in your life? And what was your experience in handling such people?

Sadhguru: Even when Mirabai or Akka Mahadevi sought, they still saw Krishna or Shiva as a person, as a man. The embodiment was important for them. Now, coming to the present situation here at Isha, from day one, a lot of care has been taken to present this as a science, not as an embodied quality in a certain person – as a possible quality in every human being. The methods are very systematic and scientific. So in many ways, we are not giving room for emotion in the beginning of one's spiritual journey in Isha. For example, when people come to the Bhava Spandana program,[1] there is a huge emotional upsurge within them – using emotion as energy to reach a peak experience. In that space, it is very much possible that they can be attached to the person who is offering this, but a living Master always sees to it that the emotion is eventually channeled towards the thirst for the Ultimate rather than the one who is offering it.

For example, in the higher programs like Samyama,[2] all emotions are cut down and just pure awareness is brought about. With me, all methods are being handled very scientifically, not giving too much importance to emotion. As long as I am embodied, the emotional dimension of the path of Isha will be kept very low, but once I am beyond this body, we will definitely encourage people to seek through emotion. For many people it has always been so, that emotion is the quickest vehicle to deliver one to the other side. Bhakthi has always been the quickest way to realize. At the same time, if bhakthi is not tempered with the necessary awareness and alertness – if the necessary foundation of practices to create this energy and awareness in a person are not put in – it is very easy to hallucinate. Bhakthi can also be a tremendous tool to access dimensions which would otherwise take a very long time for a person to attain to. Doing *yoga kriyas*, activating your energies to reach certain states, will take elaborate practices and preparation, but with bhakthi, on just the mere strength of emotion one can move from one dimension to the other in a moment.

---

1 Bhava Spandana program : a four day high-intensity residential program offered as a part of Isha Yoga programs.

2 Samyama : an eight day meditation Program offered by Sadhguru where one is transported to explosive states of meditativeness. Held at Isha Yoga Center.

We definitely don't want to destroy the emotional aspect in a person, because emotion can be a tremendous tool if it is properly used with the right sense of awareness. My level of involvement with people, my physical presence with people, as the emotional dimension increases in them, I am just receding to a smaller group of people who understand what it is all about. With larger groups, with a larger mass of people, there is always a tendency to use emotion as a way to reach. It is a natural urge in a human being to use emotions to reach the highest, because somewhere they have known only emotion as the deepest experience within themselves. Their thought or their energy has never been so intense, but they have known intense emotions, which are bringing them to the deepest space within themselves. So there is always a natural tendency to use emotions as a way to get there. Where there is emotion, we always keep a certain physical distance where, in their understanding I am a little beyond their reach, so that they don't get too emotionally attached to the individual.

Seeker: I think I am getting somewhere, but the moment I sit in front of you, Sadhguru, I feel I am simply deceiving myself. I'm right back to square one.

Sadhguru: It is good to know that you realize the deception is on. Once, while visiting a modern art museum, a lady turned to an attendant standing nearby. "This," she said, "I suppose, is one of those hideous representations you call modern art?" "No, madam," replied the assistant, "that one is called the mirror." So Deepika, don't think. Start looking. Don't use your stupid mind. It's the same nonsense. You can't think any other way than you have been trained to up until now. Don't think. Just look. The whole idea is to drop your stupid thinking. All this high and low, right and wrong, is only in your mind. When you simply look at everything, everything seems to be okay. If you stand here and just look – the grass, the trees, the hill, the big mountain, the small mountain, are all just part of the scenery. Does the cloud look better than the mountain? Or does the sky look better than the mountain? Everything is just a part of one unit. If you stand here and think, "This is a mountain, that is a cloud," then everything seems separate. The moment you project like this, all your nonsense, lifetimes of karma confront you. If you are simply here, looking at everything as it is, you become a different kind of being altogether. You will mellow down to something totally different. Now, you said you're back to square one. Tell me, what is square one? You started projecting. The moment you project, you're back to square one, where else can you be? There is nowhere else you can be, because that is the only place your mind can be. When you are in your mind, you don't travel anywhere. You only hallucinate. The first stanza of the *Guru Pooja*[1] is just that:

Apavithra Pavithrova,
Sarvavastan Gatopiva,
Yasmareth Poondari Kaksham,
Sabahyabhyantara Suchihe.

'Anyone – whether holy or unholy, whatsoever state he has reached – who meditates upon the lotus eyed lord, becomes sanctified both internally and externally.' This means you are not involved in your own self-emancipation. You're not trying to improve yourself. You're not trying to purify yourself. You just contemplate on what you hold as the highest right now. Whatever is your highest, you just contemplate upon that. Your inner and outer purity will happen naturally. If you try to emancipate yourself, to improve yourself or to purify yourself, the more and more you do it, the more of a mess you will be. You simply contemplate on what you hold as the highest. Maybe God, maybe the Guru, or whatever you hold as the highest. Or just contemplate on the sky; it is enough. Simply be with it, don't project God or anything on it. It is simply *smaran*. Smaran means remembering or contemplating on the highest. Now, everything changes; inner and outer purity naturally happen. Why temples are not working for people is because they are projecting about God. If they shift from projecting about God to smaran, there will be a tremendous transformation in them. People cannot remember God. If you have to remember, you should have seen Him somewhere or in something. Maybe in a child's face, your wife's face, your lover's face, maybe in a flower, in the clouds, somewhere you could have seen at least a glimpse of God; only then can you remember them. Others can only think. Smaran means it has happened. In this smaran everything is purified. Now you don't have to work on how to correct this or that, how to make this okay. Don't worry about all that nonsense. You just remember the highest aspect of life that you have seen. Just go on remembering that. That's your God right now. Everything can change out of that.

1 *Guru Pooja* : invoking the Guru.

Seeker: How do I use every opportunity, even every hardship that comes my way, as a stepping-stone for my growth, Sadhguru?

Sadhguru: How to use everything and everybody for your growth? First of all, you grow in gratitude, not in benevolence. I don't want you to become benevolent. I want you to become full of gratitude. Benevolent people, after some time, become uncaring people. Gautama gives one sutra where he says, "It is hard to understand that by giving away your own food to somebody else and starving, you become stronger, not weaker." It is hard to understand this. How can you give away your food and be stronger? Giving away things which are plentiful to you is not it. Giving away what one needs most, one's very sustenance itself, is what leads you closer to the Divine. A monk is hungry most of the time. He only begs for his food once a day and eats. Today somebody may give a little. Another day he might get much less. Whatever he gets, the practice was that he begged only at one house per day and there would be times where he would get nothing. Over a period of time, they relaxed this 'one house' rule and extended it to three houses because people became more and more cautious with their giving. So monks are constantly hungry, and Gautama is saying that if you give away your own food, you become stronger, not weaker. This is hard to understand, but it's true. It is really true.

There is a very wonderful true-life story, which happened during World War II in the ill-famed German concentration camp, Auschwitz. Every day numbers were called out, and people were led to the extermination area, because the camp became full. Numbers were called at random, or the weak and the old who couldn't work were chosen. If your number was called today, you were going to your death. You were going to be shot and buried en masse. Now there was a man whose number was called and he was terrified. He didn't want to die. There was a Christian missionary, young and healthy, next to him, whose number was not called. Seeing the man's fear he said, "Don't fear. I will take your place." The man felt ashamed, but at the same time could not refuse the offer. He wanted to live. The missionary was shot. It so happened that the very next day the Germans lost the war and our man was freed. For many years he lived with this sense of defeat and shame and later narrated this incident in his life. He saw that there was simply no point, because his life itself was somebody else's charity. It was because of another man's greatness that he was living. Otherwise, he would have been shot that day – it was his number.

The missionary, who didn't know him – he was not a friend, a father, a son or anything – just to ease his fear and suffering, he took the call. Now that man will know life - that man who went, not the man who stayed back. Only the other will know what life is. Only he can experience something, a certain strength, a certain power within himself, that somebody who is trying to protect himself will never experience. This does not mean you have to go sacrifice yourself or some such nonsense. The man who went to his death was not thinking in terms of sacrifice. He just did it; that is all. It was not that he was waiting to sacrifice himself for somebody else. At that moment, he saw what was needed and just did it without a second thought. That's fantastic; but if you're trying to sacrifice yourself because you're going to get strength, or you're going to go to heaven, that is not it. That is really not it.

If you can run your life without the offer of heaven, you are on the path; but if by taking the offer and by cutting a deal you can still run in the right direction, go ahead and do it. If such a situation comes in your life, if such a level of maturity comes to you that you don't need any deals and you can still do it, it is good. If you have grown out of this limitation that something has to be offered for you to do something, where no increments are needed and you still are willing to work overtime, then you have a different kind of strength. The man who does only as much as is needed will only get that much. He will always remain a beggar in his life. He will never know what strength really is, he will never know what Divinity is; he will never know what Godliness is, simply because Divinity does everything purposelessly. Just see! Everything is done purposelessly.

Seeker: Sadhguru, I hope something fruitful comes out of this whole sadhana. I also fear I might not be living up to your expectations. At times I ask myself, "Why this sadhana and what is its nature?"

Sadhguru: So there is a hope. There is a hope that something will happen, that is why you do all this. Where there is hope, there is always fear attached to it about whether it is going to happen or not. When you are hoping for something, when you're looking forward to something happening, the fear or the frustration is waiting just behind. Right now, there is a big hope in a lot of people's minds that something will happen out of this sadhana. Somebody thinks he will see Shiva, someone else thinks his *Kundalini*[1] will burst into his *Sahasrar.*[2] All these are hopes. Another way of looking at hope is as an expectation. If a person has no hope he is truly blessed, because that person has no fear of failure. Fear of missing out on something is totally not there in a person who doesn't hope. How can a person not hope? The whole sadhana is that you have to do everything intensely. Life has always been like this: if you have to do something, you either need to be enticed or be pushed forcefully. Life has always been such that you think in terms of what you will get if you do something, or maybe the circumstances in your life or the people around you push you to do things. If somebody or something pushes you, it is always misery. If hope is pushing you, there is an expectation of joy, an expectation of fulfillment, which keeps you going; but as long as hope is there, there is always the fear that it will be shattered. The whole nature of sadhana is such that it is a process of growth, but sadhana can also be a barrier. When Patanjali finished with *karma kanda* and moved into what is known as *kaivalya pada* – 'kaivalya' means ultimate liberation – he said that you could have a glimpse of the Divine in many ways. This could happen in so many ways, either by using drugs, incessantly chanting some *mantra,*[3] practicing severe austerities, or by deep *samadhis.*[4]

Now, to come to drugs...Patanjali was a scientist. He was not the usual religious kind of man. He was not afraid of anything. He looked at everything. A religious man would generally not talk about drugs. Patanjali said a drug is also a possibility to divinity, but the lowest possibility. What happens with a drug? If you take a chemical like LSD or marijuana, what happens is, the nature of the chemical is such that somewhere it breaks the mind. Ultimately your mind, body, everything is just chemistry. Whatever sadhana you're doing now also is just to change the chemistry of the system. Drugs are usually described as mind-blowing. You put this drug into your system and suddenly the mind cracks up. You're able to look at the existence through this crack, without the mind, just for a moment, and it is fantastic.

---

1 *Kundalini* : Cosmic energy which is depicted as a snake coiled at the base of the spine.
2 *Sahasrar* : the highest chakra of the human system.
3 *mantra* : a syllable or a pure sound.
4 *samadhi* : state of equanimity, a merging of the subject and the object.

Everything is just fantastic. Then you get hooked on the drug. The next time the dosage will increase. There is no growth. There is no transformation. It just becomes a trip. After a while, there are most probably no more trips. The drug becomes just a helpless dependence for you.

You can't deny that at least *some* people who are on the path of drugs have big experiences, but you will see that the man doesn't grow, there is no transformation in the way he is. He remains the same. In fact, he never attains to Grace, he sort of retards. He never attains to any kind of fragrance. He just has big experiences to talk about, otherwise he slowly retards. Only the dosage increases. The dosage becomes larger, but the man himself shrinks. Even before any recording of history happened, people have used drugs on the spiritual path. The *puranas*, mythological texts, say that Shiva himself was the first to use drugs. So it starts from there. Understand that Shiva can contain it, not you.

Once, Adi Shankara was traveling with his disciples. He stopped at a place and drank a lot of country liquor and then resumed walking. A few disciples thought that by seeing their Guru drinking alcohol, it meant they could also drink. At the very next place where the liquor was available, they drank and were wobbling behind Shankara because they were unable to hold it. When they entered the next village, Shankara walked directly toward the blacksmith's and took a vessel full of molten iron and took a drink from it. Now, the disciples who imitated him in drinking the country liquor got the point. Even here, there are a few people who are imitating me and doing things that are beyond their perception. They are only asking for trouble. So drugs are the lowest possibility, but still a possibility. On the yogic path drugs are a taboo, not because of moral correctness, but because of the limitation that they are. We have other ways to blow your mind.

The next one is the mantra. Just repetition of a mantra changes the chemistry of the system, because ultimately everything is just vibration and sound; the whole existence is just that. If you use the right sound properly, with the right amount of intensity and perseverance, it will change the chemistry of your system. You can use any word, and if used incessantly with the right sense of awareness, it can cease your mind and give you a glimpse of reality. Mantras are vibrations which can transform your energies and prepare you for a higher possibility. Without the necessary awareness, they can act like any drug, deadening the mind and causing hallucinatory states. Mantras are always good preparatory states. From time immemorial, Enlightened beings have known mantras to be a very limited process, because the danger of getting addicted to the mantra is always there. There is a beautiful story in Zen. In a certain village, there was a monastery. One morning the people heard the recitation of the sutras and they knew the Master had left. When there is no live Guru, mantras become an essential support. If the right kind of atmosphere, preparation, and awareness is created, a mantra can explode you into a different level of consciousness.

A large number of people are into mantras. They are too busy chanting *Gita, Vedas, Upanishads* or other spiritual scriptures... If you remove the mantras, if you take away the chanting, so many people will become unemployed. In terms of transformation, there is none. They can give you a glimpse of the Divine, definitely, if you go into it deep enough. Today, every ignorant fool is into mantras, not from any awareness of what it is, but just from their belief system. So much *Gita* chanting and *Veda* chanting is going on that, if taken away, it could cause a huge unemployment problem.

Now, for performing austerities on the spiritual path, what it means to perform an austerity is just this: learning to say no to everything that is natural within you. Now, if you're hungry, you say to yourself, "No, I need to do my *Shakthi Chalana Kriya*."[1] You want to eat something nice, you say, "No, I will eat only dry bread." You feel sleepy right now, you say, "No, I will meditate." This is denying, making an attempt to go beyond your likes and dislikes – going on saying 'no' to the mind. This is definitely far superior to drugs and mantras, because it will lead to a certain transformation within you. As you continue to say 'no' to your mind, the mind becomes more and more subdued, it becomes lesser and lesser. It loses its edge. The mind loses the control over you, as you go on saying 'no'. Whatever the mind says, you say no. That is the practice. When you become a total 'no, no' to your mind, you will become a big 'yes' to life. That is the level of austerities that can be done. This can lead to some amount of transformation, and may also lead a person to the highest level of consciousness if he really goes into it, if he is strong enough to go through it. Definitely a person can attain to a certain level of

1 *Shakthi Chalana Kriya* : a powerful yogic practice created by Sadhguru that uses certain breathing techniques.

Grace, but a person who gets too much into this path of austerity tends to become dry. A sort of lifeless dryness enters him. He will not be the kind of person who can just look at the mountain and enjoy it. He will deny it, saying, "It is beautiful, so I will not look at it." He will attain to a certain dryness, but don't be deceived by this dryness. Dry souls are always very wise souls, but if it's not tempered with certain other qualities, this dryness tends to become a dead kind of dryness, which you will see in many yogis. They have become dry. They don't have compassion in them. They have denied passion consciously, but have lost even their compassion.

The next thing that Patanjali mentions is that you can also attain to divinity through samadhi. Now when he says samadhi, he is talking about penetration. Samadhi means to slice through whatever is the barrier. Samadhi is the state of equanimity. A mind that is neither like or dislike, craving or aversion, wanting or not wanting, love or hate. A mind that is beyond these dualities has a heightened level of penetration which can give you a steady vision of the beyond. Now these samadhis are of many different varieties. Whichever process you choose, whichever sadhana you choose, when it is based upon your hope that one day you will see something, it has its limitations. When your sadhana is based on hope and fear, you won't attain to anything. Anyway, you will miss it. This reminds me of a story about a stupid servant. One day the Master asked him to go and get flour and salt, and gave strict instructions that he should not mix these two things together. So he took a bag and reached the shop where they were selling flour and filled it. Then he asked for salt. He did not know where to put the salt, but remembered his Master telling him not to mix the two. So he flipped the bag and filled it up. By doing so, the flour fell out. So he carried the salt to his Master. The Master asked him, "Okay, this is salt. Where is the flour?" The servant just turned the bag over and the salt fell out. Hope and fear are just like this. When you start doing something with hope, whether it happens or not, both ways you are the loser. Do your sadhana joyfully, not with the hope of making it or the fear of not making it. Just do it joyfully.

Seeker: You have always been saying that sadhana should be done intensely and without hope; now Sadhguru, you're adding 'joyfully' to the list?

Sadhguru: Yes, Somu, there are even many more on the list! Now, coming back to the sadhana, make it an offering. You're hoping and hoping and hoping that you'll get something. The fulfillment always falls short of what you hoped for. The dream and what happens in reality never match. The dream is always more colorful, more vivid. It is minus all problems, minus the price that you have to pay for it. You can just dream without paying the price, but when it gets actualized, it comes with a price. Now how to do the sadhana intensely but without hope, that is the question. How can a person work intensely, but without any hope? When can a person do something very intensely without any hope about it? Only through love can one do it, only when you really, really love. Generally, what you call as love is simply some kind of hope. When you truly love, whatever you do with your love is insufficient. Even if you offer yourself, it is insufficient. It is quite hopeless, but very intense.

If anything has to be done intensely, but at the same time without hope, love is the only way. There is no other way; it has to be very intense. There should be trust also and there can be no trust unless there is love. When you don't love somebody, there is no way you can trust him. You may make a calculation like, "I trust my business partner." It's not trust. It is just a calculation. It's an adjustment that you make; otherwise you cannot function. There can be no trust. Tomorrow, if you see him packing up your office and putting it in a suitcase, immediately you'll think all kinds of things. You will not say, "Okay, let him take it away, after all he's my partner." No, all kinds of suspicions will come. The same goes for your wife, your husband, your child, or even your mother; it doesn't matter who it is. If he or she does something very unusual, you will become suspicious immediately. One day, on a whim, and feeling like really doing something loving and nice for his wife, a man decided to surprise her with a dozen beautiful red roses. The minute he opened the door, his wife started screaming at him. "This is the worst day that I have ever had. The kids have been terrible, they got into a food fight, the washing machine broke and flooded the basement, I burnt the dinner, the dog chewed my best pair of shoes, AND NOW YOU HAVE THE NERVE TO COME HOME DRUNK!"

So you might have lived with them, you might have been born out of them, and you might have shared so much, you might have shared life with each other, but tomorrow morning if they do something unusual, doubts will come, isn't it? One minute you may be falling at their feet and you may be saying, "You are everything," but if something unusual is done, immediately there will be doubt. That is not trust. There can be no trust where there is no love. Now, this word, 'love' – today it is almost obscene the way it is being used. Saying, "I love you," is like saying, "Open sesame." It is the magic mantra that will open doors for you.

When I say 'trust', I am not asking for your loyalty. There has always been a tremendous amount of stress in the tradition on the *Guru-shishya* relationship; the Master-disciple relationship has been stressed upon in so many ways. This stress, when used by the wrong person, becomes a means of exploitation. This stress could be laid by a certain person because he wants to secure things for himself. This stress could be laid by a person out of his own insecurity, because he needs the support, he wants the loyalty. If somebody is asking for loyalty, there is nothing spiritual about that place or that person, because a spiritual person doesn't need loyalty. I am not in need of your loyalty. You can do what you want. Tomorrow, if you want, you can curse me. If that is how you feel, you can do it. I will not curse you back, because we have never looked forward to your loyalty. How long will you be with me? What are you going to do here? What are you going to do for us? We have never looked at it on those terms.

Seeker: Sadhguru, I seem to have failed in all my personal relationships. I don't know where I stand with God either. I love you very much and I hope I reach liberation and not end up getting caught up with you too.

Sadhguru: Love is needed. I don't need it, but if you're not loving, you will not grow. To love, to simply be loving, takes a tremendous amount of maturity. You always need an object to love. So initially, what kind of object to choose? You choose that kind of object where the possibility of getting stuck is the least. If you love this pole, you may get stuck with the pole – at least the pole will not get stuck with you – but if you say, "I love my wife and children," it is not only that you may get stuck, the other person involved also can get stuck to you. Tomorrow, even if you want to disentangle yourself, the other person will not be willing to let you go. Now, you may love a stone, a pole, or anything. If you can really give yourself like that to even inanimate things, it is wonderful; but generally that is too far off for most people.

It happened in the Himalayan region, there was a band of *sanyasis* [1] doing sadhana on the banks of the river Ganga. On a certain day, one of the sanyasis noticed a furry rug floating down the river. Immediately he thought, "With this rug I can be so much more comfortable during the winter." He, being an able swimmer, jumped into the river and went after the rug. He got his hands on the rug and then started screaming for help. The other sanyasis on the riverbank thought he was being carried away by the current and said, "You fool! Let go of the rug and come back." The sanyasi shouted back, "I can't let go of this, it is holding on to me. This is not a rug, it is a mountain bear." So you better know what you're going after. If you fall in love with a person who has enormous needs of his own, then you will see, you have got yourself into a bear trap. This is the reason why the *Guru-shishya paramparya*, or Master-disciple relationship, has been celebrated in this culture, as the Guru is one who has no needs of his own and thus there is no bear-trap.

People say, "I love God." I am telling you, you don't love God; you just hope that God will do something for you. It's not that this will not work, but it is too far away. You say you love God and if you can really love Him, it is beautiful; but it is not the truth. It is a hope, an expectation, and a fear. Instead of deceiving yourself like that, if you can simply say, "Okay, I am scared, that is why I am coming to you," it is better. Be straight. It doesn't matter if you don't know how to be spiritual. At least learn how to be straight. It is very, very important. If you don't learn how to be straight with yourself with every feeling, with every thought that occurs within you, you will become self-deceptive. Don't give it beautiful shapes or nice forms. If it is ugly, see it that way, bluntly see life the way it is; this is very, very important. Unless you see this, the question of growth is impossible. Just forget it. Don't think of growth, because that possibility will not arise until you are a hundred percent straight with yourself. There is no possibility of growth for that person who sees his fear as love, who sees his hope as love, or who sees his greed as love.

People have not come together simply because they are loving. They have come together only out of their greed. They need something. Maybe it's physical, psychological, emotional or economic; it doesn't matter which way. Something needs to be fulfilled, so two people come together. You think only if you

---

1 *sanyasi* : one who has renounced all worldly possessions and relationships; an ascetic.

stay together you can fulfill these things. So the drama continues. Suppose you stop fulfilling all the needs of the other person; then everything breaks down, doesn't it? So you have not come together because of love, but only out of greed. Let us be straight about this, otherwise you can forget about spirituality. You will never even taste love in your life if you're not straight. If you want to experience love, you should be sincere. Without being sincere there is no question of being loving. It's not possible. Sincerity doesn't mean sticking to some code that somebody else has fixed for you; that's not the point. Within yourself, you need to be sincere.

Seeker: Sadhguru, I sense a deep stillness in you, as if time itself has stopped, but there is an underlying current of great urgency also. What is this contradiction?

Sadhguru: Yes, that's how it is. This urgency can be both a great boon and a curse. In this urgency people will grow very quickly. At the same time, because of this same urgency, many people will drop off. They can't take this urgency. They can't take the speed. It seems almost like sheer madness. Many people who have been extremely close to me have fallen off, simply because they just could not take this urgency. They read somewhere that a Master is never urgent, but they find this one is too urgent and think it's crazy.

Seeker: But Jaggi, do we have to work as if there is no tomorrow?

Sadhguru: As if there is no tomorrow? Yes, there is no tomorrow. That's what you need to understand. You said it right; there is really no tomorrow. For a person who is walking the spiritual path, there is no tomorrow. Today is the day. When tomorrow comes, we will see about it. Whatever needs to be done, it has to be done now; this is the moment. That is why this sense of urgency. There is this old photo of Ramana with his disciples sitting around him that I would like to show you one day. You should see the disciples, the intensity with which they are sitting there, whereas Ramana is completely relaxed. His disciples, they are all sitting like tigers – urgent. If that urgency is not there, nothing can be done.

Ramana seems to be relaxed, but his presence had such urgency that it set all his disciples on fire. Without that intensity and urgency, his presence could not have Enlightened crows and cows, too. That's something incredible.

Seeker: Sometimes I get lax and slip into a laid-back attitude and end up being disappointed with myself, others, and sometimes with you as well. How do I strike a balance and maintain this urgency?

Sadhguru: You have different emotions and different kinds of tricks to get yourselves into some protective cocoon or to get somebody else to build that cocoon for you, don't you? Just don't continue the same tricks here. This has been going on all your life, you playing these tricks endlessly. Now, once you step onto a path like this, it's time to stop this. Only then there are no more expectations, no more disappointments with life. The way it is, is the way it is. At every step you get disappointed with people, because they are not fulfilling your expectations. They're not supporting your ego; that's all it is. Once a young couple got married and left for their honeymoon. When they got back the bride immediately called her mother. The mother asked, "So how was your honeymoon?" "Oh, Momma," she replied, "the honeymoon was so wonderful, so romantic." But suddenly, she burst into sobs. "Momma, as soon as we returned, David started using the most horrible language. Things I've never heard before. I mean all these awful four-letter words. You've got to come and take me home; please, Momma!" "Sarah, Sarah, get a hold of yourself. Calm down. Tell me, what could be so awful? What four letter words?" "Please don't make me tell you, Momma," said the daughter, "I'm just too embarrassed and they are too awful. Come get me, please." "Darling, baby, you must tell me what has you so upset. Tell your mother those horrible four-letter words." Still sobbing, the new bride said, "Oh Momma, words like DUST, IRON, WASH, and COOK."

This is one reason you're disappointed with life, because you have your own ideas of what life should be, and also how others should live. Otherwise, how can you get disappointed with somebody? Just because somebody is not the way you expect him to be or is refusing to be exploited by you, that's all. If you want to put it very bluntly, somebody refuses to be exploited by you or is not stupid enough to be exploited by you, so you get disappointed. Once you are on this path, we will make sure that you will not only be disappointed, but frustrated as well. We will make sure that you will reach the deepest level of frustration. You have to stop your tricks. These tricks are only towards you building protective structures around yourself. How long do you want to go on doing this? You demolish one structure and build another one. The old house is out of style so all that you do is build a new house. Isn't it so?

Seeker: I have left everything behind me and come here. Why shouldn't I look at this ashram as my home, Sadhguru?

Sadhguru: This is not your home. It's just a transit point. Do you understand? You just stop here for a while, that's all. Don't make it a new home. Be unsettled. Don't try to settle down. Your whole problem is, you try to settle down with everything that is given to you and the moment it is unsettled, you're disturbed and frustrated. The whole purpose of walking this path is to remain unsettled, not to settle down into a new situation. If you pluck yourself from one settled situation and land up in another, what's the point? Moving into an ashram, moving onto a spiritual path, is not to settle down into another cocoon. It's about learning to live without cocoons. It is about being vulnerable, continuously, by choice. It is like you take off your armor and bare your chest, only by choice. Let whatever may happen, happen, not because somebody peels it off, but by your choice. When you refuse to peel it off, maybe somebody or something or even your Guru will try to slowly peel it off once in a while, but somebody peeling it off always hurts. It is better to peel it off yourself.

Seeker: Sadhguru, since I have been on this path, I have become sort of still and quiet. I question myself as to whether this is actually stillness or stagnation. What is the difference?

Sadhguru: Stagnation is a certain disease. It is anti-life. Stillness is a tremendous amount of life not manifesting itself in any way. It is just there – potent. That is God. God is stillness, not stagnation. The mind is stagnation. Sadhana is a force which moves you from stagnation to stillness, but between stagnation and stillness, when they are together, there seems to be very little difference, because your logical mind only understands in terms of moving and not moving. Not moving is stagnation, but stillness is also not moving. This non-movement, you may call it stillness or stagnation because it's purely subjective. If you look at it objectively, stillness and stagnation are about the same. Physically they could be seen as about the same, but qualitatively they are worlds apart. A person who is meditating and a person who is sleeping may look about the same. One is sitting and sleeping, another is lying down and sleeping, that is all. For a person who doesn't know the difference, that's all he sees.

Have you seen with how much sarcasm people look at meditation – those so-called dynamic people of the world? They think it's for people who don't even know how to sleep. Externally there may be no difference between stillness and stagnation. Internally there is a tremendous difference. From stagnation to stillness, from ignorance to Enlightenment, that's the difference. In a way, it is the same thing; only the quality has to change, that's all. But how can you know the qualitative difference when you're drowned in ignorance? This is why the movement of sadhana has to go in full circle. Depending on how stupid a person is, that is how long the sadhana has to be. Physically and mentally, push yourself to the limit and see what is there. If you stop for every little discomfort, you will never know what it is. Just push yourself to the limit. Physically, mentally, emotionally, in every way push yourself to the last point. Either you must go mad or you must get Enlightened, that's all there is; and we will not allow you to go mad, don't worry.

Seeker: But for how long, Sadhguru, how long? The path seems so long and gets so difficult, and it doesn't make things easy for me, especially when I see someone freaking out with joy, for no reason, as soon as they close their eyes for meditation or whenever they are around you.

Sadhguru: Your problem is like this: there was this family who had two boys who were twins, and the only thing they had in common was their looks. If one felt it was too hot, the other felt it was too cold. If one said he liked the cake, the other said he hated it. They were opposites in every way. One was an eternal optimist, and the other a doom and gloom pessimist. Just to see what would happen, on the twins' birthday, the father loaded the pessimist brother's room with every imaginable gift – toys and games, and for the boy who always sees the brighter side of life, with horse manure. That night, the father went to check on the doom guy's room and found him sitting amidst his new gifts sobbing away bitterly. "Why," the father said in anguish, "after all this?" The boy replied, "Because my friends are going to be jealous, I will have to read all these instructions before I can do anything with this stuff, I will constantly need batteries, and my toys will eventually be stolen or broken." Passing by the optimist twin's room, the father found him dancing for joy on the pile of manure. "What are you so happy about?" the father asked. The boy replied, "There's got to be a pony in here somewhere!"

What to do with someone like you who will throw away everything I give you? Whatever this existence gives you, you crib and bitch about it. What to do with people like you? Marilynn and Laurie, are you listening? If you drive yourself in different directions, what to do? A little discomfort and you give up. Sometimes when you sit there with your eyes closed, the mind goes here and there. It becomes uncomfortable, and you let yourself fall back into your old nonsense. That is not the way. Get into the sadhana full force, go like crazy, then let us see what's going on. Whether you are going to flip this way or that, let's see. That's all it takes. When Gautama went and sat under the bodhi tree, he decided, "Until I get Enlightened, I won't get up from this place. Either I will die here or I will get Enlightened." That's all. The man sat and, within a moment, he was Enlightened. That is all it takes. He didn't have to sit for twenty-five years to do it. When a man has come to that kind of sankalpa that, "This is it. This is the only thing that matters right now." How long will it take? How long can it take to see what is already here? Not even a wink of an eye. Then why is it taking so long? It is simply because it's not intense enough.

That is why I keep asking you, "What is your priority? What is it? You have to increase it." Every time I ask that question, you have to push it up one more notch. To the point of discomfort you have pushed, but don't let up; push it up one more point and yet another point. It has to be pushed to the ultimate, to the optimum. Only then can the mind dissolve by itself. You don't have to do any other sadhana. This is the only sadhana needed. All other activity in the form of sadhana is just to get this one thing done. Make it in such a way that your sankalpa is unshakeable.

Why someone is asked to go and live in the Himalayas for twelve years is not because if they live in the Himalayas the rocks could give them Enlightenment. It is because he is even willing to waste his life for twelve years, with all kinds of hardship, just to seek Truth. If that kind of sankalpa has come, that man is very close. In a way, it is like literally wasting your life. When the whole world is eating well, drinking well and enjoying themselves, you are sitting there in the cold and chanting, "Shiva, Shiva, Shiva," knowing nothing might happen. If you live there for long enough, you may come to know. Shiva probably will not come and bail you out. When you're hungry, you're plain hungry. When you're cold, you're just cold. You know it may turn out to be hopeless being there. In spite of that you stay, because the most important thing in your life is something else. When that sankalpa comes, it does not take twelve years. In one moment, it can happen. Nobody needs to wait for twelve years. This can be the moment. It is because you don't use this moment that you have to wait for the next one. This is always the moment. Are you going to tighten it up, or every time discomfort comes, will you think, "Oh, this is not for me." It is definitely not for you if this is so. I am not saying the path is difficult; it's just that you make it difficult. The path is not difficult. It is very simple. If you are simple, it's very simple. If you are all wound up, the path is very, very winding. That's all it is.

This moment, when you're very simple and at ease, life is very simple, isn't it? When you're wound up, just see how complicated it is. Don't become all wound up. There is enough nerve-racking past in you, which is already in knots. Don't create new knots now. The old knots are already causing a lot of pain, causing a deep pit inside, which is eating you up in many ways. Some of you have become aware of this, and some are yet to become aware of it, but it is there in every human being. There is one empty pit within you which just eats you from inside. That is enough, isn't it? Don't create more now. What you have created in the past is enough. Many lifetimes of opportunities have been wasted, but this one need not go to waste too. Those of you who feel the urgency, please go on unrelentingly. To those of you who think, "Anyway, another ten thousand years are there, no problem." I am saying, why only ten thousand? There is a whole eternity ahead of you. There is no hurry. After all, what is wrong with life? When I say it, it may look like a curse, but it is not a curse. I am saying, in this situation, when the energies are high like this, if you don't make use of this situation and me, if you don't see this, well then

Seeker: Master, how does a seeker use you best on the spiritual path to liberation?

Sadhguru: How to put the Guru to the best use? See, if I give you a little toy, say a toy car – you know how to make it work, you know how to use it. Even if I give you a regular car, you know how to drive it and enjoy that also, but if I give you a spaceship, you would not know the head or tail of it, isn't it so? Probably, even if I give you an airplane – when you see those hundreds of knobs and meters – you won't know what to do with it. If I give you a spaceship, definitely you won't know what to do with it. So a Guru is a vehicle who wants to take you beyond your present dimension of existence. Let us call the Guru a spaceship. You wouldn't know how to use it. You just wouldn't know how to handle a spaceship. A car, maybe you could drive around, but a vehicle which could take you to other dimensions, you don't know how to handle it. So don't try to use it, you just learn to be with it.

If you just learn to stay within the space of the spaceship, wherever it goes, it takes you there, isn't it? So just learn to sit in his space, don't try to use him. Trying to use him would be a big mistake. That is a great mistake that millions of seekers have always made for ages, trying to use the Guru. Like I was telling you the other day, that boy, that young man that I met on the way back from Kedar, was very simple. He had been with his Guru for eight years. The Guru did not give him any sadhana. "I am just serving him and waiting. When he gives sadhana, I will do it. Right now I am just there. Whatever he says, I do. I cook, clean, sweep and just wait," said the man. He will definitely know it; there is no question about it. A man who can just be this way is an intelligent man, not an idiot. If you had seen those other four people with him, they were very bright, intelligent people. They were not goat-like people, but willing to simply wait for eight years, without even an initiation into a simple process. Just learn to sit in the spaceship without getting off at every excuse. You might not go anywhere; just learn to be in his space. What has to happen will happen.

Seeker: Sadhguru, what is your day-to-day awareness in regard to your disciples? Are you aware of our every thought and emotion, or only general situations? Can we call upon you in times of need or distress?

Sadhguru: If I say what I should say now, you will start doing freaky things to seek attention. Your question is, "Are you really there for us or not?" You're just putting it in a very polite way. Fundamentally you're asking, "Are you really there for us or not?"

Seeker: Yes, fundamentally that is it, but you have said prayers can lead to hallucinations, so I'm wondering if I can call on you in prayer during times of distress.

Sadhguru: I never said that being prayerful leads to hallucinations. What I would have said is about prayer as it is being done today. If you're really prayerful, the basic condition is to have no expectations, isn't it? If you request something, then you will expect it. If you pray, how can you expect? You are just praying, but today prayer has just become a wish list. It has taken on a completely different meaning; otherwise, being prayerful is a wonderful way to be, because it's a quality, like meditation. Prayerfulness is a certain quality in which you make something or somebody else in your life so big, and make yourself very small. Not yet into nothing, not into Shoonya, but at least you have made yourself small. Now, if you're so small, how can you tell that which is so big what to do? This doesn't make sense, isn't it? In that sense, prayer is meaningless, senseless; but if you're able to sit here and see something as enormous, and yourself as small, it's a wonderful device. That is the reason why we took you to the Himalayas, so that you would feel like an ant. Suddenly, you look at the Himalayas and you feel like a little ant crawling up there. It doesn't mean anything, whoever the hell you are.

About calling me...if you are in spiritual distress you don't even have to call, I am always there. Now, am I aware of your problems, your this and that, and your day-to-day whatever? If I wish to be I am, but not otherwise. Most of the time, I am not, because your nonsense doesn't mean anything and is of no value. Today you think something, tomorrow you think something else; it just does not mean anything. It is like I set two lines, an upper limit and a lower limit for everyone. Within these two lines, whatever games they play, I don't bother them. If they go below them, yes, and if they go above them, immediately yes.

If they are playing within that playing field, it's okay, it is up to them. I don't want to meddle with them and the little things that they do. If they sink below that, immediately there will be help. If people rise above that also, immediately there will be help. If they are playing around in the middle, I just let them handle it. They have been given brains, isn't it? The Creator gave you brains and you have got to use them. Going low can take you below the physical, which can be very damaging; also for people who go above the physical there will be help. Within the physical, just play the game as you know it. There is no need for me to look at it.

Seeker: When you say, "go below the physical", what exactly do you mean, Sadhguru?

Sadhguru: These things can lead to a lot of fear and confusion among people – these types of questions. Anyway, now you asked for it! Going below the physical could mean that physically you are ebbing; the body's life is coming to an end. It is not always so; most of the time it's not so. Suddenly, today I call someone that I have not spoken with for ten years. Neither that person has come into contact with me, nor have I come into contact with him in all these years. I just call and chat with him for a few minutes. This man might die in the next three or four days. It is not that I am causing it; death is anyway coming. He has forgotten what is alive within him, so we are just making a call to remind him. Just one little reminder – it need not necessarily always be through a telephone. It can also be through any other device. With some people I use a telephone, but every time I call, don't think you have only three or four days left! (Laughs). I am not Yama or something. For those of you who don't know, Yama is the god of death in India. I'm not Yama.

As for going above the physical, suppose they are going to cross certain limits, I may get in touch with them, just to remind them to be stable. Usually, I will not talk about it at all. Most of the time I never do, because just talking about it will spoil the whole thing. Their mind will become overactive and it just takes them off in a completely different direction. Going low could also involve negative energy influences. For example, say you got angry or you became sad. Usually, you will come out of it. You must make an enormous effort to stay there, otherwise nobody can stay there. If they are going below the line, they will be reached because they could derail themselves from the track of *prarabdha karma.*[1] If they go above the upper line, there also they will be reached, either to guide them or to slow them down, because in that state they may not be able to retain their body. Between the two parallels, it is their business to handle that part of their life. If I take up all that, there is no end to it.

There are some people who might be going totally off the track, forgetting the reason why they are here. I call them and very gently coax them to come back around, but whatever I say, they might not budge. They just continue to go on with their nonsense. Then I have to tell them not only about their actions, but also about what's going on in their mind. So I just ask them, "Yesterday at ten o'clock, what were you doing?" They come up with something and then I say, "This is what you were thinking and this is what you were up to at ten o'clock in the morning." When they realize there is nothing they can hide from me, they break up. Until then, they will not come around. It's not that yesterday I was watching them. It is all there, written to be seen when they sit in front of me. So this is not normally done at all, but only rarely, if somebody is going to extremes. Otherwise, I don't want to look into everybody's nonsense. There is nothing much worthwhile in looking into people's minds. What is in there? Nothing.

Seeker: Sadhguru, when you get into the deepest crevices of my mind and everything that I call 'myself', I feel cornered, like my privacy is always being invaded. This weighs heavily upon me.

Sadhguru: The whole thing is just that everybody is looking for a loophole. When they don't find a loophole, either they have to see the point or reject the whole thing; that is all there is. Why is it weighing heavily upon you? This is simply because there is no loophole for you to escape. Who can be cornered? When can you corner a man? Physically, when can a man be cornered? Suppose this place is wide open, can you corner him? When can you corner him? Only when there is some boundary, when the man is closed in; only then can you corner him. When the man is not so, how can you corner him?

1 *prarabdha karma* : the karma allotted for this life.

You're feeling cornered because you're closed. There is a boundary beyond which you don't allow anybody. So now, when your Guru enters there out of his responsibility and tries to push you where you need to go, you feel cornered. You have set a boundary beyond which you don't allow anybody to enter. My whole effort is to break that boundary. Maybe you give this a good name such as privacy, or space, or whatever, but do see that it is a boundary and a corner. So what's your privacy? When you use a word, you must know why you're using it or at least the meaning of it. What is your privacy, tell me. What is private for you? Anything that you hold as personal and are not willing to talk about.

Seeker: At times my feelings get trampled and I just want to be left alone and seek some privacy.

Sadhguru: Being by yourself is different; being alone is different. When are you alone? When can you be really alone? Within yourself, you can only be lonely. When can a man be really alone? Only when everything that is around him becomes a part of him and when nothing else exists. That is ultimate Realization or aloneness. The aloneness you are talking about is just loneliness, just separation, just exclusion. Separation is not aloneness. When everything has merged within you, you are alone, because nothing else exists. It is when you finally realize, "I am alone here because there is nobody else but me." Only then there is aloneness.

So what is this privacy you're talking about? Whenever you feel uncomfortable, you want to be left alone. Why is this so? I don't want any philosophies; just come to the specifics. You have some, 'Sometimes I would like to be left alone' moments. Why? Now you say that your feelings are being trampled; why are you feeling that way? There is nothing that happens without a reason. Right now you feel like being left alone from everything and everybody. Let us look at this. Nobody is intruding. They don't even know how to intrude. The moment you set up a barrier, they just leave you alone and go, isn't it? Only one person is intruding into everything. Even when you set up your barrier, he will find a way in, and if you set another barrier, he will find yet another way in. Every time you set up a barrier, if your Guru had left you like that, would you be here today? I didn't give you a choice, did I? (Laughs).

Many of you are still in that state where, if you were simply told something, even if it's the best thing for you, you would get a little irritated because you still have your own personality, your own will, your own privacy and whatnot. So when I talk to you, I talk as if I am asking, but actually I am really telling you. Even if somebody tells you what is best for you, you will resist because they are telling you, so I make it appear as if I am asking. All this is unnecessary. If your surrendering is total, this is unnecessary. For a rare few, I just say, "You have no choice, you come." I never ask them, "What will you do? Will you give up your job? Will you do this?" No. For some people, I just tell them, "You leave everything and come." They never felt there was any choice; they felt they have chosen. They were only told because if given a choice, they might have done something irrelevant with their life. When there is a need for privacy, there is offense. If somebody oversteps that privacy, you will be offended. So the need for privacy means a possibility of being offended. If there is no need for privacy, then there is no possibility of getting offended, because then anything can be said or done. The only thing is, you need trust to hand yourself over so completely.

Seeker: Sadhguru, why aren't I one of the chosen few you tell what to do with their life?

Sadhguru: In so many ways I have indicated to you what is best and what could be done, but after a few days you have come back and said, "This is not for me." What to do with people like you? For most people, I don't interfere beyond a point, and don't think this is because of your individuality. Forget about this 'you'. There is no 'you' right now. As long as your being is not established, there is no 'you'. There is only a mess inside which is your mind, feelings and emotions. All the nonsense that you carry, don't consider all of that as 'you'.

That's where the whole problem is: whatever you think or feel, this is not 'you', this is only a mess that you have gathered from outside. Now when I am talking to you, I know I am not talking to you as a being. There are moments when you are with me as a being and at that time there is absolutely no problem. In those moments, nothing needs to be said, everything happens the way it has to happen, but when you come with your mess, you have to be talked to, because it is a tangle. This tangle has to be handled carefully, very carefully. If I make one wrong move, I know this tangle will run away. The being may crave, but the tangle has its own pride, the tangle has its own problems and it will run away. The being inside may be dying to be here, but the tangle – you know, the ego – has its own problems and it will run away; isn't it so? The inner being may have been crying for lifetimes, crying to just be here. This is so with most of you here around me, but sometimes the mind and the ego together will do something, which will take you away. So when we handle your mind, your feelings and your emotions, we have to tread carefully and handle it the right way. There have been moments when there is no more 'your being' and 'my being'. In those moments, there is no problem, because my being and your being are not different anyway. When you exist on that level of experience, there is no problem. This is what can be referred to as universality. In those moments anything can be done and there is no question of privacy.

Seeker: But Jaggi, everyone does need some amount of privacy.

Sadhguru: Yes, everybody needs some physical privacy, but when we look at universality, what does it mean to you? Universality means there is no 'everything' and 'everybody'. There is only 'you', or another way to look at it is, this 'you' is not there; these are the two ways of looking at it. Now the path of responsibility is: there is only you. The path of surrender is that 'you' are not there. If only 'you' are there, the whole existence is 'you', so there is no question of privacy. If 'you' are not there, again the question of privacy does not arise. Only if you exist, if the physical body exists, it needs some privacy; that is different. If you as a person need privacy, that is very different, but even in the physical sense, there is a distorted sense of privacy about your body. You can show so much of your body, but a little more than that and it becomes a problem. This is not privacy. You have instilled these boundaries which say, "This much is public, the rest is private." To protect this boundary, you will give up your life, isn't it? There are moments when people have given up their lives, just to protect this sense of privacy.

For example, when you fall in love with somebody, you no longer feel a need for privacy. You're willing to shed even your clothes. Privacy is no longer needed because you're in love, because somewhere there is a feeling of oneness. Now, suppose in this moment you are able to see your universality; will you need privacy from the world? Again, this is just an example. A yogi who walks naked on the street, he has no problem. I am clothed not because I need privacy, but because you will not be able to digest it, because you need privacy. Wearing clothes or not wearing clothes is not about me; it is just that the situation requires it. Even the type of clothes worn is whatever the situation demands, isn't it so? There is no real choice of wearing them or not. Even to look at me, your sense of privacy will disturb you. The moment love enters into your life, the need for privacy disappears. Only because love is lacking, privacy has become a big issue in your life. In moments of love, the need for privacy is not there. In fact, privacy is a barrier and you destroy everything that is precious in the name of privacy. The need for privacy is the need for separation. It is a boundary that you have put there. You call it privacy, you call it your space, whatever nonsense you want; it is a boundary. It is as clear as that.

Seeker: Sadhguru, I am unable to contain this play of energies which are happening within me. At what point in this do you come in as the Guru?

Sadhguru: If you want to seek that which is eternal, that which is all pervading, that which is all inclusive, the normal energy that you have is not sufficient. If you want to seek God, the energy that you have just to walk around, to do something, to earn some money, is not sufficient. You need a lot more. Even if you're giving yourself one hundred percent, that kind of energy is simply not sufficient. That's why all the sadhana is done, to raise one's energy. When you are seeking the unlimited, however much energy you have seems to be insufficient. Now, by channeling all this energy towards one goal, towards the one and only goal in life, there is some possibility that you may progress towards that goal. Whether you attain the goal immediately or not is not the point; you begin to progress. The goal becomes approachable. One fundamental requirement for anybody who wishes to grow on the spiritual path is to have an un-deviated flow of energy towards one and only one goal in life: to attain to the highest and not settle for anything less than that.

If there is a person who is capable of channeling himself without any break he is blessed, but rarely do people come like that. Most people lead their lives only in jerks; a few moments of running, then they stop, or maybe even take a few steps backwards, then start running again, or maybe even run backwards. Like this, life is wasted for most people. There are a rare few, once they get started, there is no stopping for them; they just go on. For those others who are 'start-and-stop' people, they need somebody to keep them moving all the time. That 'somebody's' job is to use the carrot and stick with some equanimity as the need arises. Sometimes carrots don't work, then we use the stick. Sometimes sticks don't work, then the carrot. It's like that. I think that Ramakrishna had described a Guru in his own way. He described three types of Gurus or religious teachers who were like three different classes of doctors. There is one type of medical man who, when called upon, looks at the patient, feels his pulse, then prescribes the necessary medicine and asks him to take it. If he declines to do so, the doctor goes away without troubling himself further with the matter. This is the lowest class of doctor. In the same way, there are some religious teachers who don't care much whether their teachings are valued and acted upon or not. Doctors of the second type not only ask the patients to take their medicine, but they go a little further. They expostulate with them if they show any reluctance in taking the medicine. In the same way, the Christian religious teachers, who leave no stone unturned in order to make other people walk the way of righteousness and Truth by means of gentle persuasion, can be said to belong to this class.

The third and the highest kind of doctors would proceed to use force with the patients in case their explanations fail. Such an advisor would go to the extent of putting his knee on the chest of the patient and forcing the medicine down his throat. Similarly, there are some religious teachers who would use force on their disciples, if necessary, with a view of making them walk in the way of the Lord. These belong to the highest class. Now, in every aspect of life – it's not only in terms of doctors and spiritual teachers – in every aspect of life, these three types of people are there. When Ramakrishna considers the last one to be the highest, he takes the risk of becoming unpopular. He takes the risk of being labeled cruel or being considered not at all spiritual.

Let us see why these kinds of teachers exist or why they are needed. It's because by your own nature you might not reach. Look at the frog: wherever he sees a mosquito, there he goes. Maybe he started off in this direction, going after something, but if he sees a mosquito on his side, he goes to that side, another one on the other side, he goes to it. If you go like this, you will not get anywhere. At the most you will fill your belly, that's all. If filling the belly is the only purpose of life, then wherever there is food, there you will go sniffing. Have you seen the dogs, how they go sniffing? Wherever there is food, wherever there is pleasure, there they go. Once you're on the spiritual path, once you have seen the goal of your life, this sniffing around should stop because there are many things that smell good along the way. Wherever something smells good, if you turn in that direction, you are not going to get anywhere in this world or the next. Even the man who wants to simply fulfill his material requirements works with undivided interest in what he is doing, isn't it? Even a man who wants to make money, a man who pursues his pleasure, even he goes with a hundred percent involvement towards what he wants. If that is so, when you're seeking the highest, you know how you should be. Whatever I say will fall short of how you should be. So many things may come up on the way, but you should be strong enough, brave enough, and adamant enough to go after what you want, otherwise things will not happen.

Seeker: So Sadhguru, what exactly should I do to make this happen for me?

Sadhguru: Spirituality is not for pussycats, do you understand? You can't do anything else in your life, but think you can be spiritual; this is not so. If you can take up and do anything in this world, then there is a possibility that you may be fit for spirituality, not otherwise. If you have the strength and the courage to just take up anything in the world and do it well, then maybe you can be spiritual. This is not for people who can't do anything else. Right now, this is the impression that the whole country has, probably the whole world has; that useless, good-for-nothing people are spiritual people, because the so-called spiritual people have become like that. People who are incapable of doing anything or people who can't bear the ups and downs of life, all they have to do is to wear the ochre clothes and sit in front of the temple; their life is made. That's not spirituality; that's just begging in uniform. If you have to conquer your consciousness, if you have to reach the peak of your consciousness, a beggar can never reach there.

There are two kinds of beggars. Gautama, the Buddha, and people of that order are the highest kind of beggars. All others are plain beggars. I would say the beggar on the street and the king sitting on the throne are both beggars. They are continuously asking for something from the outside. The beggar on the street might be asking for money, food or shelter. The king might be asking for happiness, or conquering another kingdom or some such nonsense. Do you see, everybody is begging for something? Gautama begged only for his food, for the rest he was self-sufficient. All others, the only thing they don't beg for is food. It is for everything else that they beg. Their whole life is begging. Only food they earn, but a spiritual person has earned everything else from within, only for food he begs. Whichever way you think is better, be that way. Whichever way you think is a more powerful way to live, live that way.

To be spiritual means to be an emperor within yourself. This is the only way to be. Is there any other way to be? Consciously, would anybody choose to be anything where he has to seek something from someone or something else? Maybe out of his helplessness he seeks, but consciously would anybody choose to do this? Wouldn't every human being want to be that way, where he is hundred percent within himself? It doesn't mean you have to become totally self-sufficient. Always there is interdependence, but within yourself everything is there; you don't have to seek outside. Even somebody's company is not needed for you. If another person needs it, you will give it, but by yourself, you don't need anybody's company. This means you're no more a beggar within. Only for external things, maybe you will have to go to the world outside. This is ultimate freedom.

Once it is like this, this person leads a different way of life. Once there is no hankering, once there is no need within him, only then he knows what love is; only then he knows what joy is; only then he knows what it means to really share. People who have missed this joy of sharing only know exchange. People generally know only the barter system. "You give me this; I will give you that!" This is not sharing. Most relationships are not about sharing; they are only about bartering – your money, your body, your emotions. Now, sharing is, "You don't have to give me anything because I don't need anything from you, but anyway, I will share this with you." Setting up a whole life of barter may be convenient, but it is the way of the weak. This weakness is the first thing that has to go if you want to meet Shiva. If you want to meet Him, you had better be on His terms. He is not going to come and meet a mere beggar. You either need to learn to meet them on their terms or dissolve; these are the only two ways. *Gnana* and *bhakthi* mean just this. Bhakthi means you make yourself a zero, then you meet Him. Gnana means you meet Him on His terms; you become infinite. Otherwise, there is no chance of a meeting.

Love, or bhakthi, looks like a much easier path. It is, but there are more pitfalls on that path than in gnana. With gnana you know where you are going, you know if you fall. In bhakthi, you don't know. Even if you have fallen into a pit you will not know; that is the way it is. Even if you're trapped by your own illusions, you will not know. In gnana, it is not like this. Every step that you take, you know. Every step of growth, you know; every step backwards, you also know. I can't say it is a hard path, but it's the path of the courageous, not of the weaklings. The weaklings can never make it, but everybody has the possibility of making it. Everybody has the capacity to do it if they rise above their limitations. It is just about whether they are willing to do it or not, that is all.

The way we think is the way we become. Whatever you hold as the highest, naturally all your energies get drawn towards that. You know there are different kinds of people, different associations in society. In a group of drunkards, the highest thing is to be able to drink a certain amount. They are always talking about who can drink more. So naturally their whole life is about that. Pleasure seekers are thinking who can have more pleasure. So naturally their whole life is about that. People who are after money are thinking about more money, so naturally their energies are towards that. Similarly, a person who wants to walk the spiritual path has to make it that way in his mind, that this is the highest, that, "This is the first and the last thing that I want in my life." So naturally all his energies are oriented towards it. Only then the moment-to-moment struggle is gone and you don't have to struggle to correct yourself.

Seeker: Sadhguru, I know what you're saying, but at times I have this inner struggle that I am still missing out on many things in life by walking this path. How can I cope with this?

Sadhguru: When this one thing is not fixed within you, then every moment is a struggle, because every moment has a doubt: "What shall I do? Maybe I am missing out, maybe I am missing life, maybe this or that may not happen to me," all kinds of things. There are so many things that we don't know about, that other people may be doing. They may be eating, enjoying and doing many other things. Nathalie, have you ever eaten cockroach pickle? No, isn't it? You missed it? But for someone who has eaten it a few times and it is not available anymore, only he misses it. It is just the way we make it in our mind. Nobody is missing anything. It is just that you make it that way within yourself. "Oh I did not eat this. I didn't go snow skiing or disco dancing!" This is simply because you have made these things important in your mind. If you fix the goal of your life, you will not miss anything. All these *vasanas*[1] are there within everybody. The past karmas have influences over you, they push you this way and that way. All your passions, all your desires, you can't fight with them. Don't ever try to fight with your passions and desires. Fighting with them is like fighting the demon, Mahishasura. If one drop of his blood falls

1 *vasanas*: tendencies or desire; subliminal trait left behind in the mind by action and desire

a thousand Mahishasuras will rise up. Your desires and passions are just like that. If you try and fight with them, if you chop them, they will spill blood, and with every drop, a hundred or a thousand will come up. There is no point fighting them. Just educate your passions, educate your desires to flow in the right direction, that is all. You can never fight them. Fighting them will be futile; it will be a waste of life.

Seeker: Then what can we do with our desires?

Sadhguru: Just desire the highest in life. All your passions, direct them to the highest. Even if you get angry, direct it only toward Shiva. Even with your passion, that's the way to do it. Every bit of energy these emotions are not in your hands for now, but channeling them in one direction is in your hands. Maybe when you are angry you cannot be loving; you can't suddenly turn your anger into love, but the anger itself can be directed. Anger is tremendous energy, isn't it? Lust is tremendous energy also. Direct it in the right way; that is all. Every ounce of energy that you have, every passion, emotion, thought, if they are focused in one direction, the results can be very, very quick. Things will happen. Once you know there is something higher and you want to be there, there should be no other question about it. Only people around you should have questions about it, not you. There should be simply no questions about it.

Now for you, again and again, this spirituality, this Enlightenment, this God-Realization looks so far away. It appears to be close this moment, the next moment it appears to be light years away. Then a certain complacency will come. They have always told you, "A bird in hand is worth two in the bush." What is there now is better than something somewhere else. What you need to understand is, it is not somewhere; it is all here and now. Only because 'you' are not, it looks like that for you. Shiva is not somewhere, he is here and now. It is you who is not. That is the only problem. It is not difficult, but definitely it's not easy. It is extremely simple. Moving from here, from wherever you are right now, to the infinite is very simple, because it is right here. Do know, simple need not necessarily be easy. It is subtle and delicate. Unless you put your whole life energy into it, it will not open up.

With half-hearted appeals, God never comes. With half-hearted appeals, Realization never happens. It has to be everything, only then it can happen in one moment. It need not take twelve years. Probably a fool takes twelve years to become intense enough; that is different. If you make yourself intense enough, it is just one moment. After that, life is just blessed. You simply live on, whichever way you want, whatever way you choose; but without creating that one moment, going on doing all kinds of nonsense, not finding yourself, if you say, "I have found the world," what is the use? You are not even present doing all of those things, but you think you have found the world. What is the use?

Seeker: Sadhguru, this initiation into sanyas that is happening today, why is this? What does it signify?

Sadhguru: A time has come when we need to establish this order. Whatever we have done all these years is not that we have not already laid the foundation for this; we have, long ago. Yet, still we kept a certain choice open depending upon so many factors that may happen. Now, this order of bhramhacharya has progressed to a certain level of maturity. Maybe it is yet to bear lots of fruit, but it has definitely reached a certain level of maturity. Somebody who does not recognize the mango tree without fruit may think it is a wild tree, maybe a barren tree. Only someone who recognizes the mango tree knows that with a little nourishment, sweetness will ripen.

This is a huge step in establishing Isha as a permanent spiritual process for the world. This is a huge step of gratitude towards my Guru. For a man like Him, though a few individuals attained around Him, and of course there is the Dhyanalinga, but someone like Him not leaving a living order of spiritual process behind Him has always been something that has bothered me. He never stayed in one place, so He did not leave any kind of spiritual order behind Him. Even though He was a man whose experience, understanding and wisdom was far beyond what most people can dream of, He did not leave any kind of spiritual order. Once the Dhyanalinga consecration was complete and after life started flowing again through my once-almost-finished-body, I've been thinking that we should set up a truly powerful spiritual order which would befit Him and which should go on with His Grace.

He Himself is a man who lived without a name. He never had a name in His life. Because He remained in samadhi for a long period of time somewhere close to the town of Palani, people just called Him Palani Swami. But He never had a name. Here, all our bhramhacharis and sanyasis have such wonderful names. These names come from the traditions where truly proud and shining, brilliant spiritual orders have come from. These people lived in such a way that gods would be envious of them. They lived so powerfully, with such dignity. We want this order of sanyasis in Isha to definitely stand up and live that way.

Especially in today's world, where many spiritual orders have fallen into bad times, I think it is an enormous responsibility. It is an enormous responsibility and also a tremendous privilege that such a responsibility has been bestowed upon us. See, all these people here are not perfect human beings... Oh, I'm making it so gloomy and serious. Let me tell you a story.

Once, there was a spiritual Master who had a servant to help him with his daily chores. This servant used to carry two pots of water hung on a bamboo on his shoulders everyday to the Master's house. He would go up and down many times. When he was carrying this water, one of the pots that he was using was slightly cracked and it was always leaking water. The other pot, which was perfect, was always mocking the cracked pot - there are many crackpots here (laughs) - so the perfect pot was mocking everyday, "See how I'm serving the Master? See how you are; you're cracked. Half the water is gone by the time you reach the house." This was happening.

One day, after a long period of seclusion, the Master came out into the garden and walked along the pathway. He noticed, only on one side of the pathway, all along, there were lots of flowers in bloom. The Master looked at these wonderful flowers and said, "Whoever is the cause of making these flowers bloom on my pathway, let him attain," He blessed. And the cracked pot attained! So there is hope for the cracked ones also. Now, don't make it your right to be cracked!

Why this sanyas, what it means is... if we can un-burn the pots, cracked or otherwise, into the basic material of clay, we can make so many things out of it. Instead of making a pot, we can make a deity out of it - a Divine vehicle. If you can bring people down to just life, just life energy, with no personality, then this life energy can be used in so many ways. Such incredible ways that you wouldn't imagine life is possible like this. That is why this order of monkhood or sanyas. People's expectations of Isha bhramhacharis are very, very big. This is not a burden. It's a tremendous privilege when thousands of people look up to us and expect something wonderful to happen out of us. It is an enormous privilege. When people expect only lowly things from you, you will naturally fall into that. So, when people expect the highest things from you, knowingly or unknowingly you have to shift your gears to the highest point.

It's a tremendous privilege. It's an opportunity for us to rise beyond our limitations. Please make that happen, both for your sake and everybody's sake. It is very, very important. It is much more important than you will understand right now.

So, today we take this step.

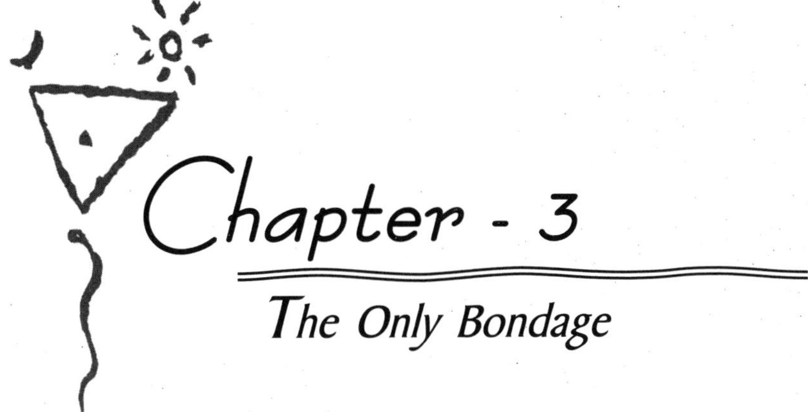

Chapter - 3

The Only Bondage

The Only Bandage

You did escape the trap
of elemental hive.

But it is your own doing
that is the ultimate trap

Till you go beyond your own crap
there is no way to break this trap.

– Sadhguru

The Yoga of Abandon. *On the night of Mahashivarathri...*

Atop the Velliangiri Mountains, in the footsteps of His Guru.

As kings and dynasties were replaced with democracies, and tyrants with popular uprisings, the twentieth century saw the quest for freedom in mankind, as a whole, reach new heights. In spite of human rights being enshrined in constitution after constitution, of nations across the globe, man remains hopelessly enslaved to his *karma* – the only and the ultimate bondage.

Unknown to the deluded being is the wicked reign of karma, seeping into the being – into every cell, predetermining how a cell, an organ or an individual behaves, controlling every breath, thought and emotion. Untold despair befalls the seeker as he realizes one day that his most prized 'freedom' is but a complex function of the karmic influences from the past.

Smitten by ignorance and unawareness, man's entanglement in this unseen web of the all-pervading karma deepens with each futile struggle to break free.

Shattering this illusion of 'freedom', so fanatically pursued in our times, Sadhguru reveals the laws of karma and offers antidotes from his inexhaustible repository of spiritual practices. Shifting the focus from action to volition, from fear and beliefs to awareness, Sadhguru de-mystifies the most widely used term in the Indian spiritual jargon, initiating the liberation of the seeker.

Seeker: Sadhguru, how do I go beyond action or karma yoga? Personally, I have no urge to do anything. I feel like drifting towards a state of non-doing.

Sadhguru: When a person has made ultimate reality the goal in his life, action becomes meaningless. Once action is meaningless, any kind of self-image is of no great significance; but right now, in the state you are in, there is still a need for action. You have not yet reached a point where you have transcended action. You are unable to be without action. So perform the kind of action you think is best right now and do what is needed for the situation. For my people, or my disciples, when I am around, I am not thinking in terms of devising a little better *karma*[1] for them. This idea of better karma is only when the *Guru*[2] is either a dud or dead. Do you understand? Better karma can only mean your Guru is either a total dud who is useless and a fake, or he's dead and gone.

Seeker: You are the brightest, the most sharp-witted and the most genuine person I have ever met, Sadhguru.

Sadhguru: Brightest and sharpest, yes. About being genuine, how do you know that this one is not a dud? On the plane that you exist, you can never know. Doubts do come sometimes, don't they? Yes, I know they come, unless you have developed such a deep trust that it does not matter whether your Guru is real or a fake – whichever way, your trust in him is such that you will anyway be with him. Until you evolve into such a state, doubts will come. And even if he is a dud, there's no way you can know. All your standards of judgment simply will not hold true. How do you judge whether the person

1 *karma* : referring to past action, the cause of all bondage.
2 Guru : lit. *dispeller of darkness*. A spiritual Master.

is a genuine Guru or a fake? Either you jell with him or you don't. That's all there is. You cannot really make a judgment about it. That's why so many of the tribe thrive. I am asking you, how will you know?

Seeker: There are certain qualities in a Guru which pull an individual beyond his logic and that's why I am here with you, Sadhguru.

Sadhguru: What are the qualities that can attract you? What can you look for? See, you are just impressed and maybe even attracted to him as a person. Maybe you like the way he looks or speaks, or even maybe the work that is being done. Your attractions cannot go beyond these things. To recognize a Guru and become his disciple, one needs a different kind of quality. When Adolf Hitler decided to start his own party, he had only a handful of friends with him. He sat in a basement with these people and spoke to them in such forceful ways that fired their imagination to great heights; he made them believe that he was going to take over the world shortly. He was just an unemployed youth, a nobody, but he was such a forceful speaker. To them, he was God who was going to rule. He was the future of this planet. This is how he built his self-image. Hitler's self-image was so powerful, he believed that he would rule the world. His self-image was so powerful that it almost came true. If you create any image without a break in it, if there is a continuous mental focus towards it, it will happen, no matter what.

There is another way to create without asking for anything, without ever thinking about anything, where things just happen. Before we arrive at that, a little bit of fired-up movement is needed. People who have never been on fire will not know the coolness of water. People who have just lived their life in a half-hearted manner, sedately, can never know the other way. Becoming a fanatic at least for a while can be useful for your energies to reach a boiling point and get moving. Then, to transform them into something else is very easy. That's the whole purpose of karma or action. Why a *sadhaka*[1] chooses action is just for this reason. We are going to perform action anyway. Now we have the choice whether we want to perform Hitler's or Mahatma Gandhi's type of action. Whichever way we feel is best right now, we'll do that. That's all there is to it. Anyway we have to perform action, so let us do it whole-heartedly, and let us choose the form of action that we want to do. Do you know the self-image that you want?

1 *sadhaka* : a spiritual seeker.

Do you want to rule the world or do you want to serve the world? Ultimately, that is the choice. Normally, everybody wants to rule the world. It is just that, because a man is half-hearted, he is only able to rule his wife. He doesn't get to rule the world, so all he's able to do is rule his children, wife or something like that, but what he really wants is to rule the world. The fool doesn't have the capacity or the intensity to do it; otherwise, he would be a potential Hitler. The man who physically abuses his child or wife because they don't conform to his ideas – suppose that tomorrow he is made the king of the world, he will use a sword instead of a stick. That's all. It is just that he's incapable and doesn't have the intensity to rule the world; otherwise, he is already the ruler.

Now the choice is just this – either to rule or to serve. Whichever kind of image you think is most harmonious, the closest to Divinity and closest to Realization, that kind of action you choose. Every moment, do it with tremendous intensity, without giving it a single moment's break. Then a day will come when action is not needed anymore. A man who does not know action – real action, intense action – can never move into inaction. If you try to, inaction will just become lethargy. Only if you have known intense action can you know inaction. People who are always resting in their life must be experts about rest, isn't it? But that is not the truth. Only a man who works intensely can know what rest is. So this non-doing business, if you really want to know it, first you must discover what doing is. You have not done that yet. In every waking moment of my life, unceasingly I pursue this work of offering myself, physically and mentally. Unceasingly I pursue it twenty-four hours of the day, every waking moment and even in my sleep, with tremendous intensity. It is only out of that, that all of this has happened in my life. It has become so powerful simply because it does not mean anything to me, but for twenty-four hours, I am at it. Now this has a different kind of power. That is the whole meaning of sacrifice. It is only out of that, that something else happens – both inside and outside – which can never be put into words.

There have been many sages in the world, Realized beings who, even today, are spreading their energy, but by themselves, they are not able to do anything. Only a few are unceasingly at it, day in and day out and only out of this, something can be created. This is how Vivekanandas are created. They are not born. This is how Mahatma Gandhis are created. This is how every powerful individual in this world is created. This is the science of creating a truly powerful being. This is not power to rule. This is not a power that can be taken away at any moment. Nobody can take it away, because wherever you are put, that is what you do. If you want to rule, you have to sit on the seat. If somebody pulls you off the seat, you will be miserable. This is not like that. Wherever you are put, you just do your work. It does not matter what the situation is, what the result of your action is, because that's what you do anyway. If they put you in hell, that is what you do. If they put you in heaven, still, that is what you do. This releases you from action. First of all, this releases you from the fruit of action. Once you are released from the fruit of action, the action will happen by itself. You don't have to stop working to be released from action. Simply, it will dissolve, melt and disappear. Once the expectation of the fruit of action is completely removed from your life, the action occurs by itself. You don't have to do anything about it.

In one of the Zen monasteries, there is an old Master who is over eighty years old. Every day, he works his heart out in the gardens. In Zen monasteries, gardening is one of the most important parts of the *sadhana.*[1] Day in and day out, people spend time in the garden. This Master has been doing this for years. Now he is over eighty and has become weak, but he does not stop. The whole day, he works in the garden. Many times his disciples have tried to dissuade him. They say, "You stop working, we are all here, we will do it," but he will not listen. He just goes on doing what he can. His capacity to work physically might have come down, but the intensity has not come down. He works with the same intensity. So one day the disciples took away his tools and hid them somewhere, as he will work only with these tools. That day, he did not eat. The next day, there were no tools, so he did not eat. The third day also, no tools; he did not eat. By then they got scared, "Oh! Because we hid the tools, he is angry. He is not eating." Once again, they replaced the tools where they were usually placed. On the fourth day, he worked and ate. Then in the evening, he gave his teaching: "No work, no food," and he went back and died. That was the last day. The four days of fasting were too much for him; but the last day he worked, he ate, then he left his body, and he just gave this teaching: "No work, no food." For this kind of a man, action is like this. Wherever he is put, that is how he will be. Hell, heaven or earth, you put him in any of these different worlds and he will be the same. Once you are like this, you are released from the external situation. By just closing your eyes, you will not become released. The moment you open them,

1 *sadhana* : spiritual practices used as a means to realization.

everything will come back and catch up with you. If you run away and sit on the mountain, you will not become free. This is the way to work it out. It has to be worked out.

Seeker: Sadhguru, does this mean that we should perform good actions that will free us from the bad karma we have accumulated?

Sadhguru: Karmas are classified in terms of *gunas*. What is a guna? It is a quality. Quality is not exactly the word. The Hindus generally talk about three types of gunas. The Buddhists classify them into seven types. It is just a classification that we can make. Karma can be classified as good karma and bad karma. What I am saying is, whether it is good karma or bad karma, it is still bondage. For people who are only interested in leading a comfortable life, this classification is important. They are always thinking how to perform good karma so that they will be born with wealth, well-being and comfort in their next life. Only a person who is living with duality, for that person there is good and bad karma.

For a person who is thinking in terms of transcending life and death, good karma is as useless as bad. To him, karma is just karma; any classification does not matter. All karma is bad for a spiritual person. Good or bad, it's bad for him. For a person who wants to transcend duality, become one with existence, for that person there is no good and bad. All karma is a barrier, a burden for him. He wants to drop all burdens. It's not like, "If you give me gold, I'm willing to carry even one hundred kilos, but if you give me one hundred kilos of garbage, I will not carry it." That's not the attitude. For a seeker it is, "I want to drop the load." Whether it's gold or garbage, both are heavy, but the other fools think carrying gold is great. Do you understand the difference, Nicholas? A man, who has become wise enough, sees that whether he carries gold or garbage, it is anyway burdensome. The other man is thinking gold will be better than garbage because right now he's carrying garbage.

Seeker: Master, is karma also affected by thoughts and not just deeds?

Sadhguru: See, the moment you say this is a good thought and that's a bad thought, this is a good deed and that is a bad deed – if somebody is doing the bad deed then he's a bad person, isn't it? "Yeah! I am a good man; you are a bad man." It's obvious! Good and bad were mainly invented by people who are selling tickets to heaven. Once a preacher of the old school was describing the events of judgment day, and of course, he used biblical phraseology whenever he could, "Oh! My friends," he intoned, "imagine the suffering of the sinners as they find themselves cast in the outer darkness, removed from the presence of the Lord and given to eternal flames. My friends, at such a time they will be weeping, wailing and gnashing their teeth." At this point one of the eldest of the congregation interrupted, "But reverend, what if one of these hopeless sinners has no teeth?" The preacher crashed his fist on the pulpit, "My friends, the Lord is not put out by details, and rest assured, teeth will be provided." These are the kind of people who invented good and bad.

Every action has a consequence. When I say, 'action', it is not just of the body. It does not pertain to body alone. Action can be of thought, emotion or energy. An action which brings a negative consequence into your life, you generally try to term it as a bad action. It is not a question of bad action, it's just that different actions produce different kinds of consequences. As a human being, your business is just this – every one of us has the intelligence to do this – if you are aware enough you can see that for every single action there is a consequence. If you can joyfully accept the consequence, do anything that you wish to do, but if you do something today and when the consequence comes, you cry, then please curtail your actions, thoughts, emotions, or whatever. Do not start something that you cannot handle. This is not about good and bad; this is just about living your life sensibly. Now you don't pick up a rock that you cannot carry – it is as simple as that. You pick up something that you can handle. So every action is just that. If you bring it into your awareness, you don't have to worry about what is good and bad; you will just do what is needed for you – nothing more, nothing less.

Seeker: Sadhguru, if I had accumulated a lot of bad karma in unawareness, in another life, will it make me suffer now, in this life? Should I try to perform good karmas to make up for that?

Sadhguru: Yes, if you are only trying to enhance the quality of your life, good karmas are useful. Good karma does not mean good action, it means action that comes from good volition. That's why there is so much talk about love everywhere. In love, you will perform good karma. When you perform good karma, the quality of your life will be enhanced, that's all. If your love becomes just intensity, beyond any sense, then it can become a process of liberation. Otherwise, love is just allowing you to do good karma.

You are always judging people as good or bad by looking at their actions. I am telling you, the so-called 'good' people never get into action. They are treacherous; they never act, because they are so cunning. They know that the moment they act, one way or the other, they are going to be found out. These 'good' people are the really treacherous people. Maybe they don't do anything physically, but this does not absolve one from the karmic processes. If you restrain yourself or your actions out of your goodness or sense, that is different, but if your fear of the consequence is all that restrains you, then the karma is very different. The 'good' people are the true criminals in the world. They never do anything, so they never get caught. They are the people who perform the worst kind of karma, maybe not in actions, but in their thoughts. For every small thing, they're willing to kill the whole world within themselves. They are like that. These are people filled with jealousy, with hatred within themselves, but they don't do anything wrong outwardly because the flesh is weak, or they don't have the courage to take action, or they are just plain cunning. That's the only thing that has stopped them.

Now there is a really wonderful person who has got a nice big house, a great wife, a very good life, but something will come up, just to remind him. Life has its ways. Once, a businessman boarded a flight and found himself sitting next to an elegant woman wearing the largest, most stunning diamond ring he had ever seen. Awestruck, he exclaimed, "Wow! That's a beautiful ring you have there!" The woman replied, "Yes, this is the Schroeder diamond. It is beautiful, but it comes with a terrible curse." "What curse?" asked the businessman. "Mr. Schroeder," answered the woman. So something will come up. If everything is right, one thing will crop up and go on bothering you, needling you. It's always like that. Otherwise, you will forget life and try to become God. You forget your limitations, so something will come up. That's your karma. The karma, though a process of bondage, is finding expression for you as a reminder of your emancipation. If you are unaware, you get entangled with it. If you are aware, it becomes the way to your liberation.

For a person who knows his limitations, even if something comes up in life, he's not really affected; it doesn't really touch him. Let us say somebody lost their child. These are simple people. If their child dies, at that moment they feel something; the next moment they leave it. There are other kinds of people whose child died ten years ago and even today, they are in turmoil. Just the thought of it and they find themselves in great turmoil. Yes, that is karma.

It does not matter what happens in life, we can blunt the edge of karma. Maybe you cannot immediately remove everything, unless you walk the spiritual path. Even a person who is not walking the spiritual path, if he's sensible, can blunt the edges of his karma and make it ineffective to a large extent. Only certain things will really take effect; other things can be minimized. Only when a person consciously walks the spiritual path, that person can definitely leave all that. If you have the urge, if you really have the character to do that, by the end of this Isha Yoga program, you can simply leave your 'load of bananas' and go. It is very much possible. The opportunity is here. Whether anybody makes it happen or not, the possibility is always wide open.

Seeker: Sadhguru, at times I am not sure if I am doing the right thing by being here at Isha. There is much disappointment at home. Am I piling up more karma by causing this pain to my family, Master?

Sadhguru: They brought you up with many expectations, which caused disappointment to them. The nature of karma is not in the action that you perform. Karma means action, but this gathering of past karmas is not because of the actions you have performed. It is the volition, the intention, the kind of mind that you carry. That's your karma. What is disappointment? Now Kumar asked this question. Let us take your situation as an example. Your wife has some expectation of you that you should be in a particular way, but you're not like that. Now you are unable to break that expectation, or you have not had the courage to break it, or you still have not had a chance to break it. Maybe there is an urge to break it, but you are keeping quiet because of society's norms. For some reason you have not broken it, but the urge is there within you. It's almost like you *have* broken the karma.

There is a story which the wonderful sage, Ramakrishna, used to tell. There were two friends who used to go visiting a prostitute every Saturday evening. On one such evening, while they were walking towards the prostitute's house, there was someone giving a discourse on the *Gita*.[1] One friend decided not to visit the prostitute, saying he would prefer to hear the lecture on the *Gita*. The other man left him there. Now the man sitting in the lecture hall, his thoughts were full of the other man. He began thinking that the other man was having the time of his life while he was caught in this place. He thought the other man was more intelligent in choosing the prostitute's place rather than a *Gita* discourse. Now the man who had gone to the prostitute's house, his mind was full of the other man. He began to think that his friend had chosen the path to liberation by preferring the *Gita* discourse to the prostitute's place, while he got caught in this. The man who had gone for the *Gita* discourse and was thinking about what was happening in the prostitute's house pays by piling up bad karma. He suffers, not the other man. You don't pay because you have gone to the prostitute; you pay because you are cunning about it. You still want to go there, but you think by going to the discourse you'll be one step closer to heaven. This cunningness will take you to hell. That man with the prostitute knows it's worthless, and seeks something else; his is good karma. So it's not about action.

Right now, why you think in terms of 'right' and 'wrong' is simply because of the social moral code. It's not your innate nature which is telling you that this is right and wrong. It is just that society has fixed some rules and they have always told you, right from your childhood, that if you break them you are a bad boy. So whenever you break these, you feel like a bad boy. If you feel like one, you become one. If you are used to gambling, maybe gambling in front of your mother or your wife, in your home, or even to utter the word is sacrilege, but once you join your gang, there gambling is just fine, isn't it? Among the gamblers, the one who does not gamble is not fit to live. It's like this everywhere. If all of you are thieves, you are all fine, isn't it? Among thieves, do they feel it is bad to rob somebody? When you fail, they think you are a no-good thief. That is a bad karma, isn't it? The question, this karmic thing, is just the way you feel about it. It's not about what you are doing. It is just the way you are holding it in your mind. Why we are talking about acceptance, acceptance, acceptance, is, if you are absolute acceptance, whatever life demands, you do. If you have to fight a battle, you go and fight; there

---

1 *Gita* : referring to *Bhagavad Gita*, sacred book of the Hindus.

is no karma. The karma is not made in physical action; it is made only by volition. It's just that some fool has formed some rules and you expect every human being to live by them. It's impossible, but society needs such rules to maintain the social ego.

Seeker: So what is social ego, Sadhguru?

Sadhguru: Society has its own ego, isn't it? For every small thing, the whole society gets upset. It need not be wrong. Suppose it's summer in the United States. Everybody is hardly wearing anything or maybe they are in miniskirts. Let's say you're fully clothed. People will get upset: "What is she doing? Why is she all covered up?" Here in India, if you dress like *that*, they'll all get upset. So this is one kind of ego; that is another kind of ego. It's the social ego which is getting upset, and your karma is becoming part of the collective karma. I want you to really understand this with a certain depth. Your idea of good and bad has been taught to you. You have imbibed it from the social atmosphere in which you have lived. See, for example, a bandit tribe, like the Pindaris, who from a young age were trained to rob and kill, they even had gods who taught them skills and brought them success in their banditry. When the British army was let loose on them, they were shot and killed indiscriminately. They were completely bewildered, as in their perception they had not done anything wrong. The Pindari ego was just to be a good bandit. The same happened for the Native American Indians also. Among some Native American tribes, unless you had killed a man in your life, you were not much of a man. They collected the scalp of the man and wore it around their neck. So what is right and wrong, what is good and bad, is all about how the social ego functions.

Seeker: Sadhguru, if a child dies, whose karma is it? They say we should not cry; what about that? Is this a part of the karmic process? Does some past karma dissolve for the parents?

Sadhguru: Definitely you don't have to cry. Whether karma dissolves or not, there is no need to cry. If you cry out of love, if tears flow out of compassion, it's good, but if you are going to cry because the physical body collapses, you need to understand, it has to collapse. Right from day one, you know this body is not eternal. Nobody is foolish enough to think it is, but people are thinking on those terms. In the West, have you heard that they are preserving bodies for the future? In England, they have started this process, with all this scientific equipment; the dead bodies are being preserved for the future. They are making blood circulate through machines, and the body is kept intact. It doesn't deteriorate. You have to pay a lot of money to keep your body like that. Now the thing is, some day all souls are going to come back, and when you come, you can come back to your own body. This is nonsense. It's really a stupid thing, an immature thing to do, simply because somewhere, Western philosophy misread the whole situation.

Jesus did not even talk about the continuation of life; he probably just wanted people to make use of this life. "You grow now, when I am here," he said. He never talked about the next life. He said, "This is it. Now, this is the chance. You have to do it now. It is now or never." That's how he spoke. Every teaching he gave was a 'now-or-never' teaching. The philosophy just stops there, with this life. So that is why the Western mind has become so tremendously active. The *Pingala*[1] has become so active because life is going to stop here. When you die, it's going to be over. Nobody has talked about what is next. There is a tremendous kind of hurry in the West, in every field, simply because for them, life ends here. A certain kind of thought comes that if you're going to die tomorrow, you want to do everything today; that's the attitude. Here, in India, we know there are many lives. What's the problem? If not this time, there is always the next one.

One day, Shankaran Pillai returned from visiting a doctor about his liver problem brought on by his heavy drinking. He mournfully told his wife that he had only twelve hours to live. After wiping away her tears, he asked her to prepare him a nice dinner. Sometime later in bed, he started to make romantic overtures and his wife, with a heavy heart, dutifully responded. Three hours later, Shankaran Pillai gently woke her up and said, "I only have seven more hours to live. I was thinking that maybe, you know…" She agreed. Still later, Shankaran Pillai, bursting into tears, realized he had only five hours of life left. He nudged his wife and said, "Please, just once more before I die." She agreed and afterward sighed heavily, rolled over and quickly fell fast asleep. Shankaran Pillai continued to hear the clock ticking away in his head until he

---

1 *Pingala* : one of the major pranic channels of the body, masculine in nature.

was down to three more hours. Again he nudged his wife to wake her, and sobbing away, turned to her and said, "I only have three more hours left, could we?" His wife sat up abruptly and turned to him and said, "Listen, I have to get up in the morning AND YOU DON'T!"

This question about, "If a child dies, is it dissolution of the parents' karma?" No, the death itself may be your karma, because for you, generally a child is a valuable possession. So losing your child is not a good experience. If your child dies, you are not going to clap, jump around, and say, "That is great; he went back to God or existence!" No, you are going to be all wound up. So it's not dissolution. It may be just that it has to happen like that for you. It's your karma. You cannot say it is dissolution. Nothing is dissolved. You are going to suffer from it. The child is gone but your suffering continues, isn't it? The karma is not in your child. The karma is only in your attitude and in your suffering.

Seeker: Is karma passed on from generation to generation, Sadhguru?

Sadhguru: Is your karma handed over to the next generation? What, Balu, are you asking whether your karmas are being handed over to your children? Hereditary karmas? See, wherever you are, or whomever you are with at any moment, whatever that man's karma, it also affects you one way or the other. Let us say, your friend is a thief. You never did anything, but when the police come and catch him, they will catch both of you. Maybe you won't get one-year imprisonment the way he does, but you will at least spend one day behind bars. This is his karma which has rubbed off on you, but it's your karma that you were with him at that moment. Similarly, the parents' karma affects the children. Whatever nonsense you do definitely affects the child. Transferring? No. If you're thinking of handing it over to your son and going, it will not work that way. It is just an influence. It's just like this: if you're next to a flower, you will get the fragrance of it, but you cannot become the flower. If you want to become a flower, you have to become the flower out of your own nature. Even if my daughter has to seek the peak of her consciousness, she has to seek it out of her own nature. Maybe being here, in this energy field, is good karma for her. She has this opportunity, even if she is not meditating, but it's not essential that she has to turn spiritual. We don't know; that is left to her. That, nobody can decide. You don't know who she is anyway, what her attributes are, what her karmic basis is. I don't want to go into that.

Seeker: You don't want to go into that, but now that you have started it…

Sadhguru: I shouldn't have started it. I started simply because you have to know. Don't look at anybody based on what they are right now. There is so much behind every person. It could be good and it could be bad, it could be positive and it could be negative, but there is so much behind every person here. If you are sensitive and subtle enough, just by looking at a person, you will be able to see his whole lifetimes of karmas, here and now. That will be your understanding of people and who they are.

Meditation may be a quick way which takes you to that level of subtleness, but for a lot of people it is not possible, because their karma, their body or their mind, something will not allow them to meditate. One purpose of doing the practices and yoga kriyas is that you become sensitive. If you just touch a person for one moment, you should know his one hundred lifetimes, and what his karma is. You may not know all the details, which city he was born in, where he lived, what he had for dinner today…that is not the point. You know the general trend of his karmas. This is not imagining or hallucinating. It must be crystal clear, just like seeing with your eyes. That is how it should be. Now the way you act, the way in which you handle people, will be with a different kind of maturity. Just by looking at them, not by looking at their present image, you will know exactly what that person needs at this moment. Even he may not know what he needs at this moment, because he only knows what he is at this moment. He does not know what he was in another lifetime, but you know what he was then; so you can handle things with a totally different kind of maturity which will not come through thought. If that sensitivity has to come, one has to work towards it; there is no other way.

Seeker: Master, you have told us many times that if we have bitter experiences in our life, it is because of our past doings. What type of activities should we do today to avoid future bitterness?

Sadhguru: Subbarao, the bitterness of any experience is not in what has happened. The bitterness of any experience is in terms of how you have received it. What is very bitter for one person could be a blessing for another person. Once, a grief stricken man threw himself on a grave and cried bitterly, hitting his head against it. "My life! Oh! How senseless it is! How worthless this carcass of mine is because you're gone. If only you had lived! If only fate had not been so cruel as to take you from this world! How different everything would have been!" A clergyman, nearby, overheard him and said, "I assume this person lying beneath this mound of earth was someone of great importance to you." "Importance? Yes, indeed," wept the man, wailing even louder, "It was my wife's first husband!" The bitterness is not in what is happening. It is in how you're allowing yourself to experience it, how you are receiving it. Similarly, whatever the past activity or karma is, is also not in terms of action, but in terms of the volition with which it is done.

What is happening with you all, if you are a little open to me or to the teaching, is just that the volition is taken away, so you just do what is needed. That is what awareness means; there is no volition. Where there is no volition, there is no karma. You are simply doing what is needed; that is what acceptance means. That is what unbounded responsibility means, that you don't have any volition about anything. In every given situation, simply whatever you see as needed, as per your awareness, as per your capability, you just do it. You build karma only with volition; whether it is good or bad, it does not matter. The strength of your volition is what builds karma.

People ask me, again and again, the same question, "What's your mission?" When I tell them, "I have no mission; I'm just fooling around," they think I'm being frivolous. They don't understand this is the deepest statement that I can make about living in the world, because there is no particular volition – just doing what is needed, that's all. In this, there is no karma. Whatever you go through, there is no karma. Whatever you are doing is just happening, as it is needed. So karma is only in terms of your need to do something. When you have no need to do anything, and you simply do what is needed, there is no karmic attachment to it. It is neither good nor bad.

Seeker: Until I reach that state of awareness where I have a choice about what I think and do, am I not accumulating more karma unconsciously? How is this choice made, Sadhguru?

Sadhguru: Swami, you are just asking me, "Until I have become aware, until that point, where is my choice?" Is that the question?

Seeker: How is the choice made?

Sadhguru: Everybody is making choices; even their compulsions are their choices. Choices made in unawareness are compulsions. Let us say you get angry right now. It is your choice, actually, to be angry. Somewhere, you believe that's the way to handle the situation, but the choice is made in such unawareness that it is a compulsion; it's happening compulsively on a different level. So you're living by choice, but choices are made without awareness – unconscious choices. It so happened, once Shankaran Pillai walked up to a bar with an ostrich behind him. After he sat down, the bartender came over and asked for the order. Shankaran Pillai said, "I'll have a beer," and turned to the ostrich, "What will you have?" "I'll have a beer too," said the ostrich. The bartender poured the beer and said, "That'll be one hundred and fifty six rupees, fifty paisa." Shankaran Pillai reached into his pocket and pulled out the exact change. The next day, he and the ostrich came in again, and he asked for a beer. The ostrich said, "I'll have the same." Once again, he reached into his pocket and paid with the exact change. This became a routine, until late one evening, the two entered again. "The usual?" asked the bartender. "Well no, this time I'll have a large scotch," Shankaran Pillai said. "Same for me," said the ostrich. "That'll be two hundred and seventy nine rupees," said the bartender. Once again, the exact change came out of his pocket. The bartender could not hold back his curiosity any longer. "Excuse me, Sir. How do you manage to come up with the exact change from your pocket every time?" "Well," Shankaran Pillai said, "several years ago, I was cleaning the attic and I found an old lamp. When I rubbed it, a genie appeared and granted me two wishes. My first wish was that if I ever have to pay for anything, I just have to put my hand in my pocket and the right amount of money will always be there." "That's brilliant," said the bartender. "Most people would wish for a million dollars or something, but you will always be as rich as you want for as long as you live!" "That's right, whether for a liter of milk or a Rolls Royce, the exact amount of money is always there," said Shankaran Pillai. Then the bartender asked, "One other thing, sir. What's with the ostrich?" He replied, "My second wish was for a chick with long legs."

Now the whole thing is to shift into making conscious choices. Even a simple act - like when you wake up in the morning, the unconscious choice is that you don't want to wake up. When the sun rises, you want to pull the sheet up a little higher over your face. Do you see this? This is the unconscious choice. Your physical body wants to remain in bed for some more time, and some more time, and some more time. For so many reasons, it doesn't want to get up. There are so many aspects of life, so many limitations in your experience of life, that in many ways, unconsciously, you're not really looking forward to the day. Let's say tomorrow you have planned to go on a picnic. Do you see, before the sun rises you will wake up on that day? Consciously you have decided the previous day; you are excited. You are looking forward to tomorrow. It is a joyful experience. You will see, you will wake up before the sun comes up. Otherwise, unconsciously, you try to pull the sheet higher up over your face because this light is not something you are looking forward to, because with light comes today's stock prices; with light comes today's problems; with light comes the whole world into your life. So you're trying unconsciously to screen yourself from that; but now we make a conscious choice. Even after you wake up, the unconscious choice is that you want to drink a cup of coffee; the body feels comfortable with that. But now you can make a conscious choice, "No, I will have a cold water bath and do my *yoga asanas.*"

Why ascetic paths were set is simply because of this: you start doing things that are naturally not comfortable for you. Once you start doing such activity that is uncomfortable for you, you do it, but you don't like it. If you have to do something that you do not like, you can only do it consciously; there is no other way to do it. Yes? Things that you like, you can do compulsively; but things that you don't like, you can only do consciously. That is why the ascetic path. You start doing everything consciously. There is no other way to be. Now, slowly, you are practicing how to be conscious in various situations in your life. When you are hungry, the natural urge is to grab food and eat. Now you make a conscious choice, "I am very hungry, but I am not eating." To stay away from food, there is no other choice except being conscious about it, but to go and eat, you don't need consciousness; you can simply go and grab it when you are hungry. These simple things are set up in life so that you start doing things more consciously. For example, we have only two meals in our day-to-day life, or sometimes only one meal. By the time this meal comes, naturally you are very hungry, but you don't immediately eat. You wait for everybody to sit down. You wait for something to go onto everybody's plate, then you utter an invocation, and then you slowly eat. This needs consciousness. Just to give that break when you are hungry – just to wait for those three or four minutes – it takes an enormous amount of awareness for a person. To grab and eat would be very simple, but you will become more and more unconscious.

This consciousness is brought into your life. Early morning, you want to drink coffee, but you sit and do your *yoga kriyas.* You can't do it any other way but by being conscious about it. Drinking coffee, you can do in unawareness. I'm not saying you cannot do that in awareness, but you can easily do it in unawareness. Now, you can't do your kriyas in unawareness. You have to be aware. So like this, you're cultivating awareness into different aspects of life. Maybe initially your awareness is only for half an hour a day, but gradually you are bringing awareness into various aspects of life like this. The idea of cultivating awareness is so that it slowly seeps into your life. In one way that is a reality; you are cultivating awareness. One thing it does is, it enhances the quality of your life, but that's not everything. The main aspect is that if you can maintain awareness in various kinds of situations in life, only then will you even become capable of being aware at that moment when you have to part with the body. Otherwise, that never arises in your life.

Leaving the body is the moment of moving from one dimension to another dimension or, in a way, getting released from a certain level of bondage. That moment is also an opportunity for one's ultimate liberation. When life has run its full course, when one is free of *prarabdha*[1] and about to shed the body, the next allotment of prarabdha is yet to happen. So this situation or space gives an opportunity for one to completely dissolve if the necessary awareness is maintained. This brief period of life where the current prarabdha is over but the next allotment is yet to happen, your situation is virtually like that of a liberated being. If you can bring the necessary awareness, it becomes a possibility for ultimate release.

Seeker: Excuse me for interrupting, Sadhguru, but does this mean that whatever we are doing in this life is trying to rid ourselves of our prarabdha karma? We don't have other karmas to work out?

1 *prarabdha* : referring to prarabdha karma, the karma allotted for this life.

Sadhguru: There are certain other karmas which will not take effect now. If you do something today, it will always wait for the next phase of your life. It will not take effect in this life. Now the spiritual process is about dropping the whole stock, or the *sanchita karma.* It is not about dealing with the prarabdha. All the moral teachings and trying to live a good life is limited towards dispensing your prarabdha alone, which means invariably the sanchita will come out with the next allotment of prarabdha, which leads to rebirth.

Here, we are cultivating awareness in the most difficult situations – *be aware, be aware.* If somebody abuses you, to abuse him back, you don't need any awareness, but to remain quiet you need enormous awareness, isn't it? So just doing things that you don't like brings an enormous amount of awareness. Like I was telling you the other day in the ashram, first thing in the morning, we eat a neem ball. "Bitterness – why start life with bitterness? Why can't we eat a sweet?" There are health and other benefits to it, but that's different. One important aspect is, neem is not something that you can like. It's bitter, but you start the day with this, because you cannot eat the neem ball in unawareness. You have to eat it with great consciousness; there is no other way. You can eat a sweet in total unawareness. Like this, certain aspects are brought into your life so that it brings awareness into different dimensions of your experience – one is on the physical level, another at the level of the breath, another at the level of the energy, another at the level of your emotions.

If you use them – the physical body, the thought process, the emotions and the energy – you will see on all these four levels you'll begin to become more and more aware, which is definitely happening; there is no question about it. So this awareness is cultivated. As this happens, slowly awareness sets things apart. As you become more and more aware of the body, you will see that you and the body are separate. As you become more and more aware of the mind, you will see that you and the mind are separate. As you become more and more aware of emotion, you and that emotion are separate. As you become moreand more aware of your physical life energy, you and that physical life energy are also separate. So what is 'you' becomes a formless thing. It may not still be a living reality that you truly are formless. Formless also means boundless. Form means bound. It may not be an actual reality that you are formless, but slowly the form is becoming weaker; that's for sure. With the practice and with the devices that are given, depending upon how intensely and how diligently you are applying these devices in your life – using these devices – accordingly, to that extent you will see, your form is becoming weaker. Your form is just a falsehood of individuality that you have created. It's just a limitation. A form means a limitation, isn't it? A form is a limit; formless is limitless. So the spiritual process means you are always seeking the limitless. That means to somehow break the form; but you cannot seek the limitless because you don't know what it is. You know the limited, so you start chipping away at the limited. If you break away everything that is limited, the unlimited is bound to happen. Unlimited is not something that you create. Breaking off the limited is all that you can do. So that's the whole process.

Seeker: Sadhguru, is there a difference between having a desire to do something and actually acting on that desire?

Sadhguru: Does action spring from desire? I don't see how you can separate this. Desire itself is an action. The desire itself is a certain action. This also springs from your awareness. If desires are happening unconsciously, that means your action is happening unconsciously. Action need not necessarily mean physical action. There is mental action, there is emotional action and there is energy action. If all these are happening unconsciously, you tend to believe, "This is my nature." When people get angry, you ask them, "Why?" They say, "This is my nature," because it is so compulsive. That's why they are saying it, isn't it? For anything that is compulsive within you, you declare, "This is my nature." That means you got yourself deeply identified with that action. Once you are so deeply identified with that action, there is no question of you being aware, or of anything happening in awareness or consciousness. Desire is not different. Desire is also one kind of action. It is not that action is springing from the desire; the desire is the beginning of the action.

The word 'karma' literally means 'action', but the action is not what you do with your hands. The quality of your action is not in what you do. Right now, I pick up this stone. This is an action. It has no quality of its own, but in my mind, I have the intention of taking it and throwing it at you. I have still not thrown it, but already the karma is done. I did not even pick it up. I have a feeling that I want to take this and throw it in your face. The karma is already done. Now if I take it and throw it and accidentally it hits your face, then it is a different kind of karma, a karma of negligence, not a karma of anger or something else. Now the stone is here, I just want to take it and throw it in your face. I have not even thrown it yet, but I look at your face and I look at the stone and I want it to hit your face. That karma is already done.

Seeker: I'm in trouble, Sadhguru!

Sadhguru: Yes, Somu, you are very much in trouble, unless you work it out (laughs). Now let us say that I actually took this stone, I was just playing with it and it landed on your head and injured you, that karma is not so serious. It's the karma of negligence. That karma is different from the karma of wanting to hit you. It also revealed that your head is empty, but that is your karma (laughs).

Seeker: Master, what about the karma of wanting to hurt the person and actually hurting him? If I throw the stone in his face, is there any difference between that and wanting to throw the stone?

Sadhguru: Now once you perform the action, there is a consequence. Do you understand? The consequence is not a punishment; it is always a way of working out the karma. The consequence is a way life is trying to work out the karma that you are constantly creating. If you do only mental karma, there is no external consequence, so the suffering is always deeper.

Seeker: Does being angry with somebody in my life and being angry with you at times – I mean, I do get angry – is it any different, Sadhguru?

Sadhguru: Being angry with me is a very bad karma; get this straight! (Laughs).

Seeker: And why so?

Sadhguru: See, the question of being angry with somebody does not arise. You are not angry with anybody, you are just angry. Your anger has nothing to do with somebody else. It's about you. Whether you are angry at a rock, God, your Guru, or whatever – anger is simply anger. It has got nothing to do with anybody or anything. You need to understand this first: your anger has nothing to do with anybody except yourself, only yourself. Only because you believe your anger has something to do with somebody, it keeps happening over and over again. If you see that it is only about you and you alone, it would not have lasted this long.

So being angry and upset about something, whether I say it or somebody else says it, comes from a strong sense of like and dislike. This strong sense of like and dislike comes from a very deep identification with a certain way of thinking, a certain way of feeling, a certain way of life – which you think is the best way to live, which you think is the best way to think and feel. If somebody is not in line with that, you get angry at those things. As your likes and dislikes become stronger, as your identifications become stronger with one thing or another, all that you are doing is excluding existence. If I say, "I like this very much," in a big way I am excluding the rest of existence at that moment. So the stronger it becomes, the deeper the exclusion becomes. The very process of liberation is to include, not to exclude. In exclusion, you become trapped. In inclusion, you become liberated.

When everything – not just everything – when the whole existence is included in you, only then you are liberated. In exclusion, you become separate. There are methods of exclusion that lead to ultimate inclusion; that is different. That is the *nethi, nethi, nethi* process that we are doing – *I am not this, I am not this* – excluding yourself from everything. Probably the word exclusion, in that sense, would be mistaken and misunderstood. It is more about dis-identifying yourself, starting with your clothes, body, house, family, every cell of your body, your ideas, thoughts, education, culture, everything, and saying, "I am not this, I am not this, I am not this." Once you are dis-identified with everything that is not you, you become all inclusive once again. So anger is just a small indicator of where you are going. Anger itself is not the karma; the exclusion is the big karma. It is because of the exclusion that the anger overflows, because you have not included somebody or something as part of yourself. Anger is just an indicator. Anger is not the karma. Exclusion is a huge karma.

Seeker: This is frightening, Sadhguru! Even my very thought can create karma? Living itself becomes difficult, because the mind is such that it can create many, many thoughts – many, many unnecessary emotions within me.

Sadhguru: Yes? It need not be scary, because every moment you have the option. Right now, if you look at this person and the very way she is sitting, one part of your mind says, "She is not okay. I don't like her." You can give an enormous amount of importance to that thought or you can just not give any importance to it. That choice you always have. The thought itself, you may not have a choice about because it is coming from a certain culture you were brought up in; but giving importance to that thought or not, getting identified with that thought or not, that choice is always in your hands, every moment. If you don't exercise that choice, then yes, every thought can become a huge karma, every thought can become a trap, every thought can become a process of self-destruction.

Seeker: Do Enlightened beings create karma? For instance, when Jesus got angry, did he create karma, Sadhguru?

Sadhguru: When a man like Jesus goes about – you know this one particular scene where he entered the synagogue, the temple, and threw out all the people who were doing business there? He literally, physically, threw them out. He went in and threw out so many people. His fury was such that nobody could stop him. He was just furious, so it was *krodha*, isn't it? It was anger; he knew that he could play with anger for a while and the next moment he could dissolve the whole thing. He involved himself in intense activity outside and then he said, "Now it is time for me to go into the mountains." He would go into the mountains, stay there, dissolve everything and then come back. Intense activity needs that break, but you know for that physical action what consequence it brought him. Otherwise, if he did not attend to it, he would have been in trouble. When the time comes, he would be in trouble. Nobody is spared, do you understand? Nobody is spared. The law is law. When you go by the law, that is the way – it is there. When you don't go by the law, you pay the price. If you understand the law, this moment you can open the door and get away. If you don't understand the law, even if you roam for millions of lifetimes, no way.

Once an intellectual understanding comes, the next thing is to step into the experiential aspect. Intellectual understanding is not a must. One can step into the experiential and an understanding flowers from within. That's also true. Intellectual understanding is needed simply because people don't have an urge towards anything that they don't understand. They're not willing to go. They are not willing to take a step, so we tell them, "It is like this. It is like that. If you do this, ultimately that will come." It has to be offered, otherwise, if it's just trust and love, intellectual understanding is not needed. You simply go for your own dissolution. If it has to be given to somebody, yes, you need understanding.

Seeker: Sadhguru, in the cycle of rebirth, does the child select the parents?

Sadhguru: Selection, yes. Selection does not mean the child chooses consciously. That's not the point. It is just like this, if we throw all of you into this hall, suddenly, the first day when you enter, everybody settles down in his own place, isn't it? There is a reason for this. That reason is your karma. Your karma may be back pain, then you will settle down near the wall. Your karma may be to always hide and look. You want to be there in the class, but you don't want to be pointed out. So you will find a big person and sit behind him. It may be unconscious, but that's how you do it. Your karma may be that you always want to be in the front row, so you just come and sit there. It does not matter where you sit, but your karma makes you settle down in some place.

Similarly, your karma makes you settle down in some particular womb, with those kinds of tendencies and with those kinds of attributes. Somewhere, there are millions of beings waiting for this. One half is there, it has to find the other half. It just finds a suitable plug and somehow gets notched up. It's not that this person is named for that person. This is not the way it works. It's just like the way many things settle down in certain ways, beings also settle down according to their attributes and tendencies. That's all it is.

Seeker: Sadhguru, is there such a thing as destiny?

Sadhguru: Once it happened that the pope went to the United States, and he had many engagements. He landed up in Cincinnati, Ohio. A chauffeur-driven stretch limo – you know the stretch limo? In the U.S., they stretch a limousine to its limits. The chauffeur was driving. The pope got a little excited because he had never driven a car like this. He told the chauffeur, "I would like to drive." How could the chauffeur say no to the pope? He said, "Okay." So the pope took the wheel and the chauffeur took the back seat. The pope started enjoying the car and pressing the gas more, and more, and more. He was hitting ninety or one hundred miles per hour. He did not realize the speed he was going at, and the Ohio police are terrible. If you go two miles over the speed limit they will catch you. He was zooming and he had the flashing light behind him. So he pulled to the side. The cop got out, and carefully, with his hand on his gun, slowly approached the car. It was the pope himself driving! He looked in the back seat and somebody was sitting there. Then he said, "Wait." He went back to his car, took the radio out and called the police chief. He said to the chief, "I've got a huge fish." "Oh come on. Who is it? Is it Ted Kennedy in trouble again?" "No, somebody much bigger than that." "Is it Chelsea Clinton, driving drunk?" "Oh no, somebody much, much bigger." "Is it the President himself?" "No, somebody far bigger than that!" "Come on, who else could be bigger than the President of the United States? What have you got on your hands?" He said, "I don't know who it is but he's got the pope as his chauffeur!"

So you don't know who is driving your car. Destiny is something that you have been creating unconsciously. You can also create it consciously. You can rewrite your destiny. What we have been trying to do with you in the last few days is just that. If you can touch that core in you, if you can for one moment see, "Everything is my responsibility," and shift your whole focus to yourself, you can rewrite your own destiny. All the time your focus is scattered, because what you consider as 'myself' is your house, your car, your wife, your child, your pet, your education, your position, your power and your other nonsense. If I strip you of all these things, you will feel like a nobody; yes or no? So what you call 'myself' is spread around you right now.

When I say '*you*', it is you, not this carpet, not this wall, not your child, not something else. When I say 'you', it's just you. If it shifts to this, you can rewrite your destiny whichever way you want. Right now, what is 'you' is spread out; you are a scattered being. You're not an established being; you are a scattered being. You still have to gather all this mess, put it inside. Then it becomes you. You still have not become *you*; you are a crowd, isn't it? The crowd's destiny is always predestined. Once you become an individual – individual means, it comes from 'indivisible'– it cannot be divided anymore; it is *this*. It cannot be here and there. Once you become a true individual, your destiny is yours. I want you to understand this. Why in the spiritual process people who are in a hurry for spiritual growth are not getting into marriage, children and relationships, is because the moment you have a wife or a husband, you cannot help it, 'me' gets identified with 'this one'. Otherwise, they will not let you live, isn't it? Once you have children, you get identified with them. Now, your 'me' includes them also. Once you get identified with them, one by one, you get identified with too many things. Now you get scattered.

Once, it happened that Indra, the king of all gods, decided to come to earth for pleasure. You know, the gods come to earth for pleasure, but people want to go to heaven. He landed on planet Earth, then had to choose some form, some body. So he chose the body of a pig, the form of a pig, because generally, in terms of physical pleasure, the pig is best. He became a pig, found himself a beautiful female pig, and they started living. Then dozens of piglets came. He got deeply involved with them. He got attached to his wife and children. Many months passed. All the gods in heaven waited and waited. They thought it was a short pleasure trip, but he did not come back. Then they came down to see what was happening and saw this whole pig business going on. They tried telling him, "You are Indra! What are you doing here as a pig? Come with us." He said, "Nothing doing," so deeply involved and attached he was to everything around him. Then they had a meeting in heaven. "What to do, how to get our king back?" Then somebody said, "He is so deeply attached to his children. Let us kill one of his children. He will realize and come back." They came and killed one piglet, one of those beautiful piglets. When one goes, you cling harder to the remaining ones. That's the way it is happening. Suppose you have five children and you suddenly lose one, you will cling harder to the remaining four. If you lose one more, you cling to the remaining three even harder, isn't it? They killed one, then they killed the next one, and the next one, and he clung to the remaining ones harder and harder. Like this, they killed all his children. Then he and his wife got busy producing more children. Then they thought, "Oh! His real attachment is to his wife. If we kill her then he will come back." So they killed the wife. With his beautiful wife dead, he was in great distress. Then after a few days, his pig friends and relatives suggested that he take another wife. They always do, isn't it? Again the whole pig business started.

The gods were at a loss. Then Narada, the celestial sage, came and said, "Why did you go about killing all these innocent beings? His attachment is to his body. If you cut his body, he will come." They went and cut his body into two halves. He came out, and asked, "What the hell am I doing here?" Then he went back to heaven.

That is how deep the bondage with the body is. It is the source of all attachments. You don't have to go on searching for non-attachment somewhere else. You don't have to go about distancing this and that in your life, but once you get scattered, your destiny becomes predestined. Whichever way your karma is, it just goes that way. If you become an individual, the significance of *sanyasa or bhramhacharya* [1] is just this: shifting your whole focus to you. When I say 'you', it is just you, not even your body or your mind. If you are unable to be like that, you just choose one more identity. When you say 'you', make it you and your Guru. You attach yourself to the Guru without any hesitation, because you have no entanglements from the other side. You can get as entangled as you want with him; he is not going to get entangled. The moment you are ripe, you can drop it. With other relationships, it is never so. If you get entangled, even if you want to become free, the other will not let you go. Either you can rewrite your own destiny or, if such awareness does not come, we can very easily rewrite destiny if you can just give yourself to me. So don't worry about the predestined thing. You just create a longing to grow, to dissolve, to know. What has to happen will happen. Why are you worried about all those things?

Seeker: Master, you say that if I have to become an individual I have to be focused on myself?

Sadhguru: Once you become an individual, your destiny becomes yours. If your destiny is in your hands, will you choose bondage or freedom? What would you choose? Freedom, because the very longing of life, the deepest longing of every life is to become free, to become free from the very process that we refer to as life or death, to become free from that itself. So once your destiny is happening in awareness, the next step will just happen by itself, because life within you has the intelligence to choose freedom, not bondage. Only because your destiny is being created in unawareness, you go about weaving bondage around yourself.

1 *bhramhacharya* : dedicated to the path of the Divine.

Seeker: According to the karma that we have when we die, can this human body become a snake or even a tiny amoeba? Our evolution, can it go down as well as up, Sadhguru?

Sadhguru: You cannot say that it is going down, because to fulfill certain aspects of life, sometimes one who has been a human may take on an animal form. Let us say right now, for example, you have certain desires which are not fulfilled. Your desire was to collect a billion rupees. You neither have the brains to earn it nor the courage or capability to go and rob a bank and get your billion. You're not made like that. So what is your desire? It is to collect. If you get ten rupees, you will save five. You will starve yourself. You will go through all kinds of difficulty. Save, save, save and save. You want to collect one billion rupees. So with this process of collecting, most probably, by the time you die, your target will not be reached. Let's say you have saved only half a billion. Now there is a big urge within you to collect the remaining amount, but you die before that with the same lust of wanting to collect. Your karma does not know what you want to collect, whether it's money or stones. What nonsense it wants to collect, it doesn't matter. It only knows it has to collect. It does not have discriminatory power. It's almost like your genes. It is a subtler gene, not a physical gene. It only knows that you like to collect. So the next time, this gene may decide to collect. Which will be the right form for you to collect? Maybe you will become an ant, or maybe you will become a bee. We don't know.

These are just examples that I am using. If a particular quality is very dominant in you, to fulfill that quality, what kind of body, what kind of physical situation would be best for you, it will seek that. It need not necessarily be an animal form. It may choose *that* kind of human form in that kind of a situation and in *that* kind of surroundings where it can be fulfilled. It could be in any way.

Seeker: Sadhguru, is spirituality the exclusive domain of the human life form or is it open to other life forms?

Sadhguru: Do other forms of life, the other creatures on this planet, know something spiritual or could we regress to that state again? It's not a question of regression or progression; it is just that life is always finding its way by its tendencies. Traditionally, we call them as your *vasanas*. Do you know what vasanas are? Vasana literally means 'smell'. Whichever way the smell is, that is the kind of thing that it attracts.

Whatever kind of stuff you hold, that is the kind of smell you emanate. Whatever kind of smell you emanate, that's the kind of thing you will attract to yourself. Suppose that tree is in full bloom. With flower and fragrance, it attracts bees. If there is some filth outside, it attracts flies. According to the vasana, that is what comes to it, isn't it? So according to your vasana, what kind of fragrance you are leaving, accordingly, those kinds of things come to you. This is not a prize; this is not a punishment; this is not progression; this is not regression. This is just nature, functioning according to qualities. It is not in terms of punishment and prize, just as per its qualities.

Let us say, for example, you are obsessed with food. I'm not saying that you are; I am just giving an example. Let us say you are too obsessed with food, and even at the moment of death you are thinking about food. Now your vasana was that. Somehow, this eating, you could not eat to a point of satisfying yourself. Somewhere it is still longing to eat. This karma in you is very strong. Now it may choose, let us say, the body of a pig because it can go on eating throughout the day. That kind of body can eat throughout the day. You taking on a pig's body is not a punishment; it is just that nature is trying to work out a certain quality. What could not be worked out in a human body is finding a suitable body to work out that kind of tendency in you. This is not a punishment, this is not regression, this is not God trying to fix you and make you a pig. That's not the point. It is just that a certain quality is trying to find its liberation. Food was so important, so it is picking up that kind of body with which food can be handled in that way. Let us not give you more examples (laughs); one is enough. So there is such a possibility, but it is rare because nature has its own buffer for you.

If you live a complete life - when I say 'complete' – there is something called prarabdha, or allotted karma. Your existence here is ruled by your karmic structure. If you have no karma, you cannot be here for a moment. I don't know if you have noticed such things. Let us say an old person, somebody who is of a certain age, cannot sleep properly or sleeps for just half an hour. Suddenly, once he crosses a certain age, you find he sleeps extremely deep. If he sleeps, he sleeps like a log. Such deep sleep comes to him because his prarabdha is getting over. Once the prarabdha is exhausted, it is not that all his karma is over, but the allotted karma, one installment, is drawing to an end. Suddenly, there is a new sense of freedom in him, a new sense of peace in him. If this comes, unless something else is created, he's coming to the end of his life. It is very clear. Oh! I should not be telling you all these things. Then if anybody sleeps deeply, you will think, "Oh! He is going to die tomorrow." So, Radhika, your mother-in-law is old and sleeps deeply; don't go looking at her with glee (laughs). Once the prarabdha is over, a certain state of balance, a certain state of equanimity comes to him. The turmoil has come down in that person, because the inner quota of karma is over. One installment is over. So the chance of somebody falling back into another kind of body other than that of a human being, or a less evolved body, is quite remote, but it can happen. It will not happen to you, those of you who are with me, because of certain things. It will not happen; I assure you that.

As for the other creatures, do they have any spiritual possibility? For the other creatures, nature is giving them a free spiritual ride. They just keep evolving by themselves. They need not know anything; it's a free ride. But certain creatures are aware. One day, Shankaran Pillai's front gate sported a sign saying: "TALKING DOG FOR SALE." A man rings the bell, and Shankaran Pillai tells him, "The dog is in the backyard." The man goes into the backyard and sees a mutt sitting there. "You talk?" he asks. "Yup," the mutt replies. "So what's your story?" The mutt looks up and says, "Well, I discovered this gift pretty young and I wanted to help the government, so I told the R.A.W. Secret Service about my gift, and in no time, they had me jetting from country to country, sitting in rooms with spies and world leaders, because no one figured a dog would be eavesdropping. I was one of the most valuable spies for eight years. This jet setting really tired me out, and I knew I was not getting any younger, and I wanted to settle down. So I signed up for a job at the airport to do some undercover security work. Mostly wandering near suspicious characters and listening in. I uncovered some incredible dealings there and was awarded a bunch of medals." The mutt sighs heavily and then says, "I had a wife, a mess of puppies, and now, I'm just retired." The man is amazed. He goes back in and asks Shankaran Pillai what he wants for the dog. He says, "Two hundred rupees." The man says, "I will buy him! Just tell me one thing, this dog is amazing, why on earth are you selling him for two hundred rupees?" Shankaran Pillai replies, "He's such a liar!"

Now if a very powerful situation is created, certain creatures become aware of something more than their physical body. The three animals that are very capable of doing this are a cow, a snake and a crow.

You know they told you, if your father dies or your grandfather dies you must feed the cow, the snake or the crow. This is because these are three creatures that are capable of a little awareness if a powerful situation is created, not otherwise.

Seeker: Sadhguru, then how could Ramana Maharshi have Enlightened animals like a cow and a crow? How could he release them from their karma?

Sadhguru: What, Kumar, do you think it would have been easier if you had come as a cow or a crow? Do you see the difficulty here of making you grow? Where is the question of enlightening an animal? You are asking how Ramana Maharshi could have Enlightened or created an opportunity for dissolution, or *mukthi,* to an animal. See, nobody can ever enlighten an animal unless the animal has come as a reincarnation of a human being. It is only possible when these beings have already seen the human form. For some reason, now they have come with the animal form. Only then such a thing is possible, by taking him back and regressing him to his human nature within that animal body and helping him out of that situation. But you can never make an animal realize, because the basic quality itself is absent; that consciousness is absent in an animal. What is there in a human being is not there in the animal. Only by regressing them into that human quality can it be done. He can be released from there, not from here, because that is the only way it can be; it cannot be any other way.

Right now, let us say you are in some other form, not in human form. So in this form, in this level of consciousness, there is no way you can attain to anything spiritual. You cannot be released from this level; but if there was a previous birth which was that of a human, then yes, I regress you back to that life and from there, I release you. Experientially, I take you back to your human life while you are still physically in the animal form. Only then it is possible, not otherwise. Let us say certain minor karmas become major in your life, like food, for example. Maybe you are a yogi in this life and you did so many things, but food became a big problem within you; you denied yourself food, food, food all the time. So somewhere, the clinging to food was not gone. Now this yogi, if he comes once again in a human form, all the hassles of a human being are there – growing up as a human being, there are so many things that he can get caught up with. Now, only food is a barrier for him. Everything else, he has mostly cleared. So he does not want to – it may not be a conscious choice – that being does not want to come in the human form and get entangled with all the other processes of growing up. So now he comes like, let us say a pig, because only food has to be satisfied. Gathering of karma for animals is minimal, that is why naturally it progresses. The evolutionary process happens naturally for an animal because he does not gather any karma as such. It is only dissolution; it simply progresses; it advances by itself into higher and higher life forms.

Seeker: So Sadhguru, we are evolving, but we may go back and forth from human form to animal form?

Sadhguru: You are going step by step, sometimes jumping, sometimes leaping, sometimes falling back. It's the 'Snake and Ladder' game that is on. As long as the snakes are there, you climb one ladder and another snake will swallow you and bring you back to square one. You climb up for a few days and again go back down. It just goes on. That's how those boards are made, isn't it? You hit a ladder, you hit the snake, you hit a ladder, you hit the snake, and it just goes on. So here, we give you a device with which you can strip off all the snakes. If you just take the responsibility, there are no more snakes on your board. You cannot build any more karma; it is over. The moment you focus the whole attention on yourself, you will see you are the source of everything that is happening here. The moment this awareness comes into you, you cannot build any more karma; it's finished. Now only what is stored up, you have to handle. It's very simple. Otherwise you will go on emptying from one side and filling from the other side. There is no end to it.

Life has been going on like this. We don't know for how long. Many, many, many lifetimes it will continue to go on like this, unless your whole energy gets centered on yourself. Once the whole focus is on yourself, it not only burns up the past but also blocks the slide; you cannot slide any more. Now there is a new strength, there is a new freedom. Isn't it so? There is a new sense of well-being. Just in a moment, all these things happen, because the slide is stopped. By just being here, you have taken a step ahead. Please look at your own life and see, from the earliest age that you remember, until some time ago, let us say a year ago, just see the heaviness that you have gathered around yourself. Just see the life-negative substances that are slowly gathering around every human being. The slide is on, isn't it? Maybe some are sliding very fast, some are sliding a little slowly, but mostly, almost everyone is sliding, in terms of life. In terms of society, in terms of money and so many other things you may be going up, but in terms of life, from your childhood until now, definitely there is a slide. It is a constant slide. By the time most people are fifty or sixty, the burden on their head is such that it shows. It literally shows, on most of them. Some people are polished enough to hide it, but it shows on most of them.

Once some awareness seeps into you, working out the past, working your way through the past becomes simple. Going to the river with a bucket to get water is one thing. Going to the river with a sieve and trying to bring water to the ashram is something else. This is what you are doing with your life. Your mind is full of holes. Your life is full of holes. With that you want to catch something. What can you catch? You put whatever grains through the sieves only to catch impurities, isn't it? That is what you catch, nothing worthwhile in life. Whether you have one hole or one hundred holes, it makes no difference. Until you plug that, you won't bring water. You'll only come empty handed.

So in every life that you come here, whether you have one hole or one hundred holes, every time people come, they go back empty-handed. Nothing attained, nothing gained, you are coming and going, birth and death. *Punarapi Jananam, Punarapi Maranam.* Only when you plug those holes you don't have to go to the river. The river comes to you; that is how it is. You don't have to go in search of God anymore. The moment your receptivity is right, God *is.* There is no need to search for God. There is no need to search for Truth. The moment your receptivity is right, Truth is. It is more essential than you and me. It is more essential than existence itself. It's not something that you search for; it is just that you are prepared to receive; that's all. It's not a piece of stone or a diamond or something to find. It's something that is everywhere, something that is always. So there is no question of finding it. It's just that you have to create the right kind of receptivity, and it is there. Plug all your holes and it is there. Are you plugging the holes? First of all, stop puncturing yourself; that's most important. If you stop punching holes into yourself, the holes that are already there are easy to close. If you stop creating new negativities, new karmas, the old holes are easy to handle. Your only problem is creating newer and newer karmas. That's the whole problem, do you understand? If that is stopped, you will see that the sense of buoyancy increases every day. Day by day, you will see that things are going up, not down any more. It cannot go down any more, because every moment, every moment here, everywhere, within you, without you – God *is;* His Grace *is.* It is just that you don't have the right receptacle to receive Him, that's all. Watch yourself and do not make new holes. That is the most important aspect of sadhana.

Seeker: Master, you said that in the Indian tradition, the cow and the snake are revered. Does it mean to say there is no compassion for other animals?

Sadhguru: No, no. Compassion should be there for the others, too. All animals are worshipped wholesale here (laughs). See, if you have to eat some animal for food, if you have to kill some animal and eat it, even towards that you should have compassion; there is no doubt about it. Even for a rudimentary man, the snake and cow have been a taboo only because these are the compulsory steps in the process of evolution of the soul. It should not matter; if you have the same compassion for everybody it does not matter, but if you are a rudimentary man who kills, you spare at least these two animals, because they are potential human beings. It's like killing a man; it is so close. If you kill a chicken or something else, the police don't arrest you. Only if you kill a human being it is a murder and they arrest you, isn't it? Why? You should have the same compassion for all life forms – it's the same loss for all life forms, isn't it?

In the Indian tradition, the laws were fixed like this: if you kill a human being it's murder; if you kill a cow it's murder; if you kill a snake, it's also murder. That was how it was fixed, but they could not fix a law to say that anything you kill is murder, because the need to kill was there, maybe for man's survival, for his food. Now the cow is one animal that has human emotions. A cow will shed tears when you have suffering in you. People have very deep relationships with cows in India, and snakes are very sensitive to certain types of energies. Wherever there are meditative situations, or rituals are performed, snakes are drawn there.

Seeker: Snakes, or the symbolism of snakes, is predominant in this culture. They are worshipped here and seem to have a significant meaning in yoga also. How come they are seen as evil in the West, especially in Christianity? Can you explain this, Sadhguru?

Sadhguru: Everybody is after my snakes; even you started now! (Laughs). Snakes, I think many times we have spoken why snakes, and what is the significance of a snake. Fundamentally, one aspect of this is that it is the symbolism for the *Kundalini*[1] because of its nature, and its similarity with that of a snake in terms of movement and stillness. Another aspect is that the snake is at a very significant step in the evolutionary process of the being. As the monkey is at a very significant step in the evolutionary process of the body, the snake is at a very significant step in the evolutionary process of the being. It is based on this that in this culture, you are not supposed to kill a snake. If you happen to find a dead snake or if you happen to kill one, then you must give it a proper funeral and a burial in India. Are you aware that a snake always gets a proper burial, like a human burial, because in terms of its being, it is very close to a human being. So killing a snake amounts to murder. That is one aspect. There are so many things; and you know, for me, snakes have always been around me. People are complaining about my garden which is full of snakes, particularly about one of my close friends who is very big, and people are terrified of him. He is very beautiful. Nobody is seeing how beautiful he is. Everybody is concerned about how big he is! (Laughs).

About the Western culture having a very negative attitude towards snakes, it is fundamentally because of a gross misinterpretation of certain aspects of the Christian philosophy. One basic aspect about the snake being a negative factor, or it being presented as a Devil's agent is because the snake came and tempted Eve to eat the apple. Now two idiots were on this planet: Adam and Eve, and they did not even know what it means. See, a man or a woman going beyond their dualities of being a man and a woman consciously, by choice, and transcending their sexual identification is a wonderful thing; but not even being aware of it is a stupid thing. They were not Enlightened and free, they were ignorant, so ignorant that they didn't know what that even means. There was no possibility of life. The snake entered the scene and tempted Eve because he found Eve to be the easier nut (laughs), and induced life on this planet.

If you believe life on this planet is God's creation, and if the snake has been the agent to induce life on this planet, you tell me whether the snake is the Divine's agent or the Devil's agent (laughs). It must be the Divine's agent, isn't it? Whatever induces life on this planet must be a Divine agent. Only somebody who is dead against the very process of life, who is stupid enough not to even accept the fundamental processes of life – the basic biology of life – such a person will think of the snake, which induced the process of life on this planet, as the Devil's agent. Anybody who is for life will definitely see the snake as a Divine agent.

---

1 *Kundalini* : cosmic energy which is depicted as a snake coiled at the base of the spine.

Here, in this culture, we see him as a Divine agent and Shiva[1] Himself carried snakes, not at his feet, but above his head, because in many ways, the snake is seen as a significant step towards life, human life, human possibilities. Because of that, in this culture, whichever temple you go to, there are snakes. I don't think there is any temple without a snake. Somewhere, there will be a little snake in almost every temple. At least all the ancient temples have snakes. Many temples that are built these days are just like your shopping complexes, probably for the same purpose. They may not have snakes, but any ancient temple you will see there is a place for a snake, because it's a very important step in the evolutionary process of the being, and in many ways, it is the inducer of life. For us, in Isha, it is very significant for so many reasons; some of them you know, some of them you are yet to know because if I speak too much about snakes, people will get paranoid. For me, they need to be constantly around me. I am very comfortable with them.

It is painful ignorance to see the snake as an agent of the Devil. If you believe God is almighty and if He did create the Devil, if He is the Creator of everything, if He did create the Devil, then He must have a useful role for the Devil also! Otherwise, we would have done without the Devil. If you are a believer in God, and you believe that everything is God's creation, and if God had to create a Devil, then you must be mature enough to understand and accept that the Devil also has a rightful place in the process of creation and his agent also has a rightful place. They must have some purpose to serve, isn't it? It is a rudimentary mind which divides life into good and bad. Anybody who knows life will not divide life as good and bad. We still choose, we make choices, but choices are coming in terms of what leads you towards freedom and what leads you towards bondage, not because something is good or bad. We have not chosen to be in a certain way because we think another way is bad. We decided to meditate, not to drink alcohol today, not because we think alcohol is bad; we meditate because we see meditation as leading us towards freedom. Alcohol was leading us towards bondage, so we chose freedom; that's all. Any conscious human being naturally will choose freedom. It's not because we have a morality, "This is 'bad' and this is 'good'," that we have chosen this. We have chosen this consciously. It is rudimentary minds which always want to divide everything into good and bad. Once there is 'good' and 'bad',

1 Shiva : lit. that which is not. The Great Lord. The destroyer in the trinity.

there is going to be a fight, and what is 'good' and 'bad' is everybody's cake. Everybody can decide what is 'good' and 'bad' for themselves.

See, right from day one, the snakes have distracted the Adams and Eves. Half the world believes that the snake is the agent of the Devil because, you know, it tempted Eve to eat the apple. Now this eating the apple was not an evil thing. If God did not want life to happen, he would not have done that. It is only eating this apple which induced life on this planet. It is the root of life. If life is God's creation, definitely the snake was a Divine agent. Only people who are against life will say it was the Devil's agent. Anybody who is for life will naturally see that the snake was the main inducer of life. So anything that induces life must be a Divine agent, not the Devil's agent.

Seeker: Is nature always working within us, Sadhguru, so that we unconsciously evolve?

Sadhguru: Charles Darwin told you that you were all monkeys, your tail fell off and you became human. When you were a monkey, you did not desire to become human. Nature just pushed you on with your evolution. Once you are in this human form, you can only evolve consciously. Unconscious evolution is over for you. The unconscious evolution is the physical evolution of the world, but once you come in the human form, the evolutionary process is in your hands now.

Seeker: Darwin's theory says man has evolved from monkeys. Given the human population, by now, monkeys should have gone away!

Sadhguru: No, Doug, too many monkeys are sitting here as humans with very minor modifications (laughs). That is what I am saying. All the process, all the steps in Darwin's theory are not essential for the being to evolve, but these two forms, the cow and the snake, are significant steps in the evolution of the being. Darwin only talked about the evolutionary process in the physical sense. He did not say every creature had to go through the form of reptile, bird, mammal and all that. He was only talking about the body, how it is evolving, how the whole of nature is evolving on this planet; that was all. Darwin was only talking about how the whole nature on this planet was evolving; how both the plant and the animal life are evolving. How, somewhere before they started, there was no plant and animal. It was a common life form.

and somewhere they deviated. Plants became what they are and animals became what they are. He was only talking about the physical evolution of the planet as such.

Seeker: So Master, since there are more and more people all the time, doesn't that mean that other life forms are evolving into human form? If so, why aren't there fewer of the other forms? How does that fit into the evolutionary process?

Sadhguru: That is simply because you are thinking in terms of quantities. Suppose one million life forms started. Now one million people are here; that means all the life forms should have been extinct. That is the logic, isn't it? That's not the way it is. It's not in terms of numbers. Suppose I create a billion bubbles and all the air is contained in them, where is there more air for other bubbles to come? That's the question, isn't it? Life does not happen that way; when we talk about the unbounded, there is no such arithmetic. Darwin never explored that sphere of life. He was not looking at how life came to be. He was only seeing how life evolved; he was only describing evolution that had been recorded on this planet, in fossils and this and that. He studied, he described, and he made a theory that said this is how life has evolved, how the physical form, the present sophisticated body has come out of that crude form that was created earlier, how it has evolved itself to this point of evolution. Darwin was only talking about that. He never talked about life as such. He was only talking about the natural evolution of physical life on this planet. Evolution and karmic laws are not against each other; they go with each other. If that is true with the body, if Darwin's theory is true with the body's evolution, a similar evolutionary process must be there for the being, for the inner nature also, isn't it? Maybe it does not happen in the same way as the body evolves, but a similar evolution should be there. Moving from the gross to the subtle is there.

Seeker: Dear Sadhguru, many times you have told us that we are functioning out of our intellect. If this is so, then how can we use this state to become more open and free?

Sadhguru: See, when you talk about openness, being absolutely open means that who you are should not be. The limited identity should completely go away. Only then, you are truly and absolutely open. Right now, if you look at it from the limited means that you have, it is an impossible thing. People believing that, "I am absolutely open," is again illusory. As I have always insisted, never think of liberation; never think of freedom; never think of openness. Always think in terms of that which binds you. Your business is with that which binds you. Right now, your hands and legs are tied up. You thinking about freedom is of no use. You just see how to handle the ropes which bind you; your business is with them. This may look uninteresting for the romantic people because they want to visualize how it is in heaven, how free they will be, how they will fly through the skies. It's not romantic. It is realistic and it is workable. Very easily, one can work themselves out of the bondages that they have fallen into. The same goes for openness and being closed. What is it that has closed you up? Before we look at how to become open, what is it that closes you up?

Seeker: Emotions.

Sadhguru: Not just emotions. There are four dimensions which could have closed you for so many reasons. Your mind could be closed because of the influences that it is subject to. Once the mind is closed, the emotions will also be within the closed circle of what the thoughts are – for the way you think is the way you feel. Your emotions are always guided by your thoughts. They may not be conscious for most people, but it is so. Another thing is, your physical body itself may be closed, and your energies may be closed. If you take two people who don't know anything about spiritual processes into a certain atmosphere, or let us say into a certain initiation, you will see that one person responds with absolute openness. Another person, even though he is mentally wanting to – even if he is praying for that to happen to him – it does not happen to him because he is closed either on the physical body level or on the energy level, of which he has no awareness.

This becoming closed has happened because of the structures that we have built over a period of time These structures are what we are calling karmas In India, we call them *vasanas or samskaras*. It means that you built limited structures around yourself These structures were essential for your survival Because your whole focus was on survival, you strengthened these structures too much. After some time, the same structure which was protecting you is now restricting you You don't want it anymore, but then you don't know how to get rid of it, because that is how your whole orientation of life has been For example, as we are heading to Badrinath[1] in this bus, Suman has pulled the whole shutter down to protect herself from the sun and dust. After some time, when there is a change in the weather, she wants to open it but she is unable to do it; maybe the bolts are stuck. She cannot open it and now it becomes a desperation

This is the situation of many human beings in the world – almost everybody – because of their security concerns, because of simply responding to their own basic sense of survival in the world. Their body, their mind, their emotions and their energy have created certain cocoons. These cocoons did, in limited atmospheres, help them to protect themselves, but when your longing reaches for other dimensions, the same things which were protecting you are a huge restriction. It is like, when you were a small kid, your parents protected you. It was nice; you enjoyed the protection. You enjoyed the comfort of being hugged and kept on their lap, but once you became a little bigger, you wanted to get off their lap and run. If they don't allow you and hold you on their lap, you will start struggling and hating that which holds you down. Karma is just like this. This is not a question of right or wrong. This was created with a certain understanding of well-being, which is limited. When that is fulfilled and naturally your being longs for the next thing, it becomes a restriction.

Whatever spiritual processes we start – on all levels of body, mind, emotion, and energy – slowly all these dimensions are handled, but one thing which is easily at hand for you is the mind and emotions. Making yourself mentally open is very fundamental and very crucial, because this is something that is immediately in your hands. Your energy is not in your hands; you don't know how to open it. Even your physical body, you don't know how to keep it open, but your mind is something that you can consciously open.

---

1 Badrinath : a place of pilgrimage in the Himalayas.

That's why a lot of talk is going on about opening the mind, not because it's the most important, but because right now that is most available for people. For opening other dimensions, anyway sadhana is there. You don't have to understand how. You just do the sadhana and it opens up, but if the energy opens up – on the level of your energy, if your karmic structure opens up and becomes more receptive, then you don't have to bother about your mind, emotions or anything, because suddenly everything changes. If you go through the mind, emotion or body, it is a more accessible way, but a very long way. If you open up the energy, it is not so accessible, but if it is opened with a certain external influence, then it's a very quick way. You don't have to understand anything. What is happening is beautiful.

Seeker: Master, if you know that your focus in life is wrong, you know you have blocks inside of you, you don't know where those blocks are, but they are keeping you from seeing goodness in life and in people – what can you focus on to help remove those blocks?

Sadhguru: You mean blocks that you are conscious of?

Seeker: I don't know, Sadhguru. I just know there are blocks there – energy, physical, mental – I don't know…

Sadhguru: Fundamentally, the very karmic walls are always like this. They are like sheets of glass. If they were like walls of brick, you could see them and you could break them, but they're sheets of glass. Everything is open, but when you try to reach out you are locked in; that's how it is. Now, what can I do to break that? Why sadhana is always set up – apart from any teaching – is just because of this: any teaching, after a certain period of time, becomes a block by itself, in a certain sense. You will twist it to your convenience. You can twist all teachings in the world. Initially, a teaching has an impact on you because it's new and you have no clue as to how it works, so it works; but over a period of time, as you begin to understand, then you will start twisting it to your convenience. You will see how the teaching supports you. The teaching is not about supporting you; the teaching is about demolishing you, but you will start using the teaching as a support for yourself. Once that happens, the teaching is no good anymore. That is why a Guru is constantly talking from different dimensions. It is Truth, but they are so contradictory that he does not allow you to settle anywhere, because the moment you settle, you start using it to your advantage. Apart from this process, the sadhana is always there – just the simple things. A kriya – in the morning you sit and breathe in a certain way – can slowly decimate these blocks. If you don't understand any teaching, it doesn't matter. You just keep doing the practice; after some time, suddenly there is a new sense of openness and freedom in you. That's always the bedrock that you can rely on, because you can always twist teachings.

Seeker: Sadhguru, whichever way I try to be, my karma comes and bombs me out. How do I work off my karma?

Sadhguru: Oh, really? Good, you admitted you have got a little bit (laughs). See, certain aspects of life are going in a certain way. Whatever the karmic structure, we're not trying to change the karma. We are trying to be free from the karmic structure. We're not talking about creating good karmas. Creating good karma still amounts to survival, a little better living. We're not seeing how to live a little better. We are seeing how to become free. So this freedom will happen, not because you are trying to change the trajectories of your karmas this way or that way. Let the karma go and bomb whatever it wants to, you are no more a part of it. That is the path that I am offering you. That is the awareness that is being created. That is the possibility that is alive right now. Let the karma go and bomb anything. You are not a part of it any more.

Once you know how to be aware, once the necessary awareness – to be away from your own body, to be away from your own mind – has come to you, don't even bother about your karmas. Just see how to deepen this awareness. Do you see, being here with me, or during the Isha Yoga programs, there have been many moments of awareness? This is the beginning of freedom. Your business is just to establish that, not to bother about your karma. Let the karmas go wherever they want to go.

Seeker: Sadhguru, if we are creating more karma just with our thoughts – to actions we can say, "It's not necessary," but the mind is not in our control. It is scary to think that even a single thought can give you a backlog of karma that you may have to work out for lifetimes.

Sadhguru: As I have already said, you don't have to watch your actions; it's a wrong idea that people have. By watching your actions, you aren't getting anywhere. It is the thought process which creates the volition, the intention. If you do something with strong volition, either positive or negative volition, both ways you build karma. If you're looking for just creating a little more pleasant atmosphere for yourself to live in, then you try to create good karma, but being on the spiritual path is not about making life pleasant. It's about seeing how to transcend both the pleasant and the unpleasant.

You have had enough of both the pleasant and the unpleasant; now you want to just drop this bag and go beyond this present dimension of existence. So this must always be understood: karma is not in terms of what you do and do not do. Karma is only in terms of what you desire to do. It is attributed to *Gautama*, the Buddha, that he said 'desirelessness'. When he said 'desirelessness', he is not stupid, to think that people can exist here without desire; he knows that without desire there is no existence. You being desireless means you have no identification with your desires; your desires are only about what is needed. You have no personal identity with the desires that you play with. Desires are just things that you play with. Without desire, there is no game at all, but now the desires are not about you anymore. It is just the way it's needed for this moment, for this situation. Once that awareness is there – once you are desireless in that sense, there is no karmic bondage for that person. Whatever he does, even if he fights a war, there is no karma for him because he has no desire to do anything like that. It's not coming out of his love for something or hate for something. It is just coming because simply, that's the way. That is the whole *Gita*. See, Krishna is constantly talking about *nishkarma* – not performing any karma, but insisting that Arjuna[1] should act. He is talking about the same desirelessness with a different language and a different connotation, but nevertheless it is the same thing. Here we are just talking about simply accepting. Just accepting everything is desirelessness, in a certain way. It does not mean you will become still and you will become incapable of activity or anything like that. It's just that, once you are truly accepting

1 Arjuna : great epic hero to whom Krishna delivered the Divine message of the Bhagavad Gita.

what is there, you're not identified with anything. Everything is there the way it is, do whatever you can do about it. That's all there is. You can be deeply involved with everything, but still not be identified with it any more.

Seeker: Dear Master, can karmas accumulated in a lifetime be done away with in a moment?

Sadhguru: See, the karma has gathered in you in so many ways. This karma that is recorded either on the level of your body, mind, or physical energies is an accumulation, but once your awareness comes to a certain point, all of this is happening separately from you. In *Shoonya,*[1] do you see, the mind is happening separately and you are happening separately? This can go so deep into you that if you sit here, everything that is not you and that which is you are separate. Once you are like this, it is all done. Your tape recorder where everything is recorded is there, and you are here. Whatever noise it makes has no impact on you. You are free from it in a moment.

Seeker: Sadhguru, is it true that karmas don't take effect upon children?

Sadhguru: Yes. As soon as you are born, your karmas do not take effect immediately. They just wait for the right atmosphere. Karma can be compared to a seed. Before the rains, the whole land is barren. There would be nothing. It rains; suddenly all kinds of vegetation will sprout up. The seeds are already there; they're just waiting for the right kind of atmosphere. Until then, they are dormant, latent, waiting there. You were carrying it with you, but it had not yet taken effect. It was simply there. When you were just born, it did not take immediate effect. It was waiting. As the process of growth happens, it looks for the right kind of situation and takes effect.

Seeker: So we can dissolve this seed of karma. How, Sadhguru?

Sadhguru: Yes, but not by chopping the plant; dissolving the seed is dissolution of karma. Otherwise there is no dissolution. Maybe it can be covered or converted into something else. You may

1 *Shoonya* : lit. emptiness. A unique form of meditation offered by Sadhguru in a live form in the Isha Yoga Programs.

make your physical suffering into mental suffering and vice versa; it is possible. You can convert one form of karma into another with certain adjustments in life, but it will come anyway. Only when you dissolve the seed, it is finished. It's very resilient.

Seeker: Is looking at past lives useful, Sadhguru? I heard that during Samyama [1] programs, people were re-living past life experiences. Is it true?

Sadhguru: In your memory, let us say you found out that the little boy next door was your husband in some previous lifetime. Many emotions well up and you would not know how to be with that boy. You would also disturb him with your emotions and in no way would it be liberating for you; it is unnecessary. Already with what relationships you have now, you are terribly attached and struggling with them. Just reminding yourself of past-life situations will not do any good, unless some specific memory is opened up for you for a certain kind of work. Otherwise, for your well-being, for your own liberation, it does not do any good. Why Gautama chose regression for the larger public is because it does not need any other preparation. You don't need any understanding, awareness or anything. The only thing that is needed is perseverance; you are willing to sit there and watch and watch. Even if you don't know anything, it does not matter. Other systems need understanding, some preparation; regression doesn't need anything. That is the reason why he chose that for the public, but in closer circles, he did not do regression.

What we handle in Samyama is much more than regression. We are not doing anything particular to regress the person. At the same time, when your awareness is heightened in a particular direction, as your awareness becomes deeper and deeper, the unconscious layers of the mind start flicking up and coming into your consciousness. It can happen physically. People can go through the whole act – whatever their past life – physically, within themselves, energy-wise or memory-wise. In the earlier Samyamas,

---

1 Samyama: an eight day meditation camp offered by Sadhguru where one is transported to explosive states of meditativeness Held at Isha Yoga Center.

too many past life memories were coming up, but now I have almost taken away the aspect of memory because later on, people can struggle. For some people it's very liberating to remember, but for many, this remembrance can be very entangling. Whenever this remembrance happens on the energy level, it is always liberating, although you might not be aware of it on the mental level. You cannot call Samyama regression, because regression methods are generally psychological exercises. What people are generally calling liberation is mainly psychological exercises. It is only giving a different manifestation of your own present psyche. It's more of a psychological exercise. It's not really about past lives. It just brings in other dimensions of your psyche which are not in your normal experience, but that is not what it should be. If you go through such experiences, it is cathartic, but it's not at the level of bringing the unconscious into the conscious.

Seeker: Sadhguru, can regression therapy to recall past lives be beneficial in any way?

Sadhguru: Psychological exercises have got nothing to do with past lives. It is all just a different projection of your present experience. See, your mind has different projections of the same thing. That is what Freud was talking about. What Freud says is that if you look at your mother, one thing is you see her as a caring, loving mother. Another thing is: you are looking at her sexuality. Another thing is: you remember her breasts from your childhood. Another thing is: when you were in the womb and coming out, you remember her reproductive organs. Because of all these projections, you have so many things mixed up in you, which make you into a complex human being. This is not past life.

There are so many images of the same thing, which are normally not in your perception. The psychological processes of regression can only bring up those things. Now, you think it's past life, but it is not so. It's another projection of your mind. Let us say you saw a film in positive. Now you see it in negative. It looks totally different. You are seeing it backwards, it also looks totally different. Let us say you saw your mother as a young woman or something else, which you have forgotten on a conscious level. When she delivered you, she was probably twenty. Today, you remember her as forty, or sixty. So 'my mother' means you have an image of a forty-year-old woman, or a sixty-year-old woman, but somewhere in your mind there is a twenty-year-old woman. So when that image comes mixed up with so many things you may think, "Oh, maybe I knew my mother in my past life." This is not the reality. It is just the layers and layers of recording that are happening in your mind. That's the significance of Freud's work. That is just a psychological exercise, and the regression processes that are happening around the world are just that.

Seeker: So Master, for instance, when I see a different time and I'm in a different place, is that still true? Say I am in France, in a cathedral, in front of monks giving me instructions, and as a result of not following the instructions, I see myself put to death by the Catholic Church. I am seeing all this happening! Even though this is not in my current experience, somehow it is coming up and I'm seeing this. What is this? What is happening?

Sadhguru: On a certain day, a drunk got into the subway train and plonked himself next to a parish priest. After a while, the drunk asked, "Why are you wearing your collar backside front?" The priest soberly answered, "That is because I am a father." The drunk said, "So what? Even I am a father with three children!" The priest explained, "No, you don't understand, I am a father to my whole congregation." So the drunk said, "Wearing your collar backside front won't help then; it's your pants that you need to wear backside front!" So Patricia, keep your mind backside front, otherwise you will have a congregation of fancy hallucinations. Too much of a Catholic upbringing has gone into you! All this is just your mind playing tricks with you. I want you to understand one thing: there is one dimension of a human being which is longing to be unbounded; the rest of it is all limited – your body, your mind, your perceptions – because the only tools that you have are body and mind. This body and mind try to do funny things to project you as something more than what you are right now – always. Some people call it romance, I call it hallucination. I don't want to take all the beauty of romance away from people's lives, but understand that if you are enjoying your dream, just enjoy it. If you are enjoying a movie, just enjoy it; that's all. Enjoy it. There is no problem about enjoying it, but don't create any significance to it. People who see such things, you will notice, are seeing so many things that don't even exist. Slowly they have become senseless about their life, about what is in front of them. Have you noticed this?

A lot of these new-age people and others who are talking about past lives and all this have no sense about the life that they are living right now, isn't it? This is simply because you are going into hallucinatory states.

You are not realizing it. If Realization comes, you will become absolutely sensible with what is here now. This is the significant difference between something that comes out of your awareness and something that comes from a hallucinatory state. Awareness spreads into every dimension of your life; not just the way you eat, the way you stand, the way you sit, but everything, the very way you exist. You will become absolutely sensible. If you are moving into hallucinatory states, you are always having huge visions of great things, but in your physical reality, you are becoming more and more senseless. This is a clear indication that you are hallucinating.

Seeker: But Sadhguru, during this Karma Samyama, it has been spoken about how people remember their past lives, and how real everything is in their experience. What is the difference between what is happening with Patricia and what is happening in Samyama?

Sadhguru: In Samyama, there is no input. There is no psychological exercise that says, "Do this, see this, say that", you know? Nothing. It is just meditation. It's simply meditation. The meditations and the processes are just aimed at pushing your energies up to such a point that your body will explode. Now, why are we pushing the energies up? To put it very simply, a very rudimentary example would be, let us say there is a light bulb here. It needs two hundred and forty volts to be fully lit, but here, in this rural power supply, we are only getting one hundred volts. If it's one hundred volts, you see only that much. If it becomes one hundred and fifty volts, you see a little bit more. If it becomes two hundred and forty volts, it will show you everything that is in the area, isn't it? So all we are trying to do is raise your voltage. We are not trying to make you see anything. I'm not saying, "Look there. This past life is there. God is coming; Jesus is coming; something else is coming." No, we are just cranking up your energy to the highest possible pitch, full voltage. In full voltage, everything that is there, you simply see, that's all. This is not suggested to you. We are not making an attempt to see anything. By wanting to see something, you will only go into imagination or hallucinations. Right now, it's dark. Let us say in the evening you come into this garden. It is pitch dark. If you try to see something, you'll imagine many things which are not there. Isn't it so? Trying to see is a stupid thing. There is no such thing as trying to see.

Samyama is not trying to see your past life. It is just cranking up your energy to the highest pitch. If your voltage is full, your awareness will spread. That also is limited to the kind of bulb that you are. Okay?

Let us say you are a big halogen bulb. It lights up a whole big space, but if you are just a little bulb, at full brightness it sees what it has to see. No matter how much we crank up the energy, this bulb will see only that much, but the business is to crank it up to the full pitch, so that whatever is possible, it will see. Once it sees and dissolution happens, this little bulb, next time it meditatively sits, it will become a little bigger bulb, a little more potent. Do you see this happening every time you go into very intense processes of meditation? Have you attended Samyama?

Seeker: Yes.

Sadhguru: The first day, when you came and sat in front of me, with what clarity did you see? Since then, are you beginning to see many other dimensions of life? This is simply because slowly, your wattage – not the voltage, the wattage – is being upgraded. As your wattage increases, your vision is increasing, but if I tell you, "See, see, see," you will hallucinate. The moment I say, "See," there is no way to see, please see (laughs). Did you get that? I want you to know that there is no way to see by making an effort. You can see only because of the light and your open eyes; that's all. You are not willing to come to terms with the simple facts of life. That's why spirituality seems to be so complex. It is not complex. You are not willing to come to the simple facts of life. You have silly ideas; that is the reason why it seems to be so complex.

So why they say that if you surrender it becomes easy is because by surrendering, you keep all your fancy ideas aside. Surrender does not mean falling at somebody's feet. Surrender simply means that you have kept all your fancy ideas aside. Everything that you consider as 'myself', you kept it aside. That is surrender, isn't it? "No, I surrender to you, I fall at your feet, but I don't like this." That is not surrender. Samyama meditations do not happen as a regression process. It is just a meditative process. Once a person moves into a higher level of awareness and a certain direction is there, naturally layers of the unconscious become conscious; that's why we call it Karma Samyama. It is an enormously liberating experience.

Seeker: Sadhguru, is it better to handle past life memories energy-wise rather than memory-wise? And if a person is energized, does past-life memory come up quickly?

Sadhguru: Right now, what is your experience in life? This moment you are experiencing life; you are sitting here and talking. This moment, what you are experiencing on one level is in the awareness of your mind. In the general awareness of your mind, if you were asleep, you would not know what I'm talking about, but since you are awake and alert now, you know what I am talking about. That's one level of experience. Another level of experience is the physical body sitting here. It has its own experience, but generally, most of it is not in your awareness. Another level of experience is your sensations. Most people are not aware unless it touches them in a certain way; energy-wise also, certain things are happening which are not in your experience. So you can bring back this situation that you are living right now, either in the form of memory, or in the form of body, or in the form of energy. Like this, you can bring it back. Energy-wise if you bring it back, people will not remember, but they work out the same karma on a much deeper level. Memory-wise if you bring it back, some people will work it out, but some people will get even more entangled than before.

Seeker: Master, are you saying that actually on all four levels, the play of the karma's manifestation is going on?

Sadhguru: It's like it is getting imprinted. Everything that happens here is constantly getting imprinted, which is having an influence on what you do next. It is easy to understand the imprints on the mind. That you can see, but people are not aware of other imprints that are also there. This memory, first it is in your energy, then in your sensation, then in your body, then in your mind. In yoga, it is said that one who has mastery over his ring finger can rewrite anybody's destiny. If I just touch my ring finger in a certain way, I can rewrite your destiny if I wish to. It is a whole science by itself. See, your finger can be divided into three portions by the lines drawn on it. The first portion of the ring finger, from the tip onwards, carries lifetimes of experiences. Everything is in this. Everything is written into this, whether you touch here or here or here (gestures), every bit, every milli, milli, millimeter is rich with life. Every micro millimeter is different. There is a whole lot of sadhana for this. If you just know how to handle your ring finger like you handle a computer mouse, you can scroll all your lifetimes just right here. If you have mastery over it, you can do miraculous things to yourself and to the external situation. The second portion of your ring finger has elaborate detail of your prarabdha. The base digit can be used to predict future possibilities, based on the past accumulations of karma and the present expressions of the prarabdha.

Always in our tradition, for everything that you do, you must use the ring finger. All the *nadis* [1] are activated by touching certain portions of the finger. If you want to take *vibhuthi* [2] or *kumkum* [3] you use this finger to apply it, simply because these are all different ways to defuse the karmic structure. Even unknowingly, if you touch something sacred that has a certain energy quality to it with your ring finger, it dissolves some karma; you get to shed some of it. Now this powerful vibhuthi here, when you take it with your ring finger, unknowingly you will drop some karma right here. The whole tradition was built like that – whichever way, you must be slowly moving towards your liberation.

Seeker: So if I just touch this finger like this...?

Sadhguru: Once you raise your energy to a certain point, in a certain direction, there are certain *nadis* which are keys to the karmic structure in the physiology. Not all the nadis are like this. Some are keys to physical life, and others are keys to different aspects of life. Certain nadis are keys to the karmic structure. So the moment you touch that, if you are aware, the moment you touch those nadis – now with great intensity, the karmic substance just pours in. If huge volumes of karma pour into your life when you aren't sufficiently prepared, or when the necessary awareness is not there, then it could lead to huge upheavals in your life. If the necessary awareness is there, when it pours in, the energy just works it out in a certain way. So the old karma, whatever it is, begins to work itself out at rapid pace. Right now, just sitting here, talking, living, breathing, is working out some karma. This is happening at a very slow pace, because in the process of dissolving, you are also creating new karma. In heightened states of awareness, you have stopped creating, and dissolution is happening at a rapid pace.

Seeker: Sadhguru, this yoga system, the *Shakthi Chalana Kriya*,[4] this also comes into our energy memory?

Sadhguru: Yes. Nothing has been taught mentally. Once it's a question of energy, everything that you know on the mental state is also there on the energy state. Do you see that many things you have learned

---

1 *nadis*: channel through which the life force or prana flows through in the subtle body

2 *vibhuthi*: sacred, consecrated ash

3 *kumkum*: vermilion or red powder that is applied between the eyebrows

4 *Shakthi Chalana Kriya*: a powerful yogic practice created by Sadhguru that uses certain breathing techniques

are there in your body without even thinking? For example, if you know how to swim, it is in your body. You don't have to mentally think about it. Almost everything you have learned is on the level of your body, on the level of sensation and on the level of your energy. If I have to teach you something memory-wise, what I know will take ten lifetimes for you to learn because it has taken that long to acquire, but if it has to be transferred by energy, it can be transferred in a moment. That is what an initiation is. Initiation is not a bundle of instructions.

Seeker: I may not know how to receive this, Sadhguru!

Sadhguru: Now transmitting and receiving is on many different levels. If we teach people certain kriyas, in the very process of teaching the kriyas, we also offer a certain amount of energy. That's why I am repeatedly saying while we are teaching yoga kriyas, "Don't try to learn mentally; we will put it in you some other way. Just be patient and receive it," but people want to write it down. It is just that energy-wise, it can be put in differently; the whole dimension is different, and it works in a different way. People think the only way to learn is to write down and memorize. This is done on the pranic level, but on the level of your etheric body also, there is memory. The subtler parts of your memory are always in the etheric body. It is very subtle energy. Right now, suppose you take a seed, or now you have genes, isn't it? Do you know genes have a memory? A gene is just a memory chip; it has generations of memory in it and it is manifesting it. That is not in your mind. If you had to remember all that in your mind, you know what a burden it would be.

If you take an apple seed and put it in a mango grove, it will not give mangos. It will only produce apples because the memory that it is an apple is deeply written into it. No matter what you do, it will only produce apples. You cannot confuse an apple tree to produce mangos or peaches, or something else. The memory is so perfect. That is what karma means; it is a deep-rooted memory. You cannot confuse it. Similarly, it does not matter where you put the man, you make him a king, or you make him a beggar, or make him whatever, his deep-rooted memory is constantly taking effect. There is a story in the yogic lore. One man loved his dog very much. So his ambition became that somehow, he had to make this dog into the king of that country. Anybody that you love, you want to put them up, isn't it? He loved his dog, so he wanted to make his dog into a king. He played some trick, and the dog ended up marrying a princess. Then they put him up on the throne. Now the dog sat on this throne, dressed in all regal clothes with the whole pageantry serving him and everything; but one day, he saw a bone out there and ran straight for it. That is what they say about the karma. What is in your deep-rooted memory, no matter where we put you, you will only go after that. Unless you move into an awareness that takes you beyond these limitations, your karma will work compellingly.

Seeker: Sadhguru, you tell us not to create new karma, but how? You say don't judge, but how not to judge?

Sadhguru: Even in the basic Isha Yoga program, the first three sessions are all about not creating a new stock of karma. Only later, we are talking about dissolution. What is more important than dissolving karma is that you learn to stop creating new karma. If you don't create a new stock, the old stock will go in its own time, or if you are aware enough, you can drop it in a moment; that's different. The important thing is to stop creating. With every reaction, you are creating more karma. Especially you, Indu, you have strong likes and dislikes.

Seeker: Yes, very strong, Sadhguru. Only you should save me! Sadhguru, I am very tempted to come to the Samyama program, because I heard one acquires the knowledge and the *sakshi* [1] not to create new karma if one goes through this.

Sadhguru: Indu, if you sit there with this attitude of getting something, you will only gather more! (Laughs). Samyama is an extremely rapid way of dissolving, an almost violently rapid way of dissolving. When your karmic structure begins to fall apart at a very rapid pace, you will see violent things will happen in the body, because it's just going through lifetimes like *that*. What would take many lifetimes is just happening in moments, so it takes on a violent form sometimes. The very way the teaching goes is about not reacting. Just accepting and not reacting is just to stop creating new karma. As you become more and more aware, natural acceptance of what is there becomes so much higher. One important

---

1 *sakshi*: lit. witness, a common way of describing the Self. Witness consciousness

aspect of Samyama is to teach you to become meditative with your eyes open. We start with eyes closed and we slowly move people to a state where they open their eyes partially, then fully, then get active with everything, just maintaining the same awareness. So once you are able to maintain that awareness with eyes open and with activity, then the question of creating karma does not arise. It is just a rapid dissolution. If one establishes himself in the Samyama state, dissolution happens. The question of creating does not arise at all.

Seeker: Sadhguru, there is a lot of teaching out there about positive thinking and how it can transform your life. Is it that simple? Can positive thinking help you get rid of karma, or at least keep you from creating more karma? Yet there's something about people who are always repeating positive affirmations that seems shallow.

Sadhguru: The reason these people have lost depth to their life is that they have become frivolous by focusing their attention on only what is convenient for them, which they call positive. They want everything quick, quick, quick, quick (snaps fingers). There is no dedication to anything. Suppose somebody has to become a scientist. He has to study for years, isn't it? Maybe he will forget his wife, his children, his nonsense; he forgets everything and gives himself. Only then something opens up for him, even on the physical plane.

If these things have to open up for you, it needs enormous focus. That steady focus is not there in the modern world, because somebody is going about teaching all the time, "Don't worry, be happy; just enjoy yourself! Enjoy yourself! Everything is fine; be happy! Laugh! Ha! Ha! Ha!" People just become frivolous and that kind of happiness will crash. One day it will crash. They'll go into mentally sick situations. One big thing that I see that is happening in the West especially is, "Be happy, be happy, live in the moment, live in the moment." Everybody will quote, "Live in the moment," because books have been written about it, all the programs have talked about it, without understanding, especially without experiencing what it is. Everybody is saying, "I am happy; I am always happy. I am always laughing." You watch those people. The moment they start this 'I am happy, I am happy' business, depending upon their lifestyles, within five or six years they'll come to a depressed state. One day, it will hit you very deeply, because your energies, according to your karmic structure, are apportioned for different possibilities. There's something for your pain. There's something for your grief. There's something for your joy. There's something for your love. This is prarabdha karma. It is not just in your mind, because the data is like that; the energy is flowing in those directions. If those things don't find expression, if you deny them, they will take root in a completely different way.

Accepting is so important because accepting means you simply see everything the way it is. You don't deny anything. If grief comes, grief. Sadness comes, sadness. Joy comes, joy. Ecstasy comes, ecstasy. When you do this, you are not denying anything; at the same time, everything is happening, but you are free from it. You're not trying to stop anything; but if you just say, "I am happy, I am happy, I am happy," this positive thinking – do you see that all those positive-thinking people went crazy? Most people who promoted all this went mad. They committed suicide. The 'Don't worry, be happy' people have committed suicide! It's bound to happen, because energy is apportioned to your prarabdha karma in different ways. Karma is data. According to this data, your energy is functioning. If you deny it, it will take root in some other way. It will find expression in some other way.

Seeker: The other day, I saw this space around you, and when you were moving, it seemed to be filled with these small, small, small... I don't know what to call it, but is that energy? Can I call it energy, Sadhguru?

Sadhguru: There are particles, the fundamental particles which constitute the basic construction materials for the atom. Today, modern science clearly says that the whole existence is just particles, moving in different patterns, but these particles have given way to energy. Even for a particle to move around there is energy behind it. So the most fundamental thing is energy. On that the particles happen, the particles become an atom, the atom becomes matter, you know? Then the other dimensions of creation happen, but the fundamental thing is absolute emptiness. Today, they have studied the radioisotopes that come from what are called black holes, which are total emptiness. They say they are very powerful. There seems to be another kind of energy there, the kind of energy which is not physical. Energy is always physical – electric, electronic, whatever – it is physical. It is a flow of electrons. In those black holes there is no flow of electrons – no electrons, protons and neutrons, but still it is very powerful. It's a different kind of energy. It is that which we have always been calling as Shoonya. It's that which we have been calling as the core of a human being, whatever it is. That is the most fundamental. It is that which we are referring to as *mukthi*[1] also – to become that which is non-physical. Whatever you see, a particle or an atom, is still physical.

There is another dimension which is not physical. In that non-physical state, there is no memory. Memory is only in the physical state. That energy, that prana, is still physical, just like electricity. Once you move into the non-physical, there is no memory, so there is no karma. That is why Shoonya meditation is so important. If you move into Shoonya, you are completely free from all karmic structures, because in that state of no-thing – you will understand it better if you put a hyphen between no and thing – it is no longer physical. Once it is not physical, there is no such thing as karma because this whole karma, or the cause and effect, belong to the physical reality. Either you can sit here and start working out your karma step-by-step – which may take we don't know how long – or you just move beyond your physical reality and all karma is gone in an instant.

Seeker: So my energy also is pure power?

Sadhguru: What do you mean by pure power?

Seeker: Electricity cannot carry the memory. It goes to the refrigerator and makes it work. It can go to the heater or to the cooler. Similarly, energy is pure. In my body, somewhere this energy is heat, somewhere it is anger, somewhere it is greed, whatever. That pure energy, one might discover as a black hole. Pure means it is not passing through the boxes. All my boxes have become neutral. The body has become very cause-and-effect-less. So the energy flows…

Sadhguru: You are talking about Ultimate Nature flowing as energy. No, Ultimate Nature does not flow as energy. It cannot flow, because it is nothingness. It can only flow from something-ness. Only because

---

1 *mukthi* : liberation, release, final absolution of the Self.

this is something it can move from here to there. How can nothingness move from here to there? It is not that which is moving. Everything that is moving is physical. Maybe it is very subtle, but it's still physical. Memory is built into that physical energy, not into the Ultimate Nature. There, there is nothing. That does not carry anything.

Seeker: So the purest of pure is not even the awareness; awareness is one type of sakshi.

Sadhguru: One of the manifestations.

Seeker: Now I got it.

Sadhguru: Oh, you keep saying that, every day. What can be of ultimate purity? Only nothingness can be absolutely pure, isn't it? Everything else has a duality. The closest manifestation of nothingness is blissfulness. It is so much easier for you to understand this if you look at it in the way yoga describes the five bodies. The closest creation, the first creation is blissfulness; from blissfulness to awareness, from awareness to energy, from energy to mind and from mind to body. It is the simplest way of putting it.

Seeker: That awareness, we were told, is the intellect.

Sadhguru: No, this is the big mistake that people make. People always mistake mental alertness for awareness. Mental alertness is not awareness. A dog has better alertness than you do. A dog or a cat has got much better mental alertness than man, isn't it so? That is not awareness. Mental alertness is still an instrument for survival, but awareness is not an instrument for survival; it is an instrument for creation.

Seeker: Sadhguru, will I shed a lot of karma in Shoonya *dhyana*[1] as well?

Sadhguru: It is not a question of shedding the karma; you are learning to create a distance with your karma. You're not trying to shed karma.

---

1 *dhyana* : meditation.

Seeker: Okay, so karma will not be a part of me anymore?

Sadhguru: Right now, you're carrying a big bundle on your head, a basket of karma on your head and you want to sell it to someone. That someone is not going to buy the whole basket, but anyway you will sell them one handful. If you sell them one handful, they will give you something in return. It may be smaller or bigger; it depends on the situation. You drop something, you pick up something else; this goes on. Now we're seeing how to put the basket aside. We are not interested in what is in the basket. We just want to put the basket aside; that's all. Once, Shankaran Pillai had to travel by train with a huge bundle of luggage. He carried it on his head, went into the train, found himself a seat, and sat with the bundle on his head. The co-passengers curiously looked at him sitting with a bundle on his head and they thought, "Okay, maybe he will put it down later," but he didn't, and he sat there quietly, as if everything was normal. The train started and still he sat there with the bundle on his head. Then one passenger, feeling concerned, thought that maybe he needed some help. So she asked him, "Sir, can I help you with anything?" Shankaran Pillai replied, "No, no. I am fine, thank you." And he just sat there. Ten minutes passed, then half-an-hour, and this man sat like this with the bundle on his head. Now the co-passengers' necks started paining looking at this. Totally flabbergasted, they asked him, "What's the problem? Why don't you put it down? If it has something very valuable and you are scared of thieves, please put it down and sit on it! Why are you carrying it on your head?" Shankaran Pillai said, "No, no, nothing valuable inside, just some clothes." "But then why are you carrying it on your head?" "Oh! I just don't want to burden the train." So Indu, please keep your basket aside.

Seeker: Then Sadhguru, that is called sakshi. I am the seer of the basket; I am not the basket. That awareness, I am awareness. I am already 'me'. This, which is reflecting, is not 'me'.

Sadhguru: You thinking, "I am not karma" is karma because you are doing all this sakshi business only to avoid the karma, isn't it?

Seeker: No, I am keeping distance from the karma.

Sadhguru: How?

Seeker: By just watching it, Sadhguru; and I have kept the basket down. I see the basket is not dissolved and I say to hell with it. I am not this basket, I am not this karma. Nothing can touch me.

Sadhguru: Your saying, "I am not this karma," is still karma. When you say, "I am not the karma," what is the intention? You want to be free from the karma. You want to avoid the karma. That itself is karma. If you sit here, your body is here, your mind is there, and you are somewhere else – it is not that you are trying to watch this or that; you are simply here – a clear space has come. Now, whatever karma that is in the mind, whatever karma that is there in the body or energy – everything has become separate from you. For a few moments, if there is a separation, you know it is possible. Once you establish this in your life, it becomes a living reality. If you sit here, the body is here, the mind is there and you are here. Once this distinction comes, now there is no karma for that person. Whatever he wants to do, he can do. Nothing touches him.

Seeker: Sadhguru, this is philosophy...

Sadhguru: Are you okay for a joke? One day a bull was grazing in the field and a pheasant was picking out the ticks off the bull's body. They are used to each other; they are sort of friends, so it's going on. Then the pheasant became nostalgic and said, "When I was young, I could fly and sit on the topmost branch of the big tree out there, but now I can't even get to the first branch." The bull said nonchalantly, "Oh! What's the problem? Just eat my dung, and it will give you all the nourishment that you need to go to the topmost branch." The pheasant said, "Really? You mean just eating your droppings will get me to the top of the tree?" "Yes, try and see!" he replied. So the pheasant hesitantly ate some of the dung, and that very day he flew up to the first branch! Every day, he started eating more and more of the dung. In about a fortnight's time it reached the topmost branch, and went and sat there. The pheasant was so thrilled, having eaten this dung and being able to sit on the topmost branch. Now when the farmer, who was sitting on his balcony, saw this fat pheasant sitting on the topmost branch of the tree, he just pulled out his shotgun and shot the pheasant off the tree! The moral of the story is: bullshit may get you to the top but it will never let you stay there. Your philosophies will not get you anywhere. Mentally if you do it, you're only trying to avoid it more and more. You are only acquiring more karma, because it is resistance. It is craving and aversion which builds the karma. You have an aversion to karma, so you're

Inner freedom for the imprisoned. His outreach programs for the prisoners. A death row inmate in His embrace of redemption.

trying to push it away. In the effort to push it away, you are only building more karma.

Seeker: But if I am detached, Sadhguru, and have kept myself so distant, even if I am having an effect of karma in my body, I say, "It is not me"; I don't react to it. There is negativity but I don't say, "Oh, why this negativity?" and shift toward the positive. If it is there, it is there, but it is not me. I am just trying to accept it.

Sadhguru: Now I must tell you a story about this Vedanta.[1] Once it so happened, Shankaran Pillai went to the Vedanta classes. The speaker, the teacher of Vedanta, was going full swing. "You are not this; you are everywhere; there is nothing like 'yours and his'; everything is yours; after all, everything is *maya*.[2] What you see, hear, smell, taste, touch, is not reality; it's all maya. There is no such thing as yours and mine; it's all one." This is Vedanta. This really sank into Shankaran Pillai in a very deep way. He went and slept over the Vedanta. He got up in the morning, totally fired up. Usually he loves to sleep but because of this Vedanta, now, first thing in the morning he started thinking, "There is nothing here which is not mine. Everything is mine; everything is me. All that is in this world is me, and everything is maya." Like this he went on.

---

1 Vedanta : a certain school of philosophy.
2 *maya* : delusion.

Sadhguru impacts global business and political leaders at the prestigious World Economic Forum in Davos, Switzerland

Then, you know, whatever philosophy, hunger comes. So he went to his favorite restaurant and ordered a big breakfast, and he ate saying, "The food is also me, I am also the food, the one who serves is also me, the one who eats is also me." Vedanta! He finished his breakfast, and with his stomach full looked around. He saw the owner of the restaurant sitting there. "It's all mine, what is mine is yours, what is yours is mine." With the same Vedanta thing going on, he got up and started walking out. When everything is yours, where is the question of paying the bill? And when he just happened to cross the counter where the cash box is, the owner got distracted by some other work and left the place, Shankaran Pillai saw a huge heap of currency in the till. Immediately, the Vedanta told him, "Everything is yours; you cannot differentiate between this and that." So because his pockets were quite empty, he put his hand into the box, took some cash, put it in his pocket and continued to walk. He is not out to rob anybody, he is just practicing Vedanta. Then a few people from the restaurant ran behind him and caught him. Shankaran Pillai said, "What are you going to catch? What you catch is also you, the one who catches is also you, what is in my stomach is also in your stomach, so who can I pay?" The owner was bewildered! He only knows *idly, dosa, vada*![1] See if a thief tries to run, they know how to catch him, beat him, thrash him; all this they know. But when he said, "The one who catches is also me, the one who is caught is also me," they didn't know what to do, so they took him to the court. There, Shankaran Pillai continued his Vedanta. The judge tried in many ways to make him understand, but Shankaran Pillai continued his Vedanta teachings. Then the judge said, "Okay, sixty lashes." First lash…reality hits. Second lash… a shout. Third lash…a scream. Then the judge said, "Don't worry, the one who lashes is also you, the one who is lashed is also you, so who can lash anybody? It's all maya. So sixty lashes on the backside." Now Shankaran Pillai cries out, "Please, no more Vedanta. Leave me alone!"

These teachings will only deceive you. When you come to a living experience that, 'This body is not me,' then there is a different kind of wisdom in you. There is a different kind of understanding in you. When you intellectually understand, it leads only to these deceptive states. When you experientially know, it's very different. Why you are saying, "It's not me," is because you don't want it to be you, isn't it? A philosophy like that will just give you some semblance of balance in your life, but it does not liberate you from the deeper karma, because you're only trying to avoid it, and in that avoidance you find a little balance in day-to-day life. But slowly, if a person does this philosophy, you will see, slowly they will become joyless. They will become reasonably balanced and stable; at the same time they will slowly become lifeless.

If you bring lifelessness into you, that itself is a very negative karma because you are just suppressing life. That is karma. The most beautiful thing that has been said about this is: Krishna said, "Hesitation is the worst sin," because with hesitation you kill life. Anything that suppresses life is the worst sin. Suppression doesn't mean, "Okay, now I want to eat; I do not eat." This is not suppression. People always think, "If I don't do what I want to do, it is suppression." No! It is just that you are not allowing yourself to experience it totally. Whether hunger or food, if you sit here and experience hunger totally, it is wonderful, it is releasing; or if you experience food totally, it is releasing. But you neither experience hunger

---

1 *idly, dosa, vada* : common South Indian breakfast items.

fully, nor food fully; this is karma. It is saying, "This is not me." See this 'not me, not me' nethi process is a very different process, but denying what is happening within you is like self-denial. If you deprive yourself of any experience – whether it is pain, suffering, joy or whatever it is – if you avoid it, that is big karma. If you go through it, it is not so much of a karma.

Today, in the name of civilization or whatever – etiquette or education – educated people are not able to experience any of their emotions fully. They cannot cry fully; they cannot laugh loudly. For everything, they have got etiquette. With this you'll see, slowly they will become joyless. A deep sense of frustration will establish itself. You will see simple people who laugh and cry as it comes, they are so much more free. They have not accumulated heaps on them yet; but people with practiced etiquette accumulate heaps on their head. The very process of life is dissolution of karma. Every living moment of your life, if you live it totally, you dissolve enormous amounts of karma. Living totally does not mean just having fun. Anything and everything that comes, you just experience it fully, intensely.

Chapter - 4

Body's Plight

Body's Plight

This toy of elemental ploy
Deceptive in its ability for joy
The pain and bondage of these miraculous five
If broken, you in liberation will fly.

– Sadhguru

Kedarnath - at home in Shiva's abode.

Sadhguru - an all-enveloping love.

The human body is the pinnacle of the physical evolution of life on this planet. The intricacy, complexity and the sophistication is unmatched by anything that modern science can hope to comprehend, far less imitate or compete with. To pack each minute cell with such an enormous amount of intelligence and to infuse this mass of billions of cells with *prana* (or the subtle life force) of such prodigious potential, is truly the ultimate miracle.

In the spiritual lore, the human body is considered supremely sacred, as this is the only mechanism that can take a being from the limited identification of the self to the unlimited, from a bounded existence to the realm of the unbounded, to the final plunge into the vastness of the Infinite.

Growing from a meeting of two cells, the body, before it withers away, goes through a series of experiences of pain and pleasure, of disease and deformity. Helplessly entangled in the tentacles of *maya*, the celestial illusion, the body is also the source of untold fear and suffering. Yet, it is the body that becomes one's deliverance. Thus the seeker's affair with the body runs a full spectrum from trauma to Bliss.

In *Body's Plight*, Sadhguru dwells at length upon the very nuts and bolts of the mechanics of the body – the *karma* that dictates its creation and dissolution, of health and healing, of diseases and miraculous cures, of depression and madness, of psychic surgeries, of death and after-death, of birth and rebirths, the choice and the choicelessness of it all.

Walking the seeker through a maze of beliefs, rituals, superstitions and myths, Sadhguru reveals the play of life culminating in what is known in the tradition as *Mahasamadhi, Mahaparinirvana, Nirvana, Moksha* or the complete liberation of the self, sharing insights on the necessary sadhana to transcend the trap of the body.

Seeker: Sadhguru, everyday I see so much disease and suffering around me. Many times it has deeply bothered me as to why a human being should suffer like this at all. It seems so unreasonable that one human being enjoys good health and another one suffers. Can you tell us, why disease? What is it? Where does it come from?

Sadhguru: There are many aspects to disease. The word 'disease', if you look at it more closely, is dis-ease. You are not at ease. Your body does not know how to rest. When it does not know how to rest, the energies become chaotic. People with asthma attend Isha Yoga programs and begin to do their *yoga kriyas* and meditate. For many of them, the asthma is completely gone. For others, it is partially gone. For a few others, there is no change. This is because the causes are different. With one person, it is chaotic energy. After three days of practicing *yoga kriyas*, the energy becomes more organized and their asthma is gone. With another person, one part of it is chaotic energy, another part has deeper karmic reasons, so it is only partially gone. For those where there is no change, there are very strong karmic reasons that are causing the disease. There might also be external situations, which have not changed.

Now how can *karma*[1] cause disease? There is something called *prarabdha*. Prarabdha means the allotted karma for this lifetime. There are many aspects to this. To make it simple, prarabdha karma is written into your mind, body, sensations, and your energy. It is most basic on the level of the energy; it is the fundamental recording. How can information be recorded on the energy? It can be recorded. I'm not sure if it is being explored scientifically, but I know that some day science will find a way of recording information on energy. At one time, whatever we wanted to record, we had to write on stone tablets.

---

1 *karma* : past action, the cause of all bondage.

From there, we moved onto books. Now, what could be written on a thousand tablets can be written in a single book. What could be written in a thousand books can be recorded on a compact disk. What could be put onto a thousand compact disks, we can now store on a small chip. Someday, what we now store in a million chips will be recorded on a little bit of energy. This is a living experience within me. I know it is possible because it is happening within me all the time, and it is happening within you also. The energy itself functions in a certain way. Everybody's energy, or *prana*, does not behave the same way. It behaves according to their karmic bondage. So the deepest recording is in the energy. This is like karmic back-ups. If you lose your mind, it is still in the body. If you lose your body, it is still in the energy; it remains in the backup systems. So energy has allotments.

There are many complexities to this. To put it very simply, there is a certain amount of energy dedicated to action, another amount to your emotion, another to your thought process, and yet another for the experiential dimensions within you. Let us say you have this much energy dedicated for emotion. Today, in modern life, in the present way of living, people's emotions are not finding their full expression. That part of the energy, the unexpressed emotion, cannot become something else. Either it has to find an emotional expression or it will turn inward and do funny things within you. That's why in Western countries there are so many mental problems. It is said that one out of every three Americans is suffering from some form of mental illness. Think of two of your best friends, Frederica. If they're okay then it must be you (laughs). One of the major factors for this is that there is no room for emotional expression. Anything emotional is looked upon as a weakness in those cultures, so it is suppressed. People are emotional, but there is no free expression for their emotions. Ninety percent of the people in the world, or even more, never find full expression for their emotions. They're afraid of their love, they're afraid of their grief, they're afraid of their joys, they are afraid of everything. To laugh loudly is a problem, to cry loudly is a problem; everything is a problem; and they call this 'modern culture'. I would say this is a restrictive culture, which causes you to behave in a certain way. So if your emotions never find full expression then that energy can turn around and do many damaging things to you.

The major portion of your prarabdha karma is the energy that is allotted for activity. The physical body is the major thing in you, even today. So the maximum amount of prarabdha goes toward activity, always.

Ninety-five percent of the time, the maximum allotted energy goes towards activity. This proportion may vary from person to person, but usually it is like this. Now, the activity level in modern life has come down dramatically because people do not use their body the way they used to. If this unused energy stays there, it could easily cause disease. The modern mind is going through a unique kind of neurosis which was not there in the past, because man has stopped using his body to a large extent. When you involve yourself intensely in physical activity, a lot of your neuroses are worked out because your nervous energy is used; but modern man has become more inactive and more neurotic than ever before. It has become a common phenomenon in society that everybody is in some level of neurosis. This is simply because the energy allotted for physical activity is not worked out. It is trapped because the physical activity is so low. Today you can see this; people involved in high levels of activity in the form of a sport – like say, a mountain climber – because of the full utilization of physical activity you will find him or her in a different level of balance and peace. You will not find such a person so entangled in sexuality and other physical drives. This is simply because one aspect of him has found full expression.

One result of this inactivity is disease; and above all, the lack of activity and trapped energy cause restlessness. It causes agitation in the body. This agitation may become a physiological disease in some people. In many people it may not become disease, but they are agitated; they are anyway at 'dis-ease'. Their energies are always struggling within themselves. There is no ease in them. They cannot even sit quietly. Even if they just sit, there is no ease. If you observe people, the very way they sit and stand shows they are not at ease. They have brought practiced gracefulness to themselves – how to walk, how to stand and how to sit. If you take away the unease in your movements, it will build into your energy, because it's not finding expression there. It shifts to yet another dimension where it is easy for it to find expression. So disease is happening because of this, because the energy turns inward.

This is one reason why our *bhramhacharis*[1] are into so much activity. Anybody seeing their level of activity would ask, "Why are these people who came here to pursue their spiritual practices or *sadhana* working twenty hours a day?" In people's minds, spirituality means someone half-dozing under a tree.

---

1 *bhramhacharis* : one on the path of the Divine, who has formally been initiated into monkhood through a certain energy process.

This is not so. Their work is part of their spiritual growth. Now that Isha is expanding - we want to bring in a significant transformation to the rural areas of Tamil Nadu[1] - our life will become twenty-four hours of activity. Right now, it is already twenty hours; it will increase to twenty-four hours.

The reason for this is, I want them to finish all the allotted energy in their prarabdha karma, let us say, in five years' time. So we keep them this active. If they expend this karma, then there will be no need for action. The action will be by choice. There will be no compulsion to be active. Now if you ask him to just sit here, he will simply sit. There will be no struggle. That's what we are doing in the higher level programs, Bhava Spandana and Samyama, immense activity, body-breaking activity, because you use up that allotted energy for activity faster than you would in normal life. This gives you a space to sit, unmoving. Then meditation will come naturally to you. When there is still unused energy allocated for activity, you cannot sit because the energy is trying to do more.

There are other aspects also to disease. There are karmic reasons why your energy functions in a certain way and causes disease. If people are diseased for karmic reasons, that's different, but many people in the world need not have disease. Today, medical science is more advanced than ever before, yet people have not become free of disease. So both the physical and emotional energies, though they are large allotments, are not being used. The only thing being used is mental energy. What is allotted for thought is being used to a large extent in today's world. For example, let us say there is money allotted in your country's budget: this much for education, this much for development, this much for industry, and this much for power. The major allotment goes toward energy, but it's not used. If you do not use it, your economy suffers. That is all that's happening in the body.

---

1 referring to the Action for Rural Rejuvenation program launched by Sadhguru. This program is to touch five million people in thirteen thousand villages in the state of Tamil Nadu, India.

Seeker: When somebody is incapacitated, like for example my mother, who has a severe disease, and is dependent on others for even simple bodily functions, she suffers so much because somebody else has to do all this 'dirty work' for her. She also feels indebted to them, and at the same time questions why this should be happening to her. How is her karma being worked out, Sadhguru? Is she adding to it with all these emotions and feelings?

Sadhguru: See, why a certain work has become 'dirty' is not because there is anything wrong or improper. It has become dirty in your understanding because of the embarrassment it causes you, and the sense of helplessness and hopelessness it brings to who you are. There never was any problem about somebody helping you, somebody doing your 'dirty work'. All these years when you were well, you had no problem with somebody doing your dirty work; in fact, it felt good that somebody was doing your dirty work. Only now this feeling and emotion has come because of your helplessness. There are various aspects to this. The helplessness is not just physical; it is much more.

Why the world is going the way it is right now - why people are pursuing life the way they are right now is - the only things that are important to people are wealth, power, and pleasure. These are the things which have become the whole guiding force of life. Somewhere in their foolishness they came to this conclusion that if they have enough money, enough power, life is going to be okay, life is going to be fixed for good. It's because of this that people are putting their whole life energy behind it. Then you see that somehow everything that everybody would wish to have, you have, and still your suffering is simply untold. It is not any different from the man on the street. Actually people who have nothing but their four limbs seem to be better than you. Then, there is shame in you, there is disappointment in you, there is shock in you, there is hurt in you which makes you feel hopeless. Above all, your pride is totally mauled by this.

This is not a problem of somebody doing your 'dirty work'; this is the problem of you being helpless, and your ego hurting so badly. So if somebody is doing all this work, what you should feel for them is extreme love, compassion and affection. What your own children or grandchildren would not even do, somebody else is doing, for whatever reason, and they are doing it pretty well. You should become extremely loving, but you become irritable, you become angry; you become all this simply because the problem is just that you are helpless. So definitely with these emotions you are adding to the karma.

About this particular person – your own mother – though she handled her disease quite gracefully at one point, it is becoming more severe and more demanding. Slowly it is beginning to hurt, emotionally and otherwise. This is not because the disease is hurting more, but because she is not able to maintain her dignity and pride, which she managed even in a wheel chair – to some extent – earlier. That's what is hurting right now. So that definitely adds to the karma.

Seeker: Sadhguru, it's very easy to say what should be welling up in you is love and not irritability. This is more easily said than done. I mean, how can this love happen in the individual unless they have risen to such a state within themselves that they are free from all this?

Sadhguru: This is a mistake that people always make. They think that to handle life properly, intelligently, you should have risen to some height. It is not so. The moment you have come here as a human being means you have risen to a certain level of intelligence. That means you have risen to a certain level of capability to handle. That means you have risen to a certain level of freedom and awareness. The moment you come in human form, it is so. You have just gotten entrenched in your own trap that you built out of your pride, your dignity and your egoistic approach to life. Somebody is doing something, which you consider to be dirty, without even making faces about it. If you look at it with openness, only love and affection will come towards that person, nothing else.

I have known many people who were very debilitated with illness; they really had to be helped with their toileting and whatever else. Suddenly, for them – their child, their wife, their husband – nobody really meant anything. That one person who was taking care of them became their everything, and they loved him or her immensely. There have even been situations where they willed their whole property to them because they felt such immense love for that person, for what they were doing. So if you just look at what somebody is doing for you, that is what will happen to you; but you're not even looking at it. You are only looking at what is happening to you. When you look at what is happening to you, pain and hurt will arise in you. If you look at what somebody else is doing for you, then definitely love and affection would arise in you, but you are not at all looking at the other person. You are only looking at yourself: "What is happening to me? What is happening to me?"

Seeker: Master, isn't it unfortunate that not even one percent of the terminally ill get this kind of realization, and use this as an opportunity to grow? In that context, what about the remaining population? I am probably very fortunate to have come in contact with you, but what about people who go through life so blindly? How is it possible for them also to get this kind of an opportunity?

Sadhguru: Whether you come in contact with a *Guru*[1] or not, whether you come in contact with spirituality or not, it doesn't matter. I'm not even talking about somebody being on a spiritual path. Once you have come with the human form, life has given you a certain sense of intelligence, a certain sense of awareness and freedom to choose what you want to be right now, in this moment. Everybody, literate or illiterate, spiritual or non-spiritual, every human being has this within him.

With the whole process of teaching this yoga, that's all we are doing, so that he gets to stand up and exercise his choice in this moment as to how to be, just reminding him that what he is doing, whether positive or negative, is still by choice. The very process of my whole teaching is just this, to make a person aware enough, to knock him on his head and tell him that whatever he does – whether it is love or hate, anger or peacefulness – whatever he does is still by choice. He is doing it by choice, but he has made his choice so one-directional – he has made himself the centerpiece of everything – that he has just discarded the other choices about life. So when you get diseased, when you get severely ill, though physically you are not wishing it upon yourselves consciously, one way or the other you have created it; knowingly or unknowingly it has happened to you, for so many reasons. Now it has come, and when you see someone doing things for you, that you yourself would not do for anyone, if you see what this person is doing, extreme love and compassion will naturally come forth in you. You do not have to create love.

"When I am in pain how can I create love?" You do not have to create love. If you just see what this person is doing for you, love will arise within you. Nature has not put this burden upon you that you have to create love when you are in pain. If you just see what somebody else is doing for you, love will arise within you, affection will arise within you; but right now your whole mental structure and the way you are looking at life has become so self-oriented, you do not want to look at anything else. You are only seeing what is happening to you; you are not seeing what somebody else is doing.

1 Guru : lit. *dispeller of darkness*. A spiritual Master.

Seeker: Sadhguru, that is because somewhere it's like, "Okay, they are just doing it for money; that's their job."

Sadhguru: No. The thing is, "Okay, I paid you money, so you clean up my shit", with this attitude you will definitely suffer. If you had seen, "Money or no money, that is not the point; this person is doing this for me. Without him or her, my life would not exist." If you see it this way, definitely love and affection will arise within you and even this diseased state, though physically painful, can become a liberating experience for you in so many ways. It can become a great realization within you, because in your normal state, the body itself is a big barrier; it is constantly distracting you. When you are diseased, suddenly you realize that your body is not permanent, that it is perishable; so all your focus and energy should shift to a higher dimension. It is a great potential. It has a great potential in it.

Now you don't have any exposure to spirituality, that's not an excuse. Everybody has the intelligence, the awareness and the freedom of choice to do this for themselves, but how many people do it is always questionable. Unfortunately, not many people do it. Even for the person who does the dirty work, instead of seeing what she is doing for somebody else, if she sees what she is doing and how, "What I would not do for myself I am doing for somebody", she will become such a wonderful human being, you understand. But if she is thinking, "Oh, I have got to do this because of this person. I have got to do this because of my economic situation", then she will also create karma. Your mother will also create karma endlessly.

Seeker: That is so in ninety-nine percent of the cases, Sadhguru. Even that one percent I am not too sure... That's how the world is right now; that's how it's happening.

Sadhguru: It's not one hundred percent. I think most of them are off and on. Sometimes they are this way, sometimes they are that way. Some moments they are Realized, some moments they are blind; that is how they go on. That is why they have some moments of joy, some moments of pain, because they are always off and on. If they constantly create misery for themselves, then it will lead to something else. They will become ill in a completely different way. An extended negative karma for a certain period of time will create a different kind of suffering for people.

However, most people are on and off in creating suffering, and most people are on and off in creating liberation also. To stay on consistently is the whole thing. If you stay on with suffering for too long, it will take you to Realization in some way, or it will destroy you. If you stay on with liberation, it will definitely liberate you, but people are always on and off, they are fickle. That is why Krishna says in the *Gita*, "The worst crime in the world is indecision." Mainly it is the fickleness, the unsteady attitude. There is no *nischala tathwam*, no 'one direction of energy'. You are going in different directions all the time. So the life energy is confused; it does not know where to go or what to do. Only with human nature has this freedom been given to you, that you can decide the direction of your life energies. For animals it is not so; the direction of their life energies is decided. It just goes that way, whichever way they go; but for human nature, this freedom has been given. It's a benediction, but you're using it as a curse.

Seeker: I have, in my own family, people who were ill and I have handled them. When I'm with them part of me does not react to anything; it does not touch me. It is not that I'm indifferent to their suffering. I can respond to life-suffering around me, but I just do what is best and leave it at that. I wonder at times what people think about me. Can you say something about it, Sadhguru?

Sadhguru: (Laughs) What they are thinking about you? I will answer the last question first: heartless. They are not even thinking; they made the conclusion long ago. Now the thing is, what is it that you are responding to? Is it responding to just some life-suffering?

Seeker: No, it could be more because it is someone in my family.

Sadhguru: Oh, "It's my family, it's my thing." That's what is causing the suffering.

Seeker: But Sadhguru, can't they see that I become dispassionate because something in me says that all emotion is only because one gets identified with someone or something as their own?

Sadhguru: Every suffering that you see – whether a worm, insect, bird, animal or human being – if your whole system, your energy or your emotions, everything – responds to it, that is wonderful. Once you start responding to everything, you will see that your response has to move into deeper dimensions within yourself. It cannot be psychological and emotional anymore, otherwise it will only lead to madness.

Seeker: Yes, exactly.

Sadhguru: See, now this tree branch is broken; my energy responds to it, but my emotions do not. Sometimes I allow myself the luxury of responding emotionally also. It's a luxury for me. Once in a while I allow myself to respond emotionally also to some type of suffering around me; otherwise, I don't emotionally respond to any suffering around me. This is coming because there is enough control over the situation. There was a time when, if I just looked at anybody's face on the streets, just seeing that they are not happy enough would bring tears to my eyes. Once it becomes so deep that you start responding to every life and whatever is happening, then there is no way to exist here. You have to dissolve; that's all there is. So naturally you will come to a deeper understanding within yourself, that psychologically and emotionally you don't respond anymore. On a much deeper level you naturally respond, but it is no more emotional and psychological, and it is good. It's a big step ahead in life, not responding to things emotionally and psychologically, not because you are putting up a barrier between you and their suffering. You're very much open to their suffering, you are very much a part of it, but still, emotionally and psychologically you do not suffer, or you are not disturbed on that level. It's a huge step to take. Now for people, the suffering is not about life going on like this. If that was it, if they had that sense, the world would be a different place altogether; but now the thing is, my father, my mother, my house, my something is suffering; that's the whole problem. So this has nothing to do with them. It's only about you.

When I was just about eleven years, maybe twelve, a certain situation occurred between my mother and me. See, an Indian mother would never come and tell her child, "I love you", or something like that. Maybe today you do it a little bit, but an Indian mother would never – at least my mother would never. Such a necessity was not there at all. Everything she did in her life was for us. We knew that, so she never had to say it. It's almost a sacrilege to say it. That's the kind of situation it was. Now something happened and she expressed herself in a tender way to me – not exactly telling me, "I love you." It's a rare thing to happen. Then I asked her a simple question – you know, my thoughts were in a certain way by then - "If I was born in the next house, would you still feel this way about me?" She felt so hurt, so offended, and with tears welling up in her eyes, she went away. I didn't think anything about it. I just asked a simple question, which was not an issue for me within myself. I knew very well that if I had been born in the next house she would not be feeling like this about me. I knew that very well; it was very clear to me in my mind. So that was why I just asked her. Then after half an hour, she came to me and not knowing what to say, still in tears, she touched my feet and went away. That also did not mean much to me. I knew she was trying to come to terms with it. She saw the point of what I was saying, but her emotions were struggling to come to terms with it. She knew it was true, but at the same time there was a struggle within, because it would have brought up many things, maybe about all her other children, her husband, her house, her father, her mother, everything. Probably it would have all come up in her mind and the whole struggle and turmoil was because of this.

So this is all about 'mine'. What is mine is just an extended me. Isn't it? The very reason why, on the spiritual path, all possessions are taken away, is so that what is 'me' becomes small inside this flesh. Right now, this big house is me, this car is me, this property is me, you know? These acres of land are me. Everything is me actually. If somebody damages the house it hurts me, as if it is me, isn't it? If somebody damages the car, it hurts me. So you're just extending the ego, extending this 'me', trying to find extensions to what you call as 'myself' outside, which is a falsehood. This is happening with a wrong identification with many things, which is the fundamentals of ignorance, which is the very foundation of all ignorance in the world – your wrong identifications. The whole spiritual process is to remove the identification even with the physical body. So extending your identification to many things outside is absolutely stupid.

Your feeling hurt because, "My mother or my child is ill" is coming from sheer ignorance. Does it mean you do not care? Does it mean you should not take care? Does it mean to say you do not do anything about it? No. You do everything that you can do about it, and there is only so much that you can do about anybody. It does not matter how much you love them, there is only that much you can do; whether they live or die is not decided by you. You will do the best you can do with what means you have. It's not even the best in the world. With the available means, accordingly you will do your best.

So all this is happening. It's just that emotionally you are not greatly hurt. You're still laughing, you're still enjoying your food, you're still going to the cinema, you're still doing everything and you're still meditating peacefully. This offends people who are emotionally attached. They will get so offended, they will think you are heartless. They will think you're a stone or whatever else, but I would say stones are better than stupid human beings, because they do not cause any harm to anybody. They are just there, not doing anything. Maybe they are meditating, because people who want to meditate always go to the mountains to be infected by the rocks. They go to the rocks to learn meditation.

I heard that an actress had said that one place which is truly spiritual for her is some rock in Bombay. She said, "This rock, I sit near this rock and I find so many answers to so many of my questions." Definitely a big rock seems to be wiser and better than any stupid human being.

Seeker: Sadhguru, how would the human race perpetuate itself if total dispassion arises? Isn't that why people fear spirituality also?

Sadhguru: People have understood dispassion as becoming dry and senseless. Dispassion is not dry and senseless; dispassion means that the bondage with life is gone. Freedom has come. Once freedom has come, how you respond to life is in your hands, isn't it? If freedom has come, in terms of your thought and emotion, you can respond. You don't have to become like a stone; you will respond as it is needed. There are situations where even if people are in extreme suffering or pain, I don't even look at them. There are situations where, for the smallest things, I will shed tears with them. So this is by choice; this is what dispassion means.

Whether it is your family or anybody else that you are taking physical responsibility for; or if there is somebody lying ill on the street, in terms of my life response, it's still the same. If my mother is ill or this woman on the street is ill, it is the same response. As far as I'm concerned, as a human being, my response is the same, but in terms of what I can physically do, it may alter depending upon my capabilities. What I could do for my mother, if I had the capability to do it for everybody physically, I would love to do it. I'm sure most human beings, or every human being who is willing to look at himself with a little openness, is the same, is it not so? If you had the means to take care of the whole world the way you take care of your mother, everybody who has looked at his life with a little sense would naturally do that; but right now it's a question of capability.

That is so even for your mother, isn't it? Even though you feel so much for her, what you can do may be limited. For many people here in India, if somebody is ill with cancer, they may not be able to do much because they cannot take their mother to America or they do not have the economic means even to seek the local treatment. So it doesn't mean that they love them less than somebody else who is capable of providing all those things for their mothers; it's just that they cannot do it. So maybe they will just give them plain water, hold their hands, sit through their pain, do whatever else they can do and allow them to die.

In terms of their karma, in terms of life, it's not any different. They let them die physically, but still everything that can be done for a human being has been done. Your life response need not change. It does not matter who it is or what it is, whether it's an apple, potato, chicken, mother, father or a tree, your response is still the same. But what you do physically is at your discretion, depending upon your capabilities, energies, possibilities, inclinations, time, life – so many aspects are involved.

Seeker: I was thinking more in terms of human perpetuation. Won't the human race come to a halt with dispassion, Sadhguru?

Sadhguru: No. Wouldn't it be very, very beautiful if human beings conceived consciously, because it is needed for the human race rather than out of their own physical compulsions? Wouldn't it be so much more beautiful if they created this very consciously – this being is needed for human life to happen and you produce it with that consciousness, rather than out of your compulsions? Is it not in many ways an indignity to the person who is born that he or she is born out of your compulsions, not out of your consciousness?

Seeker: But Sadhguru, it is not that everybody goes for a child with a compulsion. For some it is out of love for a child – maybe because it is their child, a little extension of their womb, something of theirs.

Sadhguru: See, when you say, "love for their child", where did you get love for your unborn child? When you have no love for life around you, it is still a compulsion. When I say 'compulsion', the compulsion need not necessarily be just physical; the compulsions can be psychological and emotional. There is a need to extend yourself, something that is you. Most people want to have children because they want an extension of themselves. They want something to leave behind when they go. Children are their greatest property.

Seeker: So it is more instinct, isn't it, Sadhguru?

Sadhguru: Physically it is an instinct. Emotionally, psychologically, it's not an instinct; it's a trick that you play. Physically it is an instinct, but emotionally and psychologically it is a trick, it's a ploy that you're creating to extend yourself. Do you see, when people who take up some cause in their life, whatever cause – they are fighting for the freedom of their country, they have a political cause or some other cause – when they get too intensely involved in that, they have no need to produce children because they are extending themselves in some other way where their involvement is much more?

Fundamentally, bearing a child has become such a big experience in people's lives because only by bearing a child can most people know a certain sense, or a certain depth of involvement and inclusion with life. With nothing else are they so deeply involved. They are incapable of being deeply involved with this tree. They are incapable of being deeply involved with the air around them. Their only capability is to be involved with a child, because a child does not have so much personality, or does not have personality at all when it comes into your hands. Another thing is because your identification is so much with the physical body, something that comes out of your body is definitely yours. You may say, "My house is mine," but you know you can lose it. You may say, "This property is mine," but you may lose it; but this comes out of your biological body and you cannot deny it. Even if your son denies it, still you know he's anyway yours. So it's a sure-fire extension of yourself.

People are seeking children only because of that; that's the only way they know involvement. Otherwise, they are incapable of being involved. Why, especially for a woman, bearing a child has become such a big experience is just because of her involvement; otherwise, she is never really involved with anybody for that matter. Very few people can involve themselves to that extent in their love affairs also. Even there, the involvement is because bodies touch. Because their identification is with the physical body, the only way they know to involve themselves is by opening their body. Only when a person rises to another level of experience, their involvement with something else or somebody else goes to great depths without physical involvement, because now identification with the body is receding. Identification with the other dimension of yourself is building momentum.

So a child is a deep involvement. People are hankering for children because they are seeking involvement; otherwise, what is life? If you have never tasted life, by bearing a child you're getting involved with life. With nothing else are you involved; but if you know how to involve yourself with everything around you, you will see a child is not an emotional or psychological compulsion anymore. It would be very wonderful if people chose to have children, rather than bringing them through physical, psychological or emotional compulsions within themselves.

Seeker: Jaggi, when it comes to women and children in India, it is considered very inauspicious for a barren woman to attend some of the social gatherings and celebrations, so isn't it also a social compulsion for a woman to bear children?

Sadhguru: What is auspicious? What is auspicious in the society is decided by certain people and you know how sensibly those people are living their lives, first of all! Those women who have a dozen children, in what way are they more complete than somebody who does not have children and is still happy?

One person does not have children by choice, and maybe someone else is incapable of bearing a child due to some biological reason; then she suffers, since she is incapable of doing something that is a simple biological function of being a woman.

It's like Joe, who was eighty-four years of age; he went to the doctor. The doctor asks, "Joe, what's your problem?" Joe says, "Doctor, I am not able to pee!" The doctor thought for a while and then said, "Joe, you are eighty-four years old; have you not peed enough?" It's just a simple biological function. So if the woman has chosen not to have children, she has no problems with it by herself. It is just that social stigma can come for anything that you do. Even if you sit and meditate you may get a social stigma! (Laughs)

Seeker: Sadhguru, could this stigma also have come due to the social structure? Just like a barren land is no good, in the same way, a barren woman is no good?

Sadhguru: In Indian society, the social structures were mostly agriculture based. This whole society was agriculture based at one time. For a very long time – for thousands of years – India has had an agro-based society, not a hunting-gathering kind. Only small tribal segments have been the hunting-gathering kind. Agriculture is always labor-intensive. Today we hire labor to do things, it's a different situation, but back then everybody was working on their own lands and making their own food from the land. So, how many children you had was a great asset; especially if you had male children, it was a great asset. As you know, women who have only girls are also considered inauspicious. Only when she bears a boy is she auspicious. The king determined this, because without a boy there is nobody to take over his position. He wants only his blood to take over this position, which is just an extension of himself. His son ruling the kingdom is just like him continuing to rule the kingdom after his death. If somebody else takes it, it's not good enough; that's the mentality.

So, children were a very important part of life for survival and for economic and social situations. Also, people did not experience life to any depth with any other aspect except by bearing children. It's as if you have not experienced life. Like our meditators will go and talk to somebody: "Oh, you did not experience *Samyama*? It is no good for you to be living." Just like that, a woman who has borne a child has experienced some intense moments of being involved with another being in some way. When she sees another woman who does not have children, she thinks that the woman has not known this involvement with life at all – it could be true. This involvement matures the person in so many ways, so the other is scoffing at the one who does not have a child, "You have not known involvement; you are barren with life. Not only as a physical body you are barren, you are barren with life! You have not known life." Like people are saying, "If you have not known *Bhava Spandana*[1] you are barren with life," or "If tears of joy and tears of peace and love have not washed your cheeks, you are barren." Just like that they are speaking to the childless woman.

---

1 Bhava Spandana : This four day high intensity residential program is offered as a part of Isha Yoga programs.

There are various aspects involved – social, economic, emotional, physical and biological aspects also. Over a period of time, if such a natural function as child bearing does not happen, she is a freak in some way, as far as the society is concerned. So whatever you are incapable of, people have always made fun of. If you cannot hear, they will make fun of it. If you cannot walk, they will make fun of it. It took a lot of time, evolution and culture for people to understand that if someone cannot walk, it is not a laughing matter. He needs love, compassion and support. Similarly, if somebody cannot bear a child, she needs love, compassion and support. It will take a lot of time for people to understand that. I think people are beginning to understand that now, which they did not in the past.

Seeker: Master, I have seen many people who are afflicted with different kinds of diseases come to the ashram. They are put on various practices and regimens alone, without any medication, but their conditions improve dramatically. For example, how was the physician from the US, who had an ischemic heart condition, able to trek in the Himalayas? Doug's knee, which showed torn cartilage on the MRI, is now fine and he is no longer in pain. How does this happen?

Sadhguru: The life energies within you created a whole body, isn't it? Even your brains were created by that. When you were born, your body was so small and today it became all this. Nobody is stretching you from outside, are they? Whatever is creating the body is within you. Your whole body, all the bones, all the blood, all the flesh and everything, including your brain, was created by this energy. So when it can do so much, can it not fix a little cartilage? Of course, it is not true for everybody. See here, Gina, her mother fed her with sheep brains (laughs). So even sheep brains can be a contributor! The only reason why it is not fixing it is that you're not in touch with it. You're creating a distance from it because you have formed such individual nonsense within yourself. You have identified yourself with your clothes, with your house, with cars and people - all kinds of stuff except your life energies. The more you identify with these things, the less and less of energy you become and the more and more inanimate you become.

When certain things happen and that person completely gives himself to me, at that moment, it's very easy to activate his energies in a certain way and whatever is not proper in the body will be corrected; but this energy is capable of doing that all the time. This energy is what is running your life. It is not you running this life; it's being done by this energy. Now you have read a textbook about digestion and assimilation and you think you are doing all that. Where are you doing it? At least Americans think they are, because before each meal they are reading labels about how much magnesium, how much calcium there is in the food – they are not reading the Bible anymore, they are reading labels – because they think they are doing everything. You're not doing it; this life energy has always been doing it. So if you just allow it for a moment, it will do anything.

Seeker: Sadhguru, when you say, "If somebody gives themselves in one moment," what the hell does that mean?

Sadhguru: Drop your hell! That's what it means. Right now, you are identified with everything you are not. You are functioning within the limitations of your likes and your opinions. You're sitting here, listening to me because what I'm saying is still appealing to your logic. Though we are going into the realm of the mystical, which is mumbo-jumbo to you, still it is perfectly logical. If I do not speak logically, you will not sit here. I know that. That means you have not given yourself totally; but there are moments when all your logic falls apart, you stop identifying yourself with things that you are not and you have just given yourself. In one moment, in bowing down to me, they kept their identities aside and that was all

Seeker: Where are those moments, Sadhguru?

Sadhguru: It does not matter; don't look for those moments, because you cannot create them. When you are completely overwhelmed by someone's presence, you do not exist. Otherwise, you have no way to dissolve yourself. It's a waste of time trying to do that

Seeker: Sadhguru, I am always overwhelmed by your presence

Sadhguru: Yes, but not enough, not to a point where you do not exist. Not enough yet. You can only be overwhelmed by that which is beyond you. You will not be overwhelmed by that which is you. So this talk is just that, without demanding any kind of faith or belief, we're still trying to overwhelm you. Normally, overwhelming you was done only with faith. The whole world always has been talking about faith, just to overwhelm you. Do you understand? People have been talking about miracles just to overwhelm you. Whether the miracles are true or not, consciously false miracles are also being created just to overwhelm you.

Once, a magician was on a cruise liner and he had a parrot that had seen all the magician's tricks a zillion times. He had figured out long ago how the magician made everything in the act disappear. The parrot grew to be bored, his owner growing stale and not developing any new tricks that the parrot could not figure out. One night, in the middle of the magician's performance, the ship hit an iceberg and sank. Everyone sank except the magician and the parrot. The magician managed to swim to a piece of wreckage and climb onto it. He immediately collapsed from exhaustion. Soon afterwards, the parrot flew there, and perched on the edge of the makeshift raft. It stared at the magician, and stared at the magician and stared at the magician. For a whole day, the magician was unconscious and all this time the parrot did not take his eyes off him. Eventually, the magician started to stir. Looking up, he saw the parrot eyeing him intently. Another hour went by and finally the parrot squawked, "All right, I give up; what did you do with the damn ship?" Here, we are not using those methods. With thinking and investigative minds, it will not work, so we are overwhelming you in a completely different way. Only when you are overwhelmed, you do not exist. When you are totally overwhelmed, when you do not exist, you become available in a completely different way.

Seeker: Sadhguru, if someone is ill and they give themselves to you and you activate energies in a certain way and their condition is corrected, is that true for just some people whose condition you have become aware of or for everyone?

Sadhguru: That's true for everyone. With these people something was noticeably wrong. With so many other people, just like that they're feeling so much younger and better. Is it not so? It's because the same thing has happened, but there is no specific damage that shows, that has been rectified.

Seeker: Sadhguru, is it not only with physical disease but with mental illness as well?

Sadhguru: It is with mental illness also, but mental illness is at a deeper level than physical illness, so it takes much more

Seeker: Then what does it take, Sadhguru?

Sadhguru: You are dropping your identifications only in installments. Jeanne probably had seventy-two pairs of pants. I told her, "You just keep six pairs of pants. The rest, you just give them away." She cried, "How can I give them away? They are good ones; I paid so much money." I said, "You give them away; just keep six pairs of pants. Anyway you can only wear one at a time. Six will do for you; seventy-two are not needed." Why is giving away your pants so difficult? It is because you are identified with them. When she gave them away, the first pair or two hurt, but as she gave away more and more, her identification became less and less. Now with six pairs the identification is not gone, but it is lowered. If you completely drop your identifications, you will become Realized.

Seeker: Sadhguru, I have heard that this doctor with the heart problem has recovered miraculously and trekked in the Himalayas. What was the significance of having her sleep in the Dhyanalinga[1] temple before she left on the Himalayan trek?

Sadhguru: The general and the fundamental dimension of the Dhyanalinga is spiritual, but all the other dimensions are there in it. There are temples and situations which are made for certain specific purposes. Suppose I take certain people to such places; I always make them receptive in a particular way, to that particular energy which is present in that place. Suppose I take somebody to some *Devi* temple, which is a feminine aspect, which is very powerful. If somebody needs to receive that in a particular way, then I do certain things with them so that they can receive that dimension very well.

This doctor's problem was in a specific dimension. So we just made her in such a way that she was more receptive to that dimension alone, when she slept there. You saw, the very first day, or the second day

1 Dhyanalinga : a powerful energy form consecrated exclusively for the purpose of meditation. At Isha Yoga Center.

probably after she came to India, we took her off the breathing support device she was using. She thought this was impossible because of her tracheal collapse problem. When she would lie down, her trachea would collapse and she'd suffocate. Without the device she slept here at the *ashram*, for about a week. Then she traveled on the train. No chance of having the device there, and in the Himalayas, no possibility at all. She went through the whole trip without it. Now if she starts descending from that which was offered to her, you will find, probably in a few months' time, she will need the device again. If she does not descend, if she has sense and she enhances what has been offered to her, then she will never need it; but if she just drops from that, probably in a few months' time... How long has it been?

Seeker: Three or four months, Sadhguru.

Sadhguru: Any time now, we cannot really gauge it exactly, but I would say anywhere between three to six months she may start needing the breathing aid again if she does not handle that situation sensibly within herself. I hope she does not do that to herself, but it's very much possible.

Seeker: Master, when you say, "handle that situation," what do you mean?

Sadhguru: (Laughs) Handling it improperly or handling it properly, what it means is: in a way, you were made receptive to certain energies. That energy did things that you could never imagine doing. This doctor's case is quite dramatic. With many other people it may not be so dramatically there, but it is there. Every time this happens, the first day they are all grateful, tears flowing. Within three days they just think, "It's me." The moment they get identified with that and think it is all them, then you will see it will recede, because it cannot stay in your identification. Once it recedes, all your problems will be back. The change is still only on the level of her energy. For it to manifest itself physiologically, it will take a while. If that time is not allowed, very easily people can revert themselves back to their old ways. Already, somebody told me Doug's knee is paining again.

Seeker: Sadhguru, when something is offered to any one of us and we are receptive enough to receive it, should we keep it as a gift we can use, as something we don't identify ourselves with?

Sadhguru: It's not like that. It is not like it's there as a gift to be used. Right now, you are breathing. The air that you breathe is not you; it is coming from outside, isn't it? But you never acknowledge it. So many of your diseases are just because of that. The food that you eat, it's not you, isn't it? You never acknowledge that. If you go like this, what is it that is you? There is nothing in you that you can call 'you'. In some way, the food that you eat, the air that you breathe, has gotten integrated and has started functioning as a physical body, and you call that 'me'. Because you call that 'me', it is functioning in a limited way. If you do not call it as 'you', if it's really not in your identification, then it will function in an enormous way.

For example, in Doug's case or anybody's – there are many other people like that – we have made them receptive in a particular way, a receptivity beyond the normal sense of eating food or breathing air and whatever else. It's a little above that. Before this, you were still taking in physical quantities and making them into physical quantities. Now here, you are receiving an energy situation, which changes – it's not that it changes everything, but it just triggers things in a certain way. So your whole system begins to function in a different way because of this influence. The first three days you understood it as, "This is not me; this is Grace;" but within a week's time, it becomes, "Okay, it is me and Sadhguru;" then in a month's time, "It's all me!" This is happening, isn't it? The moment you go this way, Grace recedes, because it cannot be there once you bring in your identification.

Seeker: Today, we are seeing so many people going to psychologists for treatment. It seems every single person has a shrink that he sees at least once a week. Why are we becoming so troubled? Are we all going crazier by the day, Sadhguru?

Sadhguru: Today, ninety percent of the people are in different states of mental sickness. It's just that the level of sickness is sometimes manageable, sometimes unmanageable. Let's say you have asthma. Sometimes your asthma is manageable, so you do not consider yourself as sick. You take some syrup or some tablet and you manage. On a particular day, you become really sick and you either totally collapse or are hospitalized.

Only then you consider yourself as sick, isn't it? That does not mean the other days you were not sick; you were sick, but it was manageable.

Similarly with the mental states, almost everybody is sick. It's just that they are in some manageable level of sickness. Once in a while, they flare up for some time and then they settle down again. They are managing, but the madness is very much there. Now all the psychologists and the psychiatrists have only studied sick people. People like Freud never found a meditator or a Buddha to study. He would have studied only those people who are in different states of mental sickness; either manageably mad or unmanageably mad, whichever way. They only studied mad people, and the one who is studying is also mad. He is equally mad. It's not that he has transcended his limitations.

On a certain day, it happened like this. Three psychiatrists were traveling together on a train from Germany to France, to attend the annual all-psychiatrists seminar. Sitting there, they started confiding to each other their greatest secrets. The first one said, "My greatest weakness is compulsive gambling. Every weekend, I take off from the clinic and let myself go full blast. Of course, I put all the money that I earn from my gambling spree into some charity box, and mind you, I don't start stealing from another charity box until I go drinking. Then I get sodden drunk and finish the night in the gutter." The second psychiatrist nodded his head in understanding and said, "Well, my greatest secret is that I am so dependant on taking anti-depressants all the time, and I have to gulp down an extra double dosage before I sit in consultation with my patients." The third one sat there very smug and quiet. So the other two prodded her, "What about you? We've told you our deepest secrets. Now you have to tell us yours." The third psychiatrist said, "Well, I'm a diagnosed gossiper, and I can't wait to get off this train!"

Whatever problem you have - anxiety, fear, psychosis or anything – according to that, they put you into the corresponding category and they have a treatment for that; and what kind of treatment it is! Somehow adjusting the whole situation and making you manageably mad, not making you sane. Nobody can make you sane, please know this. From unmanageable madness, they can bring you down to manageable madness. Everybody has learned the trick to manage the madness. Now this process of spirituality is not about moving into manageable madness. It's about going so mad that you become sane.

Okay? You cross the limits of madness, then you become perfectly sane. See, you're born with the madness; the karma itself is madness. The very bondages that you have created for yourself, the limitations that you have created for yourself, are they not madness?

If there is a mad man who thinks he's tied to this column - there is no rope, there is no chain, but he thinks he's tied to the column - he will only go around this, round and round. Whatever you tell him, he will not listen, because he feels he is tied to the column. Isn't this the way everybody is living, tied to some column? So it's the same madness. Being manageably mad or unmanageably mad really makes no difference. At least, if you become unmanageably mad, you can enjoy yourself in the asylum. You don't have to be ashamed of being mad anymore! You can just freak out the way you want to. You don't have to bother about controlling it. It's such a big strain to control that madness. Do you know why a person growing on the spiritual path looks totally crazy? It is because he is pushing himself to the point beyond madness, where it cannot touch him any more.

These meditations at *Isha*[1] are not about you becoming peaceful. They are about blasting yourself into bits until there is no peace and no disturbance within you; only that can be called as peace. If you get disturbed and then make yourself peaceful, that's not peace; it's just a lull. This peace is like the eye of the hurricane where everything is calm. The hurricane is blowing like mad and in between, suddenly there is total calm. Do not be fooled by this calm, it's just a small respite. The next gust will come again and it will be even worse than before. Hurricanes always move like this; because of the centrifugal and centripetal forces and the forward motion, the front end of the hurricane is less forceful than the rear end. So what you see first is nothing compared to what's going to come. That will be much bigger. The same goes with your mind.

Everything in existence is like that. Whatever blows with force is like that. It will blow, then give a little space and then again blow. The mind is also like that; it goes through a phase of disturbance then it comes back to peace. Don't ever think it is peace; it's just a break in the madness. Even mad people are perfectly

---

1 Isha : formless Divine energy. Also the name chosen by Sadhguru for the foundation he created to offer a spiritual possibility to all humankind.

sane in some moments in their life. Don't think they are twenty-four hours mad. Sometimes they are very sane and perfectly okay, and sometimes they just go off; they are more spontaneous than you. See, the man who has lost his so-called mental balance is a lot more spontaneous than you, isn't he? But you are also doing what he is doing.

Seeker: Sadhguru, does spirituality have a treatment for our depressions, our neuroses, and our madness?

Sadhguru: The way of treating madness on the spiritual path is very different. Generally, if somebody goes really mad, especially with psychological problems, what they do is take him to the master at a monastery or an ashram. See, if this person remains in the family, they try to attend to him too much, do everything for him. Now if they take him to the hospital or the asylum, there also they will attend to him, guard him, do many things. If they take him to a Buddhist monastery for example, there, they will just leave him, ignore him completely. He shouts, raves, throws stones; whatever he does, nobody reacts. Everybody just goes about doing their own work, not reacting to any madness. Within a few days this person will settle down and become peaceful, because without attention, his madness cannot go on.

Madness is just a trip of the ego. It's like a power trip, or electrical trip; it overflows. Similarly, madness is simply an overflowing of your ego. That's all it is. So just ignore the man. Put him in a corner. Don't bother about him. Don't even call him for food. Just leave him. If the fellow is really hungry he will come and eat; otherwise, he will just work out his madness and become okay. The atmosphere is right, the energy is high. Slowly, that man will settle down and then he will come and say, "Teach me meditation." Ignore the madness and it will die by itself. Your madness also, you attend to it too much. You should not.

Seeker: Master, I hope I never go mad.

Sadhguru: What makes you think that you're not mad right now? The limitations that you have set upon yourselves, are they not madness? Madness does not necessarily mean that you have to take off your clothes, go on the street and run. Mad people are of different varieties. They need not necessarily be laughing and rolling or ranting and raving. Some mad people are very serious. Others are in some other way. Madness is just the ego. It needs some expression. Now a tremendous amount of time and energy is spent to cover your madness. One way of handling it is to cover it up. Another way is to transcend it. If you cover it up, you will only fool other people who will think that you're a perfectly balanced person; but you suffer for the madness that you cover up and keep within yourself. It will grow and you will pay the price for keeping it within. If you transcend this madness, there is something else which opens up, a new fragrance, a new light.

Everybody has become a great master in cover-up jobs. Do see, you are a fantastic actor all your life. You fool the world, you fool the people close to you and you fool yourself. You tell your friends, "I think I have found inner peace. My therapist told me that a way to achieve inner peace was to finish things I had started. So today, I finished two bags of potato chips, an extra large supreme pizza with all the toppings, a lemon pie, a big box of chocolate candy and drowned it all with half a case of beer. I feel better already." Maybe you can only fool yourself like this and to that extent you can put up an act, isn't it? So much negativity you think you can drown with a beer. You cover it up so beautifully.

It is layers and layers of madness. This is not just something you gathered in a few years. It's an accumulation of many lifetimes. Layers and layers of madness have been accumulated. It has to be worked out. There is no other way. Either you drop the whole thing and walk away or slowly you cleanse the bag. The moment you lose your madness, if you really lose your madness, you are meditative. How else can you be? That's all meditation is. For a while, during meditation, you are bypassing your madness and experiencing a little bit of sanity. The mind settles down and you are just there. Otherwise it is going non-stop. The moment you're out of your madness, you are always meditative; there is no other way to be. Your mind itself is madness. Whichever way it is, it is madness. Transcending that is sanity.

Seeker: Sadhguru, are action and psychology connected? Since I was a kid, I always got into intense activity to such an extent that I would exhaust myself. I would go swimming, biking, trekking, all-night dancing or running intensely if there was nothing else to do. Was I working out my madness, unconsciously?

Sadhguru: They are connected in many ways. So Tina, if you had not been into all this activity, we know where you would have landed up by now! (Laughs).

Seeker: In the loony bin!?

Sadhguru: Yes! During the Isha Yoga programs, when you really let yourself go, you saw that the madness is a part of you and not something being put into you by anyone. Maybe it is hidden, or covered, but it's very much a part of you. All your effort in life, conscious and unconscious, is to cover this madness, this insanity which is there within, to give it a nice outlook, a nice image.

The whole world itself is going through a unique kind of neurosis, which was not there in the past. This is simply because modern man has stopped using his body to a large extent. In the past, when you intensely involved yourself in physical activity, a lot of your neurosis was worked out. Your nervous energy got spent. I know many people, especially young people, who had psychological problems. They just started swimming or playing some sport daily and then everything became okay; because of enough activity, the energy was expended.

Today, man has become physically inactive like never before – he could not afford to be so physically inactive before, he had to do so many things physically, just to survive. So he has become more neurotic than in the past. As a general phenomenon, there were neurotic people then also, but not in these numbers. Today, it has become a common phenomenon in society that everybody is in some level of neurosis. This is simply because your energy is not worked out; it's trapped. You have not transcended your madness and at the same time you're not working it out. The therapy also is not there. If you went out and chopped wood for the whole day – if you chopped a hundred logs a day – a lot of your energy would be spent, and life would be peaceful; but today it's not like that. You are not using your body the way it used to be used, so you go on generating all kinds of diseases, like never before.

This builds up into your system over a period of time. Then your physical and emotional energy need some outlet. That is how your bars, your clubs and your discotheques have come into place. People have to work out their neurosis somewhere, somehow. These discos look like madness, you can't even breathe inside. They are full of smoke and sweat but people are just going wild. You can't even dance; everybody is bumping into everybody else, but it doesn't matter. You have to work it out, otherwise you will go crazy. So on Saturday, you go work out your neurosis for the week. Then the piling up starts once more and once again the Saturday night fever comes. There is another way to drop this madness and go ahead, completely leaving it behind and going ahead where you are no more a part of it. This is what meditation is all about. Now, if you dance, you simply dance for the joy of it, and not because there is something to work out. If you're dancing to work out something, maybe it is therapeutic. It is good therapy all right, but there is a certain ugliness about it. It is lusty; u cannot dance out of love. You can only dance out of lust.

Do you know the difference between love and lust? Lust is a strong need. Love is not a need. When you love, you settle down; nothing more is needed. You can just sit here for a lifetime. With lust you can't sit anywhere; you either get into some mad action, or you are bound to go crazy. When there is a certain neurosis, a certain madness within yourself, you can only be in lust. Your lust can be for sex, for food or for some particular activity or some hobby, it doesn't matter what it is, but you develop lust for something. Without that lust you cannot live. Even your work is an effective way of throwing out your lust. It's just that it is the most popular and accepted way in the world. Today people just go on working, working and working. Not because they are creating something fantastic, but simply because they have to work, otherwise they don't know what to do with themselves.

You have to guard that madness cautiously. Nobody ever knows that you have this within yourself and you yourself would like to forget it. You do everything possible to forget it. All the entertainment in the world has come just to hide your madness. If you were perfectly sane, you would not need entertainment. You need entertainment just to cover your madness. If we take away your entertainment, you will go crazy. Do you understand? Man needs entertainment simply to hide his madness. If he was perfectly sane, he would not need entertainment. He could just sit and watch this bamboo grow. He does not really need entertainment.

Seeker: There are various types of healing going on around the world. Does the karma that is appeased through this take effect in some other way? Also, Sadhguru, in what way is psychic surgery, that is sort of getting popular now in India, different from the various other healings?

Sadhguru: See, everything always functions between cause and effect. Physical existence is always happening between cause and effect. Suppose there is an infection and the cause was bacteria. You eat or drink something somewhere and get infected; so the cause was bacteria. Now there is an effect, infection. For this you're trying to take away the cause by taking antibiotics. There, you kill the cause with medication because it is external to you. With other diseases that are not externally caused, but are happening from within the body, the cause is so much deeper compared to an infection. For this type of disease to manifest, there is an imbalance or a malfunction in the energy body, which is manifesting itself in the physical body, or sometimes in the mental body.

Now with *pranic*[1] healing – or any kind of healing for that matter – you are only appeasing the effect. In a way, what you're doing is that, with a little control or mastery over your own energies, you are able to put a screen between the cause and the effect. So the effect dies out, but the cause is buried.

It's like this: one sunny day, the owner of a drug store walked in to find a guy leaning heavily against the wall. The owner asked the clerk, "What's with that guy over there by the wall?" The clerk replied, "Well, he came in here this morning, to get something for his cough. I couldn't find the cough syrup so I gave him an entire box of laxatives." The owner yelled, "You idiot, you can't treat a cough with a box of laxatives!" The clerk said, "Of course you can. Look at him, he's afraid to cough."

So as far as nature is concerned, as far as this life energy is concerned, the effect was only its way of telling you that there is a cause inside of you. What we call as 'cause', the disturbance of energy, is trying to manifest itself in a certain way. Let us say you have asthma. Today I just remove your asthma. Without asthma in you, but still with the same type of energy, you may become some other type of calamity in a moment. The disease may not be there, but you may get into an accident. Your asthma was only an

---

1 pranic : of *prana*, the fundamental life force, the vital energy.

indication of a deeper disturbance. If we take away your asthma, it may manifest in some other way, in some other calamity. This may happen simply because your energies are still in the same situation, but its effect is gone; so it will take effect in a deeper or more acute way to inform you again. If you bring awareness to your disease, you are trying to get connected to the cause of it.

When we talk about bringing awareness to your disease, when we talk about accepting what is there, it does not mean becoming defeated by your disease. If you truly become aware of the disease, then you become aware of the cause also. The moment you bring awareness to any part of your body, in terms of energy, it will immediately become active and different things start happening there. Just as an experiment, if you carefully attend to any part of your body – not necessarily the chakras,[1] any part of your body – put your attention there and just be with that. You will see that so much energy activity will begin to happen there, because if you bring awareness and consciousness to that part of the body, naturally life energies become enhanced. Like this, one could heal something and change the energy situation to some extent.

Now you are asking about the popular healing business that is going on right now. See, one aspect of pranic healing is trying to focus your mind on someone or something, which you intend to heal. This is only one part of it. Why did the energy body get disturbed, first of all? For the energy body to be disturbed, either there is an improper lifestyle, improper thought patterns, improper emotions, or all these put together. There is a certain karmic structure that you have built which is causing a vacuum, some kind of turmoil to your energy, which is manifesting itself in the physical body as disturbed energy. So, even if you settle the energy situation to some extent with healing, or mental focus or with a certain sense of awareness, still the karmic substance which is causing this is not gone. The karmic substance is recorded in your energy as the fundamental software. It can work only within the ambit of the programmed software.

---

1 chakras : One hundred and twelve plus two points in the energy body where the pranic bodies or channels meet in triangular configuration. Of these, seven are considered foundational.

Seeker: Excuse me for interrupting you, Sadhguru, but I thought pranic healing is not about using the mind, or any such thing. It's like using the natural force that is around us, an energy force that is all around us, which we are also part of. The healing is said to be done like that, not by the mind or any such thing.

Sadhguru: If that is what somebody is claiming, ask them to focus their mind on the mountain or on the sky and do healing to the person in front of them. It will not happen. You have to focus your mind in that direction. Without focusing your mind, nothing will happen.

Seeker: But, Sadhguru, healing is done even long distance. That person could be even outside of India and I can sit here and do it. That is what is being said.

Sadhguru: Mental focus need not necessarily be within the physical limits of perception. Your mind can be focused on anything, irrespective of distance. It is not confined to the limitations of physical spaces. There are all sorts of healing processes in every town, but still the load on the local hospitals has not come down in any way. I would say fifty to sixty percent of the people are not even ill in the first place. They imagine illnesses. When I say imagine, it's a self-created situation. Medical science experimented with this just by giving placebo medicines, placebo surgeries. People became perfectly well. That means they never really had any illness; it's just a certain situation. All they need is just some placebo effect. This placebo effect was very effectively used in our tradition in India because the wise of the past understood that most people are ill by choice. They have chosen illness as a kind of defense against some other life situations within them. So all they need is a placebo. I'm talking about that segment which only needs placebo treatment and nothing else. So if somebody is praying for you and calls you up and says, "I have done healing for you. Don't worry, everything will be okay," it may just make you okay. See, people always need psychological support. Many people cannot step out of their house in the morning unless they get a phone call from somebody else saying, "Everything is okay. I'm blessing you, I'm praying for you." This is their psychological condition.

So what happens long distance is really not relevant to the earlier question that you brought up. Healing can be done, people can be relieved, but if you truly want to heal, you must be willing to take their karmic substance upon yourself, because as far as nature and life energies are concerned, where this karmic substance is does not really matter; life is life. The distinction between you and me is only in your mind. As far as life energy is concerned, one part of life energy is getting rotten right now. That's all it is. So you can shift it upon yourself, into your own energies, and it will naturally manifest in your body.

Now, suppose somebody has serious asthma, or a cardiac problem or something else and I take it away. In my body, it need not necessarily become asthma or a cardiac condition. Sometimes it can manifest the same way, but many times it will manifest in some other way, depending upon how my body reacts to that particular energy and karmic situation. All I am doing is taking that karmic substance into my system. Now this karmic substance in the other body, for that level of awareness, may take ten years to dissolve, if he does not add anything more, but in my body, I might be able to work it out in ten days.

As a preparation for the Dhyanalinga consecration process, we had drastically altered the karmic structures of a few people – physiological and other kinds of disturbances in them – so that they could be part of the work. As a result of this, you have seen on that particular initiation day, I vomited more than three-fourths of a liter of blood. This means my liver was in a complete mess and as per medical advice it needed emergency treatment without which one cannot recover; but you know very well, within forty-eight hours or a little more than that I was perfectly okay; there was no need for any doctor. So when a situation comes like that, what is being done is a certain kind of psychic surgery. See, surgery can be performed with various instruments. In ancient times, they did crude machete surgeries, then surgery evolved using finer instruments like scalpels. Now technology has taken surgery to the realms of the laser, which is a certain kind of light beam, which does the work more effectively than a machete. So without blood, without gore, without opening up wounds, surgery is performed and the body goes through all that it would during normal surgery except for the physical pain.

Similarly, with the sharpness of your psyche you could cut through and perform a surgery. Certain people have certain inborn psychic capabilities that allow them to perform such an act. It can also be developed through a certain type of yoga sadhana. It is always more reliable when it has come to you with conscious sadhana; otherwise this capability in you may be on and off. So psychic surgery is a completely different thing compared to healing which is so much on the surface. See, with surface healing, the karmic substance will always take effect in some other way.

Another part of this whole activity of trying to heal somebody is, in some way, you are trying to play God, trying to manipulate energies in a certain way. Here we are teaching yoga kriyas to people with which healing is naturally happening. The objective is not healing, but it's definitely happening; but this involves sadhana, which is karma by itself. In the so-called healing processes or clinics also this is being done, but with a lack of understanding and depth. Just laying your hands on somebody and relieving him of pain and things like that, is not a good thing unless you are capable of taking the causal substance of it.

Seeker: Master, you were explaining earlier how you have taken upon yourself somebody's karma and how it affected your energy system. You knew how to handle it. What happens to that individual whose karma you affect? What happens to his energy form, his karmic structure? Is it being altered?

Sadhguru: It is just like he is completely free from it because the fundamental cause of trouble itself is taken away. It's like you have a bad engine in your car and you sold it to your enemy. It's not there anymore, that's all.

Seeker: Master, why do you need to do it? Shouldn't everybody work it out themselves through sadhana?

Sadhguru: Yes, that's what I said. In normal conditions we will never do it. It is not just to relieve him of his disease that it was done. This was done in a very special condition where we were working towards the Dhyanalinga consecration with certain time limitations. What objectives we wanted to fulfill had to be fulfilled within a certain time span, so many things had to be pushed. If there had been more time, so many more things that we did, we would not have done. We would have handled it with much more ease and in a different way; putting people into longer stages of sadhana and not having to take these drastic steps.

Seeker: Sadhguru, Jesus performed many miracles to create faith among his followers. He even raised someone from the dead.

Sadhguru: This is all your nonsense, because when Jesus asked the fishermen to follow him and they started following him, one of them - I think it was Peter - said, "My father is dead; can I bury him and come,

Master?" Jesus said, "Leave the dead to the dead. You come. You just come; follow me." He is saying his father is dead, and he is saying he will bury him and come, but Jesus says no; leave the dead to the dead. Do you know what this means? It means leave the dead to the dead in the village; those people are dead anyway. Leave the dead to the dead and you come follow me. Such a man, would he bring a dead body back to life?

Seeker: Maybe it was for some other reason, because he wanted people to have some faith?

Sadhguru: How did Lazarus die? Did he have leprosy? See, in those times, whenever people became ill, the tradition of the Jewish culture was to put them into seclusion in caves; it was their way of avoiding infections. Food and water were just dropped inside. So they thought Lazarus was dead. When they told Jesus that Lazarus was dead, he went to see – I am just trying to reconstruct the situation; it may not be true. So Jesus went to see and probably he found that Lazarus was still alive. Jesus was brought up by the *Essenes*[1] and other people who were healers; he might have nurtured him back to health. Jesus went into the cave and came out after some time, isn't it?

Seeker: Yes. He stayed inside for some time.

Sadhguru: Probably, he nurtured him and then he brought him back. So people said, "Oh! He has brought the dead back. Lazarus was dead and now he is back." In people's perception, maybe it was so. I am just saying how things can get, you know... A miracle means, raise the dead. So much for miracles and healing.

---

1 Essenes : a secret school of mysticism which is known to have aided Jesus during his life.

Seeker: Sadhguru, I have a phobia – a fear of disease – and I run away; rather, I am repulsed by diseased people, sick people. This is quite a hindrance for my growth, isn't it?

Sadhguru: Nobody wants disease, of course. Nobody would choose to be diseased, isn't it? Nobody wants to be ill; everybody wants to be healthy. It's okay, but at the same time, you must understand that once you have a body, illness, old age and death are natural processes of life. You are not choosing to be ill, but you know that once you have a physical body, illness may happen at any moment. All right, you take care to see that you're not ill, but if you become excessively concerned about illness or health, that itself becomes an illness. Just trying to avoid illness is an illness. Illness restricts you, that's why you do not like it, isn't it? Why you do not like illness is that in some way it's going to restrict your life; but just the fear of illness also restricts your life and maybe your life span too, isn't it? It's an illness by itself.

This is not just you, there are so many people who have this fear. Especially once they cross forty, forty-five, their fear of illness becomes huge. When they were young they did not think so, because they thought they were immortal (laughs). Until they are forty or forty-five they are immortal, isn't it? Only after that the fact that you are mortal comes to you. Your fear is not of illness. Your fear is of death. Illness is the passage. You know illness is the first step towards death. So the fundamental fear is always of death. Now you're still not addressing death directly, but you're addressing illness, because you know, if illness comes, the other will follow.

Generally, in social situations, people have been telling you, convincing you, that after all, fear of death is natural. The problem is whatever the majority is doing, people say it is 'natural'. If the majority of people were smoking cigarettes people would say, "Smoking is a natural thing". Yes or no? Certain groups of people, even now they say so. "What's wrong with smoking? It's just natural." A human being is not made to smoke; you're not an automobile or something! (Laughs). It's not natural for you to smoke, but people will make it natural. So the fear of death has been made natural by social situations, but it's not so. Fear of death has come because of a certain sense of ignorance and unawareness. It's not natural. Maybe the majority has ascribed to it, but it's not a natural process to fear death. If life happens, the natural process is death. Being afraid of a natural process is unnatural. Isn't it? The fear of death comes simply because you're not in touch with reality. The fear of death has come to you because you've gotten deeply identified with this body. Your identification with this body has become so strong because you have not explored other dimensions. If you had explored other dimensions of experience, if you had established yourselves in other dimensions of experience, the body would not be such a big issue; but now your whole experience of life is limited to this body. No matter what kind of teachings other people give you, this is me, isn't it?

It doesn't matter if somebody tells you, "You are not the body," somebody tells you, "You are *atma*,"[1] whatever nonsense they teach you, in your experience, *this* is you. Whatever *Gitas* they may read to you, your experience is limited to the physical body. The fear of losing it is natural, but if you reach other dimensions of experience, if you establish yourself in other dimensions of experience, the body will become an easy thing to handle. Life or death will not make so much of a difference. Life or death is only in terms of what you are doing. For example, you started a project. It's only in terms of whether you'll be able to complete your project or not before you die. That is all it is for me, at least. Right now, I have a project on my hands. Whether it's going to be completed or not, whether I should start the next project or am I going to shed the body before it is complete, that is all my calculation about death. My calculation of death is only in terms of, "Okay, for the people involved, can we do this for them within this time frame or not?" That's all. The question of shedding the body is not a big issue, because if your experience of life is established beyond the physical body, it's a very simple affair. When you want to change your clothes, you change them, isn't it? Or if you do not like them, you throw them away and walk naked. It's up to you; both are possible.

Once, when I was in the ninth standard of school, this girl, my classmate, during the *Dussehra*[2] holidays, died of pneumonia. This just left me wondering, where could she have gone? Somebody who was just about my age died. How could someone just disappear like that? The way I was made, my nature was such that I would explore everything that came my way. Even on my way to school, I would at least climb up half a dozen big trees, look at the eggs in the birds' nests, eat the fruit on the tree; only then would

---

1 *atma* : individual soul.

2 *Dussehra* : a festival of color, dance and music, which celebrates the victory of good over evil and takes place on the 10th day after 9 days of fasting and praying.

I finally reach school. I just wanted to explore anything and everything that came my way. Now this death, I just had to see for myself, so I acquired ninety-eight Gardinal Sodium tablets from my father's medicine cupboard, as he was a physician.

In preparation for death, I distributed all my property to my friends. My property was a lot of small, small things, my prized catapults which were most difficult to part with because I held them very high and valuable and did not allow anybody to even touch them, my pet birds, the pet turtle that I released into the local Kukkarahalli water tank, the pet cobra which I released on the Chamundi hills. You see, I had a whole zoo going on the terrace of my house. I also gave away all my money, about one hundred and twelve rupees – in those days, a fortune for a young boy of my age – which I had earned through my self-employment as a snake catcher from house gardens, college and institution grounds; all of them I released on the Chamundi Hills. I distributed all these and one fine day told all my friends that today I was going to die. They thought this was one more joke. That night, I refused to take my supper and on an empty stomach, took all these tablets and went to bed. I wanted to know what would happen.

After three days, I woke up in a hospital bed. Everybody was anxious as to why I resorted to this step because until the last moment, I was that boisterous, crazy boy who was going around, doing all kinds of strange things. Even if my father scolded me or sent me out of the house, I just waited for that, and then I would just go away for a trek into the forest for a few days. That's how it was with me. If I had to find out something, it did not matter what was the price. About dying also, I never thought I was going to lose something, that I had to look into my parents' eyes one last time, nothing. I just took the tablets, closed my eyes and slept. The only heartache of this whole episode was that I could not get back all my possessions. Half the money I did get back after a lot of threatening and fist fights.

When your wanting to know something is so intense that you're willing to die for it, then knowing is not far away. So now you know what kind of crazy man you are with. When life and death make no difference for you, nothing is needed anymore. When life and death make a lot of difference, only for that fool there are so many problems. For someone who does not differentiate between life and death, there is no problem; he can live with a lot less limitations. Once this body has run its course it will go anyway, whether you like it or you do not like it. Whether you approve or disapprove, it will happen. As long as you retain your body, taking good care of it is definitely your business. Isn't it? Now if you are paranoid about ill health or death, you will not take good care of it. In your anxiety you will destroy the body. The very anxiety that says, "What may happen? What may happen to this body?" will destroy the body.

Now this fear of illness – even on seeing a dead body people are terrified. Is that so with many of you? Just by seeing a dead body you are terrified. Every day people die, all right. I am not saying it's a small thing for the people who love them, for people who care for them. For them it is a big thing, I understand, but why are you afraid just seeing a dead body? Living bodies are dangerous. They can do many things to you. What will a dead body do to you? A dead body is the safest thing, but you're afraid of it! (Laughs). Just look at this: living people are capable of so many things. They can put up very good pretenses, but tomorrow they may kill you, they may do something else to you, they may do anything. Dead bodies are so safe, but still people are afraid of them.

When I was about fourteen or fifteen, I spent an enormous amount of time in the cemeteries in Mysore. Something, somehow, drew me there. I would go and sit in the cemetery the whole night. People would set fire to their relatives' bodies which would go on burning; it's a long affair, you know. They don't have the patience to wait, so they wait for half an hour or one hour and then leave. I was the one attending to all those dead bodies. Somebody's head falls off, I would pick it up and put it back in the fire. Why I'm telling you this is because it's good to expose yourself to death. It's very good. I know that in your homes they have told you, you should not even utter the word 'death', because they have a stupid hope that if you don't utter the word, it will not enter your house. Do you think that if the word death is not in your vocabulary, it will not come to you?

I would like you to practice death. If you are willing, tomorrow evening we will set up a situation where you can consciously practice death. Are you willing, Indu? If every day, or at least for a few times in your life, you practice death consciously, then you will see that it is not the way you think it is. It's very different from what you have known. Death exists only for ignorant people. If you are in awareness, there is no such thing as death. The process of yoga is all rooted in death. In fact, you will become spiritual only if you start facing death. If you think of God, you will not become spiritual; you will invent stories. If you think of God, you will seek more survival and well-being and prosperity. Isn't it? Why are you thinking of God? Because you think he is easy currency for well-being, yes or no? Thinking of God is not spirituality; it's just another desperate attempt to live well somehow. Only when you are confronted with death, you start looking: "Okay, beyond this body, what the hell is there?" What is beyond the physical body is what we are referring to as spiritual. Your ideas of God are not spirituality, they are just another tool for survival. Only when you truly start seeking what is beyond the physical body, the spiritual processes open up for you.

Everything that we have been doing here from day one is just that, to somehow give you an experience that is beyond the limitations of the physical body; but every time something new comes up, fear and resistance is what you see within yourself. That's why the process is so slow. If you had just given yourself to me, many wonderful, liberating things could have happened to you. Right now, you want to go very cautiously. You don't want to step into anything that you don't know. At the same time, you want to know new things. There is no way. You are just defeating yourself all the time. You don't want to step into anything new without knowing it. How will you know it if you do not step into it? There is no way to know it unless you step into it, but you're not willing to step into it unless you know it. "You tell me what it is; only if I know I will step in."

Every day, just spend five minutes reminding yourself that you are mortal and today you may die. It is possible that today you might fall dead, isn't it? Just remind yourself; wonderful things will happen to you. Have you heard of Gurdjieff? Gurdjieff was a wonderful Master, but he was known as a rascal saint – a rascal, but a saint. His methods were so drastic; he did crazy things, terrible things with people. So Gurdjieff gave a solution to the world. He said, "If you want to have the whole world Enlightened, we must plant a new organ in everyone's body. Every day, twice a day, this organ will remind you: you will also die." Every day, twice a day, it reminds you. That is what the *Shoonya*[1] meditation that you are initiated into is. It's not implanted; you have to make it happen. Every day, if you sit for meditation, you will see, everything that is you will die. The fear of death is not in the body, I want you to understand. The fear of death is in your personality. You, as a person, are going to die. That's the problem. Suppose you have grown old and God offers you a deal: "Okay, you give me this old body. I will give you a new body."

---

1 *Shoonya* : lit. emptiness. A powerful meditation offered in Isha Yoga programs.

Won't you take it? You will, won't you? So the body is not really the problem. The problem is that based on this body you have created a personality. That's what you are really attached to. When you sit in Shoonya meditation, do you see that your personality has dissolved and just a certain presence is there? Like this, every day, twice a day, you die consciously. The personality is dissolved. Just the presence is there. This will release you from everything.

This happened to me. A few years ago I was in Bangalore city and I went to the vegetable market, just taking a walk. I like walking through vegetable markets, so I'm just walking there, talking to the vegetables…why, Poornima? Why do you look so shocked? You think I am only capable of talking to your kind? Suddenly, I see this one vegetable vendor who is all bright and lit up. I can't believe a man like this is selling vegetables. I look at him, and instantly our eyes lock and I laugh and he also starts laughing. I could not believe this man is selling vegetables. Then I went to him and we started talking. I asked, "How come you are here selling vegetables, a man like you?" He said, "No, I am doing my work here." I said, "What do you do?" We were just bantering. In his life he was selling vegetables, just a plain vegetable seller. Then one day he became ill. He became so ill, he thought he was going to die. For over four months, he remained so ill that every day he thought, "Today I'm going to die." He went through this process of, 'Anyway I am going to die' for four months, and then he recovered. Then, something wonderful happened to him. He got Enlightened, I am telling you. So he says, "Anybody who comes to my shop, I bless them to have a long illness." (Laughs). I said, "That's great, but if people ever come to know, you've had it!" He blesses every customer who comes to him, "Let them have a long enlightening illness."

Whatever it is – illness, death, calamity, anything that happens around you – you can either use it to liberate yourself or you can use it to entangle yourself. Especially these calamities, illness and death, are a tremendous opportunity to look beyond the limitations of what you normally understand as life, isn't it? You thought that getting up in the morning, having a coffee, having breakfast, going to work, doing this, this, this, again eating, doing that, that, that, throwing yourself around on everybody, and coming back in the evening, you thought this was life. If one day you're bed ridden, suddenly you'll see, life seems to be something else, something very different from what you thought it was, isn't it?

This need not happen to you. If you're intelligent, do learn from other people's experiences. Everything in the world need not happen to you; you must learn from other people's experiences.

You have heard about Gautama,[1] isn't it? He just saw one sick man, one old man and one dead body and he Realized that any day, this could happen to him. There is no point in running away from it. Let us look at it and see. If somebody is ill, I want you to sit with them and see that this could have been you and could be you any day. The most horrible illness that somebody has – we do not want it and we are not wishing for it – you could get it any day. It doesn't matter whether you are eighteen or eighty; it could be you today or tomorrow, isn't it? It's important to face everything with a stable and balanced mind. Avoiding it is not the solution. If you avoid it, you only get entangled. So do not avoid illness or death; face them. See that it could be you. Remind yourself. Tomorrow we will put you through an experience, but you must allow it to happen. If you are constantly resisting, it will not happen. It's a very subtle, simple process that can happen easily if you are willing.

Seeker: Sadhguru, you are saying you can make us experience death?

Sadhguru: I am walking death in so many ways. 'Guru' means 'death'. Do not take death in the negative connotation. It is the death of the limited, always, because only the limited can die. Can the unlimited die? So 'Guru' means 'death of the limited'. In His presence it is always like death. Why you are uncomfortable but at the same time you want to be there is because you know He is death and on another level you know He is liberation. Still, there is not enough maturity to come to terms with it. So my presence always influences the death meditation simply because all the time, my very energies are like that, to release you from the limited or the physical.

1 Gautama : referring to the Buddha.

Seeker: Sadhguru, in many ways we have been a witness to a drastic deterioration in your health and body in a short span of time since you started the Dhyanalinga consecration work. We believe you can do something about it. Don't you want to stay back and see us through?

Sadhguru: Nobody will stay back. Everybody goes (laughs). Don't have hopes like that. For all you know I may live until seventy, you never know. In the next four or five years, after the Dhyanalinga consecration, I want to attempt this and see, literally recreating life. Theoretically, it's very much possible. It's just a question of whether we make it happen or not. The formula is right. I know that if I put all the ingredients in a proper way it is bound to happen. We will experiment with that. If it succeeds, I will live on; otherwise, I will go without regret.

There is one aspect which is unchanging, which is always there. In Isha, we don't usually talk about it because words like *being, atma, consciousness*, whatever, have been badly misused. I made it a rule not to talk about it. Here, it is always referred to as 'the beyond'. What is beyond limitations is reality. So that is absolute. The physical body, we know, is very transient; it's changing every day. Prana is also physical in nature, but very subtle. It is this prana that connects you to what is being referred to as 'soul', and to that which is the physical body. Prana is life. Prana is the liveliness that you see, the flowers blooming, the birds singing, us sitting here. All this is because of prana. The soul cannot do this. The soul has no quality of its own. It cannot do anything.

Seeker: Master, what exactly do you mean by 'prana'?

Sadhguru: What you are referring to as a 'soul' is not an entity. Just to bring an understanding to people, the Hindu culture used a word to describe that which is unbounded, which is unfortunately misunderstood. That which is unbounded is never an entity; it cannot be. But the moment you put a name on it, it becomes an entity. Whether you call it *atma*, soul, self – whatever you call it – the moment you stick a name to it, it becomes an entity. That's where the misunderstanding and the struggle is with people. Why we are making jokes – if somebody says 'soul', I immediately look at the soles of my feet and make fun of it – is to make them understand that whatever they have thought about it, is not it. It cannot be like that. I just joke about it and destroy their concept of what the soul is.

At the Master's feet. *During a trek with the bhramhacharis.*

People say 'good souls'. In the West, they say, "Oh, he is a good soul." There is no good soul or bad soul. Soul is beyond all identification, all entity, all everything. Another way to look at this is that there is no soul as such. That's why Gautama went about saying, "You are *anatma*. There is no atma." If asked, "Then what is it?" he would say, "Ah, it is nothingness." He's just giving another name, just to deceive you out of your misconceptions. To get you out of one, he's getting you into a new word, that is all. So tomorrow you go about saying, "I am nothing, I am nothing, I am nothing." That also becomes an entity. When that happens, we use another word. See, it's not that the word is trying to describe what it is. The word is trying to destroy your misconceptions about what it is. That's all. My life and my work is just that – to destroy all your misconceptions. Just trying to destroy one concept and giving it another name will not take anybody to reality. The Master's role is to just demolish everything that is untrue. That's all. One can never get anybody to reality, but if you're ready to have all untruths destroyed, you'll arrive at it.

Sadhguru - the Master tackler.

Now you're asking about prana. This has been looked at in yoga in a very wise and wonderful way, just looking at everything as body, this physical structure as body, physiology as body, mind as body, energy or pranic system as body, and etheric substance also as body. Everything as body, even the soul as body. It is a very wise way to look at things. When we say *anandamaya kosha*, still we are not referring to the ultimate; but even that is seen as a body, because that's how it is right now. That's the only way you can grasp it. You do not talk about anything there (pointing in the distance). You talk about how to transcend one limitation and then go to the next one. When you transcend all limitations, what happens, happens. Why should you think about it now, because whatever you think, you think only from your limitations. Nobody can think of anything which is not in his present dimension of experience. Nobody!

There is no point talking to you about something which is not in your present level of experience. So in yoga it is said, everything is body. Mind is body, prana is body, etheric substance is body, everything is body. In other words, as I have been describing this, if you take your body as a whole model of creation, it's like a paint smear – starting with a very gross substance, becoming subtler, subtler, subtler – becoming nothing. So from the physical body, to the mental body, to the pranic body, it gets subtler and subtler. The physical body and mental body are more substance. The pranic body is the energy which fires all this. So that's what keeps you in touch with the body. When prana drops, you drop. Your body drops dead, or in your experience, you drop dead – whichever way. So what you're calling death is only that the prana has lost its vibrancy. Either due to old age or disease or some other damage or injury, prana has lost its vibrancy.

Now, another way is, if I shoot you in the head, your prana may be vibrant but still you will be dead. The physical body is broken and so the prana cannot immediately reconstruct it to keep it going. The physical body collapses. Suppose I shoot you in your thigh muscle. In cases where the body is not broken enough, it will allow enough time for the prana to reconstruct the damaged part. Why it is said that if somebody dies in an accident, his ghost will be going around, is simply because that man is moving around with more substance than one who dies a natural death. So there are more chances that people may feel him. Do you understand what I am saying? Suppose somebody died of old age, his prana would become very weak, the vibrancy would be lost, and then the body would fall apart. So you will not feel him. He is too subtle.

Seeker: So the prana of this person who died in an accident is felt more? And that is again the subtle body, isn't it, Sadhguru?

Sadhguru: No, let me come to that. As we saw, there are five bodies. We know that. Now, the pranic body is fully vibrant in a person, but as he becomes older and older, the pranic body loses its vibrancy. What you're doing with your kriyas is just keeping the vibrancy. No matter what your age is, just keeping that vibrancy. How vibrant it is, that is how the mental body and the physical body will be. So we are just trying to keep the pranic system in proper vibrancy, always. Now somebody is young and vibrant, but the body is destroyed - the physical body. Either by an accident or a gunshot or whatever, the physical body is destroyed. The pranic body is still very much vibrant and intact. So now, anyway, he has to part with the physical body because it's ruined. It is physically damaged. He can't do anything about it. Now when he leaves, the vibrancy of the pranic body is still intact. So he's felt much more easily by people.

Seeker: Yes, Sadhguru, but for how long would he be able to keep this pranic body which is still intact? When you say "still intact", is it a subtler body?

Sadhguru: No. Even the person who dies of old age has a subtler body, but it is too subtle for people to feel.

Seeker: So Sadhguru, this pranic body will stay intact until rebirth?

Sadhguru: Yes, until it's capable of finding another physical body.

Seeker: Finding or creating, Sadhguru?

Sadhguru: In a way, creating. In one way, creating, because without the pranic substance, the body cannot form itself.

Seeker: So Master, does creating mean when a woman conceives?

Sadhguru: A woman conceives just because two physical cells meet.

Seeker: Yes Sadhguru, one of these energy bodies finds its way to the womb at the time of conception.

Sadhguru: No, it's not then. At that time, it is not there. As the physical body slowly starts developing within a woman's womb... see it's just like there was a nest. Some bird built the nest; some other bird came and laid its eggs and made a life there. It's just like that. Some two fools came together and they started creating a body. Somebody else who is ripe for that is always looking for a body; he finds it and in that there is some choice. Depending upon how consciously he has lived, there is a little bit of choice as to what kind of body he chooses.

Seeker: Is that choice always there, Sadhguru?

Sadhguru: There is a little bit of choice, always; but when I say choice, it is not like you go into this shop and buy this shirt or whatever. It's not in that sense. There is a karmic choice. There is a natural tendency for the person to go in a certain direction, towards a certain womb, towards a certain body. That natural tendency is there. See, even when you're alive here in the physical body, you have a natural tendency to seek out certain people, because that's how your karmas are. So, similarly, when you do not have a physical body, it's much more unconscious, but still the karmic substance that you carry with you seeks out a certain type of body. So once it has found that body, it is the vibrancy of the prana which enhances the quality of the physical body. It's not just the mother who is making the baby. See, there are millions of instances where probably the mother is weak, undernourished, on the street, and yet she delivers a very healthy baby. Any number of situations like this are there. Somebody coming from the best of families, where everything is taken care of and who is very well fed, gives birth to a very fragile child. This is the pranic substance, pranic vibrancy of the being who has taken on that particular body. That's why this distinction is there. Depending upon the kind of vibrancy the pranic body has, accordingly it creates a certain type of body. So the creation of the body is not just the mother's work. What kind of being came there, also creates this in a certain way.

Seeker: So Master, when exactly does this prana enter the body that has been conceived?

Sadhguru: See, until about forty to forty-eight days after conception, it's still a body. Why it is said that if the woman has gone over forty days past conception, it should not be aborted is because the being has come in by then. Before that it was not a being. Not only because of the smallness of the body, but the being is not yet there. It is just a bundle of cells. Now this bundle of cells becomes a being, maybe not yet a person, but in many ways a person. His personality might not have manifested in the sense that we understand, but the very way the baby kicks around in the mother's womb is different from baby to baby. You had two; were they the same?

Seeker: Definitely not, Sadhguru.

Sadhguru: They were not the same; the very way they kick around is different. They already have a personality. Depending upon their karmic structure, they have a certain personality. It's not so manifest, but it is there. To what extent that little person can manifest, to that extent he's manifesting. The very moment he's born, he has his own personality. Isn't it?

Seeker: Oh, very much Sadhguru.

Sadhguru: The very way he yells, the very way he demands things is different. It's different from one baby to another. Because their area of activity is so limited, people think all babies are the same. It's not true. Every baby, the way he cries, the way he behaves, the way he looks up, the way he goes for food, everything is different from baby to baby. You just see four puppies, they're all different. All four of them, though delivered from the same womb, just see the way they are. They're different. It depends on the kind of vibrancy that he has come with, the kind of karmic substance that he carries; accordingly it is. So the diminishing of the karmic body, the diminishing of the pranic body, is what is called 'old age'.

Now the karma, as it is impressed into your physical body and mental body, is also impressed into your energy body. As the allotted karma or *prarabdha* is reaching completion, the pranic body's ability to hold on to the physical body recedes. Life, as you know it, which is physical, will begin to lose its vibrancy, but at the same time, the subtle body gathers more vibrancy because the physical body is losing its grip on the subtle. This is the reason why many of you might have noticed, even a person who has lived a gross life, the last few days before his death, seems to carry an ethereal peace about himself.

Seeker: Sadhguru, how does a decimated pranic body regain its vibrancy before it acquires a physical body again?

Sadhguru: One thing that we are doing through yoga kriyas is rejuvenating you when you are here, in the physical body. It could happen in so many other ways. Just a walk in the forest can rejuvenate you. Good food can rejuvenate you. Yogic practices can rejuvenate you. That's a different dimension. All this is when you have the body. Now, after you leave the body, if the pranic body is too vibrant, let us say it's in full life when it died, he cannot find another body for some time. He needs a certain settling down of the pranic body. Only then he can find a body. That's why we are saying that if they die now in an accident, they will remain disembodied – what normally people refer to as ghosts – for a long time.

Seeker: Is that why the rituals, Sadhguru? To appease them?

Sadhguru: Yes, to pacify him, because he's still vibrant. His pranic body still carries desires, longings, everything – so it will not settle. It remains in that form for a long period of time. It has to run its course. Initially, when they die because of an accident, they're very vibrant. That's when they are felt very strongly. Then when the prana loses its vibrancy they just hang around. In the Indian way of life there are certain practices and processes to hasten the course so that he does not have to hang in there. He's in limbo. You want to hasten that process of being in limbo for that person. Some of it is true. If somebody who is doing it knows what he's doing, it can be done. Some of it is just psychological solace for the living, so that they feel that their son or husband or child is not hanging there. "We've done something; he will find a good space." Still, it's also true that those who know what they are doing, if they do it, they can hasten the process for him so that he does not have to be around for too long.

If these pranic and subtler bodies have to take another physical body, they should come to a certain sense of sedateness. Only if they come to a lower sense of vibrancy or sedateness can the being find another body; otherwise it will not find it. If it is fully vibrant like this right now, it cannot find another body. It has to become sedate. Such a process can also be set forth willfully. *Samadhi* states can be very intense or very sedate, almost like death. Beyond a certain level of subtleness, the structure is not so firm, so it is easy to mix things; but when it's like this, with the proper structure of the physical body, when the body is firm, you cannot do this because it is vibrant. So samadhi is almost like death. With natural death that's what is happening. When somebody lives a long and proper life and dies peacefully – people are always thinking of dying peacefully – it is understood that his prana has run a full course and has simply gotten disentangled.

It's just like a ripe fruit fell off a tree. The moment it falls off, with the ripe fruit around it, the seed will immediately find root with the necessary food around it. See, the fruit has the necessary manure around it. Fruit is actually manure. We are just eating it before it actually becomes manure. So now there is a mango. The flesh is created by the tree. One thing is to attract animals so that they will take it elsewhere, carry the seed and drop it in other places. Another thing is, when the fruit falls down, it has the necessary food in it so that it works as manure. We call it manure, but it is the seed's food. It comes with packaged food, so that when it falls on the earth it has food from which it grows. So when a person goes through a full cycle and when he comes to that point, we say he died peacefully, because he has run his full course. There is no struggle, there is no disease, there is no injury. There is nothing. The prana has reached a certain level of sedateness and disentangled itself, without any struggle or disturbance. Now what we call *Mahasamadhi* is the same thing: to bring the prana to a certain state of passivity with a certain level of intensity in the structure, a certain level of maturity, so that it disentangles by itself. We are looking forward to that kind of death, because when you die like that, it is proper, because it is just a simple disentanglement, it is natural. If you die with a disease, if you die from an accident or an injury, there is violence in it. That violence is carried in so many ways in the subtler bodies.

Seeker: Jaggi, we say when a person dies of old age, prana loses its vibrancy. Then let us assume that it takes another body; does it mean to say that the prana starts getting vibrant again?

Sadhguru: Yes, it is rejuvenated. To enter the body it must be in a certain state of passive inertness. Only then it can find a body. Once prarabdha karma runs out or wears itself out, prana will lose its vibrancy, its dynamism, without a karmic substance. Once the prarabdha or allotted karma completely wears out, after a short span of time, the new installment of prarabdha will begin to manifest itself. As this new prarabdha begins to manifest, the prana regains its vibrancy and by then it will regain a body again.

Seeker: When one reaches *Mahasamadhi*, isn't that person's prana in full vibrancy? And if it is in full vibrancy, how is it that it dissolves by itself, that it does not seek a body again? What is the basis of that, Sadhguru?

Sadhguru: See, when you die of old age, you die peacefully. If somebody dies in his sleep, people say it's so wonderful because he got disentangled from the body naturally, without any violence. In a way, it's a good way to die. Now we are trying to create the same thing consciously, because it's not necessary that when it happens naturally, it will happen consciously. It may happen in your sleep. It may happen here when you are sitting. It may just happen to you, and along with that life will dissipate. Because prana is dissipating, when it comes to that stage, you may just become senile, lose your memory and not be conscious of what is happening. All these things may happen with dissipation of prana. Why an old person is becoming senile or getting lost is simply because of this. It is again like a second childhood because his prana is losing the vibrancy that it had in youth. It's again becoming like a baby. So he is going back to the same state where he took on the body. In what level of passivity his prana was, if he reaches the same level of passivity, he will die. He will leave the body like he took on the body, very naturally. All other forms of deaths, whether you die from infection, accident, suicide or whatever, all are considered unnatural. Now, what you're talking about as Mahasamadhi is to bring about that stage of dying naturally, consciously. So now one thing is, with yogic practices, it's becoming more intense. Your energies are becoming more intense. Now how can this person's energy be inert? If you know anything about energy, that which is of tremendous intensity is always stillness. Yes? This is a scientific fact. If any vibration reaches tremendous intensity, it will become still. In that stillness, the person will leave. It is in absolute stillness, not inertness, that he leaves. Once again it looks like the prana has become inert or passive as far as the physical body was concerned. In a way, you can say you deceived the body. The physical body thought that your energies became totally inert and it dropped. In a way, consciously, you deceive the body by creating a high pitch of vibrancy. This extreme vibrancy can be set with awareness; with razor-sharp awareness one can get there. One can also come to this with *bhakthi*, intensity of emotion. One can also come to this by doing the necessary practices like you are doing now. Let us say tomorrow morning you sit and do one million *kapala-bathis*;[1] at the end of the day you may leave the body. It's possible. If your energies become so intense, they'll become still. The physical body cannot contain it. It will think it's over and it will drop.

Seeker: Sadhguru, would that be *Mahasamadhi*?

Sadhguru: Yes, it is! For twelve years you do kapala-bathi, at the end of it you reach one million, okay? If you raise it to that pitch, it becomes absolute stillness. The physical body feels that it's over and disentangles because your energies become vibrant but still, because of the practice: That's very good

---

1 *kapala-bathi* : a certain powerful yoga kriya which is taught in the basic Isha Yoga program.

for you. Right now, you may think you have taken on the body. That's true in one way, but in another way, the physical body is holding you. You can't leave it. Many people, when they get into the first stages of sadhana, they say, "The hell with this body," but it will not happen. All the spiritual-thinking people believe they have taken on the body. It is true in one way, but the body has taken over you; that's another thing. It will not release you even if you want to be released. So if you push your energy to a certain pitch, with whatever method you know, then it will become still. In that stillness, the body may be deceived and dropped. Stillness is the most intense aspect of life.

Seeker: So Master, this prana which is in full vibrancy, will it not seek another body?

Sadhguru: It will not seek because it has come to that level of vibrancy.

Seeker: Realization! That is Realization!

Sadhguru: You can call it Realization, but usually we use the word 'Realization' only if somebody realizes and lives on. You can call it Enlightenment. It's the same, but you use the word 'Realization' because he is Realized. Realizing is a sort of knowing. Mahasamadhi is not necessarily knowing. He became free, that's all. The moment of freedom is also a kind of knowing, but there is nobody to know, so the knowing does not arise. Dissolution of the individual means joining the unbounded, and that's the ultimate knowing also.

Seeker: Sadhguru, when we die, the prana we carried dissolves, disintegrates and just sort of gets mixed up with something?

Sadhguru: It is just like a bubble. The bubble burst; where is the bubble? What happened to the air inside? There is no such thing.

Seeker: Sadhguru, why is the population always increasing? When you are saying that everything is one…

Sadhguru: That is because all crawling and climbing creatures have become human beings. The insect population is coming down compared to the human population, isn't it, Kiran? (Laughs). This question itself comes from the ignorance of believing and thinking of existence numerically. It's not like that! Life does not happen that way. You must understand this. Now if I say, "The bubble in the air," suppose I create a billion bubbles and all the air is contained in them, where is there more air for the other bubbles to come? That's the question, isn't it? When you are talking about the unbounded, there is no such arithmetic. Don't take the example literally, but I think it clarifies many things.

Seeker: The question, Sadhguru, was like, if you sum up all the beings or all the...

Sadhguru: The thing is, you are thinking there is a being. What if there is no being? That is why Gautama went on saying you are *anatma*. It was total sacrilege for the Hindus; he is saying, "You are anatma." So if it is anatma, how many anatmas, how many non-beings can you create? If it is atma there could be any number; if it's anatma, how many can there be? How many non-beings can you create? How many 'emptinesses' can you create? That's the question. You're always thinking materially, which comes only from the dimension of your experience, which is very limited.

If you go on producing bodies, they will get occupied anyway. If you produce bodies, life will happen. So where will the karma come from for them? Where is the karmic substance for them? Where is the mental substance for them? There is plenty of this substance. In reality, if you want, this person who is sitting here right now as one person, can take on a million bodies with the same karmic content that he has now. It's possible. There are many situations where yogis have taken up two bodies and gone around – the same karmic substance has taken on two bodies. In a way, producing our teachers is just this. I'm trying to take on a hundred bodies and go around the world. Their individuality is intact, their intelligence is intact, but just one aspect of their life, one part of their karma is superimposed. So the numbers, the population, that's not a relevant question. It's a very logical, mathematical, arithmetical question. Life does not happen like that.

Seeker: Sadhguru, what do you mean by recreation of life?

Sadhguru: Let us say this life has run its full course, which means the prana has lost the necessary vibrancy to keep the body and the being together. This can happen either due to old age or disease or as it is with me, excessive usage of the pranic body. Now you recreate it once again. It is almost like being born again, but not going back to the womb, right away. The normal way is to go back to the womb. The natural way is, if this is over, to leave it and again go back to another womb. Now without going back to the womb, recreating it here itself; same body, but a different life force. Same body, same mind and same awareness, but that which supports life, that energy has to be completely changed. We started a small process towards this kind of rejuvenation a few weeks ago and it worked well. It really worked well, so let us see. We'll make it work but we need fourteen people. We need seven *Idas* and seven *Pingalas,* masculine and feminine energies; which does not necessarily mean man and woman. They need a lot of preparation to go through a process like that. They need a tremendous amount of preparation.

We have to work on these people to bring about heightened levels of vibrancy in their system and energy body. A kind of vibrancy that will disentangle them from their physical form, except for a small connection to avoid disembodiment, or in other words, to maintain certain levels of samadhi and still have enough mastery over their systems to maintain physical activity. With such people, their energies will be so fluid that you can recreate another one. It is like I've said, if you are making clay pots, let's say you make ten clay pots; before they are dry or yet to be burned, you can again reduce them into clay and make eleven pots out of it.

What we did right now was a small thing, but it worked well. It shows on me. It has worked well. I have not heard about it anywhere, but somehow, within me, the details are just falling into place as I look at it. I can see what has to be done. The formula is clear, quite clear. It's just that, let us say, you know the recipe, but still the cooking may turn out bad. It all depends on how we put things together. It needs an expert cook. Just the recipe will not make the food tasty, but the recipe is a proof that we know it is going to work like this. So making it happen is always in our hands. We make it happen or we do not make it happen. Maybe it also depends on something else, which is beyond us; it also depends on that.

It depends on the existence also, about how badly the existence wants you; but it's possible. I see it is possible. More than wanting to live more, just the challenge of making it happen excites me.

Seeker: Sadhguru, you just said it depends on how badly existence wants you back, what do you mean by it?

Sadhguru: See, existence is not interested in any person. When the energy is mature, it takes you back, it will absorb you into itself. That's all. This question comes up in your minds because of your emotions and your insecurities, because there is a whole spiritual career in front of you. You feel you have to safeguard what you have invested in. All this is involved in the question. We will do our best. Still, it is subject to many things. It's not one hundred percent foolproof. You're not like a god who (snaps fingers) like that, it will happen. It is not so. Things have to be done. For example, we can promise you that we will lay the garden in a year's time, but it is subject to many things. We know if you plant this bamboo here, it will grow in a certain time, but still it is subject to so many things, isn't it? One day an elephant may walk in and take away your bamboo. Similarly, life is subject to many things.

Seeker: Sadhguru, how badly does Yama[1] want you?

Another audience member: Amma???

Sadhguru: Somu, Yama, Yama, not Amma! Existence and Yama are not the same, he is only the recycler. Yama is just a dispatcher – from here to there and there to here. Amma[2] is the one who delivers you here. Yama is the one who delivers you there.

Seeker: And why would the existence want you? Is it because the existence loves you so much, you are so precious that the existence feels you are better off there? And why would it want only you, not any of us? In what way are you so special, Sadhguru?

---

1 Yama : the Lord of Death.
2 Amma : mother.

Sadhguru: Somu, as I said just now, existence is not interested in anybody. Existence does not know any love. If you look up in the sky during the day, you see the sun. That becomes most dominant in your experience. In the night, if you look up, the stars become very dominant in your experience, but both the sun and the stars – and the sun also happens to be a star – are very puny little things when compared to the vastness of the sky. Generally though, that is never in your perception. So true existence is the vastness of the sky. The sun, the stars, you and me, are just small happenings, brief happenings really.

Today, modern science is telling you that even the sun has a life span. It's going to burn itself out. As you are burning your life out, similarly, the sun is on fever and he's burning his life out too. Your normal temperature is ninety-eight point six degrees Fahrenheit or whatever; his normal temperature is some ninety-eight million degrees, but he also has a life span. He is also burning up. One day he will do himself in. So whatever you see as physical existence is just a small happening. The true existence is the vastness, the emptiness that is there, the space. So when I say existence reclaiming something which is right now sitting here as a person, it's just that what you call a person is just like a bubble. This bubble doesn't have any substance of its own. The air was around. It just created a shell around it, so suddenly it has a different quality of its own. There are thick bubbles, there are thin bubbles, there are strong bubbles, there are weak bubbles, there are big bubbles, and there are small bubbles – just like people. Just like every other creature too, but when the bubble bursts, the substance that's inside the bubble, where is it? The air has reclaimed it; the atmosphere has reclaimed it. Similarly, a bubble is formed in the form of an etheric body, in the form of a pranic body, a mental body and a physical body. The physical body we can shoot down any moment we want to. It is within our power to just cut the physical body in two if we want to, but the other bodies we are not able to cut. Only what you call as existence, only that can do it.

What you are calling the spiritual process is just that. It's a deeper way of suicide. This is not about killing the physical body. You're trying to destroy the very fundamentals of creating the body within you. You're trying to destroy the very fundamental structure over which a body can form. The physical body is possible only because of the necessary karmic substances that are there in the form of etheric, pranic and mental bodies. So you are trying to destroy that through the spiritual process. With your awareness, with your practices, with your love, with your devotion, all you are trying to do is destroy the possibility of taking on another body, destroy the very foundation over which the physical body can happen. Or, in other words, you're trying to take away the possibility of going through the recycling bin over and over again. A mother's womb is only a recycling bag. Again and again… (laughs) going through the same process. So you want to take that away.

Once energies have matured to a certain point, where the other substances – the necessary foundation for another physical body – have been removed from it, energy has become just pure energy. It becomes more malleable. It is no more within the structure of the physical body. So now, even when the person is alive, he begins to experience himself in many ways beyond physical limitations. Once this energy starts maturing this way, now existence reclaims this energy. It is not that existence reclaims it, this energy is mature to a point where it cannot take on the limitations of any form any more. So naturally, it merges with existence.

To what extent your energies mature, that's what we're talking about. Or in other words, when we want to do certain work – even if the energy is mature enough to leave, you still want to retain your body and perform certain activities – then you consciously create a certain amount of karma. You create a certain amount of sturdiness to your physical, mental, pranic and etheric bodies by doing certain karmas and kriyas. Karma is the way of bondage. Kriya is the way of release. Karma is outward action. Kriya is inward action, but both can be used either to bind or to release. Both internal and external action can be used either to bind you strongly or it can be used to liberate you. Like for example, us. We are teaching basic programs with certain kriyas, and we are reassuring the participants that this is not about leaving your life and going away. This is about being more effective at what you're doing, because we are teaching kriyas only to that extent which sort of roots them in their life, makes them more effective, makes them more capable. Many more possibilities of life open up for them. The kriyas and the physical processes are taught only to that extent where it roots them in the body. The same kriyas, if they are practiced in a different dimension, with a different understanding and a different intensity, will start loosening you from the body.

So these kriyas and karmas, the external activity and internal activity can be used either to liberate you or to bind you. Once your energies reach a certain peak or certain level of maturity, when holding on to the body becomes an effort, then you start doing karmas and kriyas to hold on to the body, because you have some unfinished work. See, as karma can be binding and releasing, yoga kriyas also can be binding and releasing. Both karma and yoga kriyas can be used either to bind you or to liberate you. So this is the problem, or this is the situation that a Realized being who continues to live always has. His energy is always disentangling itself; it cannot be associated with the body, but he is doing everything to keep it rooted in the body, because he still has something to do. What we are talking about, re-creation, is to re-manifest those areas of the pranic body which are destroyed. Another thing is to create the necessary karma and kriyas within yourself to root the energy into the body so that this form of life can continue for a while longer.

Seeker: Sadhguru, how come even some Enlightened beings have physical afflictions? Why don't they cure themselves? For example, Ramakrishna Paramahamsa had cancer.

Sadhguru: Ramakrishna Paramahamsa was not interested in all this physical business. He was in the bliss body; simply blissful. The physical body, he was not bothered, mental body, he was not bothered, pranic body, he was not bothered. When a person is like that, the body may rot. He does not care. When Ramana sat for meditation, he just sat for fourteen years and his whole body was full of sores and insect bites. Animals came and bit him and he just sat because he had nothing to do with the body. If it heals, it heals. If it doesn't heal, it doesn't heal. He treats the mind and mental body the same way. If cancer comes, he doesn't care. He doesn't even feel he has cancer because he feels it is not in him.

Only people on the path of kriya yoga are capable of attending to the body in a scientific way. Others do not pay attention to it. Usually, they are incapable of too much activity. A Ramana or a Ramakrishna would not be able to trek with me to the Himalayas, let alone at my pace. Physically they are very incapable, because they were not bothered about taking care of their bodies. Their growth did not involve building a certain body. So they never attended to those things. They attained through their own intelligence and their own intensity, not following any system. Only people on the path of kriya, the Realized yogis, are physically very fit and their bodies will be properly kept. For them there is no problem. They cross the border and they come back. They smuggle things across (laughs). For them, it's a daily affair. That's the difference between a saint and a Guru. Saints somehow cross the border. They are wonderful people. They will bless you and their blessings are good to receive.

A Guru is not somebody who is just a saint. A Guru is somebody who has the methods and technologies for everything. He's somebody who is good both ways. A Guru's ways will not be saintly at all. One moment he's this, the next that. He can be in so many ways. He is just playing a role because he has all the technologies in his hand. He's not always a good man; he can do anything, but a saint is always a good man, always gentle, always loving and always happy. A Guru is not like that. He will do what is needed. If needed, he can stand up and fight.

Seeker: Sadhguru, in the past you have talked about how *Shakthi Chalana Kriya* helps with death. Would you please explain this further?

Sadhguru: The *Shakthi Chalana Kriya* that you are doing is a way to transform your life energies from just manufacturing a mass of flesh to manufacturing something so much subtler and so much more enduring than flesh. I'm sure you have no illusions about this, that the nature of life is such, this body is on loan for you from the earth. Mother Earth has loaned it to you, isn't it? She doesn't charge interest, but the loan is one hundred percent recovered. Not a cell or atom you can take with you; it's one hundred percent recovery.

Now when you have this body, you can manufacture something else, which the earth cannot reclaim. So the whole spiritual process is just that, trying to earn yourself something that the earth cannot reclaim from you. Whether you do *Shakthi Chalana Kriya*, meditation or something else, all you're trying to do is to earn something that the earth cannot reclaim. If you do not earn that, then when the loan collection comes, the earth will take everything and will not leave anything with you. Then, you know, the next part of the journey will not be good. If you have cash in your pocket you travel more comfortably, yes? Otherwise, you'll be in trouble.

You are preparing for the journey of your life with qualifications, with money, with clothes, with homes, with families, with relationships, fully knowing that all this has only a brief existence. It's needed, right? It is fine, but it need not be made into such a big issue. It should not be a life-consuming issue. A certain part of your energy you can dedicate to take care of your well-being, your physical and mental well-being, your comforts and your things, whatever you need. You are capable of that. You have the necessary intelligence and energy to do it. It's only because your life is all messed up that it does not produce what it has to produce. If you streamline yourself, you will see, earning your living and living well is very much possible without twenty-four hours of dedication; but you know very well that you have to drop all this. If you sit here for a moment with eyes closed, you can see that you seem to be something a little more than this body. You may not know what it is, but you can feel that you are something a little more than this body, isn't it?

If anybody just closes his eyes for two minutes and looks, he can see that what he calls as 'himself' is something more than the body. When the body is reclaimed, if you do not have anything with you for the next part of the journey, it won't be good. This is not only about the next part of the journey, but right now, this part of the journey also won't be very good. You may have many valuable things, you may have many people with you, you may have everything, but you, as a person, will never know one moment of peace if your energies are not good. So both for this journey and whatever may be beyond it, it is important that you begin to manufacture subtler dimensions of energy around you. The *Shakthi Chalana Kriya* that we teach you here is for this. This morning and evening *Shakthi Chalana Kriya*, if you keep on doing it, slowly you will find every breath becomes a source of manufacturing subtler forces around you. Pranayama does not only mean breath. This must be understood. *Shakthi Chalana Kriya* means to control the vital energies. Control of vital energies need not necessarily mean using the breath.

Even if I move my fingers like this, I can have total control over my energy. I can shift my energy wherever I want it. Not just in the body, anywhere, literally anywhere in the world. Whenever you wish, you can have your energy anywhere once you have certain mastery over your energies. Initially, you are using breath as a means. Breath is only a tool, but it's not about the breath. Even without the breath it can be done. It has nothing to do with the breath really. The breath is just used as an initial tool, but once a certain amount of mastery is there, it just does not matter. So *Shakthi Chalana Kriya* is not just about morning and evening. As you keep the practice going, you will see that the very quality of your breath throughout the day is different. Do you feel this? The very way it is, is different. In a way, yes, *Shakthi Chalana Kriya* is a way of preparing for the last breath and beyond.

Seeker: Can you do anything at the moment of death to help someone who has not completely reached the point of liberation? I know a meditator who told me you helped her sick father who was painfully dying of cancer with his death. What did you do, Sadhguru?

Sadhguru: Deepika, where do you collect all this information from? Now if he has run his full course of prarabdha, which is not true for most people, we can help him die consciously rather then in an unconscious state because there is a conducive atmosphere. Dissolution is possible. He is liberated. When they die of disease before the prarabdha is complete and prarabdha is still due, if I try to dissolve him, it's not going to work, nor am I going to do that. All we can do is help him to die with awareness; then he will have a little enhanced life somewhere else.

Seeker: If he has run his full course and you help him, then he's liberated for good? How is that possible, Master?

Sadhguru: Yes, he is liberated for good and this is possible only when someone has run the full course of prarabdha. Now everything is over, he's in a certain space where there is a karmic break. There are many people who die of old age; they may have lived as utter fools, but the final few days, suddenly there is a new sense of wisdom within them, a new sense of awareness about them, because their karma allotment has finished.

Just the minor things are left and the next quota of karma has not come in yet, so that's a blessed period. Even for a person who lived an ignorant life, you'll see that suddenly he knows, "In the next three days I will die." Do you know this? Aged people, who are perfectly healthy, they will just know. Such people we can dissolve very easily because they have come to that blessed state where there is no karmic bondage. There is a stock somewhere else, but here there is a little space of no karma. No karma means no individuality. Do you understand this? No karma means no substance for individual process to happen.

It has come to a point where you're almost like dissolving because the next quota has not been released yet. The current quota is over and in that space, dissolution is very simple. If one has not reached that space, if one is approaching death because of a broken body, either because of injury or disease or whatever else, such a person we can help him to die in a little better awareness so that he has a little enhanced life elsewhere.

Seeker: Is that so even for somebody who doesn't know you, Master?

Sadhguru: There is no one who does not know me; I want you to understand this. As a person, whether you know me or not, is a different thing. There is nobody who does not know me because, when I'm talking on this level, I'm not talking about myself as a person, myself as some bundle of habits and patterns and things. That which I call as 'myself' is you also. There is nobody who does not know me. We are talking about that dimension. In that dimension there is no individual person.

Seeker: So Sadhguru, every time someone is born he just gets a pack of karma to work out in this lifetime?

Sadhguru: The warehouse is there. One truckload has been taken out, to be worked out now. The warehouse is always sitting there in your head. Now what we're doing with Samyama,[1] you're not going into the prarabdha. You're going into the *sanchita* aspect of your karma. You're bringing out, you are opening up the warehouse. That's the reason why, when a person walks the spiritual path, in many ways –if they don't handle the situation properly – they will suffer much more than someone else, because they are bringing up large volumes of it. Others are just handling what is allotted to them. Now you're trying to take up the whole portion, you want to get your Ph.D. today, so you're not going step by step. That is the reason why so much discipline was always brought into yogic practices, so that when things overwhelm you, you are able to handle that situation. Otherwise, if you open up things for which you are not ready, karma can just smother you completely.

---

1 Samyama : an eight day meditation program offered by Sadhguru, where one is transported to explosive states of meditativeness. Held at Isha Yoga Center.

Seeker: So Sadhguru, people come in this life to work out some karma, a part of karma, but end up with even more karma?

Sadhguru: Yes, that's why it's like an endless circle!

Seeker: In many cases you have said to your disciples, "I can only show you the path. I cannot liberate you. If somebody says, 'I can dissolve your karma,' do not believe him; no Master can do it." This means that all these people who are with you - thousands of people who have given themselves to you - just because they die of natural death without pain, their karma will not dissolve, but somebody who is sick and suffering, say my mom or dad, you dissolve theirs? Why not mine, Sadhguru?

Sadhguru: Yours also. Now I'm teaching you programs and I'm asking you to take your life into your hands so that you live gracefully and sensibly. I am not talking about death when I talk to you about these things. I'm talking about your present life so that you can live this life fruitfully. Do not wait for me to pull the plug and live a stupid life until then. I'm telling you to take care of your own life, work towards your own Realization so that you live an elevated life here. Now those who have given themselves totally to me, even for a single moment, they do not have to worry about their liberation. Liberation is assured. To live gracefully or not, that's not assured. That is something that you have to earn; there is no other way.

Seeker: Sadhguru, let's say my neighbor, who is a crook, is dying and you dissolve him just like that. Here I am doing this sadhana day in and day out. I would feel very cheated.

Sadhguru: The sadhana is to live gracefully, to live beyond the present level of limitations. I told you that dissolving you comes only when you have given yourself totally. Now the reason why sadhana is done is that life is not one hundred percent in your hands. Many people may not run their full prarabdha, either because of injury, accident, disease or for any reason. Most people may not run their full course of prarabdha. Most people die in hospitals today because they are not running their full prarabdha. How many people die every day, without any ill health, just out of old age? It's a small percentage, isn't it?

Sadhana is done so that you create a certain sense of awareness and you're hastening the process of the dissolution of karma so that your prarabdha gets finished faster and faster. If you dissolve some aspects of your prarabdha, generally you're working towards the mental and emotional dimensions of your prarabdha so that you can live in a blessed state for a longer period of your life. If you dissolve them, your physical prarabdha is still there, so you continue to live, but without the struggles of the mind, without the struggles of the emotions. That's a blessed state. When physical prarabdha is over, the body will drop itself. The possibility of liberation is so much higher.

Seeker: Sadhguru, what happens to all the layers of bodies that contain this being at death?

Sadhguru: The physical one drops back here because it was picked up from the earth. It has to go back there. The next one is the mental body. The grosser conscious part of the mind also, you drop here. It's only the karmic part of the mind which travels with you. So next is the energy body, or the pranic body, which is the *pranamayakosha*. This is still physical, like electricity is. That goes. This is why we are working on your pranayama, to make the pranamayakosha so vibrant that when it leaves this physical body, it still has a good existence, a mind of its own, some amount of choice. Once pranamayakosha is functioning by choice, not by compulsion, evolution is very quick. When your energies are just functioning unconsciously, they function one way; but when your energies become a higher level of consciousness or awareness, suddenly you have a choice. Now, where you need to be born is your choice. Destiny slowly begins to come into your hands, if your energies are completely aware.

As I have been telling people, do not mistake mental alertness for awareness. That is not awareness. If you look at it that way, the birds are more aware than you are, isn't it? Physically, they are more mentally alert than you are. If a snake comes here, you will not know, but if you just put your foot down here, all the snakes within one hundred meters will know. So they're more alert, both mentally and physically. That alertness is only useful for survival. You'll survive better, but that's not the awareness we are talking about. If your energy becomes aware, your life begins to move from compulsions to choice.

That's the first step you have to take, to move your energies into higher levels of vibrancy. How you get there is not the point. You may get there singing, dancing, breathing, or you may get there with your love; whichever way. If your energies are high, in a high pitch of vibrancy, your life naturally is no longer a compulsion. Everything slowly becomes by choice, to such a point that death and birth become a choice.

Seeker: Sadhguru, you stopped at the energy body...

Sadhguru: The spiritual body and bliss body cannot hold form by themselves, in the sense that they have no structure of their own. Only because there is a karmic body – which has manifested itself right now in your physical body, in your mental body and your energy body – only because of karma, the other two inner bodies are there. If you take away the karmic body, even the mental body and the energy body cannot hold themselves. That's why we're calling karma the only bondage. If you remove that, your other bodies will just spill. Like if you're carrying fluid in a plastic bag, and if the bag bursts, then it's all over, finished, back into the ocean.

Seeker: Is that what you mean when you say 'dissolve', Sadhguru?

Sadhguru: Yes. You just burst the karmic bag. Once the karmic substance is taken away, it just goes. It is the karmic substance which is giving you the sense of individuality. The individual experience is there only because of the karmic substance. Even now, when you're in the physical body, if you just forget your karmic structure for one moment you will not know who you are on the level of the mind itself. Suppose you got drunk, then you don't know who you are. See the sense of freedom, how joyous you become? You become joyous because just for some time you forget who you are. At least your identities have melted away a little bit. That's why you like to sit there in meditation so much, because sometimes your identity melts away. In a way, you become free of your karmic structure for a moment. It's not totally gone, but it is somewhat gone. Just that 'somewhat gone' stage itself is so beautiful because it is imprinted in other dimensions. It's still there, but on the level of the mind. If you forget your karma, it's an enormous freedom, isn't it? If all the karma is removed from all levels, then it is total freedom.

Now you are playing a game, but you forgot it is a game. You think you're this and that, missing so much freedom. If you put down all aspects of the karma, it is dissolution, total freedom, the end of bondage.

Seeker: So Sadhguru, when I reach the level that I can decide when I die and where I will be born, is this earth the only choice that I have?

Sadhguru: Yes, and also no, in a small way. Yes, in a huge way; I would say ninety-eight percent.

Seeker: Tell me about the small way, Sadhguru.

Sadhguru: It's only two percent; don't bother about the two percent. Leave it alone. If your concern is your liberation, you just learn how to dissolve that which binds you. Don't go on a curiosity hunt.

Seeker: Sadhguru, after the physical death, can people who have known each other in this realm reunite in another? Is there some recognition?

Sadhguru: Most relationships are either of the body or on the level of the conscious mind. Very, very few relationships cross that. Once the body and the major part of the mind are dropped, you don't know anything about the other being. It may so happen that all the people that practice *kaka kriya,*[1] their energies have become a certain way. It is true, in a way it's true, but I'm telling it as a joke. Suppose that by practicing this kaka kriya, your energies have become a certain way, which is not the case for most human beings on the planet. When you leave your bodies and if you're not fully liberated, then all these kaka kriyas' bodies may come together. Not because they recognize that all of us were in Isha yoga, it's not like that; but because of a certain tendency of the energy, they may cluster together; it is possible. Not just possible, in certain situations it's very much a reality. As we were talking earlier, beings are clustering here because this kind of energy draws them – because somewhere, when they lived, they were into yogic practices, which naturally attracts them here. So in that way, yes, but not like, "This has

1 *kaka kriya* : kriya which makes one less available to gravity, taught in the basic Isha Yoga program.

been my wife, my child," no, because the deepest thing that you know about your relationships is just emotion.

Seeker: Yet in some of your other publications Sadhguru, you talk about determining specific individuals' place of rebirth and things of that nature. When you talked about the Dhyanalinga, you related that you had some individuals born in certain wombs. My assumption from that is you have the ability to take someone who has died, their energy, recognize that energy and direct that they go there for a specific purpose. Or, did they decide?

Sadhguru: No, they did not decide. It is just that with the kind of contact that they had in that life they could have easily been dissolved, but for them, their Enlightenment, their liberation, did not mean anything. Their Guru is everything for them. They are not even interested in getting dissolved or anything. They just love him, that's all. These people do not care for liberation. They aren't even looking for Enlightenment. Such beings have no quality of their own. They have just become Him. So it's easy to plant them where you want because it is just you, in a way.

Seeker: Master, what is it about people doing something at death to negatively influence a person's death and rebirth?

Sadhguru: When people curse somebody else they say, "Go to *naraka*. Go to hell." So when the moment of death comes, at that moment, they want to create some kind of desire or some kind of situation around him so that he goes to the worst possible hell. At this final moment of death, any kind of man, simply because of the disentangling process of the body, tends to become peaceful and empty. They want to disturb that. So they will create all kinds of situations where he will get desire, so that he'll suffer for a long period when he leaves the body. You don't know all the sciences. Many times they want to create the desire of lust or revulsion in him because these are very strong physical emotions. If his eyes are open, they get people to copulate in front of him. Seeing this, a little desire arises in him. Suppose someone hates you, now they are putting you to death. Now they don't just put you to death, they torture you to create revulsion within you. If someone dies with a strong desire, all evolution is gone. They just go back to the most basic state.

When the moment of death comes, no matter what kind of life you may have lived, it gives you an opportunity to settle certain things. A certain space is created no matter what kind of karmic baggage he carries. Now these vicious people want to take away that opportunity because they know that if they create a desire, he will carry his suffering beyond his physical body. There are people who can access this and tell them what kind of suffering that man is going through. So they create various kinds of situations around the dying man to make sure he gets the worst possible suffering or the worst possible hell. They want you to get the worst accommodation down there (laughs).

If loved ones are there, if spiritually aware people are there, they try to create a different kind of atmosphere for the last moment of death. That is there in every culture, isn't it? These days you think a good atmosphere means your wife, husband or child hugging you, kissing you; but you should not die with your family, really. In India, when people who are a little aware want to die, they always go away from their family. They want to die in a space of non-attachment. They want to die in a way that has nothing to do with their body, their attachments, their struggles and their things. They want to die in a space which is more spiritual in nature. Dying with your family is not a great way to die. Some amount of love is good, but there are so many attachments. The last moment of your life, if you look at your son, your daughter, your wife or husband, not just love will come. So many other things will come along with it, isn't it? Yes? Their faces are a reminder of many, many things in your life, not just of love, because the relationship has not been just about love. It has been so many things and all that will come. So always, at the moment of death, it is suggested in India that you should not be with the family. I know it's unthinkable for you Westerners. You have always thought that dying means die with the family. This is not out of love, it's out of fear. Do you understand? Because there is a deep fear, you want someone you know around you.

Seeker: What other rites are performed for the dead in India? Would you talk about them, Sadhguru?

Sadhguru: Every culture in the world has its own type of rituals for the dead. Generally, a lot of it is to settle certain psychological factors that will anyway come with the death of the dear and near ones; but in some way most cultures have known certain rituals which actually have a certain relevance and science behind them. Probably no other culture has such elaborate methods as the Hindus have. Nobody has looked at death with the kind of understanding and depth that this culture has. Right from the moment that death occurs, or even before it occurs, in yoga there are whole systems as to how to help a person die in the most beneficial way. The Hindu way of life, having thousands of years of background behind it, is very cunning. They want to extract something out of everything. Even if death is going to occur, even that they want to make use of in some way. So they have rituals for the dying, and rituals for the dead.

Now when the moment of death is approaching, those who are aware of this generally move the dying person out of the house and keep them in a north-south alignment with the head to the north. If death is certain and they want it to happen with ease, they take the body outside because if the body is still in the house, inside constructed atmospheres, the being does not leave the body with ease. So they want the body to be outside a constructed atmosphere and placed in a north-south alignment because it further eases the disentanglement of the being from the body.

Even after clinical death has occurred, still the prana is not completely gone from the physical body. The physical body is not totally broken. So the being still tends to hover around the body; but if you place it in a north-south alignment, the being will be pulled away from the body because of the magnetic pull. Certain changes happen in the physiology, or certain changes happen quickly within the body that has been discarded, so that the being realizes that it is futile to hang around that particular body, because it can no more access it once it is placed in the north-south direction. A certain distance arises between the being and the body. Because most people live totally identified with the body, as far as you're concerned, death has happened, but as far as the dead person is concerned, he has just slipped out of the body. All his life he lived being identified with the physical body. Suddenly he is out of it, which leaves him bewildered and he does not realize that it's over. So he tends to make attempts to get back into the body, which is unfit to sustain life. This can lead to a certain energy in that place which is neither good for him nor good for the people who are living around that space. So placing the body north-to-south is one precaution; it distances the being from the body.

Another thing that is known in India is, when a person dies, the first thing is they tie the toes together, because if the toes are not tied together, the remaining aspect of the prana tends to leave from the *Muladhara,*[1] and it also tends to become a passageway for the being to again enter the body in a partial way, if the Muladhara is open. If the anal outlet is left open, then the being will make an attempt to re-enter from this lower passage, which is not at all good for that being, nor is it good for the situation in which the living still exist. It can cause a very negative situation, so the toes are always tied together so that the Muladhara is closed. If you put your toes together, you will notice that your anal outlet is always tightly shut and that's the precaution that you are taking when you're doing the yoga kriyas. When you put your toes together, your anal outlet gets naturally closed. The same thing is done with the dead, so that this play of trying to get in and repossess the body cannot happen. This wanting to possess the body through the Muladhara, or the anal passage, need not necessarily be by the being or the person who left the body. There are other beings who will seek such a passage.

If somebody wants to do certain occult practices where freshly-dead bodies are used, it's always the Muladhara which is made use of because that's the easiest passage. Other passages will not be easily available. So if you leave their legs open, one thing is, the body tends to become distorted and the legs will naturally spread across, spread wide when death happens. So putting them together – one thing is, not to distort the body, another thing is to ensure that the anal passage is properly closed so that it cannot be misused by any other hovering spirits which are always looking for such a possibility. It can also be misused by people who are into occult practices. They can use that body for other purposes, which would bind that being in so many ways. Whenever a person dies in this culture, a certain atmosphere is created. Certain mantras are chanted, and certain care is taken to ensure that people who are into these practices, who are always looking for the freshly-dead, cannot make use of the body of your loved ones for such purposes. So the moment it is identified that the person is dead, the feet are tied together, or the toes are tied together so that such misuse will not happen.

---

1 *Muladhara* : the psycho-energetic chakra located at the perineum.

Seeker: It is generally said that the body should be burned in the next four hours. Is it so, Sadhguru?

Sadhguru: This is because until the body is destroyed, there is a tendency for the being to hang around and not proceed. What should happen will not happen, simply because the being is still not aware that it is over. So as quickly as possible, the body should be burnt. In ancient times, the rule was that within an hour and a half after death, the body should be burned.

When that was so, certain mistakes were made sometimes because, unlike today, there were no doctors to exactly say that somebody is dead, and there have been instances when they were put on the pyre, when the fire touched them, people sat up. Once, a funeral service was held in a synagogue for a woman who just passed away. At the end of the service, the pallbearers were carrying the casket out when they accidentally bumped into a wall, jarring the casket. They heard a faint moan, so they opened the casket and found that the woman was actually alive. She went on to live for ten more years and then died. A ceremony was held again at the same synagogue and at the end of the ceremony the pallbearers were again carrying the casket. As they were walking, the husband cried out aloud, "Watch out for the wall!" So later on they extended it to four hours to ensure that the dead are really dead and then they burn it as quickly as possible. Today, because of your attachments, you are keeping the body for days on end which is not a good thing, neither for the dead nor for the living.

Seeker: Sadhguru, in other cultures they keep it for three days before burying it. The Christians...

Sadhguru: That's because of Jesus. They're hoping that after three days they'll get up.

Seeker: What about the ashes, Sadhguru? Is there any significance to what happens to the ashes?

Sadhguru: It is forty days after the conception that the being enters the body. Similarly, up to forty days, the being still takes time to completely leave the body. When I say completely leave the body, even if you have burned the body, it will look for certain elements of the body like the ash or anything else, something that belongs to them, maybe their used clothes. If you do not know this, in the Hindu families, the moment the person dies, all the clothes that the person used, especially those clothes which touched the person's body, like underclothes, are all burned. This is because the being still looks for elements of the body, maybe the sweat, maybe the smell of the body, maybe something for which it seeks again, because still the realization has not come that it's over. All that is there. They want to just get rid of it. If you keep the ashes in one place, there is a tendency for the being to look for that. So they are put in a river where they are spread, that way they cannot be found. It's all gone. Everything possible is being done to make the being understand that it's over, and it's also for the living to understand that it is all over.

Seeker: Sadhguru, why do they offer food on the third day?

Sadhguru: On the third day after death, there is a tradition or a ritual to offer milk and water to the grave. One thing is that there is a psychological need in you to still feed them, still take care of them, though they are dead, though you can't do anything. All the milk and water or food, whatever you can offer, only a body can consume. One who is bodiless has nothing to do with all this. It has a very deep psychological implication for the living. The other aspect of it is that the one who has left the body, the dead – this is not true with everybody who dies, but with certain people – when he dies in a certain unfulfilled way, or if he dies without running the course of his prarabdha karma or the allotted karma for this life, such a person could be quenched by making certain offerings. This is not always true. In some cases it's true, so they just made that a general ritual so that in case the dead in your house has such a requirement, it is taken care of. Above all, it quenches the psychological thirst in you, wanting to do something for somebody that you care for; and generally, when they were living maybe you were not on talking terms. Maybe when they asked for a glass of water you did not bring it, but now you want to do it. All this knowledge has come out of people's awareness of experiencing those dimensions which are beyond the body very clearly. They have been established in the Indian culture, but over a period of time, they get distorted and people start doing very silly things, not realizing exactly why certain things were said.

Seeker: Sadhguru, are there words that you can convey that will help me understand what the 'nothingness experience' is like?

Sadhguru: There is no experience. When you do not exist, where is the experience? All experiencing stops. Only because you are experiencing you exist, isn't it? When you are asleep you don't exist because you are not experiencing. Your existence itself is just a certain level of experiencing. Suppose we compare you to insects, birds or other animals; your levels of experiencing are different from what they experience. So your experiencing is a huge deception. We want to take away the deception.

It happened like this: there is this old priest who got sick of all the people in his parish who kept confessing to infidelity. One Sunday, on the pulpit he said, "If I hear one more person confess to infidelity, I'll quit!" Everyone liked him very much, so they came up with a code word. Someone who had committed an infidelity would instead say they had fallen. This seemed to satisfy the old priest and things went well, until the priest passed away at a ripe old age. A few days after the new priest arrived, he visited the mayor of the town and seemed very concerned, "Mayor, you have to do something about the sidewalks in town; when people come into the confessional, they keep telling me they have fallen." The mayor started to laugh, realizing that no one had told the new priest about the code word, but before he could explain, the priest shook an accusing finger at him and shouted, "I don't know what you are laughing about because your wife has fallen three times this week!"

See, if we take away the deception, there is nothing to experience and nobody to experience it. It's over. You just blew a bubble and you believe it is real. If you just prick the bubble, what are you going to get? Will something else fall out of it? Nothing else will fall out of it. It will just disappear, that's all.

Seeker: So where is the energy, Sadhguru? The energy still stays, correct?

Sadhguru: But that is not you. There is no such specific thing as 'you' as energy. It's just a vast energy. Let us understand this right now in a more limited way. Right now, your body is sitting here. It can experience many things, the body itself, isn't it? It can experience light, it can experience sound, it can experience touch, smell and taste. Now if you die, you leave this body. It falls here and becomes a part of this earth. So where is your body now?

Seeker: In the earth.

Sadhguru: Nothing like that. It has become earth. It was earth to start with. It was just a piece of earth that stood up and pranced around a little bit and again fell back. The same thing happens with your energy also, on a different level. What you call as 'my being' is also a certain amount of energy. Just like your body came out of the earth and played a game and fell back into the earth, similarly energy came out of the unboundedness and played a little game and fell back. Spirituality means you realize that you are just a little bit of energy caught in your karmic structures. Just remove the karma and the energy falls back to what it was. It has always been that. Even today, even now, that's what it is. You imagine it is something else. You think it's you. There is no such thing. It's just the same energy playing a game. So you put it back where it belongs. You return the loan. You settle your debts and there's nothing left. You do not like it. You still want to go to heaven and be there and look down upon us, because they told you God would be waiting there with a long white beard. He will welcome you and treat you well. That's a fairy tale! It's like this: once, Jesus was strolling through heaven when he saw an old man with a long white beard sitting on a cloud and staring into the distance. "Old man," said Jesus, "This is heaven! Why are you so sad?" The old man did not bother to turn as he said, "I have been looking for my son and have not been able to find him." Jesus said, "Tell me about it." "Well," the old man said, still gazing at the sunlit horizon, "On earth, I was a carpenter, and one day my son went away. I never heard from him again. I was hoping I would find him here in heaven." His heart pounding suddenly in his chest, Jesus bent over the old man and said, ever so softly, "Father!" The old man turned and cried, "Pinocchio!"

Seeker: But Sadhguru, they talk about heaven in religion. Would that be liberation, while incarnation is hell?

Sadhguru: When you talk about heaven, there must also be a hell, isn't it? Or if there is a hell, there must be a heaven. So heaven and hell are part of the duality and duality can only exist as long as you're identified with the physical. Once the physical is completely dissolved, once the deeper modifications of your mind are completely dissolved, there is no question of duality. Once there is no duality, there is no possibility of heaven or hell.

Seeker: Sadhguru, when we die and are not liberated, if we don't go to a heaven or a hell, what happens? Is it either a heaven-ish or hell-ish state before rebirth?

Sadhguru: I don't know how it is exactly described in your Lebanese culture. I think it has just been mentioned as different kinds of pleasures or sufferings. In India, there's a whole lot of description about different types of hells, different types of heavens one can go through. See, going to heaven or hell is not a destination, it's just a certain state. If you die and are in a certain state of pleasantness, we say that you're in a heaven-ish state. If you're in a state of unpleasantness, we say you are in a certain type of hell. Any experience is either pleasant or unpleasant when you are in duality. Isn't it? So when you are still experiencing, it's either pleasant or unpleasant, cool or hot, light or dark. It's always like this.

You are bound to be somewhere, either a mild or a deep hell. Or it can be a mild heaven or a high heaven. So the question is just the intensity. Unless one dies with a certain sense of awareness, where they have maintained a certain sense of conscious choice even as a disembodied being, only then they have a certain amount of choice; but still they are in pleasantness or unpleasantness. Others go just by their tendencies. See it is all a comparative experience. I have a joke for you.

General Eisenhower, being the man who brought World War II to a decisive end, went to heaven. One day he said, "I want to visit hell." God asked, "Why?" He said, "I want to see what kind of suffering Adolf Hitler is in." So they gave him a pass and he went to hell. He asked the guards there, the devils, which way to Adolf Hitler's torture chamber. They guided him and he went to the chamber. There Eisenhower saw that Adolf Hitler was standing in a septic tank up to his neck in shit with a big grin on his face. Eisenhower first noticed only the shit and he was happy and said, "You deserve it, man." Then he noticed that Adolf Hitler was grinning. "You shameless creature, standing there in such filth; what are you grinning about?" he asked. Adolf Hitler laughed and said, "I'm standing on Mussolini's shoulders!" (Laughs). So, pleasantness and suffering is comparative, you know?

Chapter - 5

Realm of the Mystic

Realm of the Mystic

Even a blade of grass is pointing towards you
A pine tree of course is reaching out for you
Every pulsating cell of protoplasmic shell
Has to ceaselessly tread your mindless will
My longing and thrashing was a veritable hell
This merging has become blissful and still

Now I can say your Will is my Will
And when I Will, you Will.

– Sadhguru

At a cave in the Velliangiri mountains that He loves and reveres.

In another realm.

From the caveman's time when everything, from the sound of thunder and rain, fire and floods, were all too mystical, to the present day where anything that's not within the tenets of rudimentary logic is a matter of scorn and ridicule, man has certainly come a long way. Exploited to the hilt by impostors of all sorts, trivialized to palm reading, crystal gazing and aura cleansing, mysticism today is more a frivolous pastime than a sacred dimension and the key to the elusive mysteries and the purpose of Existence.

Obsessed by the mundane and ensnared by the prowess of the logical, over centuries, man has obliterated the mystical from his life. Yet, whether it is the process of birth or rebirth, or a miracle healing, whether it is stepping-out of one's body or transmigration of the soul, black magic or occult,

Enlightenment or *Mukthi*, it is the Realm of the Mystic that rules the world of the seeker and Existence.

Speaking sometimes cryptically like a Zen master to his adept disciples, sometimes like a master story-teller weaving tales of another time and another world, sometimes like the gray-haired scientist expounding with utmost simplicity the most profound aspects of the cosmos, Sadhguru takes the reader on a startling tour of the mystical, leaving the reader choicelessly humbled about his own importance in the Universe.

Quoting extensively from first hand experiences and separating truth from myth of the tradition, Sadhguru's irrefutably logical narration dares the reader to seek the Realm of the Mystic – the abode of the Enlightened.

Seeker: Sadhguru, can you please speak about the phenomena we refer to as miracles, healings, and things like that, which cannot be explained by medical science?

Sadhguru: Life functions in many ways. Anything that you don't understand, you call it a miracle. Let us say you don't know anything about electricity. You do not know what electricity is. This hall is dark. If I tell you to just press this button and the whole hall will be flooded with light, will you believe me? No. Now I just do it, and light appears. What will you call me? The Messiah, the son of God, or maybe even God Himself – simply because you don't understand how electricity works. Similarly, life happens in many different ways. You have limited yourself to just the physical, the logical – physical in experience, logical in thinking. Anything beyond this, you are calling a miracle. That's why I have been trying to remind you that if there is a miracle, then everything in the existence is a miracle; every atom is a miracle, isn't it? Can you believe that a little atom – these three things rotating around each other – if you break it, it becomes an enormous bomb that can destroy the whole planet? Is it not a miracle? Every atom is a miracle. Otherwise, there are no miracles and everything is just the way it is. It is natural. Whether you call it natural or miracle, it's the same thing; just different words. Anything which is not in your perception or your experience, you tend to call a miracle. There are no miracles in the way that you are thinking. It is just that medical sciences are limited to just knowing the physical body. If anything happens beyond that, you think it's a miracle.

The last time I was in the United States, Doug's knee cartilage was torn. He was in excruciating pain. He had already been in India for a year, training to be a teacher. He went back to the United States and suddenly his knee began to hurt terribly. He wasn't even able to sit in *vajrasana*.[1] At the same time,

---

1 *vajrasana* : a simple yogic posture.

something else was happening in his mind. He was doing funny things around me, but I just let him be. In so many ways, he was trying to tell me, not actually in words, but with his actions, comments and gestures, both consciously and unconsciously, that his knee was bad and going back to India would not be possible for him. Then he went to a doctor in Chicago; the doctor said he must have an MRI. They took the MRI scan and they told him, "The cartilage in your knee is torn; you must have surgery immediately." They said, "It's not just torn; the pieces of the cartilage have gotten between the joint. That's why there is so much pain." When he moved, he felt excruciating pain. So he brought the MRI to me and said, "The doctor says I must go through surgery. It costs ten thousand dollars. I'll have to get a job to pay for it. I can't come back to India." I said, "Don't worry about what the doctor says."

Then, there were just about four or five days left before I was to leave the country, and Doug was also supposed to leave. He came to me and asked, "What shall I do? I'm supposed to go through the surgery." I said, "Anyway, you told me you want to meditate." He said he wanted to meditate, and experience deeper and deeper states of meditation. For a meditator, one big problem is the lower part of the leg. Isn't it? Now if your knee and below is taken off, you know, it's so wonderful to sit and meditate…no pain in the leg, nothing. I said, "We'll amputate both your legs, in India. Then you can sit and meditate all the time. You told me you want to become a meditator. You want to go into deep meditation. So what's your problem? We will remove the leg and you will meditate."

"No, no, no, don't do that!" he said (laughs). I said, "It's up to you then; you do what you want." He struggled and struggled, then he came back to India. At the time, everybody was getting ready to go to the Himalayas. On the Himalayan trek, we trek over eighty kilometers in total, over a period of twelve days. Then it happened that we took a group of people trekking up the big mountain behind the ashram, and he came along. Once there, he came and asked, "Can I come to the Himalayas?" I said, "I thought you were due for amputation. Where is the question of Himalayas for you? We don't want to kill any mules there, but, okay, you come to the Himalayas." Then he remembered: "But my leg…" I said, "Leave your leg and come."

He came to the Himalayas and walked all eighty kilometers, keeping pace with me. Generally, I leave everyone behind me and go. He carried my bag and kept pace with me, wherever I went. So I went about advertising to everybody, this man tried to con me for ten thousand dollars (laughs). He showed me a fake MRI." He asked, "What happened to my leg? Really, it was hurting so much and now it's not hurting at all." Now you can call it a miracle if you want. I just call it another kind of science, that's all. It is another kind of science. Life functions in so many ways. You have just limited yourself to the physical and the logical. Anything beyond that, you think is a miracle. This life energy in you created your whole body. These bones, this flesh, this heart, this kidney and everything, can't it create a piece of cartilage? If your energies are kept in full flow and proper balance, it is capable of recreating the physical.

Seeker: Is all energy a vibration, just different frequencies of vibration? Is it gross energy versus subtle energy, just a difference in the frequency of vibration?

Sadhguru: Energy, if it vibrates, takes a form. Now you want to put a line between what is physical, and what is beyond the physical. When you are talking about energy as modern science does, you're still talking about physical energy. We refer to this as prana, which is the source of all physical creation. Beyond that also there is energy. That energy is not manifest as physical, but it is still energy. That's what we're calling the etheric body and the bliss body. Or these days we are calling it nothingness.

Nothingness is bliss. It does not make sense logically. You can speak logically only up to *pranamayakosha.*[1] Beyond that, it will not make any logical sense. How can nothingness be blissful? People feel depressed when they feel like nothing. What I'm saying is, when you experience your nothingness, you feel blissful. That's not logical. So that realm of going beyond the *karma*[2] cannot be approached logically. It's just that you understand that the physical contains something else. It's wrong to call it 'something' because it is no more a thing. We can use the word 'something' and all this '*thing*' business only when it is physical. So when we say 'nothing', probably you would understand it better if we put a hyphen between no and thing, because it is no-thing anymore, but still it is, so that is where logic ends. That's where

1 *pranamayakosha*: the energy sheath or body. One of the five sheaths of yogic physiology.

2 karma: lit. action. Referring to past action, the cause of all bondage.

modern science ends - with the physical. The whole spiritual process is to go beyond the physical, to know something which is not physical. That which is not physical has no dimension. That which has no dimension has no sense of here and there, now and then, nothing like that. Only the physical has here and there. Only the physical has now and then. That which is not physical does not subscribe to all these limitations.

Seeker: I have heard you sing, 'Nadha Bhramha', Sadhguru. What does it mean? And can we use sound to attain to mukthi?

Sadhguru: *Nadha* means sound. *Bhramha* means Divine, the All. Fundamentally, there are three sounds in the existence. Out of these three sounds, any given sound can be created. Do you know something about your color television? In your color television, there are only three color webs. Given these three color webs, any number of colors can be created. Similarly, given these three sounds, any number of sounds can be created. Right now, with an experiment, you can find out. See without the use of the tongue, there are only three sounds you can utter: "aaa", "ouuu", and "mmm". Even if you cut off your tongue, you can still utter these three sounds. For any other sound, you need the use of the tongue. You are using the tongue only to mix the sounds. There are only three sounds, and you are mixing them in many ways and producing all the other sounds. There are so many millions of sounds you can create with your mouth, isn't it? You know a mute person can only say: "aaa", "ouuu", and "mmm". He cannot say anything else because he has not learned how to use his tongue. Now if you utter these three sounds together, what will you get? AUM. AUM is not some religion's trademark, although they may be using it as their trademark. AUM is the fundamental sound in the existence.

It is said that the Great Lord Shiva can create a whole new existence just by uttering three AUMs. Now, this is not a fact, but it is a truth. Do you know the difference between a fact and a truth? Let us say you are sitting here as a woman; does that mean that your father has made no contribution towards you? Does that mean that your father does not exist within you? No. So the fact is, you're either a man or a woman. The truth is you are both. It's not that Shiva is sitting somewhere and uttering AUMs, that's not the point. What is being said is: see, today modern science proves to you beyond any doubt that the whole existence is just a vibration. Do you know this? There is no matter. After the theory of relativity and the quantum theory have come about, there is no such thing as matter. Everything is just a vibration. Yes, this has been proven beyond any doubt. Wherever there is a vibration, there is bound to be a sound.

Now this steel rod (touching the microphone stand) is not really a steel rod; it's a certain vibration. In other words, this is a certain sound. "If this is a sound, why can't I hear it?" This is the question, naturally. Why you do not hear it is because your ability to hear is limited to just a small band of frequencies. Anything above that you cannot hear; anything below that you cannot hear. The frequencies which are above your hearing level are known as ultrasonic frequencies; those below your hearing level are known as subsonic frequencies. Let's say you bring a transistor radio here and tune it to some frequency. A song is playing. Where is the song coming from? Is the radio singing? Right now, where is the sound? It is everywhere. It's in the air, but you cannot hear it. Right now, there are a lot of noises in the air, but you don't hear them. If you bring a transistor and tune it to a frequency, suddenly you hear. What the transistor is doing is converting a frequency that you cannot hear into a frequency that you can hear. That is all it is doing. So you know there is so much here that you cannot hear and the whole existence is just a sound.

Now, there are many ways to look at this. Have you been to Kedar? Has anybody been to Kedarnath? Having been born in India, if you do not go to the Himalayas, you're missing something very huge in your life. Before you're too old and no good for anything, you must go to the Himalayas once. It is something that everybody must do. Forget about anything spiritual, just the mountains themselves are too much. Everybody must see them once in their life. Being born in India, if you don't see them, you're missing something. Kedar is a very powerful and wonderful place. Above Kedar, there is a place called Kanti Sarovar. Generally people do not go there; it's a tricky climb. I just trekked up to Kanti Sarovar, and sat on one of those rocks there.

It's very difficult to put this into words, but after some time, everything turned into sound in my experience; my body, the mountain, the lake in front of me, everything had become sound. It had taken on the sound form, and was just going on in me in a completely different way. See, I have had, at many stages in my life, deep appreciation for Sanskrit as a language, and I had opportunities to learn it. I chose not to learn

Sanskrit, because the moment you learn Sanskrit, you'll end up reading the *Vedas*, the *Upanishads,*[1] and all the scriptures. My own vision has never failed me and I didn't want to clutter myself with all this traditional whatever, so I did not bother to learn Sanskrit. Here I am sitting, my mouth is closed – I am very clear about that – but my own voice is going on loudly, as if it is on a microphone, loudly singing a song, and it's in Sanskrit language. We will sing this together; just sing after me; close your eyes. Feel the sounds and just sing after me. Sing after me; you will know what it is about.

Nadha Bhramha Vishwaswaroopa
Nadha Hi Sakala Jeevaroopa
Nadha Hi Karma Nadha Hi Dharma
Nadha Hi Bandhana Nadha Hi Mukthi
Nadha Hi Shankara Nadha Hi Shakti
Nadham Nadham Sarvam Nadham
Nadham Nadham Nadham Nadham

(Sound is Bhramhan, the manifestation of the universe, sound manifests itself in the form of all life, sound is bondage, sound is the means for liberation, sound is that which binds, sound is that which liberates, sound is the bestower of all, sound is the power behind everything, sound is everything.)

Seeker: Sadhguru, your knowing seems to be inexhaustible. Is all this recorded in you or are you just getting it from somewhere?

Sadhguru: Karma is recorded in many ways: memory-wise, sensation-wise, physiology-wise and energy-wise. Similarly, knowledge too. There are some things which are transmitted to you on the level of your mind, others on the level of your body. Do you see how once you know how to swim, your body knows it? If you fall into the water; you will swim. You don't have to remember how to ride a bicycle; once you

1 *Vedas*, Upanishads : sacred scriptures in the Hindu Culture.

know how, if you sit on the bicycle, it goes, isn't it? Even if you don't ride a bicycle for twenty years and then you get onto one, you might be a bit off balance at first and then you just go, because the memory is in the body. It is no longer in the mind; it's just in the body. Transmission is also on many different levels.

Everything that I know just happens to me in a moment. When I'm walking on the street, I'm not carrying the burden of this knowledge. If you sit with me longer, longer, and a little longer, you will see. You'll be surprised. I do not know anything, but at the same time, I know everything. If you ask me anything concerned with the inner dimensions of a human being, I will come out with the answer, without any hesitation, with absolute clarity. Even if somebody says the *Gita*[1] is saying something else, I will simply say that maybe *Krishna*[2] does not know; what can I do about it? It is so crystal clear within me that it cannot be any other way. It's not that Krishna does not know. It is just that maybe you are not able to see what he's saying; that's the difference. What I'm saying is that this is not coming from a certain remembrance. It is coming in a completely different way, because it was transmitted in a different way. My association with my *Guru*[3] was just for a few moments. Somehow he didn't even want to touch me with his foot; he touched me with his walking stick. (Spreads his arms with a mock sense of pain and laughs). What cannot be learned in ten lifetimes was transmitted in one moment. It was all there. It was not just about knowing myself this way; it was also about various technologies, about how and what to do in every aspect, with absolute clarity. When it is transmitted like this, in the form of energy, not in the form of memory or in the form of knowing things logically, then the burden of knowledge is not on you. This is the difference.

People who have studied knowledge will become heavy with it. They will become serious. Studied people cannot even laugh usually, but somebody who is coming from his Realization – he knows, but the burden of knowledge is not sitting on his head all the time. He carries it very lightly, because this is a different technology altogether. See, what is in a thousand pages, today can be stored in a microchip. Similarly, what cannot be contained in a million books can be stored in a certain arrangement of energy.

---

1 *Gita* : the sacred book of the Hindus.
2 *Krishna* : Divine incarnation, historically over three thousand five hundred years ago.
3 Guru : lit. dispeller of darkness. A spiritual Master.

I do not know if modern science is working in this direction or not, but let me tell you, someday modern science will come up with ways to store information in a certain arrangement of energy. I know this clearly as that is the reality in us. Your energy system, or pranamayakosha, carries stupendous volumes of information, which is so easy to carry, which has no burdensome-ness; it's so simple.

Seeker: Now whatever you are speaking, is it recorded somewhere in your energy system?

Sadhguru: Whatever I say, is it recorded somewhere, is that what you are asking? What is already recorded is what is being spoken and what is being spoken is not something which I am thinking of and speaking. What is being spoken is what life is. It is recorded all the time, everywhere. We don't have to re-record it again; it has always been there. Whether I exist or I do not exist, Truth is; it is always there. We can talk about it if you want to, or we can just see it as it is. Do not worry; it will never be lost (laughs).

Seeker: What is the meaning of 'Sadhguru'?

Sadhguru: Sadhguru means an uneducated Guru. Sadhguru means somebody who has not gone through a so-called formal spiritual education. The only thing that he has is his inner experience; he has no spiritual education as such. He's not coming from the *Vedas, Gitas, Upanishads,* or any kind of training for that matter. The only thing he has is his inner experience. Do you see, I am quite ignorant about everything else except myself? The only thing that I know is myself, and that's all that is worth knowing in the existence. Really, the only thing that is truly worth knowing in the existence is yourself. If you know it, everything that is worth knowing is there within you. So the word 'Sadhguru' fundamentally means somebody who comes from within, not somebody who has been trained by somebody else. That means that usually a Sadhguru does not come from any particular tradition; he just sprang up like that. Maybe the support of the tradition is there, but he does not belong to a lineage because he does not come from anybody as such – no pedigree (laughs). That's why it takes a long time to find acceptance in the world, because there is no pedigree.

Seeker: Then books are useless on the path?

Sadhguru: See, whatever spirituality I'm talking about has not come to me because I studied with somebody or studied the Vedas or the Upanishads, or something. I might have just done some casual reading; bits and pieces here and there, but I have never even studied the Gita. The moment I hear a word, I know what it means. I like literature, and I like Asterix and Dennis the Menace. That's different. There is a lot of wisdom in that – sense, simple sense about life. When it comes to anything spiritual, I haven't found a book that is truly worthwhile in any way, so I usually don't read them. If I just open one book, and read any page somewhere in the middle, I know exactly what kind of mind is writing this book, and what are the possibilities. There is no point reading all four hundred pages of the book.

Seeker: When an Enlightened person opts for rebirth, is he born Enlightened? How was it in your life?

Sadhguru: I wish to correct the question a little bit. No person is ever Enlightened, because the personality is only your unconscious creation and your person is just a sum of that. Only when he has gone beyond his personality is there a possibility of Enlightenment. So when he's Enlightened, does it mean to say he has no personality? He has one, but it's a conscious personality; something that he has created to carry himself around, otherwise he can't do anything in the world. The question of a person or a being who is Enlightened and then is reborn – before we go into this, one should know that for most people, their moment of Enlightenment and their moment of leaving the body happens at once. When their energies reach a certain pitch, they leave the body. That moment of leaving the body is also Enlightenment. So the question of coming back does not arise, unless they have a certain mastery over the mechanics of the body, and they manage to retain their body because they have some specific work to do. If your objective is just liberation, then Enlightenment and leaving the body will always be together. If you have other objectives of wanting to do something else with what freedom you have found within yourself, with what liberation you have found within yourself, then there is something more to be done. Let us say there is a prisoner in a prison. If you release him from the prison, he is liberated. He goes away. Never again does he want to go back to the prison. Now, there is somebody who is ambitious enough or stupid enough to become free from the prison, but he wants to run the prison. He wants to become a prison officer. He was a prisoner then, now he wants to become a prison officer. Only when you have this kind of a problem, you retain your body. Otherwise, the normal prisoner's aspiration is somehow to get out. He would go anywhere in the world, but he doesn't want to go to the prison again. So an Enlightened being who is here right now as a person, is a person with this kind of problem. He has some work to do with the prison. He is liberated, but he still has some work to do. Now the prisoner has become the prison officer, managing things in the prison so that he can liberate all the other prisoners. The normal prisoner wants to get out of the prison; he does not care what happens inside the prison. See, when you're imprisoned in some way, what imprisons you doesn't matter. Once you realize that you're imprisoned, the only aspiration in you is to be liberated, to get away from this. Now, a few people want to become free and still want to be there to do something for the whole situation. So that's when this 'taking on a body again' comes up.

The fundamental question that you have asked is, "A person who is Enlightened, will he be born Enlightened? Or if not, does he get a reminder of his Enlightenment only at a certain stage in his life? Why so?" Let us say, for example, there are mango trees here; they have all the qualities of a mango tree. They're capable of bearing mangoes. The problem is, if the moment the sapling springs out the mangoes appear, the tree could die. The little plant would die if a huge mango came out of that little plant. It takes time. Nature is allowing time for this mango sapling to grow to a certain sturdiness, a certain strength, a certain maturity and balance, a certain capability to hold its ground. Only then it flowers and bears fruit. Similarly, an Enlightened being has certain qualities that are enshrined in him, which cannot be taken away. When he is born, he's born like anybody. The qualities are still inherent in him, but they will wait for a certain time and space where they can find expression. Until then they wait; this is nature's intelligence. It knows exactly when it should flower to find maximum fruit. If it flowers too early, it will not find its full potential. So it will wait depending upon what type of work he is intending to take up.

We know bala yogis, many of them, who at the age of six or seven became Enlightened. Most of them never reach the age of twenty-five or thirty. We have known this in India, where people get Enlightened in their childhood and never reach thirty. Before that they will go, because they cannot sustain the body

Meditating in the lap of the mystical Himalayas.

at that intensity of existence. Sufficient space has to be given so that the mind, the body and the emotions develop and mature in a certain way before the other dimension becomes alive in that person. Then he can hold it much better. If the reference is to me though, there is an experience of two lifetimes behind me. Living an Enlightened life, why did I have to wait until I was twenty-five? The very reason why, in this lifetime, this body had taken this amount of time is fundamentally for the consecration of the *Dhyanalinga.*[1] To consecrate the Dhyanalinga, Enlightenment is not enough; one needs a perfect body in many ways. When I say perfect, I'm not talking in terms of athletic perfection, but a perfect body in terms of management of energy and what can be done with it.

This is not possible for a child. In those twenty-five years of activity, I was not aware why certain things were coming to me. Now as I look back, it's so simple to see how everything happened in perfect progression. My childhood, my adolescence, my youth and further. Whatever happened with my life happened in such a way that everything that was necessary for the development of this body and this mind, for the stabilization of my emotions, naturally happened as a process of living.

---

1 Dhyanalinga : a powerful energy form consecrated exclusively for the purpose of meditation, located at Isha Yoga Center.

Mahashivaratri, a night of the Divine. Each year over one million people spend this nightlong sathsang with Sadhguru, engrossed in powerful meditations.

Seeker: Master, how did you become like this? You were born like us, yet you are so exceptional, so much ahead of us. How did it happen for you? What did you do to become like this?

Sadhguru: Even when I was a child this is how things happened to me. I never really was a child in my life. When I look back and see, I can remember clearly all the things that happened around me. I even remember situations that occurred during my infancy. My mother would be stunned when I could describe situations and conversations that I witnessed when I was three to six months of age. Even as a child I was thinking the same way as I do now. Probably this was the reason why no one in the family could hold me and kiss me. Maybe my presence was like that.

When they put me in school, school never meant anything to me. Since my fifth and sixth standards, I always wanted to go trekking. I had my own bicycle to go to school, a *tiffin*[1] box and water bottles and I was equipped for the day. I would just go climb a tree, reach the highest branch and just hang there. I would be there the whole day. I would eat there, drink my water there and wait. Just sitting and swaying there on the branch, after some time, something used to happen to me. I would become very ecstatic and it was blissful. At the time, I didn't realize what it was. Only after tasting meditation I came to know that

1 *tiffin* : snack, here referring to a lunchbox.

unknowingly, I had been in meditation. It is unexplainable. I liked it so much that every time I could skip school I would be there. The only thing is that they didn't give me a watch until I was in tenth standard, so I would not know the time. When I saw the kids going back from school in the evening, that was when I got down, got on my bicycle and went home. It used to be so beautiful being there. So the first few meditations I started teaching people, I always had them swaying. I would just make people sway and sway and get them into meditation; that's how I initiated people to begin with.

So I was doing everything like everybody. I went to school, and passing examinations was never a problem for me. I just got across, but that education didn't matter to me, whatever they did. Sitting in the classes was impossible for me because, when somebody was talking, I could see that they were talking about something that didn't mean anything in their life. It was just a job they were doing, so I did not want to listen. I knew that whatever they were saying, I could read in a book and get it myself, very easily. This continued until my college days. I was not interested in education, so when I passed my pre-university courses, I declared that I was not going to college. My father was a prominent doctor, so he wanted me to become a doctor. I refused, saying that I would not go to college that year and I would educate myself.

In that one year, everybody became my enemy. I spent most of that year in the library. Every morning, before the library's doors were opened, I would be there. I would pick up any book that I fancied and read. I spent one whole year in the library. During this time, I picked up an interest in English literature. When the next academic year commenced, my mother cajoled me into joining college. My parents wanted me to study engineering or medicine, but I refused. Then they came down to a degree in commerce or management. Again I refused. I was vehement that if at all I went to college it would be for English literature. They asked me what I would do reading poetry, but I never thought I was going to capitalize on my education. I joined B.A. English Literature, and college commenced. Every morning teachers would come to class and start dictating notes. We would do nothing else but write down dictated notes. Then I got up and asked the lecturer to give me her notes so that I could photocopy them and save her time and energy as well as ours. This irked the teacher so much, but she just could not do anything about my questions. So they all got together and decided to give me attendance for the next three years. I didn't have to go for attendance any more, so I landed in the college garden and people started coming to me to share their problems. It was almost like running a court there. I did not choose this, but it happened like that. My friends and I also formed a club on the university campus which was known as the Banyan Tree Club. It was under this Banyan tree on the campus, where all my friends met and many things were talked about. We used to talk about how fast you can drive a motorcycle and how to make this world a better place to live in. That's the range of subjects we talked about. There was no real organization; anyone who came and sat under this tree would be a member. The basic slogan was: 'We do it for the fun of it!'

I loved to travel, to explore nature. If in the middle of the night I felt like going to *Goa,*[1] I would start in ten minutes. All I would have to do was pack a bag – the motorcycle was always ready – and I would just go. Sometimes some friends would come; we had gone to many places like this. There are some people who go on planning, but something always turns up at the last moment, some excuse, and all their planning is wasted. These people will never go, whether it is going to a place or walking the spiritual path. Those who are talking spiritual, thinking spiritual, never take a single step. College passed away, and the final year came and I wrote about fifteen papers at once. Somehow, they gave me the second highest marks in the University and my father wanted me to immediately start a Master's degree. I told them enough was enough and that I had already read that syllabus. I thought I would make some money and ride all over the world in the two years that it would take me to complete the Master's degree. So I decided to start a poultry farm. I thought I would sell it after some time and go around the world. The poultry business was in a big boom in those days and I made a lot of money and things were going quite well. My father was astounded. He did not want to tell people that his son was rearing chicken. When I was into this poultry farming, everybody – my dad, my friends and ex-teachers – were constantly telling me, "Why are you wasting your life like this? We thought you would do something, but you are wasting your life like this." I never gave in to anybody's opinion and advice in my life. I was not wasting anything. I was very happy because the poultry farm was like this: in the morning, I would take care of the farm for four hours and after that I was completely free. So I meditated, swam in the well, hung on the trees, wrote poems, and read poetry. It was wonderful for me, really blissful; but everybody was telling me I was wasting my life. I had been practicing yoga since I was twelve years of age. I was not the kind of person who

1 Goa : an Indian state on the western coast known for its pristine beaches.

would do something because of discipline. Somehow it just happened; I got up in the morning and yoga happened for me. Every day, all these years, it just happened to me. Wherever I was – I could be trekking in the mountains – yoga would happen. I never did things in a disciplined way. See I was quite wild, but somehow, wherever I was, it happened. I was very successful and everything was going well, the way I wanted. When everything is happening the way you want it, you begin to think the world is revolving around you – not around the sun, you know? So I was like this, super-confident in everything I did.

Do you know Chamundi Hills? Have you been there? It's a little hill, a place where I trekked, as a child. When I was ten or eleven, if I got ten rupees in my hand, I would buy three loaves of bread and about four or five eggs. I would boil them in secrecy and go, leaving a small note. Then I would just disappear into the forest for three or four days. If I asked for permission it would not be given, so I always left a note and returned on the day I had said I would. I wouldn't come home until the bread was finished. I just walked in the forest, slept in the trees and hung around here and there. I was very good at catching snakes. I would have a bag full of snakes caught in three days and I kept them all with me. I loved to do this. In my family, they took a lot of care to see that I did not lay my hands on five or ten rupees, because if I did, I would disappear into the forest! (Laughs)

So this Chamundi Hill is very important to me in many ways. I spent a lot of time there. It was like a racetrack for me and my friends, riding motorcycles up the hill and sitting and meditating there. We would have parties there; I even had business meetings on Chamundi Hill. One afternoon around three o'clock I went there and parked my vehicle. I was just sitting on this particular rock. I had my eyes open, not even closed. I thought it was about ten minutes, but something began to happen to me. All my life I had thought this is me (pointing at himself). Suddenly, I did not know which is me and which is not me. The air that I am breathing, the rock on which I'm sitting, the atmosphere around me, everything had become me. The more I say, the crazier it will sound to you, because what was happening is indescribable. What is me has become so enormous, it is everywhere. I thought this lasted a few minutes, but when I came back to my normal senses, it was about seven thirty in the evening. My eyes were open, the sun had set and it was dark. I was fully aware, but what I had considered as myself until that moment had just disappeared. When I was eight years of age – I remember this incident very well – something happened and I cried. That day, I made up my mind that I would never cry again; I should never cry. I held myself like this (showing a closed fist) and whatever situations I came to, I did not shed a single tear, from eight until twenty-five. And here I'm sitting, tears are flowing to the point where my shirt is wet, and I'm ecstatically crazy! I do not know what is happening. When I apply my logical mind, the only thing it can tell me is that I'm losing my balance. That's all my mind can tell me, but it is so beautiful that I don't want to lose it. I'm not somebody who had been brought up in any kind of spiritual tradition. I had been fed with European philosophy – you know, Dostoevsky, Camus, Kafka and the likes. Of course, being the sixties, the era of Beatles and blue jeans, that's how I grew up. Here I am exploding into something; I don't know what it is. The next time it happened – after about six or seven days I was sitting at the dinner table with my family. I thought it was for two minutes, but seven hours had passed. I was sitting right there, fully aware, and this me is not there; *everything* is there.

This started happening more and more often. Every time I sat like this, I neither ate nor slept for many days, sometimes for up to thirteen days. I simply sat down in one place and that was all. I am just blowing my top off, and I do not know what is happening. The only thing I know is that I do not want to lose it. Then people saw me and they said, "Oh, he is in *samadhi*."[1] Somebody wanted to put a garland on me, or touch my feet. It was all crazy; I could not believe that these people wanted to do this to me (laughs). I had no words to describe what was happening to me, but it was going on like this. In about six to eight weeks, it became like a living reality. During this time, everything about me changed dramatically. What happened inside was indescribable, but my physical body – the shape of my eyes, my voice and my body structure itself – started changing. It changed so drastically that people around me could clearly see that something was happening to me.

Then suddenly, I called the people I was working with and told them, "Starting tomorrow, I won't be part of the business; I don't know what I'm doing here. I don't know what I will do next." I just traveled and sat around for one year. I gave up my business, my poultry farm and everything I was doing. I didn't know what I would do next. Then a whole flood of memories, lifetimes of memory, just descended upon me. The skeptic that I was did not want to believe anything. I was not the kind to believe anything.

---

1 *samadhi* : state of equanimity, a merging of the subject and the object.

I was not somebody who had ever entered a temple. I was not somebody who believed anything I could not see and understand. So I followed up all these memories. I followed the leads the memories gave; I went to those places, checked, met the people and did so many things. I knew this was true, crystal-clear, but my mind would not accept it. I had to go through the whole process. From that day, the Dhyanalinga became the single-pointed agenda in my life. We started working slowly, creating the necessary goodwill and making it happen. The making of the Dhyanalinga involved so many complicated processes. People who were witness to it know all the things that happened. It is too much of a fairy tale for anybody to believe. I would not believe it if somebody told me; that's all I can say.

Seeker: So what is the mastery an Enlightened being has which allows him to come back and retain a body?

Sadhguru: Once a person reaches the point of Enlightenment – all the years or lifetimes he worked to dissolve his karma – now he is consciously creating karma, because if he does not have enough karma, enough balance on his side, he can't stay in the body. Ninety percent of the time, the moment of Enlightenment and the moment of leaving the body are the same. Only a person who has a certain amount of mastery over the mechanics of the body can hold onto it; others cannot. There are many ways to do this. If you don't have mastery over the system, the other way is to go on creating karma consciously. I don't want to talk about myself at this point, how I go about doing things.

Let's take Ramakrishna Paramahamsa, for example. Ramakrishna was a very crystallized consciousness, and a very wonderful human being. Beyond all limitations, in many ways, but he was just mad about food. He would be talking to a group of disciples and he would say, "Wait." Then he would go into the kitchen and ask his wife, Sharada, "What's cooking today?" She would feel so ashamed; this man is godlike, everybody worships him, but he's so crazy about food. All the scriptures tell you that if you're turning spiritual you must lose your interest in food, isn't it? Here is a man who's being worshiped as God, and the man is mad about food. Many times she asked him, but he just avoided answering her. Everyday Sharada would serve him food in a *thali*,[1] and he always sat on the swing and ate. One day, she felt

1 *thali* : a large dinner plate.

terrible and told him, "I am ashamed of you. Why are you mad about food? The people that come and sit in front of you, they are not thinking about food. They're willing to just sit there without food. You are crazy about food, why?" Then he said, "Sharada, the day you bring the thali to me and I show no interest, please know I only have three more days." Seven years later, when Sharada brought the thali to serve him at his usual place on the swing, Ramakrishna showed no interest in the food; he turned away. Then she knew the time had come, and she broke down. Ramakrishna said, "Now there is no point crying; the time has come." It comes for everybody. This was his way of creating karma; creating a conscious desire for food. Desiring food all the time, consciously and intentionally. Without this desire, he could not hold onto his body. People who are close to me know all the tricks that I play to keep going. If you do not consciously create the karma, you cannot hold on to the body. Without karmic structure, you and your physical body have nothing to do with each other.

Seeker: Sadhguru, I don't really know how to ask this properly, but is it possible that one person's karma can take on two bodies?

Sadhguru: In so many ways, it does. Probably your question is not clear. Are you asking whether one person can take two bodies, or whether the effect of the karma can take two bodies? A single quality can take many bodies. Right now, I'm sitting here and performing some karma. This karma, this quality, can take hundreds of bodies, but this person cannot take two bodies. Still, it can happen. Let us say I die today, but I'm in a hurry to complete some unfinished work. This body has become defunct and I'm unable to sustain it. So I have to leave this body, but I'm not willing to be born through a womb, grow up and maybe get lost, and again have to do *sadhana.*[1] If I have sufficient awareness, I will wait for a suitable adult body which is going to be discarded by somebody, get into that, continue my sadhana and finish the karma off. Maybe I need five more years to finish my karma. Somebody who does not want to take that risk of getting lost by being reborn, if he finds a suitable body, just gets into that and continues his life. Now this person who is dead and has taken up another body will be in a lot of confusion. He has to face

1 *sadhana* : spiritual practices which are used as a means to Realization.

all the social problems, or he has to leave that place and run away all of a sudden. Something has to be done. So things like this have been done.

The karmic material can definitely take on more than one body. It is definitely capable of supporting more than one physical form. When I say a persona or a personality, it means it is just a front that has been taken up in a specific situation in which one lives. The same karmic substance, placed in two different kinds of situations, will take up two different personas, or masks. Such a thing happened with me. When I was here last time, in my previous life, when I was Sadhguru Shri Bhramha and life situations made it impossible to continue, I took on the body of a bala yogi who left early, and made a futile attempt towards the consecration of the Dhyanalinga. The body of Sadhguru Shri Bhramha was alive, but the physical term for that karma was set to be over in a few months. We have known yogis who have maintained two different bodies to fulfill two different types of karma. There have been yogis who lived with one body living as an ascetic, and another as a *grihastha*, a householder. They had taken upon themselves to fulfill different dimensions of activities which could not be carried on with a single body. Similarly, the reverse is also possible. There have been situations where two yogis have shared a single body. When one of their physical bodies ran its full term but could not fulfill the karmic compulsions, he decided to share another yogi's body rather than going through the process of finding a womb.

One classical example is Karthikeya or Subramanya, who is also known as Shanmugha, the six-faced one. As many of you know, Parvathi[1] had six children of six immutable qualities. She thought that if these six immutable qualities could exist in one body, it would be so magnificent. In terms of action, it would be so transforming for the world. She, being an accomplished yogini, merged these six beings into one body. Hence, Karthikeya is known as the six-faced one. There is a place in South India, in the state of Karnataka, where Subramanya – who is known as Kumara in those parts – attained Mahasamadhi. Kumara, after fighting a gory battle to establish order, killing hundreds a day with his sword, came to that place. There, he washed his bloody sword as a symbol of relinquishing violence for good, and then went up to the mountain peak, in the western *ghats*, which today is known as Kumara Parvat,

1 Parvathi : consort of Shiva.

or son's mountain. He stood on top of this peak for forty-seven days and then shed his body on the forty-eighth day. Generally, when a *yogi* wants to shed his body by will or consciously, he does it in a sitting posture or sometimes lying down, but Kumara left his body standing. When I went there, close to the peak, after a hard day climbing up the mountain, we were required to camp at the very base of the peak. I just could not sit down the whole night. Even when I sat down, the energies there would push my body into a standing posture. I was supposed to sleep in a tent just over three feet high but my body would just stand up, dismantling the tent. If you go up this peak, you'll see innumerable small pebbles, all six faced, as if they had been neatly cut. These are known as the Shanmugha lingams, the six faced Lingas. These are highly energized stones. They became like that because that was the type of energy this *yogi* left on that mountain peak.

Seeker: Master, why do we get so drunk on you? What wine, what grapes, what vineyard are you?

Sadhguru: That must be Hoda (laughs). On the last day of class in Paris, we got Hoda so drunk without any spirits. Today also, for the New Year's celebration, we don't have any bottles and spirits, but if you are willing, we can get you totally drunk. So totally drunk, in every possible way, but no hangover. No addiction, no hangover. What grapes, what wine, what vineyard…? How can I say? Keep your hands open, close your eyes and sit.

[A meditation process takes place.]

Now that you understand everything in the form of wine…This is just a drop of wine that was put into me by my Guru. I thought it was just a drop, but it was an ocean. So when you contain an ocean within you, it spills. You cannot hold it. Whatever you do, it spills. If you sit quietly, it spills too much. If you run, it spills. If you walk, it spills, if you love, it spills, if you get angry, it spills. Whatever you do, it spills, when you contain an ocean within yourself. I cannot help it. If you get too intoxicated, you must seek an antidote.

The only reason why one will not get madly intoxicated with this is because you want to deduce life. You don't want to experience life, you want to deduce life. 'A+B=C', this deduction will take the life out of you, and even if you take the life out of yourself, you still won't know what it's all about.

Once, there was a great scientist. He was experimenting, so he found himself a frog and started making deductions and conclusions. He asked the frog to jump. It jumped twenty feet. He cut off a leg and told it to hop. It then hopped fifteen feet. He again cut off another leg and again told it to hop. This time, it hopped ten feet. Then he cut off another leg and told it to hop. It hopped five feet. He then cut off the last leg and told it to hop. "HOP! HOP! HOP!" he said. The frog did not hop. He recorded all of his findings in his log book: four legs, twenty feet; three legs, fifteen feet; two legs, ten feet; one leg, five feet; zero legs, FROG DEAF.

This is where deductions will lead you to. If you're trying to deduce anything which is beyond the physical, this is what will happen. Your deductions are fine only with the material aspects of life. If you are seeking anything beyond the physical, your deductions, your calculations, will only get you further and further away from life, never close to it. You don't have to make any attempt to get close to it, because you are in it. It is just that if you put a little bit of this wine into you, it becomes more intensely alive. Just because you're not sensitive enough to see it the way it is, I'm just cranking it up for you so that even you can feel it. We're trying to make a frog without any legs leap.

Seeker: Sadhguru, in many ways you have been the biggest experience in my life, and I have seen you in so many different ways, but whichever way I look at you, I'm not able to grasp what you are. What kind of mystic are you?

Sadhguru: What kind of mystic am I? Probably there has not been one around wearing blue jeans (laughs). I do not think there has been another one like this. What kind am I? I wish I could tell you – not just about the clothes, about everything. All I can say is that there isn't another one like me; that's for sure.

There are a few, but they do not open their mouths. They will not come anywhere near people. Actually there is only just one more who has three Enlightened lifetimes behind him, but you will never get to see him. He has only four more years and then he will leave. You have seen, many times, by the snap of the fingers, I can have hundreds of people roaring with new levels of energy, to be in such deep energy contact with me that you will have to physically carry them out of that space. People have to do many things to get to some state of experience. Simply just entering a space and going like that is unheard of. I'm the only one like this, who is stupid enough to go around and try to do something with people. I am the only one, really. I'm not bragging; this is the reality.

Seeker: Sadhguru, you are able to be so many different things in different situations, like in *Samyama,*[1] you're a perfect Guru, but here in the Himalayas you sit with us as a friend and even play frisbee with us. So you're able to turn yourself up and down?

Sadhguru: Yes, of course. If it is up all the time most people will get burned up. They'll get fused out. They will not be able to take it. Even there, the weak ones can get fused out. If I keep it up for seven days in Samyama, many will get fused out. They do not have the physiological and psychological strength to take that kind of energy. Low voltage bulbs: if you put high voltage, "Pchit, pchit, pchit!" they'll go off. It is done carefully, in a graduated way. Sometimes you blow it up and sometimes you bring it down. You cannot let people stay in that kind of energy for too long. Very few people are capable of staying there, others need lots of sadhana. That's why sadhana is so important; it prepares you.

See, to have one big experience any moment in your life, we can give that to anybody, but to live like that, you need proper energy, an appropriate body and mind and also stable energy; otherwise, you can't live like that. This is the only reason why people are not always living like that. Many moments of really unspeakable ecstasies have happened to people. Moments, but they are not able to stay there simply because they don't have the right kind of vehicle to carry that kind of speed. Somewhere downhill, even your Maruti car will touch two hundred kilometers per hour, but to drive at two hundred kilometers

---

1 Samyama : an eight day meditation program offered by Sadhguru where one is transported to explosive states of meditativeness. Held at Isha Yoga Center.

per hour, you need a Lamborghini. Isn't it? It's the same thing. Sadhana is just trying to get yourself into a Lamborghini state. Then it can be high all the time and still be okay; it is like normal.

Seeker: So where is he, the other one like you, Sadhguru?

Sadhguru: Here! Here and there is only your problem (laughs).

Seeker: Is he an ascetic?

Sadhguru: Not really ascetic. Maybe for the sake of the world he may put on a certain appearance, but he does not belong to anything. For him, his whole life is open.

Seeker: So in this lifetime, he has not been with people at all? Then why is he here after his Enlightenment? Do people know about him?

Sadhguru: You don't do work just by being with people. You can do enormous things without being with anybody; actually you can do more. You can do much more if you're not with people. People who are aware, they will know of him. In yogic circles, they will know. Nobody can ignore him, but otherwise, by advertisement, you will not know. No one can ignore a being like this on the planet. All those who have eyes will know the sun is up today. Blind ones will know only by information; somebody will announce to them, "The sun has come up." The majority have become blind ones, and that is the norm in the world. Somebody has to tell them, "A yogi has come." Unfortunate, but that's how it is. So once you're going by information, all kinds of fake ones will inform, "I am the yogi." That's how it's happening. The blind ones, in the night also you could tell them, "The sun has come up." They will all say yes, isn't it? Still, other faculties are working so they are able to feel, but suppose along with their blindness they also have no sensation, you have to just announce the arrival of the sun, isn't it? Even now, for the sleeping ones, we have to announce the sun is coming up, isn't it?

Seeker: So why are you wearing blue jeans?

Sadhguru: To cover myself! (Laughs).

Seeker: No, I mean why are you dressed like us, like a regular guy?

Sadhguru: If I did not have the Dhyanalinga work, I wouldn't be like this. It got me involved with people in very deep ways.

Seeker: Is that other yogi doing some kind of work? Some kind of work brought him here?

Sadhguru: Is the sun working every day? No. It's just there, and everything happens. Does the sun get burnt out? Does the sun get nourished?

Seeker: You only had to come back to fulfill the Dhyanalinga. So he did not have a purpose, but he came back? Was it out of compassion?

Sadhguru: Not compassion; he just likes to look around the Himalayas.

Seeker: Did you visit him?

Sadhguru: Why would I visit him? I have no intention or need of really visiting anyone, for that matter. As per people's needs, we do something. He has no needs, so why the hell visit him? I'm not longing to be among such people. I can make myself into ten people and enjoy their company if I want, but I'm not longing to be in anybody's company. Oh, this is all too much mystic's musing for one day! Come, let's take a walk.

Seeker: Dear Master, you talked about carrying awareness from one life into another. The only thing that you carry forward is awareness. Where does this process end? Is there an end? Is there a beginning? Was I a blade of grass at some point? Was I a monkey, was I a lizard, was I a rock on a mountain? It is all forms of energy.

Sadhguru: A blade of grass, I don't know; monkey, I will not dispute! (Laughs). So the question is a bundle of many things, or I can call it a bundle of confusion – awareness, energy, or carrying awareness beyond what you call as life right now. Where did life begin? Where does it end? Where it began, let us leave that at this point, because it is already here. What you consider as 'myself' is already here. How to go beyond this – what you call as 'myself' – that's our business right now. The beginning was not caused by us, obviously. Going beyond has to be because of us. It has to be a conscious process; there is no other way.

Now if everything is energy, where did you spring from? You never sprung up; you just anointed yourself. "Does it mean to say I am not real? Are you telling me that nonsense about everything being *maya*?"[1] No. It's just that life is happening. Okay, how did this life begin to happen? For example, let us take planet Earth, which has its own individuality compared to other planets. As you have your own individuality compared to other people sitting here, so does this planet. No matter how many forms life takes, it still has the capability to take on a unique form – a unique quality about itself. Whether it's the whole planet or you as a person, an ant, your own little finger or even the hair on your head, it has a unique quality about itself.

This is the manifestation. At the same time, this uniqueness you see does not last forever. You as a person, being here – you as a body – you know it will end one day. Right now it is unique; your body is also unique. When it ends, this body will not retain its uniqueness anymore. It will become a part of this earth. Still, the earth is retaining its uniqueness compared to the other planets. As your body dissolves into the earth, this earth also will dissolve into the lap of something else. Now we're calling this Mother

1 *maya* : illusion, delusion.

Earth simply because we understand that, in some way, we have come from it. What you call as 'myself' right now – which is sitting here, which is walking about here – this body, is just a lump of earth taking on a different form and doing all these things. One day it will just sink back and become very much earth.

Similarly, this earth, which has taken on a certain form and a certain individuality or uniqueness about itself, will also dissolve into a larger lap and become that – whatever that is. Right now, because you have no perception of that – we are referring to it as Shiva, let us say. As we have repeatedly said, the word 'Shiva' means 'that which is not'. When we say 'that which is not', it does not necessarily mean that which does not exist. It means that which is not in your experience right now. Only physical creation is in your experience. That which is the basis of creation is not in your experience. So that which is the basis of creation is being referred to as Shiva – that which is not.

That which is not became that which is, and took on a certain quality of its own. In that, millions of forms came up. All of them took on their own individuality for some time. Right now, when you are busy – active in your life – that is life, that is everything. Tomorrow morning, if you fall dead, suddenly life becomes something else. This person, who was so active, doing all those things, suddenly disappears and everything is still fine. Only somebody's thoughts and emotions are disturbed; but as far as existence is concerned, everything is perfectly fine. Isn't it? It is only in the people who are around you – in their thoughts, in their emotions – that there is a disturbance, which will settle after some time. Or maybe somebody will keep it for life; it's okay. It is only in their thoughts and emotions. As far as life is concerned, as far as this energy is concerned, as far as this existence is concerned, there is absolutely no disturbance because nothing has happened. This just sprang up, played for some time and went back - just like a little wave in the ocean. It rolls and falls back. There is no disturbance; nothing right or wrong about it. It is just that in your individual experience or in people around you, in their individual experience, this is a great calamity. All these calamities exist only in your thoughts and emotions; it has nothing to do with life. Only when your awareness, your aliveness, has risen beyond your thought, emotion and body, only then the question of going beyond also arises. Right now, your awareness is limited only to these dimensions. So the question of carrying it beyond this life does not arise. So where does it end? If your awareness is perfect – if your awareness is very clear between that which is physical and that which is not – that's the end of it. If one leaves the body in full awareness, it can happen only out of choice.

When one is aware, everything is a choice. Only when one is not aware, everything is a compulsion. If you are truly aware, being in the body and not being in the body also happen by choice. Once such a choice has come, that's the end of the game. Now what was functioning as 'me' will not exist anymore. Everything has become as it should be, as it was. Whatever I say verbally is bound to be wrong. You can say it's like the rivers we have been passing. This river that you see now is Mandakini; what you saw just a little while ago was Alakananda; what you saw yesterday was Bhagirathi. Down at Haridwar, the foothills of the Himalayas, everything becomes Ganga. All these rivers had their own individuality. There, in Haridwar, they lose their individuality and take on another kind of individuality. This Ganga flows into the ocean and there it loses that individuality also, and becomes something else; it becomes the Indian Ocean. Now if you look deeper, there is no Indian Ocean; there is no Pacific Ocean. It's just an ocean. So all that will be gone if your awareness separates the physical from that which is not physical. Everything merges as one. It's like children blowing bubbles. If you blow a bubble, there is air in it. This air has a certain individuality because it's in the body of the bubble. The moment the bubble bursts, where is that air? It is just air, isn't it? Similarly, once you burst this (pointing at himself) with your awareness – if you know how to burst it, the physical, which is holding life energy in a certain bondage – then energy is just energy; it's a whole sea of energy. So spirituality means, not growth – spirituality means self-destruction, self-annihilation. When it is self-annihilation, it's not about physically torturing yourself or something like that. It is just destroying the individual and becoming the universal. This is why Shiva is worshipped; he's a destroyer. If you're not a destroyer, you have nothing to do with spirituality.

Seeker: After doing the *mandala*[1] kriyas, I feel something within me is stirred up and turning me upside down...

Sadhguru: These kriyas act upon the pineal gland in such a way that your present level of experience dissolves, and you move into a completely different dimension. You move into states of absolute ecstasy

1 *mandala* : physiognomic cycle, an area within the body or the cosmos.

and a certain sweetness, even in your physical body. The kechari mudra, which is crucial for a successful mandala kriya, is not really complete with you. There are certain schools of yoga; they take a thin slice of bamboo reed and use it to liberate the tongue from its bondage with the lower palate so that the tongue becomes available to form a perfect kechari. This will leave a person always soaked in ecstasy. One can enjoy ecstatic states of samadhi for a whole lifetime. See, samadhi states are available to people only in certain periods. Here, one lives like this all the time. It's an ecstatic way of living, which is very close to liberation.

When you practice these kriyas, suddenly the prana finds a forceful upward movement, demolishing all the limitations within you. Some Native American tribes have their own system of spirituality, which you can say is a small aspect of the *tantric* [1] culture in India. In India, we have developed the whole system as a science. There, they have just discovered this one aspect of it and used it very effectively, though in a very limited way. Can I tell you a joke? A man who was traveling through the prairies of the U.S.A. stopped at a small town and went into an inn. He ordered his food, stood outside and lit his cigar. He stood there quietly, blowing smoke rings. After he blew nine or ten smoke rings into the air, an angry Native American stomped up to him and said, "One more remark like that and I'll smash your face!"

Among the Native Americans, there are many masters who are well accomplished in matters of the occult. When I was in Vancouver, I happened to meet this man and his daughter who were traveling in a fully loaded pick-up truck. They were simply ranging the country. There are no more horses, so they were using a pick-up truck. So this man was wearing blue jeans and a shirt, but he was still like that. He was an old man, maybe about seventy years of age, his daughter about thirty, and they were traveling together. We just happened to stop in a place for gas or something. This man just walked towards me, came and just knocked on the window. Then he said, "The winds have been telling about your coming, brother," nodded and went away (laughs). They always speak in these terms; for them, it's always the winds. He said that, nodded and walked away. They're very sensitive people, who had a different sense of

---

1 *tantric* : practitioner of *tantra*, the science of using *mantra*, the sound and *yantra*, the form. Refers to an esoteric Indian spiritual tradition.

life all together. In a way, the occult dimensions of yoga were very alive in these traditions. Maybe they do not really have a science like we have. It's a much segregated science; it is just one aspect of the whole science. Changing bodies and things like this are quite common in their culture. There are many instances where people have exchanged their bodies and lived on, and again changed back whenever they needed to. This is mostly done with the use of certain herbs which are kept as great secrets; some of them can be highly intoxicating. Much research has been done on this.

Now the path of using any intoxicant and trying to grow – if the proper guidance and atmosphere are there – can be a very quick process. One can grow extremely fast because there is a chemical support to it. Right now, we're changing the chemistry of the system with yogic practices. Using a herb is not the same as using the raw chemical, which could be very damaging to the system. A herb also functions only as per its chemistry. The Native Americans do certain practices to support it, and also use certain herbs in a particular way which helps them to loosen the rigidity in a person's limitations. It's not just about consuming something and being intoxicated. That's not the point. People who are really on the path can be totally intoxicated, but still fully aware.

There is a tantric in Mysore. People who visit him always take bottles of rum with them. He's an ex-service man. He resigned from the army long ago. He's into various types of *Devi Pooja*, goddess worship and other occult processes. Normally all his devotees, or disciples, or whatever you call them, always offer him bottles of rum. This man drinks rum like water, but you will not once see him rolling on the floor. He's always totally alert. I've been there quite a few times. He will do pooja and drink rum like water. Four to five rum bottles are always there for him to drink, like water. He just drinks it up and only then sees people. He handles many problems for people related to black magic. He's doing useful work in his own way, and though he is totally drunk beyond normal human capacity, you'll never see any imbalance in him. I know people around him wanting to do the same thing who end up as drunkards. That path is like that. When you start using external chemical support to change or transform yourself, generally only one person out of a hundred comes out free. The other ninety-nine end up with a drug or alcohol problem. So the path is dangerous. When it's so difficult to be normal and be aware, imagine being drunk and being aware; it needs tremendous awareness.

The very nature of intoxicants is to make you unaware. They are using something that makes them unaware and still have to remain aware, which is a hard path, but can be a quick path if it is done in a proper presence. A tremendous experience of samadhi can be had, but people can also go on bad trips. If somebody who is always in fear takes these kinds of chemicals, he will have an extreme fear-trip hallucination. On the other hand, one who is well established in his awareness to a point that he can carry it into his sleep, for such a sadhaka, these substances could be beneficial if used under proper guidance, but subject to various limitations. The path of yoga offers enough opportunities for us to get high without using any external aids like that. If you're willing, I'm the greatest intoxicant. I can activate such deep states of intoxicating awareness. It is all within you. So don't you try to stop yourself. Just allow it to happen. Get intoxicated. Let everything turn upside down. This will neither bring you addiction, nor will you have a hangover.

Seeker: At times I get very impatient as to when it is going to be. How long is this waiting going to be? It seems to be right here, yet too...

Sadhguru: Maybe the last twenty-five days have been – blow hot, blow cold. It could have been a steady race, but this is how people are made. I'm never surprised. We are just here to see what's next; that's all. I'm neither surprised nor disappointed. It's okay. There have been ups and downs during this Wholeness program. The mind is such, a little something happens and it gets excited. Doubts will arise, questions will arise; you're still in that state. This has to go. Until this goes, many things will not be steady.

There was a Zen disciple named Tongain learning under Chuang Tzu – a great Master. In twenty years of staying with Chuang Tzu, he learned many things. Much transformation happened, but Enlightenment did not. After twenty years, he wanted to go out and make a comparative study with some other Master. Every time he goes to Chuang Tzu and asks for permission, "I want to go out," the Master just raps him on the head. He just gives him one on his head. Tongain goes back. A few days later, he goes again to

Chuang Tzu and asks, "Shall I go? I've been here for twenty years. Shall I go out for a year or two?" Again the Master raps him and sends him back; not a word, just a rap on the head. Many times he goes; many times he gets it on the head and comes back. Then he poured out his woe to a brother disciple, an elder. "Every time I go, he's rapping me on the head. What shall I do? Will you go and ask him?" So the senior disciple went and asked Chaung Tzu and got permission. He came and told Tongain that the Master had given permission, he could go. Tongain was very happy and went to thank the Master and take leave. He said, "I'm leaving". Again he was rapped on the head. Tongain was totally confused, he came back and cried to the brother disciple, "My permission is cancelled; he rapped me on my head again." The brother disciple said, "How can he do this? He just can't change his decision after giving the permission. I'll go and ask him." So both of them went to the Master and asked, "You said he can go, but again you rapped him." The Master said, "I never said that he should not go. When he comes back he will be Enlightened, I know. Then I can't rap him; I will have to bow down. So I rapped him now." Tongain got impatient after twenty years. After twenty years of waiting.

What took years and lifetimes in the past, today we're talking in terms of days and weeks. All this is possible only because of the Grace of all the innumerable great Masters; you are reaping the benefit of their work. Last night was a good opportunity for many of you to plunge; you should have become a hollow bamboo. I have fixed the plug at one end of it so it does not shoot up right now. I have fixed one end of it; you should have felt the hollowness. At moments some of you have felt it. Then thoughts come, something comes and immediately you become something else.

Seeker: What do you mean when you say you fixed one end? What's that?

Sadhguru: The kind of sadhana you are doing here would normally need lots of foundation work. Generally, on the path of *kriya yoga*, before we initiate people into this type of sadhana, a sadhaka would have gone through an enormous amount of foundational work in terms of energy. This is to establish the body's *Muladhara*[1] in a very substantial way so that when he does sadhana which pulls the energy

---

1 *Muladhara* : the psycho energetic chakra located at the perineum.

upward, the body does not snap or the ability to hold onto the body is not lost. In the present circumstances, in today's world, people are unable to give themselves to that kind of sustained practice and the time it takes to make this happen. Very few people would be able to sustain a sadhana like that without the lower end of the *Sushumna* [1] being tied; the Muladhara properly tied up. If sadhana to elevate the energies is done very forcefully without fixing the Muladhara, one might leave the body instantaneously; a person could easily slip out of the body. Even if he does not slip out of the body totally, it could cause withdrawal from certain areas of the energy system, which will leave a person incapacitated.

So before we attempt such sadhana with sadhakas who don't have the necessary foundation work, a yogi always fixes the lower end of the sushumna, which is the Muladhara. This can be done only in an atmosphere where very intense energy situations have been created. Many of you have seen and experienced, in the last few weeks of being here, how the energy can be turned up and down. It is clear that there is a very strong energy situation around you. So using this energy situation, I'm tying up the lower end of the Muladhara for everybody who is sitting in this hall, so that when they do their sadhana, when they really get their energies moving, the foundation of the body, which is the Muladhara, remains intact.

Seeker: Jaggi, you are fixing a person's Muladhara, but can't he always leave through another *chakra*? [2]

Sadhguru: The word 'Muladhara' itself means foundation. By stabilizing the foundation, which is the basis of this life energy existing in the body, it is ensured that such things do not happen. It's just like, if you want to hold a big ship in the harbor, only one rope is needed. If you tie it down, it stays there. Now the situation is like this: we have chained the boat to the shore, but at the same time, we are rowing it just to get a feeling of going somewhere. Actually, you're not going anywhere, because you are tied to the shore. So that's what we are doing with this sadhana. To make a person experience a moment of moving beyond the physical – at the same time not leaving the physical; that is ensured by tightening or

1 *Sushumna* : the central channel in the energy body which conducts the kundalini or spiritual force.

2 *chakra* : lit. *wheel*. Here, it refers to the seven main junctions of the nadis (subtle energy pathways) in the human body. Each chakra has a distinct color, form, sound and quality.

establishing the Muladhara. The question of somebody slipping out through this chakra or that chakra does not arise here. The tying of the Muladhara is not to see that he does not slip out of that chakra. The purpose of this tying up is so that he does not slip out of any chakra. The foundation is tightened so that he cannot slip out from any chakra. Tying up is not to cease downward movement of energy. The tying up is to control the upward movement of energy. So it applies to all the chakras.

Seeker: But Jaggi, the ultimate in yoga, or on the spiritual path is to attain, isn't it?

Sadhguru: Yes.

Seeker: What if the person is ripe enough to shift his energies and get out of his body? Would this tying up one end stop him from leaving?

Sadhguru: The 'tying up one end' is a temporary thing, and in the process of yoga, there are many situations where a person can leave in a moment of intense practice or sadhana. Generally, this is not considered as a right thing to do. By doing sadhana, we're only trying to get mastery over our life energies so that we can leave by will. If you leave while doing sadhana, it is still good, it is still wonderful, but that's not the highest way to leave. It's not happening by conscious will. Still the total realization of, 'I am not this flesh' has not arisen both intellectually and energy-wise. With the intensity of sadhana one may leave, but that's not the best way to leave. With sadhana, you generate the necessary intensity and control over your own systems.

Later on, you'll be able to just sit down and leave quietly, because you will have mastery over that; that is the highest way to leave. We have no intention that anybody should leave during sadhana. As I said in the earlier analogy of rowing the boat that is tied to the shore, as your control increases we can tie longer and longer ropes. We can allow the rope to be a little longer, so that you have much more feeling of leaving, but you're still in control of the body. When there is total mastery over this, then you don't intend to leave during any kind of intense practice; you leave quietly when everything is normal.

Seeker: Master, in this whole process of doing this intense sadhana and these kriyas, if one acquires certain powers, are you telling us we should not use them?

Sadhguru: Let me tell you a story. Many of you must have heard of Kaushika. He was a *Brahmin*[1] sadhaka. For his sadhana, he found himself a place in the forest close to a particular village. There, he practiced sadhana to make himself more powerful and to gain *siddhis.*[2] One day, while he was practicing, a bird's dropping fell on his shoulder. He got mad and he looked at the bird. The intensity of his look was such that the bird just burst into flames and the ashes fell. He was very happy that his sadhana had worked. "If I just look at somebody, they will burn." At lunch time, he went into the village to beg and eat. He went to a particular house where he said, "Bhikshandehi." That means he wants food. In India, when a spiritual person comes to your house, you never say no. Whatever you have, something you give. So the housewife called from inside, "Please wait, I'm serving food to my husband." He waited for a few moments and then again said, "Bhikshandehi." She said, "Please wait, I'm coming." A few more minutes passed and he was getting angry and he shouted loudly, "Bhikshandehi." Then she came with food. He yelled, "Who do you think I am that you can keep me waiting?" This morning's incident had suddenly made him feel very big. Then she said, "I know you are Kaushika, but please don't glare at me; I am not a bird that you can burn up." Kaushika was shocked.

He asks, "What is this? How did you know that today I burnt up a bird? How do you know what happened in my life this morning? What sadhana are you doing?" She says, "My only sadhana is to serve my husband." Then he falls at her feet and asks her to take him as her disciple. She says, "No, I cannot take you as my disciple." She sees there is another problem with him which is adding to his inflated ego – his caste. He is a Brahmin. So she tells him to go meet another Master whose name is Dharmavada, who is a *Shudra*[3] by birth and a butcher by profession. She says, "You go to him, he's the best Master for you." This Master lives in a far away place, so Kaushika goes there. The story goes like this, but now what I'm asking you is, if this woman's only sadhana

1 *Brahmin* : member of the priestly Hindu caste system.

2 *siddhis* : powers, paranormal or supernormal accomplishments.

3 *Shudra* : member of the menial labor caste in the Hindu caste system.

was cooking and serving her husband, how did she know of Dharmavada who was far away? He was not a well-known Master; he was a butcher. So how did she know of him?

Now don't come to a stupid conclusion like thinking that women only have to serve their husbands and they will attain. Don't simply concoct the whole story to your own convenience. By serving her husband, a woman might attain to peace or to love. What the woman in the story said and what she did clearly shows that she was into some sadhana. She had her own sadhana in her life. She had been to a Master, she had learned and she was well versed in what she was doing. This intensity had come into her life not just out of doing simple acts. She could not have known about the spiritual masters – unknown spiritual masters of those times – if she was not on the path. One reason why I immediately walked out of my business was just this: somehow I thought it was unfair of me to continue because the other man does not know what's going to happen next, and I know it. I can always outsmart him in many different ways; make a fool out of him. People who are doing these kriyas may sometimes develop visions of the future. So what to do about it? Capitalize on it? Tomorrow, a billboard will extol your magical skills.

Seeker: No Jaggi. I won't do that.

Sadhguru: At least, won't you see into your children's and your family's futures? Suppose you develop the vision to look; won't you look? It could very easily happen, but we have put some blocks on it right now. With these intense practices you could develop minor siddhis in spite of the precautions. We have put certain stoppers on it, but some day you may blow the stoppers off. The stopper is there not to restrict you. When there is not enough maturity in you, if these things fall into your hands, you are ruined. Right now *Kundalini* [1] is playing with you. If you get a little vision and use it, the Kundalini will die and go back to the Muladhara. That's all that will happen. The moment you use it, it's finished. All your sadhana is wasted. Your only consolation is that you can change your profession and become an astrologer. It's a great profession in the world today.

See, when a person goes into a state like that, there are many possibilities. There are many ways of being in samadhi states. Powerful siddhi states can happen. You saw what happened to Srinivas. His energy

---

1 *Kundalini* : Cosmic energy which is depicted as a snake coiled at the base of the spine.

was going towards this, and I was not interested in anybody acquiring some kind of power or getting established in some state of pleasure. This state could have easily led to certain siddhis or situations within himself where he could use his energy and do certain things in the world. I wanted to pull him out. He was just trying to settle down, but I made him work. It's okay not to experience anything and come back, because there will be another day. Either you go to the highest or remain normal; that is better. Either liberation, or let us live like normal people. Those in-between states are wonderful states to experience, but they become a bondage by themselves over a period of time. Somewhere inside, there is a certain intelligence which acts by itself. Deep down, that intelligence – which is creation itself, that intelligence which is the source of all creation – takes charge. Now it knows, either you come back to the normal state or you go to the peak. In-between, it will not allow you to settle.

Seeker: Sadhguru, I saw you used something on him, a wooden stick, and then he came out of this state. What was that?

Sadhguru: See, if you get established in one of these states, you'll take years to come out of it and move to a higher level, because it is nice. It's pleasant, it's powerful. Yesterday, if I had not brought him down, he would have taken another few weeks or months to come back to a normal state. So once I put the wand on him, he came back to the normal level of consciousness. In the last four days people saw this wand, just a piece of wood, which became so powerful. You felt the energy. This tool has been sort of consecrated in a converse way so that it sucks in the energy rather than emanating it. It's like a damper: when certain moving objects are there in machines, there are dampers to keep control and slow down the process. Similarly, this is like a damper that pulls down the energy in a certain way, and you saw how it worked right there, when I applied it this way. Dhyanalinga is many fold more powerful than this, but emanating energy. This wand is not forever. It will work for a certain period of time, then it has to be recharged to become like this. I don't personally need this. I'm experimenting in producing tools that would be useful for situations when I'm not around.

Seeker: So this wand acts as a damper?

Sadhguru: The wand does not have specific qualities of trying to dampen something wherever you apply it. It tends to pull the energy in a certain direction. So it can also be used positively if it is applied in a certain way. Applied in another way, it can dampen the situation. It can also become a positive tool in raising energies if it is properly applied.

Seeker: Sadhguru, some people go to soothsayers or fortune tellers, these kinds of people who seem crazy, make inquiries about their future. Is this okay?

Sadhguru: This has come from the understanding that somebody who is in a higher state of energy has a clearer vision. If your energies build up, if you are in a higher state of energy, you see things more clearly than other people. It's from that understanding that they are going to them, but I know there is a whole lot of drama, misuse and so many things; that is different, but there is a basis to it. That reminds me of Goraknath. Goraknath is one of the most well-known yogis in India, even today. It is one of the largest spiritual paths – a wild path. They are generally known as kanphats, which means, 'a hole in the ear'. They are always recognized by this hole in their ear. Goraknath's Guru was Matsyendranath. He was barely human; he was too far beyond. People even today believe that Matsyendranath was the reincarnation of Shiva himself. He lived a secluded life, except for a few fierce disciples who lived with him. Goraknath was one of those.

Many wonderful things happened around Goraknath – a very, very fierce man. Once, Matsyendranath saw that Goraknath was getting too attached to him as a person. So he sent him away for fourteen years of sadhana somewhere else, away from him. He said, "Don't come to me. Just go away into the forest and do your sadhana." So once the Guru said this, he just left. After fourteen years, he came back – these fourteen years he lived, just longing to see his Guru again. So when he finished his fourteen years, he came straight back to where the Guru was supposed to be. There was another disciple guarding the entrance of the cave in which the Guru was supposed to be living. At first, the disciple did not allow him to enter the cave. He said, "No, Matsyendranath does not intend to see you." Goraknath became furious. "Fourteen years I have been just burning to set my eyes upon my Guru. Who are you to stop me?" He pushed him aside and went into the cave. The cave was empty. He came out and asked him, "Please tell me where he is." The disciple refused to tell him and said, "I cannot tell you, nor do I want to tell you. Leave this place." Out of his sadhana, Goraknath had acquired many siddhis, and in his fury and his longing to see his Guru, he used his occult powers to read the disciple's mind. Like this, he found out where the Guru was and immediately went there. When he reached there, Matsyendranath was waiting He said, "All the sadhana I gave you, you misused today. You went into your brother disciple's mind to know what was happening there. You had no business to do that. Now for another fourteen years, you go." Now Goraknath went another fourteen years, and he sat in an extremely difficult asana. This is known as Goraknathasana even today; it's a terribly difficult asana. He stayed in that posture, balancing for fourteen years.

Goraknath came from the west coast; that's where his Master, Matsyendranath was - even today a mountain there is named after him. Just last year, I happened to be there. Even today, there is still a band of people living there. Once, Goraknath saw his Guru go to Assam to see somebody, and he did not come back. In his vision he saw that his Guru was into physical pleasures. He was aghast - "How could my Guru be like this?" So he went walking from the west coast to Assam, which is around three thousand kilometers away; he walked all the way. There the Guru was sitting in a prostitute's house with two women on his lap, fondling them, seeking physical pleasure. He could not believe this- how could this happen to Matsyendranath? He is Shiva Himself. He had experienced him in so many powerful ways - and here was this man, sitting with two prostitutes. He told him, "You must come with me," and he scared the prostitutes away with his fierceness. He drew his Guru out and brought him along. On the way, Matsyendranath went for a bath. He gave his handbag to Goraknath and said, "Take care of this- something precious is inside - you must take care of this." He went for a bath in the river. The bag was too heavy, so Goraknath just opened and looked, and he found two big bars of gold. He was so heartbroken, "What has happened to my Guru? First with the prostitutes, now he is collecting gold! If he wants, he can piss on a rock and make the whole rock into gold; he has that much occult in him, but he is attached to two bars of gold. Why?" Then he took these two bars of gold and threw them into the forest and the two of them walked back. Goraknath was in great distress that his Guru was getting lost and he was feeling proud that he walked three thousand kilometers to save his Guru from being lost. When this pride came into him, Matsyendranath put his hand on Goraknath's head, and suddenly Goraknath realized that he was sitting right there. He had neither walked to Assam, nor had he seen the prostitutes, the gold or anything. It had all happened in his mind. Then he was in total distress, absolutely broken, thinking, "I imagined all this about my Guru." It was all real. He actually walked, he went there, he saw. All this happened because of the occult of the Guru. He created everything around him, in reality. Goraknath was in absolute distress: "I did all this. I imagined that my Guru was with prostitutes. I imagined my Guru was lusting for gold." He was in total distress. Then Matsyendranath said, "It's okay. At least you were willing to walk three thousand kilometers to save me. That's good for you. Don't worry about saving me. You were ready to walk all this way to save me, that's great for you; keep that going in you." So some of you are getting certain notions and certain thoughts, and it's good. I always have self-appointed personal advisors around me, too. They tell me what I should or should not do, but it's okay. They are always there (laughs).

Seeker: Master, I have heard you say that people who go into long periods of meditation or samadhi states can get caught up in their own world. Can you explain this for us?

Sadhguru: Gautama [1] never sat for twelve years in one place. He never sat in meditation for long hours either. He never went into that state where he could not come back. Many of his disciples, many Buddhist monks, went into very long meditations and never came out for years. Gautama himself never went because he saw it was not necessary for him. He practiced all the eight, he experienced all the eight kinds of samadhis before his Enlightenment and discarded them. He said, "This is not it." This is not going to take you any closer to Realization. It is just moving into a higher level of experience and probably you will get more caught up, because it is more beautiful than the current reality. Here, in meditation, at least there is pain in your legs to remind you of the present reality. There, there is no pain to remind you, which is in one way or the other, more dangerous. Many yogis have been trapped in realities like this. They have created their own worlds.

1 Gautama : referring to the Buddha.

Now I'm going into an area which is a twilight zone. There are many yogis who have created their own world around themselves. A yogi goes into his cave and he actually creates his own universe and lives there. This is not a joke. He creates everything that he wants. His own kind of planets, his own kind of earth, his own kind of everything, and he lives there happily. A universe is contained inside the cave. In an atom's space, you can create a whole universe, because there is no 'this much' or 'that much'. That is all the creation of the mind. There are many yogis like this, but they are no closer to Realization than you are. He lives in a different world, that's all. He is probably more caught up than you, because he is the creator also; he has learned the art of creation. Do you understand? So this does not become an ultimate release. This just becomes a different kind of action, a different way of doing things. An artist is just drawing a new world on a canvas; a yogi is actually creating it. The artist's creation is two-dimensional, whereas the yogi's is three-dimensional. This is more deceptive. An artist gets so involved in the world that he is creating that he starts believing it is true, and it is true for him. A poet believes that whatever he writes is the truth. Similarly, a man who is painting, if he's deeply involved, believes that what he is painting is the truth. When two-dimensional things are like this, if you create three-dimensional things around yourself, definitely you're going to be more caught up with them. So, going off either into this state or that state is not the thing. This will not lead you to liberation.

There is sufficient energy here to take a lot of people into samadhi states. If you want to go away like that for three or six months, it is possible, but what is the purpose? If a karmic situation arises and there is a need to go off, to hide yourself from the external world for a while, then with that purpose, it is done. That's different. That's the best samadhi you can have. You can live in heaven. You can do what you want, but this does not lead to dissolution. It doesn't lead to a blissful state. Maybe it creates happiness, maybe it creates peace to some extent, but it does not release you from everything. It's just another kind of karma.

Okay, right now, either fortunately or unfortunately, you've had certain glimpses of another dimension of life. What difference has it made? In terms of Realization, has it gotten you any closer? No. If the goal is set, if you have made Realization the top priority in your life, then whatever you do, if it does not take you a step closer, is meaningless. A man who wants to go up Mount Everest, for instance, will not take one step sideways unless it's absolutely necessary. Every ounce of his energy is spent only on reaching the summit. When you want to transcend your own consciousness, you need every ounce of what you have, and still it is not enough.

Seeker: You have written about darkness, which disturbed me a lot. And today at the gathering, the sathsang, it was the first time I have been in this type of situation. Why the sudden reaction of these people with sounds, noises or emotional explosions? It disturbed me a lot. I just kept my eyes closed. I wanted to see what experience I was going to get; I was waiting for my experience. Nothing was there, but I just listened. Whatever it was with me, I don't know. Is this an occult science we are stepping into? I'm afraid, Sadhguru.

Sadhguru: Now, the poem, 'The Dark One', is that the one you are talking about?

The Dark One

When I first heard the sounds of
Darkness and silence meeting within me

The little mind argues for light
The virtue, the power, the beauty

Light a brief happening could hold me not
All encompassing darkness drew me in

Darkness, the infinite eternity
Dwarfs the happened, the happening and yet to happen

Choosing the eternal
Darkness I became

The dark one that I am
The divine and the devil are but a small part

The divine I dispense with ease
If you meet the devil you better cease

If I want to teach you about God, when you are operating within the limitations of your mind, within the parameters of your intellect, then I should always refer to God as Light, because with light you see; with light everything is clear. Clarity comes with light, isn't it? But once your experiences are beginning to transcend the limitations of the intellect, then we will refer to God as Darkness. You tell me, in this existence, which is more permanent? Which is more basic, light or darkness? Darkness. It is in the lap of darkness that light happens. What is it that holds everything in the existence? Darkness, isn't it? Light is just a brief happening. It is burning; it will burn out after some time. Whether it's a light bulb or the sun, it will burn out after some time. This will get burned out in a few hours; that will get burned out in a few million years, but it will get burnt out.

So before and after the sun, what exists? Darkness. What is it that you are referring to as God? Everything springs from that; that is what you are referring to as God. What is the root of everything in the existence? That is what you are referring to as God. You tell me now, what is God, darkness or light? Nothingness means darkness. Everything comes from nothingness. Science proves it to you and your religions have always said it. God is all-encompassing, and only darkness can be all-encompassing. Shiva is the dark one. Do you know that Shiva is the destroyer because He is darkness? He is not light. Light is but a brief happening. When you are living within the parameters of your intellect, we refer to the Divine as Light. If you have transcended, if you have a little experience beyond the intellect, then we refer to the Divine as Darkness, because darkness is all-encompassing.

Light is just a little source and burns itself out, but whatever happens or does not happen, darkness always is. Intellectually you have always ascribed the quality of evil to darkness. That's why you have this problem. That's your problem; that is not the problem of the existence. That's not the problem with the existence. In existence, everything springs from darkness. Light just happens on and off. That's why I'm telling you, Enlightenment means absolute darkness. You can't imagine darkness. You can only imagine light. That's why in yoga, always we say that the Divine is darkness, because you cannot imagine darkness. Only when you are beyond the mind, you will have a taste of darkness.

Now you are asking, "Is this occult science?" This is not occult and, first of all, what is the idea of the occult that you have? If you learn the technology of using energies in a certain way, it is called occult. Generally, it's used in the negative sense because that's what is known to people, but there is any amount of positive occult also. Now we have established the Dhyanalinga. It is a whole technology of creating energy in a certain way; it is occult. When you're doing yogic kriyas, if you get mastery over your energies, it is a kind of occult. You become healthy with kriyas. If your heart disease goes away it is occult, because you have learned to handle your energies. Normally, the word is used in the negative sense because this black magic is more well-known. So people think occult means something negative. It's not so. If you learn to handle the energies, that is occult. Which way you handle them, positive or negative, that is always there. Some people will use the sword to save a life; some people will use the sword to take a life.

Here people are bursting, not emotionally, but because they are so energy-sensitive. If you're willing, we can have you in such a deep energy contact that we will blow your fuse off and we will have to carry you out of this temple. You cannot walk out; you will be so blown out. Right now we are not opening you up that way because you're not prepared for anything like that. So don't worry, this is a free country; everybody can go crazy. They just went crazy for ten minutes; now they are perfectly normal.

Seeker: When I close my eyes I am in darkness. Does this mean I am with God, or is it just my imagination?

Sadhguru: Most people see light when they close their eyes, isn't it? Everybody is claiming that the moment they close their eyes, they're seeing light. Now when you meditate we are asking you to close your eyes, because you are a little nearer to your Creator with eyes closed than with eyes open. Isn't it so? Isn't that true in your experience? All your experiences are deeper when your eyes are closed. It's like this with everything; when you really enjoy something, you close your eyes. When you're kissed by somebody, you close your eyes (laughs), because with eyes closed, it enhances the whole experience. Isn't it? You get closer to yourself with eyes closed. So definitely you are closer. You have not become that, but at least you're one step closer just by closing your eyes.

Seeker: What does the occult include? Is anything that is beyond the physical existence occult?

Sadhguru: No, occult is physical, it's still very physical. Occult is of the physical realm, but it's on the energy level, not the physical level. Somebody can chemically poison you; that's physical. Somebody can poison you with energy, with negative energy so that some harm will befall you, some disease, or death. Usually they use some kind of medium. Let us say I give you this banana, poisoned not with any chemicals, but with negative energy. If you eat it, you'll get a terrible disease, which no medicine will cure. It's not a physical chemical so you cannot use an antidote; it's on a different level. People even die like this. This is only the negative part of the occult. There is also a positive part to it. Occult means using physical energies in whichever way you want. It can be used to enhance life or destroy life. In a way, practicing kriyas, technically is a kind of occult. You're learning to use your energies in a certain way. Now, Doug's cartilage is suddenly fixed, it's occult. Most of the time we never get into occult, because if you do something physically, you acquire a kind of karma. If you achieve the same thing with energy, you acquire a hundred times over more karma.

Seeker: Even if it is something positive?

Sadhguru: Whether it's positive or negative. Positive or negative is just your social relevance. As far as the existence is concerned, there is no positive, there is no negative. It's the way you're meddling with life. Why I say all these healings are stupid, immature acts, is simply because of this. You're trying to use the energies. You don't even have mastery over the little bit of energy which you can activate, but you're trying to use it to heal this or heal that. There is a very deep ego involved. You are trying to play God or something. The karmic levels are too much. Not only for you; even for the person who goes through it. See, usually people who are into the occult die terrible deaths. Do you know this? They're very powerful people, but they die terrible deaths. When they are living they are extremely powerful people.

They can get any spirit (snaps fingers), anything, catch it and just store it in a bottle. This is real. They bring bottles, just glass bottles, catch all kinds of beings and put them in there, then use them for their benefit.

Seeker: So when these people who practice the occult get a little older, when they are weak, do the spirits get them?

Sadhguru: Yes. The spirits get them. Not only do the spirits attack them, the energy of life also gets at them. They die terrible deaths. Dying a terrible death is just one part of it. It goes even further, because the level of karma that they gather is so enormously high. All people who claim to heal will suffer. They will suffer, and they'll make the people they have meddled with also suffer. People whom they have healed will also suffer, because meddling with energies amounts to the occult. The occult is not a good thing to meddle with.

If I have to do any occult, I create enormous amounts of buffers before I attempt anything like this. When we did the *Vishuddhi* [1] consecration for the Dhyanalinga, it was occult. To use that particular being for the consecration process is occult. It may be for a good purpose; that's not the point; it still is occult. You're entering into another realm of activity, where karma is all multiplied. So a whole system of buffers is created, where it is no longer me doing it. I initiate a certain process and leave the rest to happen. Only one part of the consecration process was occult. Another part of it was not physical. Establishing the triangle was occult. Making it like a vortex that draws this energy which is not physical; that's of a different realm, it's not occult. The physical thing that you set up, the instrument that you set up to draw the energy, is occult. Enormous care was taken to see that the people who were involved did not acquire unnecessary attributes. Lots of care was taken; but if you start doing it all the time, it will cause immense damage to you.

This happened with Sadhguru Shri Bhrahma: this event occurred during the British rule of India, in the Nilgiri mountain range. One day, the army issued orders saying that nobody should walk across the

---

1 *Vishuddhi* : of the seven chakras, is the center of power and vision. Located at the pit of the throat.

railway tracks near the station. The ashram was located just across from the station and to go to the town, he had to cross the tracks. He ignored the orders and crossed. The soldiers, seeing this fierce, wild-looking man blatantly disregarding orders, asked him to turn back and leave. Sadhguru continued on his way. So they arrested him and put him in jail. He had no time for such things. He had something to do, but these people were locking him up. So he just walked through the bars and walked away. Now they knew this was not an ordinary being and they did not know what to do with him, but they had orders to arrest him. So they followed him wherever he went. A few of his devotees gathered and said, "Don't you touch this man, this is our Guru", but the soldiers had orders to arrest him. Then the people reminded them that this was not an ordinary being, but they wanted to see something more. The kind of person that Sadhguru was, he didn't want to be bothered by those people, so he just called one boy who was standing there. He placed his hand upon the boy's head and said, "Walk upon the lake." That boy just walked around on the water, he walked upon the water, across the lake and came back. A crowd had gathered, and the soldiers were frightened by the whole thing. They hurried away from that place and left Sadhguru to his work. You never do these occult aspects for your personal benefit. People who are greedy, you know, for money or power, they start doing this kind of thing all the time. They always die terrible deaths.

Seeker: When Sadhguru moved into the body of the bala *yogi*, was this occult?

Sadhguru: That's a little more than occult, but part of it is occult. More than one aspect is not in the realm of the occult. Right now, someone can come and kill you with a sword or with a laser gun and you'll be dead; but with the occult, it is like this, there are no bullets, no sword, no knife, nothing. They can kill you right here and no one can arrest them, because there is no proof. They can have you dead right here with an occult process. Everyone knows who did it, but no one can do anything because there is no physical proof. No physical means are used, but it is still physical. It's very subtle, but it is still physical on another level. Unfortunately, only the negative aspect of the occult is well-known, but there are also positive aspects to it. As far as existence is concerned, there is no positive or negative. It's just that you are meddling with another dimension of life for which there is a price to pay.

Seeker: So you defined occult as the use of energy. What kind of energy are we talking about?

Sadhguru: *Pranamayakosha.*[1] That's why I said even doing the yoga kriyas is a kind of occult. In another way, it's not the same thing. There are many people here who have gone through intense sadhana. If they want to use their energies to heal or predict people's future or anything like that, they can do it very easily. They have the capability to sit in the city and make a lot of money or whatever, but if they even as much as look into somebody else's mind, I just push them back; for one point, ten points down. They know that, so they don't dare do it. People who think they have more compassion than others, stupid compassion, misplaced compassion, want to do everything for everybody. Such people who would like to do such things, we just roll back their life, because they do not know that in their foolishness they will acquire unnecessary karma for themselves and others. If it was just going to affect them, then it is up to them what they do. "Oh, out of my compassion, I want to relieve somebody. I don't care if I gather karma; it's okay." You could be thinking like this, but it is not so. You cause harm even to the person that you meddle with. In both ways it is harmful. There is no point in allowing it unless you have the mastery over doing things with yourself and with situations, so that occult karma is created and dissolved right there. If I do any occult, I create a situation, a kind of boundary within which occult karma is created and right there it is dissolved. Only then I step into that realm. If I just walk out of that situation without dissolving the karma, it's a huge karma.

Seeker: So materializing objects like rings or such things, is that occult too?

Sadhguru: Yes it is. It's not even about materializing. Most of these people are not capable of materializing anything from thin air. They're only moving things from one place to another. Many people are producing watches, gold rings, gold chains, even whisky bottles with 'Made in Heaven' labels on them. They're not creating anything, they're just moving things. A little bit of occult. Let us say somebody has a warehouse somewhere full of watches, jewels or whatever. Now when he gives it to you it seems like he has produced it from thin air, but really, it is just moving things – from there to here. As to miracles – one morning, a man came into the church on crutches. He stopped in front of the holy water, put some on both his legs, and then threw away his crutches. An altar boy witnessed the scene and ran into the rectory to tell the

---

1 *Pranamayakosha* : one of the five sheaths, composed of the life force or prana.

priest what he had just seen. "Son, you have just witnessed a miracle", the priest said, "Tell me where is this man now?" "Ah… he's over there, by the holy water, on the floor, still trying to get up", says the boy.

Seeker: But Sadhguru, you have not answered the question. Is it occult if you can materialize things or you can move things?

Sadhguru: Yes, Sue, you can also materialize things, but in most of the cases it's just moving things. Materializing and de-materializing, both are possible with the occult. One way of looking at materialization is that you're not totally creating something; it's just that you're converting one thing into another. If you look at it scientifically, what's the difference between this stone and gold? It's just the same protons, neutrons, electrons, but the arrangement is different. The numbers are different, that's all. Isn't it? With the power of your mind and energy, you can rearrange those things. If you give me a piece of stone, I can make it into gold and give it to you. That's why with so much disdain, Goraknath says "If my Guru pisses on a rock, he can make it into gold."

Seeker: So have you used the occult many times? Did you go through some occult training?

Sadhguru: I have not learned the occult that way. It's just that when you are spiritually aware, this also comes into your awareness. I have not done any sadhana as such for the occult. It's just that when you become aware, you become aware of everything. That's also there. One aspect of the Dhyanalinga is the highest form of occult. At the same time, I'm not well versed with occult practices of doing things to somebody or producing things. If I sit down and work at it, I can do it because I know what it is, but I'm not practiced in occult.

Seeker: You had talked during the Lebanon sathsang about consecrating spaces. What do you mean by consecrating a space? For example, when you consecrated the *Spanda Hall*,[1] during the opening ceremony, what were you doing and what is the purpose of consecration?

Sadhguru: Do you know what desecration is? Just the reverse is consecration, in a sense. See, consecrations can be done in so many ways. Different types of consecration are done for different purposes, for different uses. For specific purposes, spaces can be consecrated. When we consecrate a certain space, it needs to be kept up; otherwise, it will not stay that way. Usually we use another kind of tool, where there is a basis, where there is a constant process happening all the time to keep the space like that. Spanda Hall is used mainly for Bhava Spandana and Samyama. Right now it is consecrated in a certain way, but we will be bringing some other tools to consecrate it; powerful energy situations happen just like that (snaps fingers).

Many people go into the temple, the Dhyanalinga temple, and come out with tears in their eyes without knowing why. This is not just here; there are so many powerful temples like that, where if you just enter the space, your energy gets heightened in a certain way. This depends on which way that space has been consecrated. It's like preparing the soil. If you want to grow paddy, you prepare the soil one way. For wheat, another way. For carrots, some other way. It's just like that. To grow different kinds of crops, you consecrate the soil in different ways. If meditativeness is what you want to create, you consecrate it one way. If occult is what we want to do, we consecrate it another way. We're just creating a conducive atmosphere and energy. As we have been saying, everything is energy. Health is one kind of energy. Ill health is another kind. Peace is one kind of energy; disturbance is another kind. Joy is one kind of energy; misery is another kind. So we are just creating a certain kind of atmosphere, of peacefulness, joyfulness, blissfulness, or healthfulness. That kind of energy is being created so that people can make use of it.

---

1 Spanda Hall : the venue for advanced Isha Yoga programs. Spanda Hall at Isha Yoga Center is a 64,000 sq. ft. meditation facility which can seat 5,000 people.

Seeker: Can we learn how to do that?

Sadhguru: Can somebody learn? Definitely, but how can you learn? It is all subjective; it's internal. If you want to learn certain external ritualistic processes, you can. For example, people do *agnihotri yagna,* using the element of fire. With *yagnas* and *yagas* they consecrate the space. That is one way of doing it, but it's an elaborate system, and it's not one hundred percent foolproof.

Seeker: Is it possible to consecrate people also, for any reason?

Sadhguru: We do, actually. Initiation is consecration. I do consecrate people in so many varieties of initiations – not just *Shoonya* initiation. Shoonya is rather a general initiation which is very powerful in terms of liberation. There are other kinds of initiations that I do for specific purposes for people, which is in a way consecration. After such initiations you feel some parts of you, some aspects of you, are completely changed. Consecrating people – it's the wrong word to use. We should call it initiation, not consecration. In a way, if you want to call everything consecration, it is consecration – creating a certain atmosphere within a person.

For example, when I initiate *bhramhacharis,*[1] just look at them – in twenty-four hours, the kind of change that comes about them. Have you seen, the last time? What an enormous change! It's not the same person anymore. It's a very powerful initiation that is done with a certain preparation. If people had a little more patience, if they could just wait for a year or two without anything, just hang around, clean, sweep, and just wait; this prepares them. That is what we're doing at Isha. I don't even talk to them. They are not called into any meetings and I don't answer any of their questions – nothing. They just hang around. Now the initiation is powerful because, you know, they're prepared.

Seeker: The blessing of the *rudhrakshas,*[1] is that also a consecration?

Sadhguru: If you bring about some kind of change in the energy situation from a little gross to a little higher state – you're one step up – it's a kind of consecration. When we talk consecration, when we talk

---

1 *bhramhachari* : one on the path of the Divine who has been formally initiated into monkhood through a certain energy process.

2 *rudhrakshas* : sacred beads, seeds of a tree found mostly in the Himalayas also known to have many medicinal and transcendental qualities.

about it in terms of the Dhyanalinga, it's of a completely different dimension. We are preparing the rudhrakshas; we're not just giving them out. Rudhrakshas are always kept in the shrine for a certain period of time. Only after that is done they are given. What you buy in the shop won't be like that. When I bless them, it's different; I do something individual for them.

Seeker: Master, can rudhraksha be used for protection against negative energies?

Sadhguru: Rudhrakshas create a cocoon of your own energy, so that negative energies from outside cannot affect you. Do you have such a thing in your culture, that some people use negative energies to cause harm to somebody else? Is it there? I don't know how many of them are really effective. In India, this is an old, evolved science by itself. One Veda, out of the four Vedas, called Atharva Veda, is all about manipulating energies for your benefit and somebody else's detriment – how to cause injury, disease or even death to a person. There are various methods generally known as black magic. It's a kind of specialization. Do you know? Specializations are there in certain fields. It's not just a question of belief. It's a science; it works. It definitely works. It's just that, because it's a subjective science, it involves a lot of inner work.

Most people who want to do something negative are coming from a certain greed, anger or hatred and they will not have the stability to stay in sadhana. So they don't fully master the art. They know a little, but the rest is psychological. Let's say somebody wants to perform black magic on you. Without doing any black magic, if they just bring a human skull with a little blood on it and leave it in front of your house, it will start working on you. Ninety percent is just psychological, but there are people who, without doing anything, can destroy you from long distances. There are people like that. Any number of people who get affected like this keep coming to me for help. There are so many things we do for these people. Many times this black magic may not necessarily be directed towards you. Now somebody wants to do something negative to this person sitting here. He's not receptive to it, but if you're sitting next to him, you might get it. It's very much possible. Just like if two people are shooting at each other, but somebody next to them gets hit. So most of the time these negative energies won't be directed at you; they'll be directed at somebody else and you'll be the recipient. Yes, if you're wearing rudhraksha, it creates a cocoon of your own energy.

Seeker: Can we wear them all the time? I see people having them wrapped around their wrist; is this just as effective?

Sadhguru: Yes, you can wear them all the time. You can keep them on. They have to be worn around the neck, not on the wrist. Only a certain type of person should wear them on the wrist. If you do, you have to maintain your life in a very rigid way, which is usually not possible. People in family situations should wear them around the neck, not on their wrists; it's not good. I even wanted to tell some of the young ladies who are here that wearing rings on their thumbs is not a good thing to do. You will attract all kinds of things that are not necessary for you. You can wear rings on your ring finger, but don't wear metal on your thumbs. On any of these four fingers is okay. The ring finger is the best, but never wear metal rings on your thumbs. You'll become susceptible to certain kinds of energies that are not necessary for you. Especially metals like gold and copper on the thumb will lead to attracting occult forms – certain forms created by certain occult people. Becoming susceptible to these forms, which are in someone else's control, is not a good thing for you. As it is, having a ring on your ring finger got you into somebody's control (laughs).

Seeker: Is it harmful to do massage or reflexology? Through massage, could you activate something that you are not supposed to?

Sadhguru: Actually, it's not really harmful. People are not that sensitive. When I am in a certain way, I don't allow people to even touch my feet. Otherwise, I will let everybody touch my feet, what's the problem? It's a good way for people to receive. Bowing down is not just for exercise. If one knows how to bow down, if one touches the feet of someone in a certain way, one can receive enormously. Not everybody who bows down and touches feet receives. Only when it is done with reverence and surrender, something can happen.

There is a whole science behind this. In yoga, there is a whole system called *angamardhana*. *Anga* means limbs or parts of body, *mardhana* means to annihilate. It is a system of massage that will take you to a bodiless experience. Generally, massage is catering to the pleasures of the senses, but angamardhana is a system that takes you beyond your senses. In yoga, people did not write down these things or do these things because then, every massage parlor would start activating chakras without knowing what is what. That's not how it should be. Some activation is happening, even when you're walking. Massage is not just about relaxing your body. There are other aspects involved in it. There are certain ways to do it. There are certain chakras that work only in the clockwise direction and certain others which work only anticlockwise. Only by pressing the body in a certain way, the chakras are activated.

Now if you start talking about these things, everybody will start doing this and doing that and messing things up. That's the reason why it is not talked about, because you're operating in a field which is physical, but not only physical. With just the physical you can do whatever you want. If it is non-physical, there is nothing you can do. Here, you are operating in an area which is on the borderline, so things are different. Just your logical way of doing things, your physical way of doing things, is not everything. There are other aspects to it. For every little thing that yoga does, there is yet another aspect to it, but once that other dimension is missing, then the whole thing is reduced to gross physical yoga.

Seeker: Sadhguru, why is there so much significance attached to the feet of a Guru? Why has it always been said in spiritual lore that we should bow down to the Guru's feet?

Sadhguru: There are certain very important aspects to feet. Bowing down and touching the feet in a certain way is an enormous opportunity for one to receive things. Yesterday, you saw that group of people who bowed down to my feet. Did you notice how they held my feet? Traditionally, they have been told the importance of it and how to hold the feet. These men they just held my feet and they were all in tears. These were full-grown and balanced men, running very large businesses of their own. They just know how to hold the feet. That's all.

Since the consecration of the Dhyanalinga, I've been wearing socks. I didn't want people to touch my feet because my whole energy system was so fragile. Most saints also do not allow anybody to touch their feet because they're in a certain state. Sometimes touching feet takes away too much. People who do not know anything about this don't mind. It feels very good to have somebody touch your feet! There is a certain way of receiving things. Now in many ways I have demonstrated how, just the ring finger, what are all the things it can do to a person. Just one touch can do so many things. Similarly, in the feet also there are areas and spaces through which one can receive enormously. All the chakras have manifestations in your sole : S-O-L-E sole, not S-O-U-L soul. In the soles of your feet, the seven chakras are manifested in a certain way. In the ninety-day Wholeness program, all the participants were taught to activate the chakras in each other's feet. Even when the National Hockey Team was here for a program, their feet were pressed to activate their chakras. It made such a big difference for those guys. We just pressed certain chakras and activated their energy. Also in the Dhyanalinga temple, the steps are made in such a way that the heel of your foot is pressed and this activates the nadis.

Now today, I think it's called reflexology. Those people press everywhere and just hope to touch something. This is not like that. In yoga, it is clear-cut; it is known exactly where each chakra is located in your feet. Everybody's chakras are not in the same location. By looking at where one's chakras are located, you can know everything about that person, even his karmic structure. In so many ways, it is written in the body, including in your hands. Your karma is all written there, at least most aspects of it. It is based on this that people are trying to read your future; because the past is written, they are trying to predict the future.

Seeker: What is the reason for the anklet you are wearing?

Sadhguru: Oh, just to keep me stable on the ground! (Laughs). You might have noticed that every bhramhachari and almost every other inmate is wearing a copper ring. Have you noticed this?

Seeker: Yes, it's in the shape of a snake…

Sadhguru: The snake is just symbolism. Fundamentally, it is a copper or metal ring. We cannot afford gold so we use copper (laughs). This is so because when people go into intense sadhana, there are possibilities that they may accidentally slip out of their bodies. Just to ensure that people don't fall out of their bodies accidentally, we fix a metal ring. If there is metal on the body, it can't happen. Many of you are already wearing a lot of metal. People who are on the spiritual path do not wear any metal or jewelry.

So we always put a copper ring on their ring finger, because it's a sensitive finger. As I have already mentioned, there are certain nadis present in this finger. It can be activated and made to be very sensitive. People who are into certain types of sadhana are very much aware of it. We put on a ring so that the person is held and accidental slipping out won't happen. Once a Guru gives a ring to the disciple, he's not supposed to remove it. He's never to remove the ring without permission, because we don't want such things to happen.

The Dhyanalinga consecration required samadhi states with intense activity which could be dangerous for the people involved; they could slip out at anytime. Then certain things happened; one of the persons involved left. After that, people around me were very concerned that I may leave. So they put a big shackle on me (laughs). It's just a device to get you a little more integrated into the body.

Seeker: Will that prevent you from going?

Sadhguru: Accidental slippages can be controlled. It gets you a little more integrated into the body.

Seeker: And what's this thread attached to it?

Sadhguru: Why don't you touch it and see?

Seeker: It's like a pulse…

Sadhguru: Indu, if you hold it too long, you'll become young; you'll have to live your life all over again. (Questioner laughs) Do you feel something?

Seeker: Yes, it's as if I'm holding a pulse. It feels alive…My whole hand is going… tick, tick, tick … Sadhguru, why do you keep this thread tied to your anklet?

Sadhguru: I'm still on life support. Certain nadis are still not functioning in me since the consecration process. I'm still existing through somebody else. If I take it off, immediately I will become…

Seeker: So it creates a link? The thread creates a link between you and somebody?

Sadhguru: Yes, it's connected to somebody else. Some process has been done with them, which creates that link. If the thread is removed, within three days my energy will start becoming low, because certain parts of my energy body are still not well established. I must do it; it has been too long. I need to take some time off.

Seeker: This knowledge of nadis, is it within you, or has some other Guru or nadi expert told you about it?

Sadhguru: Indu, you're really something! Nobody has told me anything. This is just that you know your system, so you find a device. Probably nobody else has done anything like this; nobody has used the nadis this way. I'm sure someone might have, but in different ways. Probably nobody would have done it this way. I just found a convenient method for myself and used what was available.

Seeker: This anklet is touching you all the time and the thread is an antenna or something?

Sadhguru: Okay, you can call it an antenna; it's not really an antenna. It is more like a wire. From here onward though, it's wireless. I used certain people this way; I used certain situations, sometimes maybe even a tree. If anything happens to me, it will affect their body in a similar way. Let us say I hurt my shoulder, immediately there will be pain in that person's shoulder.

Seeker: That person with whom the thread is connected?

Sadhguru: Yes, they'll have pain in their body. So they know something is not okay with me. Then they will take a little extra care. They'll do certain practices, more sadhana. They have been taught some practices. Suppose the system does not function properly; immediately they'll do certain particular practices and bring in more aliveness and more intensity into the system. So they do all the practices for me (laughs).

Seeker: Wherever you are, even in another country, this linkage works?

Sadhguru: Wherever does not matter.

Seeker: You mean to say someone is doing some practice and it helps to cure you?

Sadhguru: Yes. See, the way I injure myself and the way I recover is quite miraculous. Medically, it's not possible. If I tear my muscle, it's clearly visible that it is torn and swollen. You'll see, tomorrow morning, it will be gone. I don't do anything about it. They know once the pain comes, they have to do certain processes. They will do those things.

Seeker: Sadhguru, you're a wonder of a man!

Sadhguru: It is not that I'm a wonder; I have wonderful people around me.

Seeker: You have taught them this whole science and that's how the linkage is established?

Sadhguru: They do not know what exactly it is, but they know it works like this because experientially, it's true for them. They don't know exactly how to make this happen, but they know that if this happens in their body, they must do a certain practice, like we are teaching you variations of *mudras* to direct energy to different parts of the body during your practice of yoga kriyas. If your head is paining, you hold the mudra, your hand, this way; if the pain is in your back, you hold it another way. Usually, only three or four varieties of problems will come to me. So for those things, I have told them what to do. If it is something else, then I have to tell them how to do it. They will handle normal problems. During initiation, sometimes problems will occur. If there are too many sick people in the class, it will affect me – even though I don't take it upon myself – at times, in a different dimension, because in some ways things open up. So if the percentage of sick people is high, especially mentally ill people, suffering from depression or manic situations, those types of things will affect the system. For those things, the support system knows what to do. If I'm too low, they will feel low and they will do what has to be done. Another area, this part of me (pointing to the liver area) is totally un-established. After the consecration, this part has always been trouble for me.

Seeker: What, the liver!?

Sadhguru: Yes, the liver and just around it. Because this area was in trouble, the liver also was affected. Earlier, that was the main thing. At any moment, lumps would just appear. Big lumps. Two or three days later, the lumps would just dissolve themselves. If the energy got disturbed, it would produce something in my body; but after that celestial snake visited me, it got all settled. There is no trouble there now. Otherwise, my lower chakras become too low, while the upper chakras become too high. Then I'll be too alert – overly alert and too bright – but physically I'll be receding. So for that, they know what to do. These are simple problems that I normally face. If something else happens, I'll need to talk to them.

Seeker: What, a snake? A snake visited you? What is all this, Sadhguru!?

Sadhguru: After the consecration of the Dhyanalinga, my health situation was quite bad. I was in a terrible state, but I started recovering. Many processes were done. A few people really dedicated their lives to making me well again. This involved so many things – which are too otherworldly and unbelievable for you to understand. It's too fairytale-ish for any logical mind to believe. I started recovering and started functioning okay, but certain parts of my body – especially the right side, just beside my navel – were like a vacuum, creating problems. Tumors started forming there. People who had observed me witnessed how big lumps used to form one day, and disappear after a few days.

In order to stop being nagged, I went and got a medical opinion. When they checked my blood, my RBC was excessively high; the iron content in the blood was too high. This was because my liver function was starting to fail, because that part of the energy body was totally destroyed. We could have fixed it, but I needed time – at least a month or two for myself – that time I never got. I was always talking about taking a month off and fixing my body, but it never happened. So this condition kept getting worse. If it had been allowed to grow, it could have slowly become cancerous and destroyed the body. I never got the time to really fix it. Off and on, we did small patch-up jobs here and there, but we never really did a proper job on the system, because of time and other compulsions.

About eight or nine months ago (referring to December 2001), it was early in the morning. I was lying down in my bedroom at the ashram. At around four forty-five, I opened my eyes and saw a huge snake sitting next to me – larger than normal proportions. Its hood was raised. This was a huge cobra that was sitting right next to my bed. I have always kept a little brass cobra next to my bed; that is what says good morning to me every day. Now there was a big one, a live one, standing up, with such a giant hood. I opened my eyes and saw it clearly, it was just sitting right there. I was looking at it and then it came towards me and bit me, next to the navel. I closed my eyes and it remained there for some time, and then it left. This bite caused wounds to my belly – four fang marks, with blood oozing out. I showed it to Bharathi – the wound was still open and bleeding when I showed it to her.

After that day, people who have been in the ashram and around me have seen how dramatically I have been improving in the last eight months. Four years ago, when we went to the Himalayas, in Gangotri, I wasn't even able to start the climb. So I just stayed back while the rest of the group climbed to Gomukh and Tapovan and stayed for two days. Two years later, I was able to make the trip to Bhojwas and Gomukh, but every kilometer, people needed to massage my legs, and I needed a lot of support along the way. This trip, if I wanted to, I could have passed you all, but I slowed down my pace so we could go together. I could have run to Tapovan if I had wanted to. I'm not doing any great physical activity to improve my physical body, but the improvement is distinctly there.

From that day, the space or the vacuum is gone; the celestial snake took it away from me. So what's all this? It's very difficult to explain. All I can say is, during the course of many lifetimes, I have made as many friends – from this world and the other – as I have made enemies. The enemies are not worthwhile kinds of people. My friends are. I never ask them to do anything for me, nor do they come and bother me unless it is needed. Somehow they just intervened and this happened.

Chapter - 6

Beings of the Beyond

Beings of the Beyond

The ruthless debtor that she is
claimed back earth that you fancied was you
To leave you so naked and bare as to be bodiless
dead they think you are when you wait for another lease

Since earth's debt you repaid
ones who claimed to love you abhor you
With me the wanderer of the twilight world
you can rest upon my breast, to annul your destined course.

– Sadhguru

Everything that is worth knowing can be known from within.

- Sadhguru

At ease with all kinds. *With Sadhguru even the venomous turn docile. At one time, Sadhguru lived with over twenty venomous snakes in his bedroom.*

Whether it is spirits or ghosts, angels or demons, the devil or gods, man's interest in the Beings of the Beyond has been phenomenal. During childhood, fed with an overdose of mythology, where the sky is not the limit, many of us even believed we were one such being ourselves. Then came the science teachers who instilled '*seeing is believing*', and the rationalists who goaded the masses to seek '*scientifically verifiable proof* ' and finally, the Relativity freaks who questioned the reality of not only the unseen, but even that which is *seen* and felt.

Today, we would like to believe these beings do not exist. We hear so many stories but never get the proof. The stories can be dismissed, but the feeling, the certainty that there must be more to what we perceive, lingers in us all our lives.

Driven by an unquenched desire to communicate and relate to these Beings of the Beyond, often in desperate pursuit of solutions to nagging worldly situations, man has ended up more often in the gory and the ghastly than with any real clarity.

Far from frightening little children and speaking to the voices in the dark, this much-misunderstood aspect of life has a rightful place and purpose in Creation. Here, as always, maneuvering deftly between fact and fiction, Sadhguru, elaborates on the spiritual aspects of the Beings of the Beyond. In a series of questions and answers, Sadhguru, perhaps for the first time in print, reveals the cause of their existence, what they can and cannot do, their sadhana and salvation. Thus creating a no-frills understanding, freeing seekers from frivolous desires and unfounded fears, preparing them to receive possible situations of the Beyond with grace and humility.

Seeker: In an article in the *Forest Flower*,[1] I have read that someone who was present at the *Dhyanalinga* consecration experienced the presence of disembodied beings that were present during certain processes of consecration. This is beyond my logical understanding. Can you throw some light on this?

Sadhguru: Now, 'throw some light'…you must understand this. With your eyes, you can only see that which stops and reflects light. Right now, you can see my palm because it stops light. If it just allows all the light to pass through, you will not see my hand, isn't it? So throwing light on disembodied beings is a little difficult (laughs). The only reason you do not see them is because they don't stop light. Whatever I'm going to talk about now, don't believe it. At the same time, don't be a fool and disbelieve it either. Life exists in many dimensions. I want you to keep just this much openness. Now I'm going to speak so blatantly and illogically that you will need to look beyond your normal levels of understanding. Wouldn't you like to explore all dimensions of life, no matter what they are? Once you are here, wouldn't you like to know every aspect of what your life is about? Or would you just explore that which is convenient and comfortable for you?

All beings, embodied or disembodied, are in many ways functioning or playing their lives out as per their *karmic* structures. When you're embodied, there is more possibility of using your will. When you're disembodied, depending on one's level of awareness, depending upon what level of subtleness one has evolved into, accordingly the disembodied beings function just as karmic play. As their qualities are, accordingly they are drawn to different areas or different spaces. Whenever we create a certain energy space, a certain powerful situation of energy, a higher possibility of energy, then naturally these

1 *Forest Flower* : referring to the Isha Foundation's monthly newsletter.

beings are just drawn there. A few are drawn by will, by choice; the rest, they cannot help it. When such energies are created, they are just drawn towards it. It was not just during the Dhyanalinga consecration. I should not be talking about these things, because I know there are people who have wild imaginations.

In many situations in my life, they have been around me, and they still are, especially where I live. They are very, very much there, because the shrine at the house is made in such a way that it just draws these kinds of beings. It's like an everyday thing for me. As there are trees and plants, I have many of them just moving around; they never get in my way, so I don't mind. They don't eat my food, so I don't mind (laughs). Many of them who were in a certain state of evolution, in the last few years I have just completely dissolved them. There are others who are not of that quality; they have to wait, but if I take it upon myself, I can draw many more of them, trap them and dissolve all of them completely. It is possible.

Seeker: Why trap them? What does it mean to trap them, to dissolve them?

Sadhguru: In one dimension of life, dissolution is absolute freedom. In another dimension of life, it is slaughter. Naturally, that dimension will try to struggle and escape. Whatever is being threatened naturally tries to defend itself to escape that situation. Now, there is another dimension which longs to be there. It's like a marriage: those who are in are trying to be out, those who are out are trying to be in. It once happened that an old farmer had a wife who nagged him unmercifully from morning till night and sometimes even later. She was always complaining about something. The only time he got any relief was when he was out plowing with his old mule, and he tried to plow a lot! One day, when he was out plowing, his wife brought his lunch to the field. He drove the old mule into the shade, sat down on a stump and began to eat his lunch. Immediately, his wife began haranguing him again. The nagging just went on and on. All of a sudden, the old mule lashed out with both his hind feet, caught her smack in the back of the head and killed her dead on the spot.

At the funeral, later, the minister noticed something rather odd. When a woman mourner would approach the old farmer, he would listen for a minute and then nod his head in agreement. When a man mourner approached him, he would listen for a minute and then shake his head in disagreement. This was so consistent that the minister decided to ask the old farmer about it. So after the funeral, he came up to him and asked the farmer why he nodded his head and agreed with the women, but always shook his head and disagreed with the men. The old farmer said, "Well, the women would come up and say something about how nice my wife looked, or how pretty her dress was, so I nodded my head in agreement." "And what about the men?" the minister asked. "They wanted to know if the mule was for sale." So that's the whole struggle all the time, especially for a disembodied being, because he has no conscious will. He is only going about according to his vasana – the karmic tendencies in him. He needs to be trapped; otherwise, you cannot do anything to help him.

Seeker: So how do you trap them?

Sadhguru: Trap does not mean physically trapping something, like trapping an animal. It is just that one dimension in you is longing to become free. Another dimension has known only limitations and it only knows limitations. If one has to transcend the limited into the dimension of the unlimited, it takes a certain amount of coaxing and seducing of that being. So seduction is a trap. It's a trap. Enticement is a trap. Any attraction that you create is a trap. Right now, the very fact that you are listening to this talk is a trap, a logical trap to take you into that which is illogical. We can further say that the only reason why you're here is because right now, I appeal to your logic. What I want to offer you is not logical. So the logical dimension of what I am speaking is like a trap to offer you or to deliver you into that dimension which is beyond logic.

Seeker: So how do you make this trapping business possible?

Sadhguru: We need to create a certain situation to make those things happen. A few of you who were in the ninety-day Wholeness Program witnessed this. When the sadhana was taken to a certain pitch, when the energies became a certain way, certain beings started almost physically appearing around us because that kind of energy just drew them. Those few beings that some of you witnessed came by choice. These were certain yogis who left their bodies unfulfilled, and they were conscious enough not to take on another physical body. They did not want to go through the whole process again so they were just looking for situations through which they could dissolve themselves. Especially those seven or eight who were constantly around throughout the Wholeness Program, over a period of time I took care of all of them, because they were there consciously. There were a few others who were around us, some of them consciously; some of them were just drawn there.

So what is a disembodied being? See, the physical body that you see right now is something that you picked up from the earth. It is just the food that you have eaten. What you call as 'my body' is just a heap of food. It's a piece of earth, right now standing up and prancing around like this. Again it will fall back and become earth. Even before you picked up this much earth, you were still very much a complete being. Even when your body was very small, you were still a complete being. So the physical body is being constructed with some other substance. That substance is still intact. If you shed the body, it's simply because your time to pay back the loan has come. The physical body is something that you have borrowed from the planet on which you're living. When the time comes, the planet will claim it back, no interest claimed, but you have to pay it back to the atom. It won't let you keep even an atom of it. You have to shed it totally.

Now the other dimensions of you, especially the karmic shell, continue to play, seeking another physical body. If it is completely unaware, it naturally seeks another physical body. If it is aware to some extent, it can hold on for a certain period of time. If it is in a certain level of awareness, the disembodied being is in a certain state of pleasantness. It is this state that is referred to as heaven. These beings are in different levels of pleasantness, or you can even say certain ecstasy within themselves, because they have left their physical body in a certain state of awareness; now they have acquired a certain sweetness about them. They enjoy the sweetness for a certain period of time, a holiday, a vacation, before taking on another physical body. This vacation is what you refer to as heaven. Similarly, if people leave or die in certain states of fear, anxiety, anger or ignorance, their karmic shell will have acquired a certain kind of unpleasantness about it. This unpleasantness is what you refer to as hell. Like this, there are many layers of hell and also many layers of heaven.

One who is on the spiritual path is not aiming to enter into these spaces – pleasantness or unpleasantness. He wants to drop the whole structure. Traditionally, especially in this culture, many methods, hundreds of different ways were taught with which you can acquire certain good karma or certain pleasantness about yourself, and through which you can live in states of heaven, so that when you drop this body,

The lesser known dimensions. *Sadhguru rests outside an occult temple on the way to Kedarnath.*

you don't go through suffering. You don't go through unpleasantness. You go through a certain state of pleasantness or ecstasy within yourself, which will naturally decide what kind of physical situation you will choose, which womb you will choose. As the tendencies are, accordingly you choose. In India, we call these vasanas. Whichever way your vasana is, that's the kind of body, mind and life you choose. This choice is happening unconsciously, but if one is in a certain state of evolution, this choice can also happen consciously.

Once, a bunch of friends were sharing an apartment. One of them was a regular drinker and all he could afford was cheap whisky. Every night, he would drink his fill, get dead drunk, run to the kitchen sink and puke and puke and puke. His roommates quickly grew disgusted by his routine and warned him that if he didn't stop, he would lose his stomach one day. This didn't do much good. So they decided to teach him a lesson. The following night, they disemboweled a chicken and left the bloody guts in the sink. Sure enough, the young man came home drunk as usual, headed straight for the kitchen and immediately began heaving with great vigor. A few minutes later, he appeared in the living room doorway, white as a ghost. He announced, "It happened, it happened! Just as you said it would, I vomited up my insides,

Sacred space for Self transformation. At the Spanda Ha of Isha Yoga Center, a 64,000 sq. ft. meditation facility.

but the good news is, by God's Grace and help, I got them all back down. Now grab me a drink, quick!" See, just like you, disembodied beings exist by their tendencies. Only their physical body is gone; everything else is there. They are as much a reality as you. It's just that, because they don't stop light, you're unable to see them. Your vision does not allow you to see them. If you had a little keener sense of vision, if your experience of life was a little more than that which is physical, they would be very much a reality for you.

Now, don't start seeing them in every nook and corner of the ashram (laughs). That's the danger of talking about this. During the Dhyanalinga consecration process, they were here in huge numbers; the room was filled with them. We had to push our way through them; they were all over. They were too excited about a possibility like this. Most of them had not come there by choice; they were just sucked into that vortex as the energy became subtler and subtler. To understand this physically would be like – you know, the winds always move from high pressure to low pressure? Everything moves in the direction of low pressure. Wherever the energy becomes very subtle, we can say it's a kind of low pressure. So naturally all these beings move in that direction; they're just drawn in that direction. Wherever the energy is gross, it's high pressure; everything tries to move away from it.

These beings are drawn here, especially into my presence, which has a certain significance. At the same time, they will never be drawn into the temple because whenever we consecrate a temple, we also create a certain situation where these kinds of beings are not able to enter the temple space. It happened that a few people came to me who were possessed by some other being that was tormenting them. We just took them to the temple. In ten minutes, they were perfectly okay because that being could not enter the temple. A certain safeguard is always created when we create a temple. Since these beings resent that they cannot enter the temple space, in order to entertain them, traditionally in this country, if we build a major powerful temple, a little away from the temple, another kind of temple will be built which will attract these forces. These are usually used for occult purposes.

Those of you who were walking with me to Kedar in the Himalayas this time, remember that we spent some time at an occult temple on the way. That temple was built so that those beings could come, and also so that those who have certain mastery can use those beings in a certain way. It is also a kind of protection for the main temple, so that it cannot be misused. Before I go, I will set up an occult temple for the Dhyanalinga. This will ensure that future generations cannot misuse the Dhyanalinga in any way. We will establish an occult temple, which is like a guardian for the Dhyanalinga. Not that it needs a guardian, but it will take care of those kinds of beings who want to be there, but cannot. These energies are such that they are drawn to the temple and are being repelled from it at the same time. We don't want to leave them like that, because there is nothing wrong with them; they are just other kinds of beings. Whether they carry a body or not, what's my problem? So we will be creating a small occult temple to entertain all these beings. Then you'll have them in big company (laughs).

Right now, the shrine at the house is in that kind of condition, because it has seen different aspects of consecration. Above all, the shrine has seen the reconstruction of my own body, which needed certain factors. Because of that, it acts like a magnet for those beings, but they don't usually enter the shrine unless I invite them. I have brought some of them in by the hand (laughs). I should not be talking about these things. All these days I have spoken so logically and sensibly; suddenly, you're making me speak like this on the last day of the year! Anyway the New Year also comes like those beings, without a sound. Look out!

There have been some beings who came and sat on the rooftop continuously for months. They would not leave; they were just waiting and waiting. After the consecration, my body was unstable, so I didn't bother with them. See, these beings do not have brains, they just have tendencies. So if the body is not stable and you take them on, they can just turn against your own system. After the consecration, I just left them alone; but in the last ten to eleven months, I have taken many of them into the shrine and just dissolved them completely. They make the shrine more and more exuberant in energy. If they had to come back into the body and find Realization, they could get caught up with so many things. Do you see, once you have this intellect, how difficult it is to Enlighten you? (Laughs). If you did not have a body, I could have done anything I wanted with you. If I do something with you now, your body will fall dead right here. We would have to explain so many things, which could be very difficult. If you did not have a body, I could do anything and nobody would know.

All beings are seeking dissolution, whether they are aware of it or not. Out of their limitations, fears and misunderstandings, they may think they are not seeking it, but every being is seeking dissolution, always. If your body would not fall on our hands, it would be so easy to dissolve you. That's why a Guru always waits until your body becomes ripe enough. When the moment of death comes naturally, he will interfere and do what he has to do. Maybe he will make you leave a few days early.

Seeker: Sadhguru, all these stories we hear about ghosts and spirits, is there anything to them?

Sadhguru: What you are calling *peyi-pishachi*, or ghosts, are those beings who left their body, usually in an unnatural way. Let's say you have strong *prarabdha* karma left unfinished, either because you were killed in an accident, murdered, or even died of a disease – you can cause a disease to yourself by drinking too much, smoking too much or doing something to yourself that breaks the body. Somehow, you broke the body by hanging by the noose, shooting yourself, or drinking alcohol everyday. You somehow damaged the physical body so much that it could not sustain life anymore, but your prarabdha is still not complete. This being will have a denser presence, and its tendencies are very strong. They are active in a certain way so you could see them more easily. They don't have to do anything; they just appear.

If you happen to just see them, because of your own inhibitions and limitations, you may get really paranoid. It's a psychological situation; it has nothing to do with the beings. Suppose you see a headless man, what's the problem? Most people don't have a head anyway, or even if they have a head, it's not worth much (laughs). It is just that if you see a headless man, you'll go through all kinds of weird emotions. This is not necessary; it's a psychological situation which has nothing to do with these beings.

Seeker: Sadhguru, these disembodied beings that we're speaking about, these spirits or whatever, where do so-called angels fit into this discussion? Are angels disembodied beings or are they beyond them? Are they evolved to the level of dissolution?

Sadhguru: Don't use the word 'angel'. The word 'angel' has too many hallucinatory meanings, you know?

Seeker: It does, but is 'angel' just a term that a certain sect of humanity decided to call this kind of disembodied being?

Sadhguru: Here, in this culture, we have identified different types of angels. Different levels of bodiless existence are referred to as *yakshas, gandharvas,* or devas. It's like they are at different evolutionary levels, or we can say they are on different types of vacations. Somebody is in first class, somebody is in second class, somebody is in another class, and somebody else is in hell. There are those beings who are aware, who have refused to enter any of these vacations, and they are looking for ways of dissolution. We call them *celestial beings.* They have not become yakshas, gandharvas, or devas. They are just keeping themselves loose, still looking for liberation. Do you understand?

Seeker: Is that a better position to be in?

Sadhguru: Yes, in many ways, because they're still looking for liberation. These other beings are enjoying their vacation. They are enjoying some type of heaven, some kind of pleasantness and joy in them, some kind of luxury around them. Luxury does not mean the kind that we know; somehow, they are pleasant, but their vacation will end sometime and they will take on another physical body. Nobody remains a yaksha, gandharva, or deva forever. He enjoys it for a certain time then he again takes on a physical form. There is nothing new about this in India. Ever since ancient times, it has been talked about. I'm not talking about something I have read. I'm talking about something I see. It is all very much a reality.

Seeker: It seems the Indian culture just knows about these things. Whether they have experienced them or not, they know about them; they have been told these things. But most people in the West have not been brought up with this rich a culture.

Sadhguru: They also believe in angels and vampires. I know so many meditators in the United States who initially kept telling me that angels were coming to them. Now, after being with me for some time, they don't dare talk about those things anymore, every day telling me many fanciful things. It's all too hallucinatory. That's the reason I have never talked about these aspects before. The moment I talk, you'll see, the most idiotic ones in the ashram will be the first ones who will see gandharvas. The intelligent ones will not see them. Only the idiotic ones will start seeing celestial beings everywhere, because they have no control over their imagination. It will just fly and they will start doing stupid things and claim that angels guided them. All these UFO cults, the ones that committed mass suicide, they said that aliens came and told them to do it. People can do these kinds of stupid things with this information. That is the reason why we have not talked about it before.

Seeker: We have focused primarily on human disembodied beings, up to this point. What about non-human disembodied beings?

Sadhguru: There is really no such thing as non-human disembodied beings. For example, does a grasshopper go about hopping without a body? Is there such a thing? Not really, because when a grasshopper dies, whatever does not die in it is at a very rudimentary state of evolution. Usually, it just clings to the earth. In India, we have been told that you should never walk on grass at night. One reason for this is your own safety: to avoid snakes, insects and whatever. Another reason is because all these beings, which are in a very quick transitory state – it's like a transit port – just cling to the earth. Suppose a grasshopper dies; it immediately wants to find the next body, but there may be a little time span in-between.

Most animals and insects die in the night, not in the day, especially the lower level of animals. They may get eaten by a bird or some animal; that's different. If they die by themselves, it's mostly at night, and the being tends to cling to the earth, because they are very much like the earth. They are even capable of merging with it. In this culture, it has been said that once the sun sets, you should not walk on the grass because these beings will get trampled in some way. So for them the transitory state is very short. They are going completely by their tendencies, so the transition happens quickly for them.

A disembodied snake can possess a human being. In this culture it is a common knowledge called *naga dosha*. This can particularly affect certain layers of your skin and create a very strange sense of stillness and movement. A snake has a more substantial presence of being. That's one reason why in this culture, people are told not to kill a snake, because it has a more substantial presence about it. In case you happen to kill a snake, it needs to be cremated or buried as we do for a human body. Similarly for the cow and crow, the being of a cow always tends to linger on around certain types of trees. The *Pungai* tree is one of those which attract the bodiless cows, but their period of transition is very brief. So in India it is understood that if you spend time under this particular tree, you'll be blessed with nourishment, as cow's milk has always been the very symbol of nourishment.

Seeker: So does everybody, when they die, become a disembodied being?

Sadhguru: When you drop your body, you are disembodied.

Seeker: So everybody enters this state?

Sadhguru: Yes, everybody. The span of time varies. If you finish your prarabdha and leave, or if you die with very strong desires, the span of time may be short, the interval is brief. Finding a womb is almost instantaneous.

You may be back within days or weeks. Now what if there is no appropriate womb for that being? That's when it falls back into animal nature, and regresses back to work out all those desires.

Seeker: Regarding these disembodied beings or celestial beings, what is the difference in the process for their next life choice? Is it conscious, partially conscious or totally unconscious?

Sadhguru: We use the words 'celestial beings' to refer only to those beings who still have some choice. The others, we refer to as 'disembodied beings'. We can call them ghosts, *bhootha prethas,* gandharvas, yakshas or whatever. We are using the words 'celestial beings' only for those who have a certain sense of choice, because they lived and died in a certain sense of awareness. The others, the disembodied beings, are just functioning by compulsion, the same way you are.

Seeker: Do any of these disembodied beings serve us as guides or are they doing their own thing?

Sadhguru: If they knew any better, they would have found liberation. Why are they just wandering around? Because they don't know any better. See, somebody is rich, somebody is poor in the world, but when it comes to basic life, the rich man doesn't know any better than the poor man, isn't it? Similarly, when it comes to Realization and liberation, that disembodied person does not know any better than you. He's also stuck, like you. The only thing is that it's a little more pleasant. If you are rich, you eat well, you dress well, you live in a more comfortable home, but you don't know any better about life. It's all the same.

Seeker: Can these disembodied beings adversely impact a seeker on the path? Conversely, can they assist the seeker on the path?

Sadhguru: For someone who is seeking liberation, I want you to understand, what you are seeking is self-annihilation. For one who is seeking self-annihilation, who can cause any more damage than he can cause to himself? You want to cause the maximum – not harm – you want to annihilate yourself. When that is what you're seeking, if a ghost or a beast comes and helps you, what's your problem? It's okay. For a seeker, nobody can take anything from him if he's a real seeker. If he's a fancy seeker; who is just trying to add spirituality as entertainment in his life, maybe. If he is a genuine seeker, anything that happens to him – even the most disastrous thing – is also a plus, because it only annihilates him a little more.

Traditionally, the first thing a seeker does in India is to go with a begging bowl, even if he's a king. Being a beggar is the worst possible thing that can happen to a human being. So a king chooses to be a beggar, he has already done the worst possible thing to himself. Who or what else can do anything more to him? It can be your choice; otherwise, life will choose for you and make you endure many things.

One Sunday morning, everyone in this bright beautiful tiny town got up really early and went to the local church. Before the service started, the town's people were sitting on church pews, talking about their lives, families, just chatting. Suddenly Satan appeared at the front of the church. Everyone started screaming and running to the front door, trampling each other in a frantic attempt to get away from evil incarnate. Soon the church was empty, except for one elderly gentleman, who just sat there calmly, not moving, seemingly oblivious to the fact that God's ultimate enemy was in his presence. This confused Satan a bit. So he walked up to the man and said, "Don't you know who I am?" The man replied, "Yes, I do." Satan asked, "Well, aren't you afraid of me?" "No, I'm not," said the man. Satan, a little perturbed by this, asked, "Why aren't you afraid of me?" The man calmly replied, "I've been married to your sister for over forty-eight years..." After that no ghost or beast can do anything more to you, isn't it?

Seeker: Can these disembodied beings take over a person? Can they feed off our energies?

Sadhguru: Yes, definitely. They can very easily get into your system. Such a thing is possible, though we never think on those terms. These things are done and beings are used in many ways. If there is a *mantric* who has some power over a certain spirit, he will put the spirit into some person out of whom he wants to get something. That person will then do whatever he is asked to do.

Trapping these beings has its limitations. You can't keep the being trapped forever, even if the trap is very strong. It can get released when the person who has imprisoned it dies. The power of most mantrics does not go away upon death; it goes away before that. Somewhere, they lose their hold on it and the beings desert the mantric. Have you read Shakespeare's *The Tempest*? In it, the sorcerer depicted does many things like this. They can extend their hold only on the grosser spirits, the wicked ones. They have no hold on the evolved beings. These beings will not hover around such an atmosphere, because they can feel the energy and what kind of a person is there. An unaware or ignorant spirit may get easily trapped. These evolved beings won't get trapped so easily. Even here, with me, they were very cautious in the beginning.

Now someone who has died without completing his *prarabdha* or the allotted karma is leaving with his karmic structure still intact. The only way you can die when your prarabdha is still intact is if your body breaks. This can only happen because of an accident, injury or disease. You might be thinking, "Isn't disease a natural cause of death?" See, disease is also one way of breaking the body. If you die of a heart attack because of excessive stress, it's just like murder, suicide, or an accident. One part of the body broke, and life is not able to sustain itself in a physical body anymore, so it leaves, but the karmic structure is still intact. This being continues to be very much present. When I say very much present, it's more 'experience-able,' because the karmic structure is left intact. If a person runs the full term of his prarabdha – the prarabdha is gone – then he's too subtle; most people will not be able to feel him. When his prarabdha is intact and he dies, many more people can feel him. That's why traditionally in this culture they say that if you die of murder, suicide or in an accident, you become a ghost. Everyone becomes a ghost; this is a more solid ghost, a denser ghost that can be experienced by a few more people. Only people of a certain refinement can experience the more subtle ones.

Beings whose prarabdha is still intact continue to have human tendencies. They want to eat, sleep and copulate. They want to do everything, because their karma is still intact. The others don't have this.

Their karmic structure is gone, so such things do not even exist in them. That's the difference. If you work out your karma quickly, you're free from all these compulsions. Even with these disembodied beings, it's the same reality. If karmic compulsions are there, such beings can feed upon you, because they are not able to satisfy their tendencies by themselves. For example, everywhere in the world, there is rape. With rape, no one experiences any pleasure. It is just that there is a compulsion. He wants to do it, that's all. He's seeking pleasure, but there is really no pleasure in it. It is just a compulsion. At any cost, he wants to do it. There are people who get possessed by gluttonous beings who only want to eat. Such beings, when they possess somebody, that person will start eating five to ten times a normal human's diet and still not be satisfied. Even when this being eats like that, it is not able to experience the food. He cannot experience eating. It's just a kind of compulsion for him. Even if he makes that person eat, he cannot experience it, because the eating process is only for the physical body. It's a compulsion. So the possessed person will become more and more desperate, and demand more and more food. Still, he can't experience the food, nor can he dislodge this being from his body. That's why in India it has been taught that when you eat food, you should not eat gluttonously; you must eat gently. You must put the food in front of you, bow down to it, sit quietly for a minute and then eat. If you're very aware, you just put a little bit of water around the plate, so that this kind of being is not attracted to you. If you eat gluttonously, these kinds of beings will want to get into you, because they have the tendency towards gluttony within them. Now when people on the spiritual path do sadhana, their energies become more positive and subtler. Then they may tend to attract different kinds of beings. When energies become subtle, disembodied beings may come.

Seeker: Sadhguru, really, are you saying that because of our sadhana, we tend to attract disembodied beings?

Sadhguru: All these beings want to come here because this is a very pleasant energy for them. It's just like when we go and sit under a tree to enjoy the shade of the tree. Now if I allow everybody to come and sit under this tree, they may not just be satisfied with the shade of this tree. One person wants to pluck something from it; another person wants to climb it; somebody else may want to cut down the tree. It's the same thing with these beings; they are all here for different things. So that's the reason why, once somebody starts sadhana, we encourage them to wear *rudhraksha*,[1] because it creates a cocoon, and they become unavailable to these kinds of things.

Seeker: Then why don't you wear rudhraksha?

Sadhguru: I'm not wearing rudhraksha because I don't want to make spirituality into a bundle of symbols, which can destroy the true value of it. If you go up north, you'll see somebody wearing a huge bunch of malas – no sensible man can wear that many malas – and he thinks he's very spiritual. His hair is long and he's wearing twenty-five malas. I don't wear rudhraksha because I don't want to make people ever think that wearing this or that will make you spiritual. It's not true. I'm not out to protect myself from anything. I don't need the protection. You see, these disembodied beings exist on this plane only for a short time. So these things are very rare. Maybe in today's world, these things happen a little more than before because we are a little more accident-prone than we were before.

Seeker: Are you saying that today, in the twenty-first century, with all our technology, we are more accident-prone?

Sadhguru: Yes, only because of the technology. If there was no technology, at the worst, what could happen? How often do you climb a tree and fall down? Not too often, right? But today, there are any number of situations where accidents can happen. You can wreck your car. You can crash in an airplane. You can get electrocuted. So many things can happen. Never before has the world been as accident-prone as it is today. So there are more beings dying without completing their prarabdha. Also because stress levels are high, which can cause more diseases, more people are dying without completing their prarabdha. So it is possible that there are more accidents today. Now you should not think along those lines, because it just creates a whole lot of fear and it will mess you up psychologically. Worrying about accidents will not solve anything. Keep yourself in such a way that you are not available to these kinds of things.

---

1 *rudhraksha* : sacred beads, seeds of a tree found mostly in the Himalayas, also known to have many medicinal and transcendental qualities.

Seeker: Sadhguru, the ashram seems to be a place that attracts many of these disembodied beings... is it a safe place to be?

Sadhguru: The ashram is not the only place where these beings are; they are everywhere. It's just that we are aware of them here. If there is a safe place, this is the safest place. With the energies of the Dhyanalinga, there is absolutely no need for concern for one's safety from these kinds of beings here.

Seeker: Once a disembodied being is completely liberated, is it able to remain in non-physical realms? If so, why would he do this?

Sadhguru: It is very rare that this would happen, but there have been some beings who have done that. There are yogis called *nirmanakaya*. *Nirman* means 'to create'; *kaya* means 'a body'. These yogis are of the highest accomplishment and are able to recreate their body at will. They do not need to be reborn. See, when you are born through a womb, you are also creating a body. Your own energy is doing it. You take nutrients from your mother, and you create a body – it is not the mother who is creating it. After you are born, you are still creating this body, isn't it? You are creating it in the same way that you are now – taking nutrients through food, through the air that you breathe, the water that you drink and the sunlight. Before you are born, that mechanism has not come yet, so you are using the mother's mechanisms of eating, drinking and breathing to structure the body, but it is your own energies which are doing it.

One can acquire the capability to create a body without the help of a mother's womb. You are able to create it by yourself. Now you don't have to create this small body. The small body is created because only that can fit into the mother's womb. When you sit and create it, you can create an average sized body or one that is twenty feet tall. So these nirmanakayas are in subtle states and use elaborate processes. They have chosen to be in that state. Some out of their compassion, some because they have been - what can I say - ordained by their masters, who have told them, "Don't worry about your *mukthi.*[1] Just do this." The span of time in which they do this may be very long in normal human terms. It could be a couple of thousand years to even ten thousand years, but even this has a certain span to it; eventually, they will dissolve. These nirmanakayas have chosen to be in their subtle body. Once in a while, they may create a gross body to come back and do certain things - there are such beings. Without them, I would not be so knowledgeable.

Seeker: Do disembodied beings remain in the sphere of the earth? Are they captive to its pull, or are they free to roam the existence? Are they all around us? When we die, do we just float around this existence?

Sadhguru: There is no such thing as existence (laughs).

Seeker: Is that all you are going to say, Sadhguru?

Sadhguru: That's enough, isn't it? Some yogis even create their whole existence while sitting in a cave.

Seeker: If a yogi creates his entire existence, his whole universe, in a cave, what's to say that all of us, sitting here today, right now, even you, are simply not players in the existence of some yogi sitting in a cave somewhere? Do you know? It's like infinite…

Sadhguru: (Laughs) I think you can go and join a UFO cult. You have all the qualifications. Okay, about what you asked just now, all these time and space problems exist only in your conscious mind. It is a trick of the conscious. Once you transcend certain dimensions of the mind, there is no space and time. It is all one. What is here is there; what is there is here. What is now is then; what is then is now. So when you ask, "Can they roam the existence?" Yes, you are also roaming the existence right now, isn't it? As you are living in the realm of the conscious mind, it's like if you are here in India, you cannot be in America. Once you transcend that, there is no America; there is no India. It is all here. So when somebody says

1 *mukthi* : liberation.

that they have seen me and experienced me in two different places at the same time – it was not that I was in two different places; I was in the same place. They think these are two different places. It is not so. Einstein told you that your existence is relative. Indian philosophy has always been telling you that it is all an illusion. It seems to be there, but it is not there. It is all here. It is all now. The beginning is here. The end is here. Eternity is here. For one who is lost in his mind, there are many places, but for one who is totally here, everything is here and now. Do you understand?

Seeker: But the tendency is, you said, to go to certain places. If there is no here and there...

Sadhguru: For you there is here and there, isn't it? It is a reality.

Seeker: Yes, but then what do you mean?

Sadhguru: Let us say you are in Chennai right now. So all the beings in the existence are in Chennai, and Chennai is everywhere. Now you really understand the realm of the mystic (laughs). I told you, logic is only a trap because that's the only thing you understand. Do you know how it is to spend a whole lifetime, even with the people who are closest to you, without ever getting to talk about what really matters? Do you know how it is? That's how it is to be a Guru.

Seeker: But Gurus are supposed to have lots of patience.

Sadhguru: It takes a lot more than patience, but you don't have the right to test it! (Laughs).

Seeker: Sadhguru, one cannot talk about disembodied beings in a logical manner, but the way you put it together for us, with such confidence and clarity is convincing, whether it is logical or not.

Sadhguru: That's all. That's how it is. It's the clarity and authority with which I can say what I'm saying that is able to convince people, but what is being said is still illogical.

Seeker: It's just like what Ramana used to say when people would ask, "How do I take this back to America with me, what I have here at Ramanashram?" He would say, "Who's going to America, and who is here?" He's saying the same thing. When this has touched you, it makes no difference where you are or what time you are in, in terms of time and space.

Sadhguru: Yes.

Seeker: Then what is this effort towards liberation? We already are liberated.

Sadhguru: It is not that you are already liberated. You are not bound, but you believe that you are bound. All you are trying to do is to destroy an illusion. That's why it's so hard, because you can't destroy an illusion. You can only wake up. Trying to destroy an illusion is a stupid thing. If you destroy the illusion, and say, "Yes, I have destroyed the illusion", then you're in a deeper illusion.

That's why we're saying don't get into mental games, because you go into deeper and deeper illusions. All you have to do is awaken yourself. To put it logically, between sleep and wakefulness, there is a difference for you. In sleep, you are alive. In wakefulness you're also alive, but wakefulness is a more intense aliveness than sleep. It is a heightened level of energy, a heightened level of awareness. Isn't that so? In sleep also, you are fully alive, but there is no experience of anything. The moment you awaken, suddenly this whole world opens up in front of you. What is it that has happened? All that has happened is that you have moved to a heightened level of energy and awareness. That's all that happens between sleep and wakefulness. Now what we are talking about in terms of Realization is moving into a higher level of energy and a higher level of awareness. Suddenly, you are awake in a different reality altogether, which we are referring to as the Ultimate Reality. That makes it very simple.

Seeker: Can you tell us a specific instance where you have helped a disembodied being?

Sadhguru: Let me tell you about the woman on the roof. We have done many things with such beings, but this particular one hung around for more than a year and a half, maybe two. After the Dhyanalinga consecration, my body was in a certain state of instability, and I did not want to meddle with her because they have – what can I say – no sense of judgment. They just have a longing. It's like somebody who is in a deep state of desire has no judgment about life. He just has a longing for something. Somebody wants to drink; he wants to drink. Somebody wants to rape; he wants to rape. It's not because they are good or bad that they're doing it. They have no judgment about life; they only have longings. These beings are like that. They have no logical judgment about life. They just have longings and certain vasanas – according to their karma. They simply go by that.

There are other kinds of creatures, which have gone totally out of shape; they have not been able to retain their human form – they have become subtle – but this is a woman who has retained her feminine form well, with a heightened sense of femininity. No woman in the world will be like that. She is extremely beautiful and is in much larger proportion than normal. She also creates an illusion of wearing beautiful dresses and presenting herself well. Her vasana is femininity, which is always in counter to masculinity. So if you try to meddle with her, naturally she will come as a woman. She won't know any other way to approach. This can lead to so many unnecessary situations, but she would not do anything on her own. If I had invited her into the shrine to dissolve her, in a moment it would have been over.

As my body was in a certain state of fragility and instability after the consecration, I did not want to deal with her. In the night, she would be walking in the inner corridor of my house, anklets sounding, *jing, jing, jing, jing*. It was not just me who heard her. Whoever stayed in the house would hear her walking throughout the night. If you opened the door and came into the corridor, she would be up there, sitting on the roof with a forlorn look on her face, all the time. She sat up there for almost two years. She would not enter the shrine. She did not dare to, but she kept walking and waiting. I did not do anything with her. I just left her there. I didn't try to ward her off because she was so forlorn and longing, seeking something. The longing was not just for the masculine, though she had taken on this excessively feminine kind of state. She was just seeking to go somewhere; some awareness had come into her. See, once a being has such tendencies to identify itself with the feminine, naturally the same tendencies will long for the masculine. This is not something that she's choosing – "I want this person or I want that person." It's just a natural tendency. After the celestial snake took away certain disturbances from my damaged energy body, I brought her down and took her into the shrine and the job was done in five minutes. It was over; she was gone, totally dissolved.

Seeker: Sadhguru, when this 'woman on the roof' came with total, utter femininity, somehow she was seeking masculine energy. So how did she know? Did she see you as a man? Was she looking for you?

Sadhguru: Yes, she was. See, me being a man is in a completely different dimension. This woman, the way she retained her form and all that, had a little more awareness in her than just being a disembodied being. This being was definitely a little more aware. She saw me as a certain being; she saw me as a certain light; she saw me as a possibility. That possibility is always identified as man. Whether it's a man or a woman, sexually, it doesn't matter. If you attain to a certain level of sadhana and certain level of liberation within yourself, then for those beings, or for anyone for that matter, you will be seen as a man. It is Purusha. When I say 'man', it's not necessarily in terms of man because of some body parts. The whole Hindu philosophy goes about like this, the first basic form, the formless thing, is mother. Mother goddess is most basic. Prakrithi is feminine, formless, un-manifested. The first manifestation is Purusha. That is considered masculine. Any manifestation is considered as Purusha or masculine. That way, if you attain to a certain level of liberation within yourself, as far as the existence is concerned, you are seen as masculine, not as feminine. Or, you can put it this way: it is no more receptivity. It's more a giving kind of thing, outgoing, so it is seen as masculine. Feminine means it is receptivity.

Seeker: So she left her previous body in a certain state of awareness? That's why she could be like this, waiting on the roof?

Sadhguru: Yes, in a way. We could look back at her karmic structure if we wanted to, whatever she had, where she came from, what she had done, but I already have enough people on my hands (laughs). It's unnecessary.

Seeker: Did she have awareness as you were taking her into the shrine? Did she have awareness of what you were doing?

Sadhguru: Not really. For her, after that long wait, just being asked into the shrine itself was enough. Somewhere, on one level, yes, but what I was going to do with her was not the concern. After all, when she felt my energy, she knew this would only lead to dissolution.

Seeker: Sadhguru, pardon me for asking, but I am just so curious; was she wearing clothes? Are these beings clothed? If beings are disembodied, how do they wear clothing? Can they see our style of clothes? Would she look at our styles as well? Once the body is gone, why clothes?

Sadhguru: These disembodied beings, except for those few celestial beings who have evolved to a certain level of awareness and capability within themselves, operate simply out of their tendencies. Even when they are embodied, most beings are still operating and living their life according to the quality of their tendencies. Very few people living here are functioning out of their awareness and choice. When you're embodied, you have so much more choice or discretion. Why human life is considered as higher than that of the yakshas, gandharvas, and devas, is because there is discretion. That means one can evolve by choice. Disembodied beings evolve mostly by tendencies, not by choice, not by discretion, because there is no intellect. Intellect is the biggest barrier. An intellect is also a tremendous possibility because it gives you discretion; it gives you choice, which other beings do not have. They don't think. They are just energy. They have certain tendencies and they function out of that.

For example, this woman who had been sitting on the roof for a long time, waiting, was clothed very well, sometimes even with lots of jewelry and things like that. Her clothing was vibrantly colored, like that of Rajasthani women, a long skirt and a drape around her upper body; very beautifully clothed. Her clothes ranged in the shades of yellow and orange. She had also made herself a little larger than normal, something like six and a half or seven feet tall. These things happened not by conscious choice; they happened by her tendencies. These things were deep in her karmic structure – wanting to be beautiful, to look and dress in a certain way. This was very deeply ingrained in her and she found expression that way. It's not that she was consciously wearing a yellow or orange dress. What was deeply within her karma as beautiful was finding expression. In reality, there is no beauty, ugliness, or anything. Her karmic tendencies just found expression in a certain way.

Seeker: So her features were not her features? She could just make herself beautiful or ugly?

Sadhguru: They were her features. There are some beings that don't have a proper human form. They do not necessarily have hands and legs. They are more like a human-shaped amoeba, they don't have proper features, but this particular being had proper features, and a very well formed body and face, because this was very deep in her karma, wanting to be beautiful and wanting to be in a certain way. She had certain desires and longings within her karma, which were deep-rooted, and she was able to find expression like that. There are beings for whom this is not important, so they don't have proper features. There are beings whose tendencies or vasanas make them horribly ugly – not really ugly; they are not in the normal human form. Like what's inside your body, if it hangs outside, you think it's horrible. Suppose your stomach bag or your heart hangs out, you think it's horrible. So there are beings like that who have twisted-out proportions because their minds and their tendencies are like that. Accordingly, they have taken certain forms. These forms are not consciously created. It is not by their choice; it's by their tendencies that they have created it. So you can say in a way it's their creation.

Like how you are right now is your creation, but it is an unconscious creation. The rules are about the same. It's just that when you are embodied, you have more discretion. As you become more aware, you gain more discretion. Once, an explorer in the depth of the Amazon jungle found himself surrounded by a group of bloodthirsty natives. Upon surveying the situation he cursed to himself, "Oh God, I'm cooked!" Suddenly, a ray of light fell from the sky and a voice boomed out, "No, you're not cooked. Pick up that stone at your feet and bash it on the head of the chief standing in front of you." The explorer picked it up and started to bash the life out of the chief. Then he stood above the lifeless body, breathing heavily, surrounded by a hundred natives with looks of disbelief and shock on their faces. The voice boomed out again, "Okay, now you're cooked!" This is how life takes over when your intelligence isn't used. As you become less and less aware, you have less discretion. As a human being, if you don't make use of your awareness and discretion, human life is wasted on you; you're cooked! These disembodied beings are in the level of awareness in which they left. They can't gain or lose awareness. They're in a kind of a limbo; it's a stagnant state. There is nothing they can do about it. It is progressing, but they can't do anything about it – it is only happening as per their tendencies. It is like a light bulb. You keep it on. It has a certain life span, after that it will burn out. The bulb cannot choose how long to burn or when to go out. It burns for so many hours then it goes out. It's just like that. You cannot evolve; you cannot regress. What you have, you just experience, that's all.

Once you are embodied and you're here as a human being, you can either evolve or regress. Both are possible for you. That's the beauty of having an intellect which can discriminate and choose. It can make you progress; it can make you regress. Once you don't have this intellect, you just function by tendencies. Animal nature is functioning by tendencies. Similarly, disembodied beings also function by tendencies. Unless – and that applies to just a small number – they were in a certain degree of evolution before they left the body, then they are there by conscious choice. We refer to these as celestial beings, those who exist by choice, just to create the distinction.

Seeker: Sadhguru, so in the process, because there is no body, could this lady switch to a masculine form?

Sadhguru: There is no body, but she has no choice. Whichever way her karmic structure is, this is just being reflected. For example, another disembodied being, 'the lady with the beard', became very popular with people during the ninety-day Wholeness program. She wanted to be masculine; not being masculine for the sake of sexuality, but masculine as a spiritual possibility, because of social reasons. So somewhere in her mind there was a deep regret that she had not been born as a man. Spiritual possibilities were denied to her just because she was a woman. This huge karma within her caused her to wish that she was a man, but her body did not change. Because she saw yogis with beards, a beard gathered around her face. A full-grown beard, like a man's beard. It's not that she was creating it, but her tendencies and her longings – probably many times, if not consciously, then unconsciously, she had thought, "If I just had a beard and I looked like a man, I could be there." That thought gave her a beard. It's not that she was wearing a beard.

Seeker: Master, you say the karmic structure does not differentiate between the masculine and the feminine. Then what is it that makes a disembodied being come as masculine or feminine?

Sadhguru: It is the tendencies, the vasanas that they carry. Suppose in your previous life you were masculine and now you're feminine. If those masculine karmic tendencies are much more powerful, or of a deeper impression than the present karmic tendencies, then as a disembodied being, you will most probably go around in a man's form. Whatever is the tendency of the karmic structure, that's the kind of form it tries to find. Or sometimes it may be mixed up. One part of your body may be masculine and another part feminine. It's very much possible. It may also be neither. It may be just a distortion of the two, not knowing what to become. It could be anything. This is the reason why people, because of some confused perception, become distorted beings. As I have said, these beings don't always have perfectly formed bodies. The 'woman on the roof' was deeply into her femininity, so she had a perfectly formed body. This is not always so. It could become anything, as per the dominant tendencies.

Seeker: Let's say you have the masculine form; you have masculine energy. Then why would you choose to come back in the feminine form in another lifetime?

Sadhguru: That's very much possible. Especially if your masculine tendencies are very strong, naturally they will seek to become feminine. This is nature's way. If a feminine tendency is extremely strong, it will tend to take on a masculine body because the formation of the physical body is caused by duality. So if someone's karmic tendency is extremely feminine, they will tend to become masculine in body. If someone's tendency is extremely masculine, they will tend to become feminine in the body because the meeting of the dualities has to happen. If the karmic tendencies are highly masculine, too masculine, and if it happens to find a masculine body, this will be an abnormal person.

Seeker: This will be a very powerful being?

Sadhguru: Powerful, yes, but he could be very abnormal and tend to be very violent. It's possible, but not necessarily so. You must understand that the energy has no quality of its own. It is neither positive nor negative, neither good nor bad. It just functions by tendencies. Good and bad qualities arise within you only when discretion arises. Where there is no discretion, there is no positive and negative. For example, let's say there is a nuclear reactor here. It could be lighting up the whole city. Tomorrow morning, if it leaks, it could be killing the whole city. It has no quality of its own. It is neither a good reactor nor a bad reactor. It just has tendencies; that's all. You can channel it this way or that way. This is how the whole existence is. This is the nature of the Creator. That is why, in this culture, we have always described God as Nirguna. That means He is attribute-less. He has no qualities.

He's neither good nor evil. He is simply there. He can become anything. That's why Shiva has been described as the embodiment of all the beautiful and all the ugly, all the horrible and all the fantastic, everything – simply because the Creator has no tendencies. It is just energy. It can manifest itself any way. That level of energy, that manifestation that you call as the Creator, is absolutely attribute-less.

What you call a human being is somebody who, in the process of taking on manifestations, has picked up tendencies. That's what we're calling as the karmic body, the vasanas, or tendencies. It's something that one picks up. It's like the moss that you pick up on the path when you walk. Slowly you pick it up and as it gathers you have more and more established qualities. From an animal to a human being, you have more and more established qualities, because it has run through a longer process of evolution, and picked up more and more tendencies, more and more qualities. That's why a human being seems to have a more evolved, or rather, a more established personality compared to animal nature. Though they also have a personality, it is not as established as a human being, because the human being has run a longer path of evolution, and naturally, has picked-up more karmic substance in the course of this evolution. It's all the same energy, that of animals and human beings. The whole process of dissolution is again going to that point where you drop all tendencies and just become pure energy. So when you just become pure energy without attributes, we say you are God-like. That is absolute dissolution. That is Mukthi. That is Nirvana. That is *Mahasamadhi.* Once you become pure energy, there is no such thing as you and me, this and that. All duality is lost. Duality has come only with tendencies, or tendencies have come because of dualities. Shiva, the attribute-less one, takes on the form of Ardhanarishwara, the half man-half woman state, to function in the world. Without duality there is no function. Now, these disembodied beings are incapable of experiencing anything that is physical. They can't see your physical body, your clothes or anything that is physical about you. They can only see you as an energy being, the way they are now. 'The lady on the roof' was wearing clothes, but she could not experience the clothes, nor could she see them. It was just an expression of her tendencies.

Seeker: Sadhguru, can you tell us about the science behind dissolving a disembodied being? What happens to them?

Sadhguru: The only reason why this kind of a being is able to retain its form as a separate entity from the rest of the existence is because there is a karmic structure. The physical body has been shed, but the karmic body is still intact. Only because the karmic body is intact, there is a form and there is individuality about it. There are individual likes, dislikes, compulsions and desires. So dissolving somebody or attaining to Mukthi, liberation, Mahasamadhi or Mahaparinirvana, the ultimate dissolution is just destroying the karmic body. So how to destroy the karmic body? The very desire to destroy karma is karma. Do you understand? "I want to destroy all my karma," that itself is karma. This is why, the more you go after something, the more you get entangled with it. Anything that you go after initially, looks wonderful. After some time, it becomes a huge entanglement. This is simply because the very process of seeking something is karma.

The whole spiritual science that we are establishing has been designed in such a way that you long for something and still you don't care about the outcome. In the Isha Yoga programs, I always start like this: "This is a game. I want to win, but if I lose, it's okay." That's the fundamental thing. You are setting a basis for this: "I will have intense longing, but what happens in the end is not my problem, because I don't care about the outcome." You're setting the right atmosphere, the right pitch. Now, if what happens to you matters, then immediately, the very process of longing for spiritual growth becomes your karma. "I want to go to heaven," is a huge karma, because it's a huge desire. Even if the desire of going to heaven is fulfilled, still you are in bondage. You're not free. So these disembodied beings that we are talking about, gandharvas, yakshas, and devas are all in that kind of state. They have longed for something higher and they got there. Somebody longed to be a rich person; they became rich. There are gandharvas in the physical world, isn't it? In the physical world, a rich person, a well-to-do person, is like a gandharva for a poor man. Only the gandharva, the rich person, knows his struggles, his problems. The poor man on the street never understands that a man who is driving a Mercedes-Benz could be struggling; but the rich person knows his own problems. Because of modern technology, comforts have become more available. At one time, these comforts were only available to kings. Today, as society becomes more affluent, many people have everything, but still they are frustrated. They know it's not getting them anywhere; it is not adding to their happiness. Now it is easier for them to understand the need to turn inward. So the comfort that modern technology offers can be a great enhancer to the spiritual process.

Now what we are doing in terms of dissolving that being is just breaking the karma. How do you break somebody's karma? As I have spoken earlier, karma is stored on the level of your mind, physical body, sensations and energy. Once somebody has shed their physical body, sensations don't exist. The mind is there, but it has lost its logical nature. So fundamentally, it's in the energy body – whichever way the karma has been imprinted in the energy body, accordingly it functions in the mental body. You know, the courtesans in ancient India used to wear elaborate jewelry. With that, they played an elaborate game: the courtesan's whole body would be covered with jewelry. The man would come to her, full of desire, and would be unable to get this jewelry off. It would take hours to get it off. Whichever way he would try, it would not come off. Now the woman knows the trick: there is just one pin, and when she has teased him sufficiently, she just pulls that pin and all the jewelry just falls off. Both the mental and energy bodies are like this. All your karma is held by certain pins. These pins are in certain points of your body. In a way, we can say they are chakras. Not necessarily only the seven chakras; there are other points too. So all we do is pull those plugs and the karmic body just collapses.

All these fools who are talking about activating chakras are absolutely ignorant people who don't know anything about it. They can't do it. Just by chance – with some force or maybe because of a conducive atmosphere – if they happen to do something with a chakra, they'll have a dead person on their hands. That person will be released all right, probably a major segment of their karma broken, if not the whole thing, but they can't retain the body anymore. All kinds of jokers are talking about activating chakras and doing irresponsible things with them. The chakras are like pins. If I just pull them, right now I can release you, but you'll not retain your physical body. You will be liberated, but you'll be dead as far as the world is concerned, and we will be in trouble!

Many times, ailing people, when they are very old, ask me to visit them. I don't go unless I see there is enough maturity in them, and I see they are asking me to release them, not to make them well. Their prarabdha is nearly finished. People ask me to come and see their father, grandfather, or somebody when they are sick or old and dying. If I visit that person, within seven to eight days he will be gone.

People who find that their parents have reached a very ripe age and are suffering will send me a picture of them. If I look at the person's picture, within seven days he'll be gone. I do those services also! (Laughs). That's all we did to the 'lady on the roof'. She had put on a very subtle body, and it was so much easier to pull her pins than yours. With her, nothing was needed because there was no physical body. I brought her into the shrine because I wanted her to leave in a very conducive atmosphere and not get into a state of fear or disturbance. I just brought her inside and asked her to bow down to the shrine. When she did, I just pulled the plugs and dissolved her. It's finished; she is no more.

Seeker: Why should I be dissolved? Why should my identity be dissolved?

Sadhguru: It is not my intent to dissolve you. It's just that everything is moving towards that anyway. For example, Jesus said, "The kingdom of God is within you." Can the kingdom of God just be this big or that big? The kingdom of God is unbounded, and the unbounded cannot happen as long as the limited exists. So what Jesus was telling you is just that; your limited existence is blocking you from experiencing that which is unbounded, which he refers to as the kingdom of God. Now my pulling the plug or you doing the sadhana or attaining to Mahasamadhi, all mean the same thing. You just dissolve the limited, so that the unbounded becomes the reality as it has always been. It's not that we are setting a new course for life. That's the way it has always been. Every being is looking for dissolution, whether you're aware of it or not. At the end of the day, you want to sleep. This is dissolution. It does not matter how wonderful the day has been. You still want to sleep because you will dissolve for some time. Isn't it? Similarly, when you live your life, however rich your experience was, in the end you want to dissolve. That longing is always there. If you're deeply attached to the body, it will take a long time for you to realize. If you're a little more aware, you will see that very quickly.

Seeker: How do you pull the plug? I mean, what's the method?

Sadhguru: You don't need to know the method. You know that such a method exists, that's enough. It would be irresponsible to talk about methods. That's why I told you to avoid going to people who are activating chakras and doing all those stupid things. This has become a huge thing in the West, but it is not the thing to do.

Seeker: There are also lots of literature and workshops in the West that talk about activating the light body, using meditations with merkabas which involve creating the star of David in your mind and moving into different dimensions. Is that also dangerous?

Sadhguru: Definitely. It depends on what kind of methods they are using and how capable they are. If they are just making a profession out of it, it's their business. There are fools to be exploited, so there are smart ones to exploit them. That's their problem. As long as spirituality is not being exploited, I don't care to stop every bit of nonsense that is going on in the world. That way you make enemies. They are all just commercial forces. You can't stop commercial forces. They have got nothing to do with spirituality, and it's not my job to see if the commercial products in the world are using the right ingredients or not (laughs). I can't go about finding out whether they are selling good milk powder or bad milk powder. This is also just like that.

Recently, the psychic hotline on the psychic friends' network had launched a hotline for frogs. Here is the story of one frog and his discussion with his psychic. A frog called the psychic hotline and was told, "You're going to meet a beautiful young girl who will want to know everything about you." The frog says, "This is great; will I meet her at a party?" "No," says the psychic, "next semester, in her biology class." This is what happens to all those people who fall for these things. You'll think you are going somewhere, but you end up on the dissection table.

Seeker: Sadhguru, how does a disembodied being, which has no will of its own, work off its karma?

Sadhguru: It doesn't work off karma. Karma wears off just by living. It is the allotted karma that is wearing off. The unfinished prarabdha karma is wearing off. Now if you just sit, breathe and live, your karma wears off. The problem is that you're acquiring more karma than what is wearing off. It's wearing off at a certain pace, but you are acquiring it at a faster pace, depending upon how you are living your life. Depending on the level of awareness in which you are living your life, accordingly you're acquiring karma. A disembodied being cannot acquire more karma. For a disembodied being, karma is wearing out very slowly. This is not the right way to express this, but let us say you have another three years of prarabdha karma left. If you leave your body with these three years of prarabdha and become disembodied, these three years may get multiplied into thirty years, or three hundred years. Karma wears out very slowly when you have no body, because there is no conscious action. Everything happens by tendencies, but you can't accumulate any new karma.

Seeker: Do these disembodied beings have any awareness of what is happening to them, or is there any suffering involved with the process of karma wearing off?

Sadhguru: Yes, pleasantness and unpleasantness is there in them. Suffering is there. Enjoyment is there. All that is by tendency, not by conscious choice, except for those few celestial beings who are at a certain level of awareness.

Seeker: So choosing to come back, to reincarnate in another body, is to work out that karma faster than it can be worked out non-physically?

Sadhguru: It's not a question of choice. Once it wears off, for the next quota of karma, it has to take another body. There is no choice about it; it will always find a womb. Once the prarabdha karma begins to lose its strength, the pranic energy will lose its vibrancy and come to a certain passivity and inertness. Once it comes to a certain level of passivity, it will naturally seek a womb.

Seeker: What about being able to choose your parents? Is it a result of everything that happened before?

Sadhguru: It's an unconscious choice. According to your tendencies, you choose. So which womb you are born in, is just the result. I have to tell you a joke: once, Mark Twain went to Paris and he was at a party when one of those French snobs came up to him and said, "You Americans, you don't even know who your grandfathers are." Mark Twain coolly replied, "Yes, we Americans don't know who our grandfathers are; but you French people don't even know who your fathers are!"

Seeker: Master, why don't these beings just take on the body of someone who just died and work out their remaining karma?

Sadhguru: These beings are incapable of such things. They can't take on the body of someone who just died because their karma and their pranic substance are still in a certain level of vibrancy. It is not subtle enough to take on a physical body. If these beings need to take on a body, their karmic substance must work itself out and the energy system has to become passive and inert. Otherwise, they cannot be in touch with another body, because a dead body has lost its vibrancy. Even if they enter a body, they cannot experience it, because of their state. So physical things are out of their view, out of their experience, but because of tendencies, they do certain things which do not mean much.

Seeker: When we were in the ninety-day Wholeness program, I saw one disembodied being who seemed to be a woman but had a beard. She never came into the open – just seemed to be clandestinely watching us all the time. Why?

Sadhguru: This was a woman who walked the spiritual path clandestinely, because it was denied to her since she was a woman. In spite of the barriers, her intensity almost saw her through. Her only longing was that she wanted to come as a man. The karma of being clandestine still remained for her. During the Wholeness program, there was enough opportunity that she could have directly approached us, and it would have been over for her, but she still carried the same habit of doing things hidden from men. That's the way women have lived for centuries. She could have approached us, but the karma, the attitude, with which she had lived and died, was a little hard for her to overcome. She was probably not able to comprehend that there were so many women there. If she could have really understood and seen that although she was in a woman's body she was also fit for the spiritual path, then things would have been much easier for her.

When you don't have a physical body, you don't see it either. To see this body you need eyes. To see that body – the body that she had – you need a different kind of eyes, and she had only those eyes. She saw me, the inner being of me, but not my body. Similarly, she saw everyone in the same way, so she was not able to differentiate a woman from a man. If she had been able to see, freedom would not have been far away for her. She really hovered around desperately. She was a person who had been on the spiritual path, whose life was extended beyond the physical body.

Seeker: What was her sadhana to reach that state?

Sadhguru: Hers was a different level of growth. It lacked certain guidance, but her sheer intensity to attain saw her to that level. The urge was so tremendous that no method was needed; just one little push and she would have attained. Nobody gave her that push until after the Wholeness program, when I dissolved her and many others.

Seeker: Did those beings talk to you?

Sadhguru: There was no communication. During the program, they would appear and disappear. They were like birds. One sudden move, one wrong move and they all would fly off. They were shy initially, but then they got bolder. They took their own time to settle down, even with me. Not once did I make a conscious effort to look at them. I just ignored them and went about doing whatever I was doing. They were a very private lot. They did not allow anybody and everybody to enter their domain. It's just like you only allow a few people into your innermost privacy. You don't allow the whole crowd into your privacy, do you? They were just around me all the time. They had gotten used to the place.

Seeker: What do you mean by 'wrong move', Sadhguru?

Sadhguru: A very brisk movement of the body or any sudden jerky action. They don't see the body, only the amount of disturbance in the energy that a movement creates. They understand and perceive it in their own way. For example, when a person is gentle and moves with full awareness, nothing is disturbed around him and they are okay. All your agitated movements and actions, you don't know how much disturbance they cause in the universe. Why a person who has become aware moves with care is because of this: he notices the disturbance that is caused to the atmosphere by his movements. So this disturbance that you cause with those kinds of movements, that is the kind of atmosphere you create around you. You create that and suffer because of it. What you create is what you have to live with.

Your own aura, your own outer atmosphere, is what you have created. Naturally, that's the kind of influence it has on your mind and body also, and those beings are very sensitive to these things. They do not like the noise that your agitated bodies and minds are making.

Seeker: There was also a being present during Wholeness wrapped in rough raiment, always sticking to corners. Why didn't he move more freely like the other bhootha prethas? Anyway, why were all those spooky beings there?

Sadhguru: These beings were all over me. I even shifted my bed to the floor from the cot in the corner, as it was very uncomfortable for them to hang around that corner. So I came down to make enough space for all of them to sit around me. One night, at about three, I was singing. I made sure nobody should hear it. I was simply humming sitting under the tree, but some of you said that you heard me. The presence of these disembodied beings was amplifying everything around. The very nature of the work also got amplified. Now, that being wrapped in rough raiment did not like the activity there, so he was in the corner, but he was helplessly drawn to this energy. Still he lived in his own habit patterns; that's why he was hiding behind his rough raiment. The same old karmas – everything is the same. It is just that the body has moved into a more subtle nature. The grossness is gone.

You asked why they were here. These are not ghosts in the usual sense. What you call as ghosts, or bhootha prethas, are unfulfilled lost beings, whereas these were beings that had walked the spiritual path, but had not yet reached the goal. Somewhere, they had just taken a little break. Some of them had consciously chosen to remain in their subtle body and work out their remaining karma. Others had been granted this kind of a state; one more chance, you can say. They did not have to be born once again. They found their way here and were just hanging around. Time for them may not be the way you think, but there is some limitation as to how long they can be in this state.

Seeker: Are they what one refers to as astral beings?

Sadhguru: It's just another name you can call them by. The only difference between you and them is that they have a subtler physical form.

Seeker: You said they were also spiritual seekers. How did they dissolve? How did they find their way out?

Sadhguru: How did they find their way out? I think that is why they were here. These beings were a little evolved; they were not just wandering spirits. They knew their way. They were not aimlessly wandering here. They were here with a purpose. They knew we could do what was required.

Seeker: So these beings, can they be trapped in this state? I have heard that these beings are good mediums to get things done; and if trapped, can they become free?

Sadhguru: These beings? Trapped? Yes, they can be trapped. A tantric or someone else who is well accomplished in the occult sciences can do this. It's like how even the greatest saint can be put behind bars. You know, they crucified Jesus. Similarly, on a different level, you can trap these beings also. If I have a being with me who does not have a body, and who does not need transport to go from here to there, can you imagine how many things I can get done through him? But I'm not going to use them in any way; my only interest is in their emancipation; my involvement with them is only on that level.

Seeker: Are they more evolved than us? Are they completely free, unlike us?

Sadhguru: They definitely have an advantage over you. People who have a body and a conscious mind have their own limitations. It's not that they don't have a mind and body; they do, but they are subtler. They could see each other. They could see you, but not your physical body. They see you as a subtle body. They understand that you have a physical body. They do not see, but they have understanding. They are aware enough not to collect any new karma in any way. Once the body is gone, the need to do karma is also gone. They can, though the possibility is very small. Even here, with me, they were very cautious in the beginning. After some time, the 'lady with the beard' was not hiding any more. They were all sitting together, except that they would always push her to the back row.

Seeker: Why, Jaggi? Only because she was a lady?

Sadhguru: Yes, maybe (laughs).

Seeker: But subtler bodies don't have feminine or masculine forms, isn't that right?

Sadhguru: Yes. There is no sex. This beard is probably a kind of joke among them. It is not really the way they perceive, but somehow they were aware that she was not like them. The whole scene was like this. See, when people are asked to take *prasad* [1] and are kept standing for a while, do you see how they unnecessarily jostle about? We still have not started giving the prasad and nobody is getting anything, but still they jostle. The scene was the same there; there was nothing being given to anybody, but still they were pushing her.

Seeker: Did you tell them, "Mind your own business?"

Sadhguru: I did not tell them anything. I just allowed them to be.

Seeker: Were you helping them out?

Sadhguru: Not yet.

Seeker: Why not?

Sadhguru: See, I can pardon you if you don't help yourself to what I am offering, but people who have transcended their physical limitations, if they cannot help themselves, there is no pardon for them. Do you understand?

Seeker: You are more strict with them…

---

1 *prasad* : token of blessing, often in the form of sweets or flowers.

Sadhguru: It's not a question of strictness. The first time you were with me, maybe you were acting stupid; that's okay. As you get closer to me, I expect you to be more sensible. When a person has gone beyond his physical nature, I expect him to be a lot more sensible. I'm here, I'm available, drink from me; take your fill. Only when you take it and drink, that's when things happen.

Seeker: How do they know you are a Master?

Sadhguru: How? How do they know? How did you get to know? They don't know your language, your 'Master' business, your 'Guru' business – all this. They only know that this bag is empty (pointing to himself). They are just seeing how to empty theirs and go; that's all. They don't know all this spiritual nonsense that you're doing here. Now when I say nonsense, I don't mean useless. I am putting my life into everything that is being done here. Whatever you do still belongs to the physical realm, but we're getting ourselves into that type of activity which does not make any sense to the physical realm, it is yet to touch the beyond.

The presence of these beings did some good to me. Did you notice how, in the last three days, I had attained to a new kind of well-being? It was visible. My contact with the body had become so minimal, my being had become too loose from the body. I needed a solid karma in order to stay here. It is not that these beings helped me in any way. I just needed something to get involved with. My energies were only from *Anahatha*[1] upwards. The lower chakras were literally lifeless. So when I struggled to push my energies down, it produced a reaction which was not good for me. I thought that maybe I would get involved with food. So I started asking for different varieties of food, but after two days that did not mean anything to me. I have always tried to use my family as a way of being involved, but that's also on and off. Now my involvement with these beings – I was not doing anything with them, but just by being aware of them, my energies became more balanced. It's just like when you get a new job, you are more involved in it than usual. It was not really new for me, but it was a break from the kind of work I normally did. I was just trying to get involved with something. Just trying to get caught up, you know? This may sound ironic. You take lifetimes of work to release yourself, and when you're released, you need to get caught up.

---

1 *Anahatha* : the unstruck, one of the seven primary energy centers in the body.

Seeker: You should learn from us Jaggi; we are experts at that.

Sadhguru: I should learn, I should really learn. What are the things that you get caught up with?

Seeker: Everything. Starting from sweets, like a laddu…

Sadhguru: Starting from a laddu? It definitely shows on you, Raja! See, my work with them was just for one moment. It is not any great teaching that I had to give them. All they had to do was empty their bags into mine and go. That's all. It was as simple as that. It is just that they had to develop that much trust.

Seeker: Even they have these issues of trust and confidence, Sadhguru?

Sadhguru: Yes, they do, but to a lesser extent than you. Mentally they have the same problems that you have, but they're free from physical problems. Otherwise their bag of karma is small; they are just carrying a handbag whereas you have a whole sack. Still, they have the same problems. It took so long for them to come and be here with me. All these days, one moment they were here, the next gone: appearing, disappearing. Finally, they were sitting here, enjoying themselves. It took a lot of time for most of you to do that. Just to be here.

Seeker: Not just during the Wholeness program, but also during the Dhyanalinga consecration, it wasn't just about seeing; it was voices we heard too. How can you actually hear something non-physical?

Sadhguru: See, if you are in a certain state of awareness, thoughts of people can be heard; actually heard, literally heard.

Seeker: Their vasanas are what is heard?

Sadhguru: Yes, but those vasanas are reacting to certain situations. You know that man who was very excited about Bharathi, he would go on saying, "*Avan than eval; avan than eval* ". He would go on repeating, "*Avan than eval.*"

Seeker: What does it mean?

Sadhguru: "He is her; he is her." He could not stop it. He knew this person as 'he' somewhere, and once he saw her, he could not stop. "He is her, he is her," it went on, because it's not like words, but the reaction was like that; the energy was reacting. The tendencies were reacting in such a way because there was some excitement somewhere else that was just reacting, reverberating as sounds clearly heard, not just by me. Even the people around me were terrified, hearing voices. You know, beings saying like, "glug, glug, glug, glug," talking in various languages.

Seeker: So when one is disembodied, does he still have thoughts?

Sadhguru: Not thoughts, tendencies. See, your thoughts are your tendencies.

Seeker: Then tendencies can be heard…

Sadhguru: Yes. Tendencies react to different situations. Your likes and dislikes are not just in your head; the whole body reacts. Isn't it? The more deeply you are embedded in your karma, the more deeply your body reacts. There is someone who, if you smear his face with some filth, will just go, wash his face well and come back. Someone else, if you smear his face with some filth, he will be revolted and puke. There is someone else who'll get angry, irritated and disgusted with it. Somebody else may just fall dead; it's possible. It depends on how strong your karmic structure is, accordingly, the reaction is that powerful. As your karma becomes lighter, your reactions become lighter. That means your whole life and existence is moving more from unconsciousness to consciousness. That's why your reactions are becoming less. The more unconscious you are, the more reactive you are. The more conscious you are, the less reactive you are.

Seeker: Sadhguru, I have heard that people use certain devices to attract disembodied beings.

Sadhguru: Do you see that tamarind tree in the village next to the ashram? That tree got very distorted. Some things can be used to attract disembodied beings. For example, in many places, some people misuse the fluids of a woman's menstrual cycle to attract the really distorted ones. The fluid is applied onto a cloth or some such thing and is hung onto, generally, tamarind trees, and for sure you'll see distorted beings.

Seeker: But would this disembodied being possess us if we go there?

Sadhguru: No, you can go with a certain protection.

Seeker: Like a rudhraksha?

Sadhguru: You can wear your cross and go, Marie-Christine (laughs), but I want you to remember that even Jesus got the worst on the cross.

Seeker: You were talking about them hanging upside down. Do they really hang upside down?

Sadhguru: There is no up and down for them, they are just hanging. When I saw them, a couple of times, they were hanging upside down, but I don't see any reason why it should always be like that. Probably, whichever way they hang, after some time, they take a certain shape and form. They don't have a certain established form. It's a loose form. It's like a loose sack with something heavy inside. So that way, yes they are hanging upside down, but there is no up and down for them.

Seeker: But Sadhguru, why a tamarind tree?

Sadhguru: Because the carbon dioxide is very high there, so it has the least disturbance in terms of life forms. None of the birds or animals will rest in a tamarind tree at night because of this. They won't go there because there is too much carbon dioxide. These kinds of beings like to hang there, because there is no physical disturbance and anyway they don't need oxygen to breathe. Somehow, they choose that.

It's not that they cannot hang on other trees, but they tend to go where there is less movement. That is also why they tend to hang around in cemeteries, corners and such places, for the same reasons. That's the way they are made. If there's a lot of movement of people, they don't like to go there.

Seeker: So was the tamarind tree in the village distorted by some such use, Sadhguru?

Sadhguru: Not necessarily. The tamarind tree might have responded to certain beings, but it could have just happened, for so many reasons. One day, we can go and do a practical search for disembodied beings.

Seeker: Sadhguru, why are these beings attracted to such gross things as the smell of blood or whatever?

Sadhguru: Not the smell of blood, I said the menstrual fluid. The menstrual fluid always means rebirth for them. They're attracted by tendencies. When they sense these fluids, they think it is an opportunity to look for a new body. So a woman always becomes more susceptible to such forces and such beings when she is close or when she is menstruating. What I'm saying is that in their perception, if they look at your physical body, they can't really make out what is what with you. If your menstrual fluids have gathered in a big way in your uterus, now they can see that you are a woman. Otherwise, they can't make out the difference between a man and a woman. See, the aura of these fluids is the aura of new life; it draws them because in some way they sense that it is an opportunity to be reborn.

It happened that two hippies in unisex clothes and typical hairstyle went to the immigration officer in the state of Texas. The immigration officer looked at them and could not make out who is the man and who is the woman. Both wore long hair, both were dressed in the same kind of clothes, same dress, everything. Being a Texan, he didn't know what to say. So he asked, "Which one of you has a menstrual cycle?" The guy said, "No, man, I got a Honda!"

One of the reasons why in India, when a woman menstruates, she is put in a protected atmosphere, why she's asked to chant God's name, why she is not allowed to go out to certain places or do certain things is because she is susceptible to so many forces. As it is, physiologically and psychologically, she becomes a little fragile at this time. This makes her available that way also.

Seeker: What do they do, Sadhguru? Can they possess her?

Sadhguru: They can easily possess her. The opportunity or the possibility of these beings possessing a woman during this time is so much more. They may not be completely possessed, but many women may just get influenced by their tendencies if they hover around. You may not know that it is a being, but just its presence makes you imbalanced, and you know, act a little crazy or aggressive. Those kinds of things may happen to certain people. Otherwise, at those times they'll go into depressions.

Seeker: So what extra care can a woman take at that time, when she has her menstrual cycle, or before that?

Sadhguru: Especially when she is having it, just the application of *vibhuthi*[1] at certain points of the body, and showering two or three times a day creates a protection. Normally, in India, it's compulsory that she needs to have a minimum of two or three showers a day, isn't it? Even if at twelve o'clock in the night she begins to menstruate, she must immediately have a bath. The fluids must not remain on the body. That's the rule. Twice a day, she must have a head bath. She just sits in one place; she doesn't expose herself to too many situations; she keeps her exposure to a minimum level. When I say in India this is what women do that does not mean it's the right thing. We are not giving any physiological, psychological, emotional and other spiritual reasons for it. It's just being said, but the modern women have broken everything.

Seeker: Why the head bath, Sadhguru?

Sadhguru: The aura is most dominant in the head region. See, why the halo is, is because it's the most visible part of the aura. When she is in that state, naturally the most visible part of the aura becomes visible for the other being also. So the first thing is to put water over the head, to cleanse the aura, to make it different. After a bath, your aura is not the same as before. That's why, in India, for anything you want to do, you always take a bath first. If you want to go to the temple, first thing is bath.

---

1 *vibhuthi* : sacred, consecrated ash.

It cleanses; it makes you more receptive and less available to these forces. When a woman is having her period, that quality is there in her aura, so when she has a bath, that quality is lowered. The other being cannot sense that quality so much. See, this sense of smell is not physical, but if the aura changes, he knows this is happening.

The next point in the aura manifestation, the strongest point for most human beings, would be the sexual region. This is where they have their maximum aura, apart from the head – and for some, this may be more dominant than their head. Only a person who is into intense sadhana and is evolved may have a different powerful center – the throat center or the heart center. Otherwise, generally, for most living physical bodies, apart from the head area, which is naturally so, you'll find that the aura is strongest in the reproductive region. Even in terms of temperature distribution, it is the warmest part of the body, isn't it? That is how the body is made. So when a woman is menstruating, because the fluids have come out, when the disembodied being tastes the aura, he will tend to go in that direction.

Seeker: In some cultures, they say that women who are going through menstruation are impure.

Sadhguru: Not true. This is the modern woman thinking like that. In India, if a woman is menstruating, she's not allowed to move around everywhere, she just stays in one space. Over a period of time, out of ignorance, people started exploiting it: "Oh! You stay there; you're not okay." That is not the idea; the idea was to protect her. What was given as a prescription for well-being became a source of discrimination and exploitation.

Once, in kindergarten class, the teacher asked the kids, "What's the most exciting thing that you ever did, or the most exciting thing that you have witnessed in your life?" One by one, the kids came up to the blackboard. One kid wrote the roller coaster, another wrote the picnic that they had last week, and like this, many things were written. Then Tom came up and just put a dot on the blackboard. "What Tom? What is this?" asked the teacher. The boy said, "It's a period." The teacher said, "And what's so exciting about a period?" So he replied, "I don't know, but when my sixteen year old sister missed one, the whole family got real excited!"

See, there used to be an enormous amount of physical activity in a woman's life. Caring for the home was not like today, turning on the washing machine, turning on the mixer. Just cooking for twenty-five people in the house used to be an enormous physical activity. So those three or four days she was given a complete break, and she did not need to handle anything. She had no family duties, no social duties and no religious duties for those few days of the month, so that she was completely free. She should not expose herself to too many situations; but slowly, over a period of time, it became like an exploitation.

Seeker: And what will happen if women get possessed by one of those beings?

Sadhguru: When women get possessed, they will have continuous periods for any number of days; do you know this? Now, somebody may have a tumor or something, that's different. When women become possessed, they may menstruate every day or off their natural cycle. Look at it in terms of life; don't think in terms of this person or that person. All that has happened is that the menstrual fluid has the smell of creation, of new life. It has the aura of new life. Your blood and flesh do not have this. It's not in the rest of the body. When they smell that or taste the aura of that, they dive for it. So they extract it out of her every day, hoping that it will happen. They're ignorant. They don't know that this cannot happen. All they know is that it's the smell of new life.

Seeker: You're saying that they don't know all those things, then how can they do it?

Sadhguru: This is also by tendencies. If you create terror in a woman she may have her period any time of the month, do you know that? If she gets terrified, she will menstruate. So they appear, or they create sensations in the body. They may appear in so many forms! She goes and looks at herself in the mirror, she may look like a demented being. She'll get terrified. This is enough; after that, her own mind will do the job. Too many things need not be done. It's not even that they are trying to create this. It is just that they became a little visible for her; that's all. The rest will happen. If he is very gross and very present - a very freshly taken away kind of life – it will go for her.

Seeker: Sadhguru, they can appear and disappear when they want?

Sadhguru: See, it is not that they appear and disappear. Some of them are dense so they become visible. It's just your capability to see or not. At a certain moment, in a certain state of receptivity, you may see them. When one possesses a person then, usually, death will happen because he will create a situation where the person will just walk off into a well or walk off a mountain. So this being possesses everything, your intelligence, your emotions and your body. One part of you may still be struggling. Now he just walks off the mountain and he falls straight down. It is not his body, it does not hurt him, but you die in the process. Your body is broken. It's as if you're driving somebody else's car; you don't care. You bang through everything and go.

Seeker: Otherwise, Sadhguru, if it is outside and hovers around her...

Sadhguru: It tends to go near where the fluid is. So once it goes there, it creates a different kind of energy and she will just bleed continuously.

Seeker: So what can she do?

Sadhguru: See, if that being is chased away, that will stop. Otherwise by the natural process it may go away, because that being becomes weak or because she enters certain spaces. If a woman comes to the Dhyanalinga, it will go away. This is also one of the reasons why they don't want women who are menstruating to enter temples, because they may bring this kind of negativity into that sacred space.

Seeker: But Sadhguru, the sacred space is supposed to be the protection...

Sadhguru: Yes, but all temples may not have been made that way. At the Dhyanalinga we have no such problem because these beings cannot enter. That is the nature of the energy there. You can always park them outside and come; they will wait for you. Even in certain temples, which are especially prepared for this, they have no problem. In these temples where they do sacred rituals, there are no restrictions. In other temples, it is a subtler energy which is constantly being kept up with the use of *mantras.*[1]

Seeker: Then the disembodied being itself can go inside by itself; why should it go through a woman?

Sadhguru: By itself, that being will not go towards that energy. It goes with the woman's aura.

Seeker: And once it goes inside, why would it want to remain there in that energy field?

Sadhguru: It's not that it wants to remain there. When it goes in, if the energy is a little subtler – the atmosphere is a little subtler – the presence of that being will be felt more. That is also one of the reasons why people who go to certain temples may feel negativity instead of positivity. Such beings may enter only certain temples, not all temples, but they have made a general prescription out of it.

Seeker: So Sadhguru, any kind of disembodied being would be able to affect any kind of person? It's not like it has to have a strong presence and the woman has to be sensitive to such things?

Sadhguru: All of them will not be drawn to this; only certain types, those who have left their body prematurely – especially when it is recent, when their prana is still vibrant and their desires and tendencies are still strong. As it weakens, as I said, they tend to hang somewhere. When they are active, that's the time when they seek this kind of thing. They are capable of moving.

Actually, people who do this kind of work – the tantrics and others who work with these kinds of beings – will want to especially use the males of these beings because the male can be used in a certain way to do things, violently. They can even use this being to go and kill somebody else. They can use a disembodied being to just go and do whatever they want. When they want to catch such beings, freshly disembodied, they actually collect the menstrual fluid from their women, apply it on their own bodies and go into cemeteries to attract them. Similarly, if they want to catch the feminine of these creatures – feminine by

---

1 *mantras* : a syllable or a pure sound.

tendencies, not by sex – for pleasure and for so many other things they use the semen as an attraction, and apply it to their bodies. Using menstrual fluid is a more common thing than using semen because usually, they are not pleasure-seekers. They are power-seekers. They want to have mastery over certain beings. They want to control people. They want to do things. They want to scare the daylights out of somebody else.

Seeker: Sadhguru, when there is no physical body, where is the pleasure?

Sadhguru: I want you to know that pleasure does not come from somebody else's body. It's from your body that the pleasure is always derived; the other form has just to act as a stimulus for you. A tantric with sufficient mastery can make this form of the disembodied being much more physical, or can add much more substance to the being, to the form, than the way it normally is. It may not be one hundred percent physical, but it has more substance. Even now, whether it is a man or a woman, you are using them only as a stimulus. Pleasure is still only of your body. You don't know the pleasure of the other body, but because there are emotional, psychological and other aspects involved, the human being becomes important, isn't it?

Seeker: Sadhguru, using a disembodied being to kill someone, would it happen out of fear, or in terms of action they can really do something? Does the person have to be vulnerable to such things?

Sadhguru: By action also. By possessing, internally it can kill. Externally it can also kill by just creating certain situations.

Seeker: Sadhguru, does the person have to be vulnerable to such things? Does the being have to be powerful enough to possess a person?

Sadhguru: There needs to be some sense of vulnerability. It's not to the same extent with everybody. If a person is well established, all these things won't have any power over him. A person who is a meditator – when some quality of meditativeness has come – cannot be possessed by anything. It's not possible, but they may create terror in you just by appearing in very distorted forms. Now you walk outside and you see a distorted being, it need not do anything. If it just stands there, it is enough. If there is somebody standing there, carrying his own head in his hands, it's enough for you. If you are very balanced, you just look at him and you go. Now there is nothing he can do, but by appearing here and there, it can kill a person psychologically. So to exercise power over somebody, they want to catch hold of freshly disembodied beings, those who are still very vibrant, since they lose their intensity after some time. That's why they keep going for a fresh hunt. It is not that they trapped one and they can do what they want. If they trap one, it may work for some time. After that, it becomes not so vibrant, so they cannot use it anymore. Then they go for a fresh catch.

Seeker: Sadhguru, these people who are using disembodied beings, whatever they are doing to others, doesn't it affect them?

Sadhguru: Oh! It's a very negative karma to do such things. It can backfire on you at any moment, but usually they have their own protection systems. They take care of themselves in a certain way and do it. Those who are skilful do it, but it is not something that a spiritual seeker should even look at. They are usually power-seekers; they seek power over life. People who have lots of pleasure in terrorizing somebody, in just putting fear into somebody, there are many people who enjoy this. That's power; it can become a means to wealth.

Seeker: Can a disembodied being be used for protection?

Sadhguru: See, now we can create a situation like that. Suppose I get one of them, one of those really unruly ones. Otherwise I get one, I make it really unruly and just leave it here in this perimeter; we set up a perimeter for it. Anyone who comes into this perimeter – except certain people who would have a certain pass – would have it. If you come in, you've had it, in so many ways.

Seeker: Sadhguru, would you use them for protection, if it was needed?

Sadhguru: No. We will never do such things. It's not the right thing to do, okay? We don't touch those things. If at all we touch them, it is only for their benefit. Never use another being, a helpless being.

It's like molesting a child for your pleasure. It just amounts to that. Only a different kind of people will do such things.

Seeker: This is what the occult temple will be used for? For such things, Sadhguru?

Sadhguru: No. See, all the occult people are not using it for their benefit. They will just do it for certain reasons. Above all, their whole purpose is to get mastery over a certain dimension of life. They will not ask anything out of it. They have total control over a hundred beings, but they will never ask for anything from it. They will just use it to learn, progress, and gain mastery over that. This needs to be clear, otherwise, people will think these tantrics are all demented.

Seeker: If celestial or disembodied beings disturb you, what's the best way to handle them? Like for example, if I see a snake, I freeze. So what's the best thing to do if I see this kind of thing?

Sadhguru: It's simple. If one is meditative, they need not bother about all that.

Seeker: So we should just ignore it?

Sadhguru: It's not a question of ignoring it; it will not even come into your experience. It's not necessary for everybody to see them. What's there to see? There are enough people with bodies to see. Why do you want to see disembodied beings?

Seeker: The idea that there is a whole world to see and that you don't see it, is not very comfortable for me. There is a whole existence that I know nothing about. I don't think I could settle with what you're saying. I know I might have to, but I don't really want to.

Sadhguru: It's like going on a world tour. Now, people who are living in this land have not seen America, Africa or Europe. They have a huge longing to go and see those places. If you go there, after all, it is just that the people may be dressed differently, colors are different, this and that, but you still want to go and see. It's like that. If you see disembodied beings, what should you do? If your energies are in a certain way, you don't have to do anything. You see them – that's all. Right now, if you see the plants, what do you do? You don't do anything.

Seeker: Admire them maybe?

Sadhguru: You really don't do anything. You just see. If you admire them, then you're saying they're good, they are nice, they are beautiful. I don't think that they are beautiful or they are ugly. They are just there, that's all.

Seeker: I'm a long way from that non-evaluative stage. In the realm of coming and going, do we treat them as trespassers?

Sadhguru: They are not trespassing; they are in their own realm and you're in your own realm. They will not eat your food; they cannot. Nor can you go and occupy their space; you can't. There is no trespassing. They are in their realm and you're in yours. It doesn't matter. If you happen to see them, it just doesn't mean anything. There are some very distorted creatures among some of them. By distorted I mean to say – your nose is supposed to be about one and a half inches long. If it becomes ten inches, it's a distortion. If everybody had a ten-inch nose, then your nose would be a distortion. So our sense of distortion is always from what we have known and seen. Let us say certain beings have taken on certain other kinds of forms; not normal human shapes and sizes. It has those things that people are afraid of, simply because they don't look like that. If a white man sees a black man, he gets afraid; or a black man sees a white man, he gets afraid, simply because their colors are different. It's just that. So if you ever see something like that, it need not cause any terror or anything, if you have kept yourself in a certain way. If you have not and you see it, it disturbs you. Sometimes people who are not on the spiritual path get access, and they suffer immensely. Their whole growth is affected. Even their physical growth is affected if they are young, because of the terror that will arise in them.

Seeker: Even that answer may cause fear in many. The question is, should I be afraid or should I not be afraid? Will they cause harm to me? Should I have protection?

Sadhguru: Should I go under the sofa or should I wear a cross? Should I do something else? Let me tell you a joke. One dark night, two nuns were driving down a deserted highway, when out of nowhere a vampire lands on the front hood of their car and faces them through the windshield. The two nuns started to panic and one nun yells to the other, "Do something! Show it your cross!" The nun in the passenger seat agrees, leans out the window and in rage, yells, "GET YOUR ASS OFF THE WINDSHIELD!!!" See, there is no need for you to have any fear about disembodied beings. They have no intentions of harming anybody, because they are incapable of holding any intentions of their own. First of all, they can't even see you as a physical being. They see you as an energy form. So the question of them coming in search of you does not arise. Of course, this question comes because you have heard that somebody was possessed, was tormented by some other being. You have heard these stories and maybe even witnessed certain situations which amount to this.

This usually happens only if there is some kind of relationship to the energy. One thing is, they could be of the same blood and the same karmic substance. In some way, it is connected deeply, and in some way, those beings are drawn to this particular person who carries that kind of thing. Let us say, somebody that you know died today without completing his prarabdha karma; he has a certain presence. His karmic body is still intact and he is present. If his prarabdha was weak, if it had run the major part of its course and was weak, there is very little that kind of a being can do. If his prarabdha was very strong or incomplete, if he has a lot of prarabdha left, then that being has a more solid or a denser presence than somebody who is nearly at the end of his prarabdha.

Suppose that in your family somebody died halfway through their prarabdha. They still have a very strong prarabdha and you happen to be wearing their clothes. Unknowingly, they will come at you. It's not that they are seeking you; it is just that these clothes carry – in some way – a part of their body and energy. They tend to gravitate in that direction. This is a part of our tradition, that if a person dies, you should never wear their rings. If someone with strong prarabdha has died and you wear their rings on your ring finger, it becomes very easy for that being to enter you. You become very accessible.

He's not trying to torment you. He's not trying to do anything. He has no such intentions. He will just function according to his tendencies, which will be a torture for you in some way. Otherwise, the situation of some disembodied being coming and tormenting you or even becoming visible to you does not arise. Such a possibility is very remote; it does not happen. Only if in some way it is connected to you, and only if the prarabdha is very strong, that being will gravitate around you and you'll be able to feel it. Otherwise, it is too subtle for you to feel, unless you have raised yourself to a certain level of awareness. If you have raised yourself to that level of awareness where you can feel these beings, you just have no problem with them. So there is no need for you to do anything to protect yourself, unless you're involved in some kind of work which involves these beings, and you are trying to draw them and do certain things with them. Only then, the question of protecting yourself arises. Otherwise, you don't have to bother about it

Above all, do not bother about things which are not in your present level of experience. Learn to concern yourself and handle yourself with utmost clarity in the dimensions that are in your present level of experience. When you have utter clarity about where you are in the present dimension, the next dimension reveals itself to you. If there is no clarity in the dimension in which you exist, then the next dimension can never arise for you. Clarity means, if your intelligence is un-entangled with your identifications and situations in which you now exist, then moving into the next dimension is a natural progression of your intelligence.

Seeker: You said they function according to their tendencies, but their tendency could be very mean and nasty.

Sadhguru: Yes, that's what I said. That's why I said they could torture you. Just their tendencies and the way they function within you could torture you, but the chances of them entering you and doing things are so remote that you don't have to consider it at all.

Seeker: Can they do things from outside without entering?

Sadhguru: It's not that they are trying to do something. Now, if you make the energy situation in this room very subtle, extremely subtle, then these beings become visible. Because you have made all kinds of weird conclusions about these beings, you may just cause terror to yourself. Let's say this wall is dark in color and you splash a drop of grease on the wall. You cannot see it. If you paint the wall white, then the smallest spot becomes so visible. In that sense, when you create a very subtle atmosphere around yourself, then these beings become more visible. It is only in that sense that I'm able to see these things and you are not. It's only because of that. If you carry a dense atmosphere around yourself, then what is subtler than what you create around yourself is not visible to you. Now how many of you, after listening to all this, would feel jumpy if you had to walk the street alone at night?

Seeker: Definitely, a normal person would feel a little jumpy.

Sadhguru: Why do you call that person, a normal person? Do you think I am abnormal?

Seeker: It depends on what context you are speaking. I think the word normal by itself means average: normal temperature, normal blood pressure. They are averages. You are abnormal in the sense that you do not go with the majority – that way.

Sadhguru: Who is abnormal? Someone who is fully developed, is he abnormal? Or is someone whose brain is half developed abnormal? A fully developed body, a fully developed mind, can you call that abnormal? Right now, if you don't have a total perspective of life, you are abnormal. Just because the majority is abnormal, don't make the normal abnormal. You have started using it like that. Normal means that which is proper. Abnormal means that which is improper; but it's okay, we are not fighting with definitions. I want to tickle you so that you look at it in a different context. Otherwise, a Buddha is abnormal, a Jesus is abnormal, a Krishna is abnormal. Are you saying that only the Marilyns and Jennifers of this world are normal?

Seeker: The Buddhas of this world were extraordinary! They were not normal, that's how we look at them.

Sadhguru: No, they were just normal. Are you seeking to be abnormal or normal? If you believe you are normal, all your seeking will disappear. Only if you see that you are abnormal and undeveloped, your seeking will become deeper. If you think, "I am normal," why would you seek to be something else? Are you seeking to become a freak? No. If your perception is undeveloped, it means you're not normal. So the only reason you are seeking is to become normal.

Seeker: Why would anyone be so afraid and jumpy after hearing your explanations of these things?

Sadhguru: Let me tell you a story. One day, a man walked into a bar, sat down and ordered a beer. As he sipped the beer, he heard a soothing voice say, "Nice tie." Looking around, he noticed that the place was empty except for him and the bartender, who was dozing off. A few sips later the voice said, "You look so handsome and the shirt fits you just right." At this the man woke up the bartender and asked, "Hey, I must be losing my mind, I keep hearing voices saying nice things and there is not a living soul in this place. Just you and me and you have been asleep." "It's the peanuts." said the bartender. "Say what!?" exclaimed the man. "You heard me, it's the peanuts. They're complimentary."

The only reason why someone might be jumpy is that they have heard stories. The old stories in their head already make them feel jumpy. Now somebody is finally confirming these stories with authority. We have confirmed these stories with so much authority that maybe we have enhanced your old stories and left you feeling a little more jumpy; that's okay.

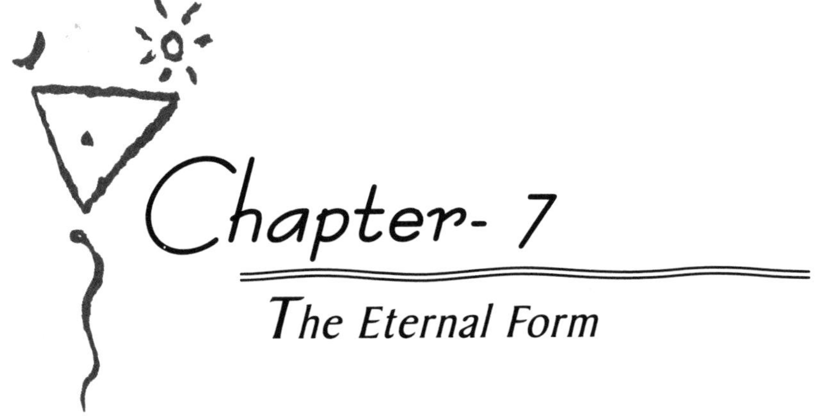

Chapter- 7

The Eternal Form

The Eternal Form

You are my Guru's will
My only obsession
In my dreams and my wakefulness
My only longing was to fulfill you

Willing to do anything
That men should and should not
Willing to offer myself and
Another hundred lives if need be

Here now that you have happened
O Glorious One
May your Glory and Grace
Stir the sleeping hordes

Into wakefulness and light
Now that you have happened
And the gift of life is still with me
What shall I do with myself

Have lived the peaks for too long
Time to graze the valleys of life

– Sadhguru

From another time. Sadhguru Shri Bhramha.

Anyone who comes into the sphere of the Dhyanalinga cannot escape the sowing of the spiritual seed of liberation. **- Sadhguru**

Entrusted to him by his Guru, the consecration of the Dhyanalinga, the dream of many enlightened beings, has been the mission and the consummation of Sadhguru's life. What exactly is the Dhyanalinga? Why is it so special that even enlightened beings wished to bequeath it to the world? Why is it that Sadhguru chose to go through the cycle of birth and death not once or even twice but three times to make it happen? Why is it that Sadhguru considers that any price to consecrate the Dhyanalinga is worthwhile? What are the virtues and the benefits of the Dhyanalinga? These are only some of the myriad of questions about the Dhyanalinga, which one can never really comprehend.

Yet, despite the limitations of the mind and word, Sadhguru dispels misgivings and in an effort to enhance one's possibility of experiencing the Dhyanalinga, shares insights on the Dhyanalinga with groups of close disciples from various beliefs, faiths, cultures and traditions, from different parts of the globe, from the devout believer to the atheist and the scholar who is clueless about an inner possibility.

Delving deeply into the very core of the spiritual sciences, Sadhguru unravels the mysteries of the little known ancient science of temple building. Answering questions on the purpose of temples, the energies of the deities and their consecration, on rituals and sacrifices, on trials, setbacks and successes, Sadhguru jokes through hair-raising revelations about temples that perhaps until yesterday one went to only ritualistically, or abhorred, but missed completely, either way.

Seeker: Sadhguru, this Dhyanalinga, which you refer to as the Eternal Form, what is it? I am very intrigued.

Sadhguru: *Dhyanalinga…* what it is all about. If you look at life today, modern science tells you beyond any doubt that the whole existence is just energy manifesting itself in so many different ways. The only thing is that it is in different levels of manifestation. If everything is the same energy, can you treat everything the same way?

We just had our dinner. There was so much variety, I was mind boggled. I didn't know what to choose. I asked Momita, "Please choose for me." I did not want to choose from a hundred different varieties for myself. Now this food, when it is on your plate, it's wonderful, tasty and delicious. Tomorrow morning, what happens to the food that you have eaten? It becomes shit. This tasty food and that are the same energy. This food that you have eaten and what has become of it, can you treat both the same way? When it falls into the earth, in a few days again it stands up as food. Again you eat it, again you know what it turns into. It's the same energy taking on different forms. This form and that form, what a world of difference, isn't it? When you make mud into food, you can call it agriculture; food into energy, digestion; stone into God, consecration. Similarly, what you call as creation is the same energy, from the grossest to the subtlest.

Just looking back, after I finished college, I wanted to make some money so I could travel; I started a poultry farm. One day, I decided to paint the wall. I dipped the brush in the paint and put it to the wall. I did not want to paint the whole wall thoroughly, so I just put the paintbrush onto the surface and walked from one side to the other. The paint started out very thick, then became thin, thin, thinner and slowly disappeared. I saw this paint smear, which started out thick, become thinner and thinner and then just disappear. Seeing this, I exploded; tears were simply rolling out of my eyes. I just looked at this and there was the whole creation right there. That's all the whole creation is: a paint smear. It starts out really thick and gross, becomes thinner and thinner and thinner, and becomes nothing. So from the lowest to the highest, it was all there, the *vishwa rupa darshana*[1] for me, in just this paint smear. I sat there going crazy and ecstatic (laughs). I didn't paint for three days. Then I started again.

What you call as creation is just that. Everything is the same energy. The rock is the same energy. God is also the same energy. This is gross; that is subtle. As you make it more and more subtle, beyond a certain level of subtleness, you call it Divine. Below a certain level of grossness, you call it animal; further below that you call it inanimate. It is all the same energy. So the whole creation is just a paint smear for me, and if you look at it, it's the same for you. What you call as the Dhyanalinga is the result of taking energies to subtler and subtler levels. The whole process of yoga is to become less physical and more fluid, more subtle. For example, *samadhi* is that state where the contact with the body is minimized to a single point, and the rest of the energy is loose, no longer involved with the body. Once energy is like this, much can be done with it. When the energy is stuck, identified with the body, nothing much can be done with it. All you can do is produce thoughts, emotions, and physical actions; but once the energy becomes free from physical identification and becomes fluid, so many unimaginable things can be done with it.

Dhyanalinga is a miracle. When I say miracle, I'm not talking about gross acts of changing one object into another. If you can go through life untouched, if you can play with life whichever way you want and life still cannot do anything to you, life does not leave a scratch on you; that is a miracle that we are working to manifest in everybody's life in so many ways. That is also the miracle of Isha Yoga programs. If a person does not realize the miracle that he is, the miracle that life is, the miracle that holds you on this planet, the miracle that makes you die, the miracle that makes you to be born once again; if a person does not understand this, does not experience this, such a fool will go about seeking these frivolous miracles or the so-called miracles of transforming one thing into another. Fundamentally, these so-called miracles are meddling with the process of life. If you have tasted life, if you have known and experienced some sense of depth to it, you will know that meddling with it is the most foolish thing to do because you can't make

---

1 *vishwa rupa darshana* : an experience of oneness of the existence.

During the initial process of the Dhyanalinga consecration, a blessed few who were present witnessed high power situations of unbelievable magnitude.

it any more beautiful. The only thing you can do is to allow yourself to experience the beauty of life, allow yourself to experience the grandeur of life. Anything else you do with it is bound to be a stupid act. From your limited sense of understanding, whatever else you do, whatever else you are driven to do with your life is very immature and juvenile. The Dhyanalinga, I call it a miracle because it is a possibility to know life in its utmost depth, to experience life in its totality. The sphere and the energy of the Dhyanalinga will create a possibility for every human being who comes in contact with it – either actually in its vicinity, or just in his consciousness – if he is willing to open himself up. It will be available to him; it will become the highest possibility for him.

You have known the pleasure and the convenience of modern science; so why the Dhyanalinga? It is because I want you to know the power, the liberation of another kind of science, the inner science, the yogic science through which you can become the master of your own destiny. That is why the Dhyanalinga. A science like this gives you absolute mastery over life itself. The whole process of the Dhyanalinga is just to manifest this science in such a way that it cannot ever be taken away, to manifest it also in such a way that it's accessible at any time to everybody who is willing. Not only to create your life the way you want it, but to be able to decide the very process of life, death and rebirth. Even to the extent of deciding the womb in which you are going to be born; ultimately, being able to dissolve at will.

Seeker: Master, you say that the Dhyanalinga offers the possibility for each human being to experience life in its totality. Can you tell us how?

Sadhguru: I think we need to bring some understanding of the science behind the Dhyanalinga. In the yogic tradition, this whole aspect of what we call as Shiva[1] and Shakthi is about the duality of life. When you experience life through your sense perceptions, the experience of it is in a certain duality. It is this duality which is traditionally personified as Shiva and Shakthi, the Ardhanarishwara.[2] In yoga, we call this the *Ida* and *Pingala*, and in the far eastern culture as *Yin* and *Yang*. You can also call it the feminine and masculine or the intuitive and logical aspect of oneself. These are the two dimensions in which you and the world around you exist. It is based on this duality that all religious sciences have grown. Based on this, life is created; without these two dualities, life does not exist as it is right now. In the beginning, everything was primordial; there was no duality, but once creation happened, there was duality. To experience and limit you to this duality is the reason why there are sense organs. You experience everything through your senses: seeing, smelling, tasting, hearing and touching. These sense organs manifest and enhance the sense of duality in the world. The sense of light and dark, good and bad, pleasant and unpleasant is what makes everything appear more established. As you get more involved with the sense perception, think, and feel life, the duality only gets deeper.

Now is there something wrong with the duality? That's not the point. Without duality, there is no creation. It's only because of these opposites that creation happened; but to be trapped within the duality is the problem. If one is limited to the duality, one does not know the beyond. It then becomes a great

---

1 Shiva : lit. *that which is not.* The Great Lord. The destroyer in the trinity.
2 Ardhanarishwara : Shiva, in the form of half man and half woman.

limitation in your life. Duality is the source of all the pleasures in the world. If there were no opposites, there would be no pleasures. At the same time, duality is the source for all suffering in the world. It is only because of these opposites that man suffers. Caught in this 'pleasure and pain' experience of life, people get wounded by life. They don't become wise with life, they become wounded by it. They are not able to handle this duality, nor are they able to transcend it.

When you have limited yourself to your sense perceptions, you're bound by this duality; you can't help it. The sense organs seem to be an access to freedom. Your eyes, for example, your vision, seems to be your freedom. If you have no eyes, you have no experience of the outside, but it is the eye which is limiting you in so many ways. The eye is like a window to your body; it's through this window that you can look out. This window seems to be a great possibility, but the window is also a limitation for you. If you remove this limitation, then you will observe that it's not the eyes that see, it's you who sees. Your eyes are only an opening to the world. So sense perceptions are just a small opening and at the same time a great bondage within yourselves.

The process or science of the Dhyanalinga is an establishment of the exuberance of the duality of life. Through the *nadis*[1] of the Ida and Pingala, through the seven *chakras*[2] and the wide range of manifestation and experience, life has happened. The many forms of life, the many levels of life, the many ways of experiencing life are there in the world only because of this duality and the seven chakras or the seven dimensions of life. The Dhyanalinga is manifested on all of these levels, but its purpose is to help a person go beyond this duality. We are not against sense perception, but seeing the limitation that it is, one needs to go beyond that. Through this manifestation of Ida and Pingala or Shiva and Shakthi, both dimensions, the logical and the intuitive, can be enjoyed and experienced. Knowing that both the logical and the intuitive are not sufficient, one has to know that which is beyond this, which in yoga we

---

1 *nadis* : channels through which the life force, or *prana*, flows through in the energy body.
2 *chakras* : seven main points or junctions of confluence of the pranic nadis or channels in the energy body.

refer to as *pratibha*, where you are neither intuitive nor logical. You have a direct perception of the world the way it is. You experience life simply the way it is, not through the interpretation of the senses.

Seeker: In what way is the Dhyanalinga unique? What's so different about it, Sadhguru?

Sadhguru: The uniqueness of the Dhyanalinga is that all the seven chakras are established. *Lingadhanda*, a copper tube with solidified mercury in it, has all the seven chakras established in their full flow, further complemented by copper rings on the outer periphery of the Dhyanalinga. Do you know what chakras are? Within your physical body, there are various centers, there are seven basic centers representing the seven dimensions of life, or seven dimensions of the experience of life. These seven chakras are: the *Muladhara*, which is located at the perineum, between the anal outlet and the genital organs. *Swadhistana* is just above the genital organs; *Manipuraka* is just below the navel; *Anahata* is the soft spot beneath the point where the ribcage meets; *Vishuddhi* is at the pit of the throat; *Ajna* is between the eyebrows and *Sahasrar* is at the top of the head.

What do these seven dimensions represent? If your energy is dominant in Muladhara, then food and sleep will be the most dominant factors in your life. If it is dominant in Swadhistana, pleasure will be the most dominant in your life. You will seek pleasure and enjoy the physical reality. If your energy is dominant in Manipuraka, you are a doer – you will do many things in the world. If it is dominant in Anahata, you are a very creative person. If your energy is dominant in Vishuddhi, you become a very powerful person. If your energy is dominant in Ajna, you become peaceful. If you attain to Ajna, then you're realized intellectually. You're not realized experientially, but a certain peace and stability arises within you irrespective of what is happening outside of you. If your energy moves into Sahasrar, you will explode into unexplained ecstasy. Whatever experience happens within you, it's just a certain expression of your life energies. Anger, misery, peace, joy, ecstasy... all are different levels of expression for the same energy. These are the seven dimensions through which one can find expression.

In my previous life as Sadhguru Shri Bhramha, I was known as *Chakreshwara.* For those of you from the state of Tamil Nadu, maybe you have heard of this. It means somebody who has complete mastery over all the hundred and fourteen chakras. It is because of that mastery that now we can have people blowing up everywhere like explosions. He was known as Chakreshwara because he exhibited certain qualities of his total mastery over the chakras. A phenomenally rare thing he did was, when he left his body, he left through all the seven chakras. Generally, when yogis leave their body, they leave through one particular chakra – whichever they have particular mastery over, through that they leave. Otherwise, depending upon their tendencies, they leave accordingly, but Sadhguru left his body through all the seven chakras. As a preparation for the consecration of the Dhyanalinga, he left his body through all the seven chakras. So this is from the horse's mouth (laughs).

So the uniqueness of the Dhyanalinga is that it has all the seven chakras energized at their peak. It's the highest possible manifestation, in the sense that if you take energy and push it up to very high levels of intensity, it can hold form only to a certain point. Beyond that, it cannot hold any form; it becomes formless. If it becomes formless, people are incapable of experiencing it. Pushing the energy to the highest point beyond which there will be no form, and crystallizing it at that point, it has been taken and consecrated.

It took three and a half years of a very intense process of consecration. The kinds of situations that people witnessed during the consecration are too unbelievable. Many yogis and *siddhas* [1] have attempted to create a Dhyanalinga, but for various reasons, all the required ingredients never fell together. There were three fully consecrated Lingas in the present state of Bihar, but their physical forms are gone now. They have been totally razed to the ground and homes have been built over their locations, but the energy forms are still there. We know where they are; I have located them. All the other Lingas were never completed. I have found dozens of places where they attempted to create a Dhyanalinga, but for some reason, they were never completed.

---

1 *siddhas* : one who has attained perfection or mastery over a certain mystical aspect of life.

An ethereal ambience. *The abode of the Dhyanalinga.*

Seeker: Sadhguru, in India there are Lingas[1] everywhere. In what way is the Dhyanalinga different from other Lingas worshipped in the Hindu tradition? Are there other Lingas in the world or is it a science limited to Indian culture? You also say it's not a religious symbol. How so? And what about the science behind the making of the Dhyanalinga?

Sadhguru: The science of Linga making is a huge experiential possibility, and has been there for thousands of years, but in the last eight or nine hundred years, especially when the *bhakthi* movement swept the country, the science of building a temple got washed away. For a *bhaktha*, for a devotee, nothing is important except his emotion. His path is emotion. It is only from the strength of his emotion that he does everything. So they just kept the science aside and started building temples whichever way they liked. It's a love affair, you know? A bhaktha can do whatever he wants. Anything is fair with him. He can do anything he wishes because the only thing he has is the strength of his emotion. That's the way of the bhaktha; because of this, the science of making Lingas receded. Otherwise, it was a very deep science. This is a very subjective science and it was never written down, because if you write it down, it will be completely misunderstood. Many Lingas have been created like this, without any knowledge of the science.

Temples created by bhakthas are places for people to create emotion. Very few people are true bhakthas; the rest are just using devotion as a currency to get what they want. Ninety-eight percent of the world's prayers are about: "Give me this, give me that, or protect me." This is just survival. There is no

---

1 Lingas : an energy form consecrated for worship.

transcendence in that. There is nothing prayerful about it. This is just seeking survival, shifting your currency from one to the other, that's all. Generally, the only Lingas that have a scientific basis to them are those created by siddhas and yogis looking at liberation as a scientific process. They are eternal vibrations. Usually, they were consecrated with the use of mantras, for specific purposes and specific qualities. If you're not aware of this, in South India, there are five Lingas for the five elements in nature. These five Lingas are created for *sadhana*[1], not for worship; this must be understood. And the most fundamental sadhana in yoga is *bhootha shuddhi.*

The *pancha bhoothas* are the five elements in nature. If you look at yourself, your physical body is made up of five elements. These are earth, fire, wind, water, and space. They come together in a certain way to become the body. So the whole spiritual process is about going beyond the physical, beyond the five elements. These elements have a huge grip on everything that you experience. To transcend them, the fundamental practice of yoga involves what's called bhootha shuddhi. For every element that is involved, there's a certain practice you can do to become free from it. That is why, to practice the bhootha shuddhi, they created five different Lingas: one for earth, one for fire, one for wind, one for water, and one for space. Huge magnificent temples were built where you can go and do sadhana. If you want to do sadhana for the element of water, you go to Thiruvanaikaval. For space, you go to Chidambaram. To do different sadhana, different types of temples were built. This is how a temple is supposed to be, a place where energy is created in a particular way for the specific purpose of sadhana. They created these temples as places for sadhana, not for worship. Indian temples have never been places of prayer; nobody ever leads prayers there. Nobody tells you that you must go there, give five rupees and appeal to God to do this or that. The tradition always told you that if you go to the temple, you must sit there for a while, because these temples are energy centers. It's like a public charging place. Everyday in the morning, before you go out into the world, you have a bath, go sit in the temple and imbibe this, energize yourself. Then go out into the world with the right kind of vibe.

---

1 *sadhana*: spiritual practices which are used as a means to realization.

The incredible thing is that there are Lingas all around the world. In Africa there are terra cotta Lingas used for occult purposes. In Greece there's a temple with a Linga below the ground known as the 'Navel of the Earth'. This is purely Manipuraka. Somebody showed me the picture and I immediately knew what type of people consecrated this Linga. It was definitely done by Indian yogis. Somebody went there five thousand years ago and consecrated the Linga for Manipuraka, probably because the local king or chieftain wanted victory, prosperity and well-being. So they created an instrument towards that purpose. As most temples were funded by kings, they mostly were Manipuraka in nature, but a few kings who looked beyond those things wanted Anahata Lingas – also called Atma Lingas. Usually these Atma Lingas are for love and devotion, for ultimate dissolution. Anahata is a very malleable kind of state, accessible to most people. There are occult Lingas which are Muladhara Lingas, very base, gross, and powerful, used for occult purposes. Those types of Lingas you can find in certain parts of Assam and Karnataka. There are secret temples, usually very small and powerful in their occult capabilities, but generally most Lingas are Manipuraka.

Right now, most of the Lingas in the country represent one or two chakras at the most. Generally only one, because the Linga is made powerful and intense with one chakra for a particular purpose and is consecrated by mantras. The Dhyanalinga, which is empowered with all the seven chakras, was consecrated by *prana prathishta.*[1] Holding all the seven chakras together was the greatest challenge. If I had wanted to create seven separate Lingas for seven chakras, that would have been so much easier, but the impact would not have been the same. The Dhyanalinga is like having the energy body of the most evolved being sitting there, or you could say, the highest being, referred to as Shiva, his energy body.

Another thing is, probably for the first time anywhere in the world, the Dhyanalinga is cared for by both men and women. Nobody has allowed women to do this kind of work before, but today, fourteen days in a lunar month – towards the full moon – women take care of the Dhyanalinga. The next fourteen

1 *prana prathishta*: process of consecration or energizing an object with Divine energies through a direct process involving the consecrator's own life energies.

days – towards the new moon – men take care of it. I think that's a big gift for the society to be able to go beyond these traditions. *Bhramhacharinis*[1] are there in the temple, doing everything that needs to be done.

If one wants to do spiritual sadhana, he can have the intimacy of sitting with a *Guru*, a live Master. That is the purpose with which the Dhyanalinga has been created. So people come, sit for a moment and go, that's fine, but those who want to do sadhana can have that kind of intimacy with that energy which is not normally available for people. It's very rare for people to have such an opportunity.

Seeker: What's the origin of this Linga form? Is there any scientific explanation to it, Sadhguru?

Sadhguru: When un-manifest energy begins to manifest itself, the first form is always the Linga. The word *Linga* means *the form*. Why we are referring to it as *the form* is: the first form in the existence is always a Linga. Linga means a perfect ellipsoid. The first form of creation is an ellipsoid. Today modern cosmologists are saying that the core of every galaxy is in the form of an ellipsoid. There are many pictures that show just this. Yoga has always been saying, the first and final form is a Linga. If you become meditative, your energies will naturally take the form of a Linga. From our experience, we clearly know this.

Something beautiful like this happened with one of our meditators. A few years ago, when I was conducting a program in the United States, there was a participant who was an intuitive artist. During the program she just kept gazing at me, scribbling and scribbling, without looking at the paper she was drawing on and never lifting the pen off the paper, just scribbling. After three days of scribbling, she had a drawing of a form. When she finally looked at it, she could not make anything out of it. She did not know anything about the Dhyanalinga and she thought the drawing looked like a doorway. She came to me and said, "I want to show you this. My intuition drove me to draw this. I was just looking at you and this is what

1 *Bhramhacharini* : a woman who is on the path of the Divine, usually refers to one who has formally been initiated into monkhood through a certain energy process.

came out. It looks like a doorway. Maybe you're my doorway." I looked at it. It was the shape of a perfect Linga. She got the essence of my energy just like that and drew a perfect Linga.

The first form is a Linga. The final form before dissolution is also a Linga. So a Linga is held as a doorway to the beyond, whether you go this way or that way. Both ways, before dissolving into nothingness, the final form is always a perfect ellipsoid. The science of Linga-making is based on this. If you give me any object, this paper for example, I can make it highly energetic and give it to you. In a few seconds I can make it highly energetic. If you hold it before and after I touch it, you will feel the difference, but the paper won't be able to retain this energy; it will hold it for some time, and again it will become just a piece of paper. It cannot sustain it; but if you create a perfect Linga form, it becomes a perennial storehouse of energy. Once you charge it, it will always stay that way.

Seeker: Your teaching is so powerful, Sadhguru, so why the need for Dhyanalinga?

Sadhguru: We can teach or impart things to you in many different ways. You know, people come to me in different ways. Some people come here as investigators, some people as students, some as disciples and some as devotees. Investigators want to find out what's wrong. That is, I mean there is nothing wrong, but they want to find out what's wrong; they are not interested in learning, do you understand? Many investigators came and quite a few of them have slowly evolved into devotees today.

Students come because they want to learn; they want to pick up something. I call the investigators shit-pickers. They always come to pick the dirtiest out of any situation; what's the dirtiest part of what's happening here. They want to pick out what's wrong. Students are also pickers; they want to pick out what's good. This is an old habit from the hunting and gathering days. Man has been gathering, gathering, and gathering, either things, people or knowledge, he wants to gather. The need for gathering has come because there is a sense of inadequacy and incompleteness. You want to gather something all the time, maybe money, maybe wealth, maybe relationships, maybe knowledge. It's just a question of taste, that's all. People who are gathering knowledge always think they are better than people who are gathering money or things, but it is not so. It is just a question of taste; somebody likes toast for breakfast, somebody likes *masala dosa*, somebody likes a whole meal in the morning. It's a question of taste. Everybody is gathering whatever is dominant in them. Socially, one thing is held superior to the other, but actually, gathering knowledge is so much more entangling than gathering money, wealth, people or anything. Knowledge is the most entangling thing, because the way you think and feel, your ways of thinking and feeling are the deepest attachment within you. People have always thought renunciation means leave your wife, leave your husband. That's easy, you know? If your wife or husband has become inconvenient, leaving them is quite easy. Now, the problem is that the deepest attachment is to your own ways of thinking and feeling. If somebody threatens your way of thinking and feeling, you're willing to leave your child, husband, wife, father, mother, anybody, yes or no? Your own ways of thinking and feeling, that's where the trap is. So gathering knowledge is not any better, but students want to gather knowledge, that's their way. The third is the disciple. The disciple has come to transform himself, he wants to become something other than what he is right now; a pretty good beginning, but a devotee is not interested in all this. He just wants to dissolve. He doesn't want to exist as himself anymore, he wants to become one with everything. These are the four ways that you can come here.

Now depending upon who you are, and depending upon what your requirements are, we start imparting things in so many different ways. We can transform your body, you know, every day in the morning bending you and twisting you? If you do *yoga asanas* for six months, you will see, suddenly you're so much more peaceful, healthier, better, everything. You will see an enormous change in your body and your mind, simply because you're doing simple physical asanas. Let us say you practice for six months or one year, and give it up for another six months, then you're back to square one. If we transform your mind...with all these classes we are transforming your mind. If you live in awareness for the next six months, there's a huge change in you, but if in the next two years you live in unawareness, you will be back to square one. The next thing is we're trying to transform your *prana* or vital energies with *yoga kriyas*. You practice for six months and you give them up for the next five years, you will be once again back to square one. This period may vary from person to person, depending upon their lifestyles and other situations – karmic situations and other aspects.

If you can impress or imprint something into the etheric body, or spiritual body, a substance which is beyond the pranic or the physical energies, you can never destroy it. It's not in your hands anymore.

That is what an initiation means. An initiation is not just a set of instructions. Why so much elaborate care is taken, I want to tell you very plainly: all this body bending, holding your breath and grinding from morning to night, everything is just to give you a fifteen-minute *Shoonya*[1] meditation. All this drama of eight days is just to initiate you into fifteen minutes of meditation; just hoping that you will be in the right level of receptivity and receive this. The seed of it, once it falls into you, you cannot destroy. It doesn't matter what you do, even if you live the worst possible life, you cannot destroy the seed. If you create a conducive atmosphere, it grows and flowers. If you don't, it will wait.

Have you seen how in summer everything seems to be dry? When you look at the land, it looks so hopeless. Probably a long summer looks like the end of life. A few drops of rain come and do you see how it all springs up? They are all waiting; they are just waiting. One drop and immediately they are up. This is a seed. Once it is implanted into your etheric body, you cannot destroy it. That's what an initiation means. That's why so much care is taken about it. The whole Isha Yoga program is just about initiating you into Shoonya. I want you to understand that. Now if I have to initiate people like this – eight days of grinding, and you know all the logistics involved in it – I can initiate only a small group of people into Shoonya meditation at the same time. Ten thousand people a day is not possible. So we created a device…I would call it a tool. Dhyanalinga is a tool. Sitting in the space of the Dhyanalinga for a while, you start as a devotee, which has a tremendous advantage over Isha Yoga programs. It starts from the other end, which cannot be influenced by the outer situation. If you transform your spiritual body, you will see that this transformation is permanent. Once you are in the sphere of the Dhyanalinga, the seed of spiritual liberation is sown into you. Whether you are willing or not, a believer or non-believer, whether you have come to investigate or surrender, it doesn't matter. When people sit in the temple, this impression will definitely happen, knowingly or unknowingly.

This seed will wait. If the person creates a conducive atmosphere, it will flower very quickly; if he doesn't, it will wait. It will wait ten lifetimes or hundreds of lifetimes, but you cannot destroy it. This is why we have put so much effort into creating the Dhyanalinga. This transformation works within you on a different level altogether – one which cannot be destroyed, cannot be undone. After we are gone,

1 *Shoonya*: emptiness, a powerful meditation offered in the basic Isha Yoga program.

what Isha Yoga will become, we don't know. We're taking a lot of care to see that distortions do not happen. We are demanding tremendous discipline and dedication from the teachers. We're putting very hard conditions on them so that distortions are not made. If whatever Gautama Buddha said, Krishna said or Jesus said can be distorted in a thousand years, what I have said will also definitely be distorted. So the Dhyanalinga is the *shakthi moola*[1] for that; it cannot be distorted. If the whole of Isha Yoga is distorted, it doesn't matter. If you just go and sit at the Dhyanalinga, everything that needs to happen will happen experientially, without saying a word; that's the nature of the Dhyanalinga. Even if a person who doesn't know anything about meditation comes and sits there, he will become meditative by his own nature. That is the quality of the Dhyanalinga. That's the kind of tool it is. It has taken an enormous effort to create it. It took three lifetimes for me. It's very hard for you to believe this. It will sound too unbelievable if I tell you the whole saga of what it took to make it happen. People who have been around me have seen all that has happened. That is the nature of this tool. If we go on teaching in the current way, with the kind of safeguards we're creating, we can never reach enough people. So the Dhyanalinga is to just hasten this process. That's why in our eagerness to share, we have created this.

Seeker: Master, you say it took you three lifetimes to create the Dhyanalinga. How did it all begin?

Sadhguru: This did not happen accidentally. It is a continuation of the past. Three hundred and seventy years ago there was a man in a small village in the present state of Madhya Pradesh. His name was Bilva. He lived a totally different kind of life. He was too wild and intense. He didn't really fit into the norms of society. There's a certain tradition in India, where people called the *budubuduku* just walk through the streets, usually very early in the morning, when it's still pitch dark. They wake you up with their drumbeats. Intuitively, if they see something, they will tell you; otherwise, they will sing songs in praise of the Lord and walk away. This is a certain tradition within the *Shaiva* culture, where this particular tribe of people is also involved in snake charming; snakes and Shiva are deeply connected. In the evolutionary process, the snake is at an important stage of development, because it is close to that of a human being.

1 *shakthi moola*: energy source.

Bilva was the snake charmer of his tribe and he was deeply in love with what he was doing. These were people who lived totally, loving life for what it is. They weren't the kind to accumulate anything. They had no sense of money, property or possessions. They simply lived, and Shiva was very important in their lives. Bilva loved snakes. Mind you, snakes, poisonous creatures! If you love poisonous creatures, you have to be a different kind of person. To kiss a snake, you must be very courageous. For a person for whom love means everything, everything else is secondary; being alive itself is secondary. That's the kind of person he was. He was someone who could not fit into the social structure and was looked upon as a rebel. For one of the many rebellious acts he did, not respecting the prevalent caste distinction, at a very young age he was put to death by a snake's bite, while he was tied to a tree.

He was a great bhaktha of Shiva. Our mantra, "Shambho",[1] comes from that era. At that time, you couldn't really call him a spiritual person; he was a bhaktha, but not really a spiritual person. Those last few moments of his life, he watched his breath. See, the cobra's venom acts on the cardiovascular system. The blood thickens and makes cardiac and respiratory action difficult and ultimately it stops. Poison was all through his body and death a few minutes away. There was nothing else he could do and breath watching just happened. It was more of an accident than a conscious awareness. It was more a Grace than a sadhana. From that breath watching, which happened for just a few minutes, a new spiritual process began which changed that person's future in so many ways. That's why, in Samyama,[2] breath watching has a feel of venom to it. It has a different quality. Isha breath watching is very different from anywhere else. Though it is the most common meditation, if you go anywhere else and see people breath watching, it won't be the same. Here, it was realized when death was close and certain. This breath watching had a different kind of intensity; it was not done in comfort. He was lying face down, almost dead, and managed to be aware of those last few minutes of life. So this breath watching has a kind of overpowering effect on people. This path is very quick, and it is because of the quality of this breath watching that we dare to think of imparting Samyama in seven days.

---

1 Shambho: another name for Shiva, which denotes his loving nature.

2 Samyama: an eight day meditation program offered by Sadhguru where one is transported to explosive states of meditativeness, held at Isha Yoga Center.

In his next life, he was a very intense seeker of the Ultimate Nature. Shiva was his way. He went through heartbreaking sadhana, but still final Realization had not happened. He was known as Shivayogi. Until now, I have never spoken about my Guru. I think it's time I said something about him. Shri Palani Swami was a Realized Master. This was not his name, but he was called so because he attained to a certain samadhi state, near the town of Palani in Tamil Nadu. He remained in this state for about two and a half years. After that, he wandered all over the country enlightening many people. He came to Shivayogi and bestowed his Grace upon him, a forlorn sadhaka. When this yogi saw him, he recognized that this was the Guru. Until then, he would not accept any human being as his Guru. For him, Shiva was the only Guru. He wanted Shiva to come and initiate him, but when he saw Palani Swami, he recognized that this being was at the very peak of consciousness and he offered himself. But somewhere there was still a little resistance because he could not offer himself to another man. He would only offer himself totally to Shiva. So the Guru, out of his compassion, appeared in the form of Shiva himself. Shivayogi surrendered. Palani Swami didn't even touch him with his hand or foot; he just took his staff and put it on his Ajna. At that moment, Shivayogi attained to his Ultimate Nature.

This contact with the Guru lasted only a few hours. After that they never met again, but they were constantly in touch. Palani Swami attained Mahasamadhi[1] in the Velliangiri hills.[2] Somehow he identified Shivayogi as a person suitable for establishing the Dhyanalinga and entrusted this work to him; not in speech, not in words, but he communicated the immense technology needed to consecrate the Dhyanalinga. So Shivayogi began working towards establishing the Dhyanalinga, but was not able to fulfill his Guru's vision because of limited resources and lack of support.

To continue the work of creating the Dhyanalinga, he came back as Sadhguru Shri Bhramha. He started the work towards this in Coimbatore,[3] but faced a lot of social resistance from people. As Dhyanalinga is the highest manifestation of the Divine, it includes all aspects and manifestations of life, so it involved men and women in very intense processes. If a man and woman sit together, people can only think of one thing.

---

1 Mahasamadhi : complete dissolution of the Self also known as Nirvana, or Mahaparinibbana in other spiritual traditions.
2 Velliangiri hills : referring to the mountain range surrounding the Isha Yoga Center where the Dhyanalinga is located.
3 Coimbatore : closest major city to Isha Yoga Center, in Tamil Nadu, a South Indian state.

A lot of resistance came up, and he was literally hounded out of the place. He became very angry that he could not fulfill his Guru's will and left Coimbatore in great fury, as if on fire. In that anger, he started to walk in no particular direction. Seeing his fierceness, nobody was able to go near him, except for one disciple by the name of Vibhuthi who followed him. Sadhguru Shri Bhramha walked without eating, sleeping or even sitting for three or four days. The disciple would follow him, see in which direction the Master was going, cook food and run to reach his Master and place the food in front of him, step aside and wait for him to eat. He finally reached a temple in Cuddapah, in the state of Andhra Pradesh. It was not pre-planned that he should go there, but he was drawn in that direction because his Guru's blessings and energies were there.

After reaching this place, his anger had still not subsided. Even after four or five months, he was still angry. Nobody could come near Sadhguru Shri Bhramha and his disciple. It's not that they did anything or harmed anybody, but they were so fierce – fiercer than wild animals – even if they were only sitting, nobody wanted to come near them. Within a few days, all the priests in the temple left, as they couldn't stay there because of the intensity of that being. Sadhguru Shri Bhramha knew that he didn't have much time. He knew that because of certain karmic limitations, he would have to leave his body within the next two years. So he sat with his disciple and plotted how to make the Dhyanalinga happen in the next life. Many things were decided there – who should be involved in the consecration process, where they should be born, in which womb, how and at what time. They plotted everything. Sadhguru Shri Bhramha even decided what kind of a person he should be born as, how his physical body and state of mind should be. Everything was created right there. The fundamental blueprint for the Dhyanalinga was made in that Cuddapah temple. Now, you shouldn't believe all these things, but disbelieving them would also be stupid.

Then Sadhguru Shri Bhramha came back to Coimbatore for the last time, where many people gathered at the foothills of the Velliangiri Mountains. He declared, "I will be back." He ascended the mountain for the last time and left his body through all seven chakras. He was one of the very few Masters who had mastery over all the seven chakras and was referred to as Chakreshwara. He was only forty-two years old at the time. Today, the place where he attained samadhi and shed his body still exists; it is very vibrant, it pulsates with energy. People who go there can feel it and experience it. The quality of this place, at the top of the seventh hill, just at the edge of the mountain where wild winds blow constantly, says everything about this man. That is where he felt most comfortable. It is a very powerful spot. Most of you have been there with me just a couple of days ago. Would any of you like to share your experience?

Srinivas: I was walking directly towards the place without knowing where it was and something was just pulling me in a particular direction. When I reached there, I sat and meditated for sometime and went into *shavasana.*[1] I was aware of everything that was going on around me. I could hear people chanting "Shambho," but I could not open my mouth. I was there for about fifteen minutes and in my experience I wasn't even breathing. Even when I inhaled, the exhalation came out immediately in one abrupt gasp. I felt very loose in my body, as if it was becoming separate from me. Sadhguru said that if I had been left alone, I would have left my body.

Sadhguru: Before Sadhguru Shri Bhramha shed the body, he made one futile attempt to achieve the work he had started. A certain yogi in Vajreshwari left his body at the age of twenty-six. He was a *bala yogi*[2] named Sadhananda who attained Realization at the age of eleven. Sadhananda spent about three and a half years in samadhi. When he came out, he was eager to share his experience, and only found five or six disciples to impart it to, but they weren't sincere enough. So he got angry and he left his body. Sadhguru Shri Bhramha immediately took hold of this bala yogi's body and tried to fulfill his purpose through it. He did this because he had no patience to be born again and go through the process of life all over again. For a few months, Sadhguru Shri Bhramha was in two different physical bodies at the same time. In this attempt to create the Dhyanalinga, he gathered a few disciples around him and tried working with them with tremendous intensity, because the time span available was very limited. When people didn't meet his expectations, he got angry, and in anger he shed that body, too.

Today, after a saga of three lifetimes, the Dhyanalinga stands in full glory. I don't really know what to say – whether I am happy, ecstatic or what – to present this, to offer this to the world. Whatever words I use would be improper, but in a way I am relieved (laughs) that it is done. This is not my will; this is my Guru's

---

1 *shavasana*: lit. corpse posture. Practiced intermittently between other asanas, it is known for the rejuvenation of the system.
2 *bala yogi*: child yogi. Refers to someone who gets enlightened as a child.

will that this must happen. These three lifetimes have been spent towards fulfilling this, with the Grace of the Guru and with so many people's love, support and understanding – knowingly or unknowingly, willingly or unwillingly, consciously or unconsciously – in making this happen. I wish to bow down to all of them; this is the greatest gift that could be offered to future generations. Today, I just feel empty. I can't say I'm happy, I can't say I'm fulfilled, I can't say anything. All I know is that today, I am absolutely empty; it has been so since the consecration day because suddenly, there seems to be no purpose for living.

This reminds me of a very ancient story that has been repeatedly told in yogic lore. It so happened, one day, there were two men. One was blind and the other crippled. They were in a forest and suddenly, there was a fire. One could see where to go but couldn't walk, the other couldn't see but could walk. So the two of them struggled by themselves for a while and nothing happened. They would be burnt anyway, because fire doesn't distinguish; it burns everything in its way. So between the two of them, they came to an agreement. The blind person, who was physically fit, carried the crippled person, who could see, on his shoulders to direct the way. They both got out of the forest fire. This story beautifully depicts the need for both the logical and the intuitive aspects of life to be met. The earlier attempts at creating the Dhyanalinga were purely intuitive. We knew how to do it from within, but we didn't successfully create a social situation that would accept it. This time, the blind and the crippled have come together successfully. We have sufficiently worked on the social situation to complete the process with people's support. Even this time, serious attempts were made to stop the process by certain groups of people. The society was treating us like the enemy, but we got through this because the blind and the crippled came together successfully. The actual consecration process took almost three and a half years. There were two ways to make it happen. One was to playfully dance through it. The other was to give up this body and merge with the Dhyanalinga. Doing that would have been the easier way, but we avoided this. I had the apprehension that this process would put so much fear into people that it might take one or two generations for them to accept the Dhyanalinga itself. So to do it like a play, to make it like a dance, it took so many things…the true significance of the Dhyanalinga will be known only after a couple of generations. Right now, it will be a point of controversy, a point of debate. It will take some time for people to know what it really means.

Seeker: Sadhguru Shri Bhramha was considered to be a very intense, wild man. How much of this streak is retained in you, Master?

Sadhguru: All of it! But I have made great efforts to dampen that wild streak to a large extent. I have brought it down. Otherwise, the wild streak, though powerful, was very troublesome. He lived his life like that and he was constantly in trouble with the people around him. His inner understanding was crystal clear, but he didn't care about the outside. He just did what he wanted. For him, others were stupid and he didn't respect their stupidity. He just trampled on them, and for that they wouldn't leave him alone. They may have been stupid, but they were strong in their own way. Stupid people can destroy the world and they're doing it, isn't it? There were only two ways you could be with him. If you have to be with a king, you have to be of his kind, or you must be his humblest servant. It's the same with Shiva: either you have to be of his kind or his humblest servant. These are the two paths of *gnana*[1] and *bhakthi*. Today, both are possible with me.

Seeker: So Master, it seems that you're saying Sadhguru Shri Bhramha was very arrogant with people around him.

Sadhguru: (Laughs) Arrogance! Not simple arrogance, it was absolute arrogance! He was simply arrogant for no reason. Not because of his ego; it was just that his energy was so fierce and people could not perceive him any other way. You ask people who knew him who are still around, they'll tell you how arrogant he was. Even if he has to call Shiva he would only say, "Hey." That's how he was. That was the only way he addressed people, but still people around him loved him very much. He wasn't at all nice to people the way they normally understand, but people close around him experienced him as the very embodiment of love and compassion. They built seventy institutions for him around the State of Tamil Nadu. When those people who knew him at that time heard that I was here, they just rushed here to be with me.

1 *gnana* knowing or perception

Seeker: Master, you said Sadhguru Shri Bhramha took up a *bala yogi's* body. What is a *bala yogi*?

Sadhguru: *Bala yogi* means a child yogi; as children they get Enlightened. Usually they're not able to retain their bodies, because they don't have the technology to do that. They are Realized, they are blissful, they are free, but they don't know the tricks to stay in the body. They don't teach anything, they just sit there. Generally, they only bless people. Their presence is very wonderful; they are at the highest state. Sadhguru Shri Bhramha took up the bala yogi, Sadhananda's body because it was ideal for his purpose. Much before the consecration, I put up his picture in my car as a reminder to me, because he left this body in anger. That's one thing I didn't want to happen this time. The situations were so against us when we were working towards the consecration. I didn't want to leave in anger. In those days, I spent a lot of time traveling in my car, so I put that picture there to remind myself not to get angry.

Seeker: Master, what's this reminder? How does anger affect you?

Sadhguru: The futility of what he was trying to do made Sadhguru Shri Bhramha leave in anger. In this life, I'm free to be in every other way, but not free to be in anger. If I get angry, immediately, below my Anahata, everything dies. The energy just thinks it is time to leave the body. Now you know Nathalie, why I am so kind to all of you! (Laughs). This time anger is not going to take us away, that's for sure. Anger is one thing which is not going to eat us up, no way. When a person has to do something with tremendous intensity and at the same time remain cool, it takes a lot of balance. When I say intensity, it means the kind that people normally don't see in their lives. Once a person, a yogi, pushes himself to that level of intensity, he will be boiling; it brings you to the very edge of physical existence where you're like a living volcano. So to maintain that level of intensity and be very cool, it took three lifetimes of sadhana and understanding.

Seeker: Why was it futile, Sadhguru? What prevented you from completing the consecration at that time?

Sadhguru: The consecration of the Dhyanalinga wasn't just about the process. It was about organizing whole external social situations also, which couldn't be done then. Sadhguru Shri Bhramha couldn't gather the necessary support. A few people gathered around him, and he tried to work with them.

With the limited time span he had, he was pushing the process and those involved in it at an enormous pace. When he realized that the people around him were not grasping the purpose of what he was doing because of their own limitations, he got angry and left the body; angry, not with anyone in particular; angry with the futility of being unable to fulfill his Guru's wish. His anger was about his own incapability to put everything together. If he didn't have the wherewithal, it would have been different, but he knew how to do it and still, for some external situations which to him were ridiculous, he wasn't able to put it together. It's like playing a game. You have the skill, and you had the chance of scoring a goal, but you kicked the ball somewhere else. That doesn't mean you're frustrated with life; that doesn't mean you're angry with anybody or anything. It's just that the passion of the moment, anger, took over.

Seeker: Sadhguru, you keep using 'us' or 'we'. Who are you referring to?

Sadhguru: (Laughs) I'm referring to my accomplice in everything I do...Shiva and me.

Seeker: Master, in what way was Sadhguru Shri Bhramha different from what you are now?

Sadhguru: Have you seen Sadhguru Shri Bhramha's photograph? That was one kind of body. That body had seen lots of physical sadhana. Physically, it was very strong and stable. That was the kind of body which could easily walk a hundred kilometers in a day and still be okay. Now, this body that we have hasn't gone through that kind of physical sadhana. In spite of that, it has the same physical traits. If that kind of physical sadhana was brought into this life also, the body would have been more stable, but then, the energy would have been a little different. It wouldn't be the same as it is now. Fierce sadhana, which brings enormous stability to the body, will also make the energies in a way that's not as approachable as it is now.

The way Sadhguru Shri Bhramha was and the way we are right now is very different. Most people couldn't understand what Sadhguru Shri Bhramha was doing. His methods were so wild and revolutionary. He didn't care what you thought about him. Now, what we're doing here is something that everybody will be able to appreciate. It's very easy to appreciate Isha Yoga, isn't it? Even if people come with resistance, the moment they see the whole structure, they say, "Oh, it is fine. That's good work."

See, what's the point in doing any work that doesn't work? What's the fun? Just for my satisfaction? To say, "No, this is the way I do it?" This looks very romantic, but it's not practical. We have matured. If you told this to Sadhguru Shri Bhramha, he might have kicked you and walked away. He didn't care what you thought of him. He only did things his way. Now we're not like that. I say, "Do it like this." You say, "No…like this." It's okay. I will walk three steps with you. Later on, I know anyway, you will come my way.

So different Masters have acted in different ways, depending on whatever they saw was best for that moment. Many of them didn't give a hoot whether people got it or not. They threw their energies in the world everywhere. Whoever had to get it would get it anyway. They thought, what was the point in trying to teach this fellow or that fellow? That was their attitude, but some Masters went in the midst of people and imparted their teachings to make them open to receive their Grace. If his disciple was acting like a donkey, Sadhguru Shri Bhramha would kick him without hesitation. We can't do that now, because we don't care to do it anymore. We have to decide what kind of situations we want to cater to, what kind of transformation we want to bring about, what level of work we want to do. Our work always has to be streamlined into a certain area; only then results will come. If you try to take everything in the world and do it, in the end, nothing will come out. However, there are hundreds of opportunities everyday for a person, even for the donkey, to see the point and come out of it very easily by himself. But we don't want to beat the donkey out of him; it is up to him to come out of his ignorance, if he wants to

Seeker: Master, was there any reason behind your choosing the Velliangiri Mountains as the place to establish the Dhyanalinga?

Sadhguru: Right from my childhood, right from my infancy, whatever I saw visually, always in the background, there were mountains. Until I was sixteen years of age, I thought in everybody's visual perception there were mountains, too. Only when I discussed it with my friends they said, "You're crazy. Where are the mountains?" But to me, they were always there in my eyes. So after sixteen, I knew that I must seek this place, but then I dismissed the idea because it was always there in my vision. If something is always there, you get used to it. Suppose there's a dot on your spectacle; you get used to it after some time. It's just like that. The mountains were always there in my eyes. Then, when the time to start work on the Dhyanalinga came, I began looking for these mountains. I traveled everywhere, like a madman. I took my motorcycle and from Goa down to Kanyakumari, I rode up and down, looking for these mountains, "Where are they?" Only when I came here, I saw the 'Seventh Hill' and I immediately knew this was the place. We didn't know who owned this land; we just walked in and said, "We want this land." In about nine to ten days, we had it registered. We didn't even know whose land it was when we came here. It just happened like that for us.

Seeker: Sadhguru, what is it that went into the creation of the Dhyanalinga?

Sadhguru: See, initially, nobody would believe it when I told them that I was going to make a temple, because people see me as an agnostic, very logical, questioning everything. I spent seventeen years of my life just creating the necessary goodwill in the society before I even uttered the word *Linga.* When I first said, "I am going to build a temple," nobody believed me. Even though I was living my life with this single-pointed agenda, nobody around me was told this even once. Only when I found there was sufficient support and the situation was mature enough, was it said. People wouldn't believe me. They said, "You building a temple? Because of you, we stopped going to temples. Now you're going to build a temple?"

Now, coming to the consecration process; the whole process was to make the energies of the Dhyanalinga so subtle, beyond which there could be no form. Beyond a point of certain subtleness, energy won't be able to retain a form. So, to the ultimate point of subtlety you take the energy and encase it in a certain way that it stays there forever. It is locked in a particular way. This consecration process doesn't involve any mantras or any kind of rituals. It is purely an energy process involving people. Right now, suppose you take ten pots. If they are burnt clay, you can't do anything with them. If you break them, they become pieces. Let's say, there's some process to make this burnt clay back into how it used to be, now these ten pots can be put together and an eleventh pot can also be made out of them. This is about making you malleable, making your life energies malleable. Right now, it's established as an individual. So developing the people involved in this process, putting them through years of sadhana, making them malleable, and using these energies, is how we created a situation where something much higher was invited into that space. That's how the consecration happened.

To create these people who could be involved in the consecration, we had a ninety-day Wholeness Program. About seventy people participated. The basic idea was to pick fourteen people out of these seventy, who could be useful to make the Dhyanalinga. People were put through very intense kriyas and other kinds of sadhana. We were in a hurry to dissolve certain *karmas*;[1] I we had no time to wait for these things to happen in their life, so everything was put on fast-forward for them. Trying to create those fourteen people who could be in such a state that their contact with the body would be minimal, but would still be stable enough to sit there and do what was needed, didn't happen – even though an enormous effort was made. Creating fourteen people who are one in body, mind, emotion and everything, is not an easy task. Though much effort was put into it, it didn't happen. Then we decided to go for a more drastic process, where only two people were involved. This was a high-risk process, but keeping two people in control was so much easier than keeping fourteen people in absolute control.

It is hard to believe this. After the two people were brought in to create a triangle of energy with me as a pivot, it was necessary that they, in their mind, emotion, and energy, became one. Now, if this person felt something on his left knee, the other two also felt something on their left knee, wherever they were. What was your life and what was their life was all mixed up in your mind. Let's say, you, me and somebody else are right now in a triangle. You didn't know what had happened in my life ten years ago, but suddenly, now, you know; and what had happened in your life twenty-five years ago, I didn't know, but suddenly, now, I know. It all got so mixed up; we didn't know whose memory was whose. It was all there, together. The mind became one; the emotions became one; the physical body also, energy-wise, became one. Anything that happened in this body happened in that body. It became like that. This was so much easier, creating these three people than creating fourteen people, but this was a very drastic process. There was an enormous risk involved for the people who were into it. This was like creating a triangle of energy as an invitation to the Divine. Once you create a triangle, it is like a vortex. It is a certain fierce possibility; it just sucks everything in. So the Dhyanalinga was consecrated through this process.

---

3 karma : past action, the cause of all bondage.

Seeker: What's this fierce possibility? What is it that it sucks in, Sadhguru?

Sadhguru: The things that happened with the people involved in the consecration of the Dhyanalinga are unbelievable. You won't believe that such things are possible in human life. My wife, Vijji, who was part of this process, was a person who normally, if she sees one insect, one shadow, would scream. She was like that, and this is a process where so many things are involved, even if a little fear appears in that moment, the whole process would be ruined. We would have to start from the beginning, afresh. So many disembodied beings were present in so many forms, moving, talking. We were able to hear them. Vijji and Bharathi were utterly confused on the first day; "Who is talking?" Their loud voices were actually being heard everywhere; many of them, dozens of them, just talking loudly. These two were totally confused, looking around, trying to see who it was.

Actually, they were not talking. These were exalted beings released from everything, but they still had a little karmic structure. Total dissolution had not happened yet. So, once you reach that dimension of energy, you can hear their karmic structures just playing on, like a tape recorder. Both were clearly able to hear many people talking all at once. Anybody, any human being would have become terrified, but it seemed very natural then in that situation because the two were raised to a higher level of energy. I never expected them to take it so well. They went through these kinds of experiences with full awareness. They were not hallucinating, they were not hypnotized, and they were not under any kind of intoxication. They were in absolute awareness, more aware than anybody could normally be.

I started the process in June – July, 1996, because I was thinking it would take one and a half years at least to get them into a certain kind of stability, but it happened within weeks. It was incredible. I didn't know how fast or how slow the process would be, but once we put them together, everything happened beyond my expectations. They're almost like two different kinds of qualities, like two opposite poles. One person was all reason, another person was all love. One person was all determination and the other person was all like…just doesn't know. When these two qualities came together, it became like one beautiful person with all the qualities; they became like a complete human being. They just went so beautifully, but then, things that happened were so incredible, it became too overwhelming. Keeping these two people rooted in their bodies became difficult, so we had to stall the process for some time. To withstand the immensity of the experiences existing in higher levels of energy, and to still be normal in everyday activity, one needs a certain level of inner freedom and mastery over the energies. One thing was, these two people have their families to take care of, their day-to-day life in which they had to be totally involved. Another thing was, they had to maintain very high levels of energy and give themselves totally to the consecration process. So, they needed to acquire the necessary maturity, balance and freedom within themselves to be able to handle this. For that, I had to stall the process for some time.

The whole purpose of the triangle was to build a vortex where intense energy could be created wherein it would be an invitation to my Guru's energy to come and consecrate the Dhyanalinga. After all, it was his dream that this should happen. I didn't want to do it myself; I wanted him to do it. That's why this triangle was being built up in different levels. Slowly, this energy was moved into different levels, and at every step, the triangle was moved into different dimensions. You can move it into such a state that this being who has completely dissolved, this being who is completely gone, liberated, now would come back and through him the consecration would happen.

When we say 'triangle of energy', in almost every possible way, the individual is melted. If you have to form a triangle, in many ways you have to merge the three individuals. In many ways, the individual structures had to be loosened. In other words, these three people had to be in a certain state of samadhi, where their contact with the body had become minimal. The individual form was being stretched into another kind of form. If energies had to be stretched like this, or if energies had to become malleable enough to form a triangle, they had to become very subtle, extremely subtle. When you form a triangle with this kind of energy, it creates a whole vortex or a swirl, where the highest energies are drawn into it. All those beings seeking liberation are also drawn into it. You can call it Cosmic or Divine energies. That's how the vortex functions. Using these energies is how the Linga form was created.

When we make things happen like this, there can be absolutely no fault in the work that we do. If I do it, there may be something in my body, some element, which can cause a little distortion in the energy, because I am still embodied and the body is never perfect. There are so many distortions in the body. For example, because of the kind of food I have eaten today there may be a little pain in my back, I might catch a cold...and this can get impressed upon the Linga. So we wanted to use His energies.

When it is done this way, the work would be just perfect. Nobody can find fault with it. There won't be an atom of fault in it.

Seeker: Sadhguru, this being who has dissolved, how is it possible to bring him back?

Sadhguru: Now, a Guru does not mean a teacher. If you have experienced Him, He is everything to you. Everything that happens is Him. The Dhyanalinga is Him, this breath is Him, the food that I eat is Him, the earth that I walk on is Him…

Seeker: Sadhguru, I think He did not come because He wanted it to happen through you, because He knew that you were more than capable of doing it…

Sadhguru: (Laughs).

Seeker: Can we also experience the various states that these two people involved in the consecration process have experienced? Is it possible for everybody, Sadhguru?

Sadhguru: Now, we had just chosen two people for the consecration. If it can be done with a hundred people, we can just blow the world! But to create the ideal kind of people, that's the challenge. They come very close, but they give up at the last moment. At the threshold, they will take backward steps. That's what I have seen with most people. If people mature beyond likes and dislikes, good and bad, you simply tell them what needs to be done and they can do it without a thought in their mind. Then, we can create a situation where a hundred people can sit together and bring down the highest energies. You want Gautama Buddha; we will have him here tomorrow. It's like that. It can be done. It's within our reach. Not only Gautama Buddha; you can bring down Shiva himself. If you can generate that kind of energy, you can literally blow the world. If you can create one situation like that, that's the best thing you can do to this world. Whatever service, and other nonsense you do, it cannot match this.

Someday it should happen that hundreds of people can be in a total state of acceptance to merge and go through experiences beyond logic. Where they are totally connected with each other, where everything becomes one, as if your heart is in somebody else's body, and your brain is in somebody else's head. During the consecration process, things started happening like this, where that person's body scent is in this person's body and this person's body scent is in that person's body. This person's thoughts are in that person's mind, that person's past is in this person's mind. Also a few glimpses of incidents that happened at an early age in one's life which the other did not know about, neither had they spoken about it – some small incidents, not some big event – now the other person simply knows about it, and asks, "Is it like this?" And the other person in surprise asks, "How do you know?" The karmas became all mixed up.

To experience this, people have to mature. There were many levels of resistance within them, many levels of strategies in their mind. If all strategies are dropped, if people can simply be, things can be done effortlessly. People have to bring themselves to that level of surrender or acceptance where they will simply do what's told, even if it is the most extreme thing, without any second thought about it. When people can be brought to this level, we can completely dissolve them altogether, but right now, the intention, or the goal, is not to liberate people just like that. We want them to make use of this energy so that they can take it to large groups of people. If it was about liberating just a small group of people, it's a very simple thing for me, but I don't want to settle for something like that.

Seeker: You had announced that you would be leaving your body at the age of forty-two, after the consecration of the Dhyanalinga, but fortunately, Sadhguru, you're still here among us. How did this miracle happen?

Sadhguru: A few years before the consecration happened, people who had been with me know this; my physical existence has always been a struggle. One day I was healthy, the next day I was finished. It had been like this, high and low. Retaining the body was a struggle. I had announced, almost seven years before the process started, that at the age of forty-two, retaining this body would be quite a challenge. The way it was going, I wouldn't have lasted beyond that, but eight months after starting the Dhyanalinga process, I stabilized the physical body in many ways by making use of the other two participants in the process. We achieved a body which would last, which might not go. This was in no way a desperate attempt to save somebody's life. That was not the purpose.

The purpose was to take life to the extreme point, where one can recreate his life; where, if he wants, he can choose the place of his birth, the womb that he wants to be born in. How it's possible for one to take the very process of life and death into one's hands, I feel needs to be demonstrated in society. People have completely lost touch with what inner capabilities they have, what potential a human being can carry within himself. Today, we see a large portion of society looking for stupid miracles; miracles to produce gold, this and that which will only deepen your suffering, your greed, your fear. Unfortunately, these things you call miracles. The biggest miracle is to play with life without allowing life to play with you. If one can go through life untouched, that's the greatest miracle anyone can achieve. That miracle, everybody can manifest in their lives. Right now, we have set the necessary foundation. How far each person goes, how far each person reaches, depends.

Seeker: You said, during the Dhyanalinga process, you went on a *karma yatra*[1] with those involved in the consecration. What's a karma yatra, Sadhguru? What was its purpose?

Sadhguru: This whole process was for the two people actively involved in consecrating the Dhyanalinga. During the process, it was found that there were certain karmic bondages, certain barriers, which were not allowing them to go beyond a certain point. That was why we went on this trip, to many places of past life significance like Orissa and Cuddapah, to name a few. We had never been to these places or seen them before in this life; you must understand this. I would just say there's a place like this – certain temples, old homes – describe them and tell these two people, "Let's go there." This is what happened in Raigarh in Madhya Pradesh. Until the last moment, I didn't know the name of the town. As we were driving down, I said, "The place we're looking for must be in Raigarh." Then we located Raigarh on the map and went there. When we went there, within minutes we were in this place that I had described earlier. It was such a powerful experience. These two people went through a fast forward of life, in a quick progression; so many events of their past life just happened.

1 *yatra*: travel, pilgrimage.

These events had happened three hundred and seventy years ago. Now, you go and make an enquiry; many facts we had already talked about to most of our meditators were confirmed by the people living there. We had never been there before in this life, but we knew. All those other places like Cudappah, Sambalpur, were like that. We knew exactly where to go, because once we started approaching that place, the vibrations were such that the past connection just pulled us there. In six days, we drove five thousand, two hundred kilometers. I would describe the place exactly before we would enter the town, so that doubts didn't arise in the minds of even these two people. They shouldn't think that they're only imagining those things. I would tell them how the vibrations would be, which chakra would get activated when you walk into the place, everything I would tell them, and it would be exactly the same in their experience; it couldn't be any different.

As I said the other day, I only wish everybody could have participated in a process like this. Every time, when we finished, we always felt this, "If only we could involve all the *bhramhacharis*,[1] how fantastic it would be," but it would be difficult to bring so many people to that level of involvement and understanding. It's not easy. Things were going like that and once we went for this karma yatra, it became a living experience for both of them. Wherever we went, actually those places were past lives only for one of them, not the other, but we chose those places because they were spiritually significant. We could have chosen so many other places where both their pasts were involved or where their pasts were separately involved, but we wanted to go to those places which were of spiritual significance. When we went there, the spiritual dimension became a living experience for both of them. So when they went through these kinds of processes, all the structures which were holding them were shaken loose. The consecration became very easy. Even before that, the urge to break the karmic bondage was there; sadhana was there towards that, but this acted like an extra boost.

Seeker: Vijji left her body before the end of the consecration process, leaving the energy triangle incomplete. How, then, did you continue with it, Sadhguru?

Sadhguru: Because my wife, Vijji, was part of the consecration process, for me in this life, the social situation was more conducive. Everything was going too well, like a dream. When things were going so well,

---

1 *bhramhachari*: One who is on the path of the Divine, who has formally been initiated into monkhood through a certain energy process.

especially with a process like this, I knew some impediment would come. Usually, the difficulty always came from social situations. So I instructed all the people around me to be extremely careful not to get into any kind of trouble anywhere; not to create any kind of resistance with anybody, because I knew something was coming. From which direction it would come, we were watching, and here it came. Vijji just dropped her body, and the consecration was left incomplete. She attained Mahasamadhi, and we were back to square one again. Ninety-five percent of the work was done. Just a little more time, in one more week, we would have completed the consecration, but now we got stuck. It took us another one-and-a-half years to finish the work.

Now I started playing both roles: hers and mine. This was like recreating another person with your energy. This is very hard to believe. She was gone, but we needed this person in that place because replacing her with another would be too difficult at that juncture of the work. To prepare another person, to bring another person to that level of sadhana, it would take any number of years. So I started recreating her energy-wise, and it became so much a reality that you could almost feel her and touch her. To that extent this person was re-created. When I sat in this process for four to five hours, by the end of it I came out totally drained, because with one person's energy, I was managing two bodies. It took such a big toll on me. You will notice if you see my pictures, in about eleven month's time, I aged about twenty-five to thirty years. I became old and sick. All kinds of bizarre diseases were there in my body. When they took my blood test in the United States, they couldn't believe it. The results were as if I had some devastating diseases in my body. I never took any treatment for that. I knew why it was happening, but I wanted a medical parameter as to what damage I was causing to my body. My liver was damaged, my heart was giving me trouble and my blood was in a bad state. They were predicting all kinds of cancers in my body. Suddenly, lumps would appear on my body and the next day would mysteriously disappear. People around me couldn't believe what was happening. The body was going through such turmoil. I thought, "Anyway, with consecration, we will close this body business," but because of certain people who stood there and gave their lives in a certain way, we went beyond that point. Even today, I am not one hundred percent okay. I have recovered to almost seventy to seventy-five percent. I never took any treatment; slowly we re-created the body. It's still not one hundred percent all right. Some amount of re-creation still needs to be done. Some parts of the energy body are destroyed, badly damaged.

Seeker: How could Vijji have left her body when the consecration process was so close to completion? Couldn't she have waited until it was over and then leave?

Sadhguru: Vijji was not an accomplished *yogi*. She did what she did with just the sheer intensity of her emotions. The last few months for her, every step, every breath, had become just 'Shambho'. She set forth towards this process in late July, and on the last three full moon days of December, January and February, she was to raise the pitch of her sadhana. As you know, the last two full moons, she cooked and served all at the ashram by her own hand. The consecration process, as it was going, was sure to be over before the 23rd of January,[1] but due to certain unavoidable social circumstances, that was not to be. What she thought would happen on the coming full moon day in the month of February, happened a month early. That day was a very special day in terms of the way energies were moving for this planet.

There was an exceedingly rare and archetypically appropriate planetary alignment, a moment in time expressed in the heavens as a perfect six-pointed star. This pattern comes on the exact day where three outer planets, Jupiter, Uranus and Neptune are conjoined together for the first time in almost two hundred years. On January 23rd, this cluster of planets centered on the first degree of Aquarius, joined by the Sun with the Full Moon opposite them all. This pattern may also be seen as a symbolic representation of the long heralded 'dawning of the Age of Aquarius'. It is also the *thaipoosam*, a day that many sages of the past had chosen for their own Mahasamadhi. Though on one level I knew this was coming, the situation around me and what was demanded out of me at that moment blocked my conscious cognition. Though her leaving was very much of conscious will, she had no moment to moment control over the life forces; but the last few minutes before she left, she was aware, and accommodated the dissolution of herself by removing all the jewelry that was on her body, as the metal would have been a hindrance. When the Divine descends, you just accommodate.

---

1 Vijji attained Mahasamadhi on 23rd January 1997.

Seeker: I heard, Sadhguru, that with a clap of your hand, you created a small hairline crack in the Dhyanalinga during the consecration. What was the purpose of this?

Sadhguru: During the process of consecration, in case I shed the body, we knew locking the energies would be a huge problem. We didn't want such a problem to happen. See, the Linga and the *gowripeeta* [1] are essentially two different types of stones. The Linga is the highest-density stone that can be found in Asia, over four-thousand-two-hundred-plus units. I have always kept it as a possibility that in case the consecration didn't happen as planned, the only way for me would be to merge into it and somebody else would have to lock the energies. Now, let's say we energized the Linga and there had been a delay in the locking of the energies; it would have been very much possible that the Linga, unable to contain the energies, would have opened up. As a safeguard against this, I effected a minute vertical crack in the Linga. You can't even chisel that stone; it is like steel. You can't work it with your hand, it can only be done with a machine, but we cracked it with just a clap. We went through many problems, but locking was not a problem; we did it very well. It is complete.

Now that it's complete, we can actually remove the stone Linga. It is not needed. The energy form is always there. The stone was used only as scaffolding for the process, but it has been fitted with certain mechanisms which make it very powerful in a different way. It is rooted in liquid mercury, and the core of the Linga has solidified mercury also. Modern chemistry doesn't have the technique to solidify mercury, but the traditional alchemy in India always solidified mercury through a technique called *rasa vaidya.* So the stone Linga has some significance, but that's not the main part. If we take it away, still nothing will change as far as the energy is concerned. As far as its power and ability to put people into meditative states is concerned, nothing will change. It will still feel the same way as it feels now. When you come and sit there, if you're sensitive, it will just shake you from the very root of your spine. Even if you don't know anything about meditation, just come and sit there; you will become meditative. That's how it has been made. It is an enormous tool, a unique mechanism.

---

1 *gowripeeta* : the base or the feminine portion of a Linga.

However, people need something to see visually; otherwise they would come here and ask, "You say there's a Dhyanalinga here, where is it?" So we're not going to remove it, because we spent a lot of money on it also! (Laughs). It is going to remain, but the Dhyanalinga is not about the stone that you see. An energy form has been consecrated, and properly locked. You can't kill it; even if you destroy the planet, you still can't kill it. That's how it's done. All those people who witnessed the various stages of consecration in those three and a half years are blessed. Many of them were absolutely ignorant; they didn't even know what was happening. Most of the time they were bewildered, looking at what was happening to somebody else, but still it didn't matter. Just being in that atmosphere has done many things to them. See, even now, when you sit here, somebody is blowing his top off; even if you don't have a clue as to what's happening, the energy around you does what it has to do. If you are open and allow it to happen, the impact would be much more, but anyway it has an impact; you can't escape it.

Seeker: Sadhguru, could you explain to us in a scientific manner the locking of the chakras?

Sadhguru: Hebbar, among all my disciples, the skeptic's skeptic, you had to ask this question! The consecration of the Dhyanalinga – the whole process was to create a very intense energy form; energy which is not really physical, but that of the spiritual or etheric body. Once the energy form is created you need to establish it with chakras, without which you cannot create that kind of form. With a single chakra you can create only one kind of form. Unless the seven chakras are there, you cannot create this form as we know it. So it has been created, but there's nothing to hold it because it has no karmic body. This is true with you also. Your form is not just of your physical body; the other bodies – mental, pranic, etheric and bliss bodies – have also taken this form. The subtler bodies are also in this form right now, and are held in place because of the karmic substance. If the karmic substance is taken away, then the inner two bodies, the deeper two bodies, the etheric body and the bliss body, will just melt and dissolve. It's like you carrying a bucket of water. Only because of the bucket, the water is separate from its source. The moment the bucket breaks, the water just falls back into the ocean and that's it.

We have created a certain energy form for the Dhyanalinga with the consecration process, but it has no karmic structure in the Linga, so the chakras have to be locked. If they're not locked, the energy will just dissipate. Very powerful energy, which has been revved up to the highest possible intensity, will just dissipate. It's not possible to maintain a form beyond that level of energy, and the dissipation will be even faster because it's at such a high pitch. So it's being locked with pranic substance, not with spiritual substance. It's locked with pranic substance, which is where the huge problem is with our own bodies; the pranic substance had to be used, and it doesn't have any tenacity unless there is karmic substance to it. Prana is still a physical aspect; without karma, the physical can't retain its form. So now, we have to create that kind of prana that has no karma in it. When you carry your body, it has karma in it. The very way your body is, is molded by your karmic substance; similarly with your mind, but it's more visible with your mind. With your mind, it is so clear that the karmic substance is influencing its functioning. The same is true with the pranic substance also. The way your karma is, your pranic substance is also.

Now, we did not want to put any prana with karmic substance into the Dhyanalinga, but at the same time, there is no tenacity to the energy you create, because without karma it would dissipate. Only because of karma, everything is in a form. I want you to understand, you are living only because of your karma. Only because it holds you in, you are alive as an individual. If it doesn't hold you in, you're gone. So that's what gives you the form, that's what makes you who you are right now, and that's the bondage also. People are not getting what spirituality is, because on one level they always enhance their karma, and on another, they want to destroy it. The urge to destroy it also becomes a way of establishing it.

The pranic substance in the Dhyanalinga was woven in a certain way. If the other two involved in the consecration were with me, I would have locked it with so much more ease. Because one person was missing, creating three threads of prana without karmic substance from three different bodies -taking it and weaving it and tying it up in a certain way - was difficult. So the karma is just these three pure aspects of prana without any karmic substance, and they're bound together. That binding is the karma. The three threads were actual nadis, one from Bharathi, one of mine and another also from me, but created in Vijji's flavor. Taking nadis out of one's system could be damaging. It had to be done with care, and elaborate precautions were taken to limit the damage. A whole process of reconstructing these nadis was undertaken, but still the damage it did to my body is not fully repaired. Though I ensured that this didn't happen to the others involved, with myself I couldn't manage it, as my role was multifunctional. This damage to the nadis is still manifesting in the form of many physiological problems.

There's no other karma in the energy. We didn't want to put our karma into the Dhyanalinga, whatever it may be; whether it's good or bad, that's not the point. We couldn't put our individual karma into the Linga. So the only way it can hold together is with the three different pranas taken together and bound together. Now the only karma they have is the bondage between the three, so that was used like a rope. If you want to understand it that way, it's like a rope you tie around the chakra wherever the intensity is focused, so it is locked. Just like tying it up one by one, all of it was tied from top to bottom. The main challenge was the lower chakras, the Swadhistana and the Muladhara. Since one person was missing, the process took an enormous toll on my body, weakening my Swadhistana and Muladhara. It was like I could leave at any moment.

When it came down to locking Swadhistana and Muladhara, it became a huge challenge. The Muladhara I locked, but the Swadhistana became a huge problem. When I locked the Swadhistana, I just fell, and there was every possibility that I could lose my body at that moment. I kept everything ready, to a point where I had arranged legal adoption for my daughter, the ashram – how it should be, how it should be maintained, everything was written down. I had the samadhi ready and I just asked them to park a vehicle outside. If I totally lose the body, that was fine, they knew how to handle it, but suppose I became incapacitated and I needed to be brought in, then the vehicle would be there. When I locked Swadhistana, it just knocked me off totally. I almost lost my body. They had to literally carry me, put me in the vehicle and take me to the shrine and then so much had to be done. For three days, I lost my speech, and I couldn't stand up. People had to help me stand up and sit down. Seeing me in that condition, they didn't think I would live. That was because pulling out these threads, pulling out your own nadis, trying to bind them to something and not taking your karma along with it, took its toll. That was not new to me, but doing it with other people and doing it with someone who wasn't there, that was the most difficult part.

Seeker: Sadhguru, why did you lock the chakras from top to bottom? And why did you lock Muladhara first before you locked Swadhistana?

Sadhguru: Now, the damage that had occurred to the lower two chakras in my system after Vijji's departure had left them very fragile, and like I said, there was every possibility that I could lose my body in the process of locking the energies during the consecration process. Locking the top chakras was more subtle, but that was not the problem for us. The lower chakras are more physically demanding. I didn't want to take the risk of leaving the upper chakras for the possible dissipation of energies in the event of any problem with the locking of the lower chakras. Here, we took the risk of slightly distorting the energy form of the Linga, but by Divine Grace, it happened in the best possible way. See, the Linga is a form of very intense energy, naturally seeking expansion. As the top four chakras were secured or locked, the bottom part of the Linga was tending to expand and lose form. After tying up Anahata, the next thing that I did was to tie the Muladhara. With the Muladhara secured, it gave us a little more time to tie the Manipuraka and Swadhistana. As it turned out, Swadhistana became the most challenging part. Swadhistana means the abode of the Self. Though the Muladhara is foundational, Swadhistana is key to one's rooting in the body.

Seeker: I understand that a mantra is a certain vibration, which in turn produces energy. In this context, Sadhguru, could you consecrate the Dhyanalinga using *mantras*?[1]

Sadhguru: Those of you who witnessed the consecration process saw that we didn't use any mantras. Our *poojas*[2] don't have any mantras either; it's a wonderful play of energies. Generally, all the energy in poojas is created with mantras. Here, we have no mantras. We don't care to use mantras. Everything is done with pure energy. You use the sound and generate energy; that is one way. Another way is: you simply have energy. You have energy to spill around, so you spill it and do things. That's a totally different way. That's also a kind of pooja, if you can call it that. It's a process where there are no mantras, but the energy is there. Actually when we say *Muladhara, Swadhistana* or *Manipuraka*, each one has a mantra.

---

1 *mantras: a syllable or a pure sound.*

2 *poojas: worship, appropriate procedure for invocation of the Divine.*

There are mantras attached to each chakra. Using the proper mantras you can activate the chakra, but we never use mantras. We simply use energy. Simply direct force, as it is. This is a completely different path and attitude. It's a different dimension of sadhana altogether. In the yogic culture, especially on the Shaiva path, which is a mixture of yoga and *tantra,*[1] both these things are mixed in a way.

Now, this whole science of sound and form – the name-form relationship – is known as mantra. A mantra means a pure sound. If you feed any sound into an oscilloscope, depending on its frequency, amplitude and other aspects of the sound, it gives out a certain form. Every sound has a form attached to it. Similarly, every form has a sound attached to it. The sound is known as mantra. The corresponding form is known as yantra. The technique of using these two things together is known as tantra. So 'mantra, yantra, tantra' means 'sound, form and technique', the technology of creating powerful energy forms. This is a very deep science by itself.

Seeker: Sadhguru, what is the significance of having three people for the consecration process?

Sadhguru: I actually wanted to involve fourteen people in the consecration, seven Idas and seven Pingalas. Creating fourteen people that can just merge into one whole is not easy, but if that had been achieved, then the rest would have been so simple and safe. If you can create more people, multiples of seven, let's say we create twenty-eight, it would have become easier still; but do you know what a huge, huge dream it is? To create twenty-eight people who are in body, mind and emotion, like one, is such a challenge (laughs). To have two people merging into one was not simple either. There are so many deep layers of resistance in people. I literally tore through their karma, kept it aside, and put them together; otherwise, there was no way these people could have come together. They were willing to become friends; beyond that they wouldn't go. Is there anybody with whom you're willing to merge and become one? It is not so, you just believe it at certain moments, but it's not so.

---

1 *tantra* : the science of using mantra, the sound, and yantra, the form. Refers to an esoteric Indian spiritual tradition.

Seeker: Sadhguru, you had chosen two people that were diametrically opposite to each other. Why was that?

Sadhguru: To represent different dimensions of life. If they were the same type, there would have been no balance. In evenness, there's no balance. It's always in unevenness that there's balance. Suppose we choose two highly emotional people; they won't be able to do much. They will only go in one direction. They won't hold two ends of the triangle. If they have to hold the two ends of the triangle, they must be two completely different kinds of people. Even to put these two kinds of people together was impossible. That's why I said it's a more drastic step. Suppose we had chosen fourteen, we would have chosen seven different qualities in fourteen different people. Now they need not be opposites, they can be alike; it is very easy to match them, but here, these two people were complete opposites. Normally, they couldn't even sit together, because they were in two totally different worlds. Now, you have to merge them together. One was pure logic, the other was pure emotion. Though they did wonderfully together when we were in the consecration process, they didn't go out of their way during other times to make it easy for me. I enjoyed it all, it was a huge challenge (laughs).

Seeker: Sadhguru, you have told all of us Vijji is no more; she truly is no more. But, at times, when we needed her to form the triangle during the consecration process, I very clearly felt her there, like almost physically present. I want to know how this was possible.

Sadhguru: Even if the flower is no more, still, the fragrance can be. And the fragrance of this flower is forever; it's never lost. It's just that it may get mixed up with so many other smells and you may not be sensitive enough to feel it; but, once it enters the air, it's always there in a certain way. The physical fragrance may die, but the energy fragrance that we're talking about can't be killed. Now, Sadhguru Shri Bhramha left his body up there on the mountain. That person is no more in the sense that he is in some other form now; but even today, if you go there, that energy is not dead in any way, isn't it? It is still very much there, and it has kept its quality. Here, the quality or the energy is different. So when it comes to Vijji, she's truly no more. We know what kind of energy she carried; that fragrance is definitely felt, even today. You can't exorcise her fragrance, it is impossible, but she can't come and do anything; there is no 'she' anymore.

We can easily create a person on the energy level. If you're willing, if you sit in front of the Dhyanalinga, you will see that it's a whole person. It's not just something vibrating, or some meditative energy, nothing like that. It's a whole person with all the seven chakras at their peak. I am surprised you asked this question now, because just four or five days ago, you saw me creating a person or the energy of a whole person, just like that. In two minutes, I had a new person going. In that sense, we can create Vijji, we can create Gautama Buddha, we can create anybody. If we know the fragrance of what that person is; the energy body can be created.

If you want to create an actual physical body, that's also possible, but then you have to get into the five elements and meddle with them, which is a deep binding karmic factor. Once you get into the five elements, then you can't do something and leave it like that; it entangles with your self in so many ways. That leads you into a different sphere of life altogether, but even that is not impossible. It's very much possible. We can re-create that physical body also, but it serves no spiritual purpose. It is only to fulfill your attachments, which is not the right thing to do. You get deeply entangled if you meddle with the five elements. Even the existing five elements in the body, which is your physical body, if you get too involved with them, you get entangled. When you do this kind of work, of meddling with the elements on that level, your entanglement will be very, very deep, which is unnecessary; but on the energy level, you can play this game and get away with it without any entanglement. This can also become a very big bondage if you don't approach it with the right kind of dispassion. Above all, you need insulation. If you know how to create insulation for yourself, you can play games without the games becoming a part of you. If you don't create the right kind of insulation, it can become a deeply entangling process.

Seeker: Sadhguru, you said that during the consecration process, you actually trapped a disembodied being, and he became a part of the Dhyanalinga…

Sadhguru: When we were consecrating the Dhyanalinga, there was no temple structure as yet. It was in the open air. We were using various people in different states to consecrate the seven chakras of the Dhyanalinga. See, it is easy to get people to do sadhana on Ajna or Anahata, but when it comes to the

Vishuddhi chakra, located at the pit of the throat, which is also the power center, sadhana is very difficult. If we start sadhana on Vishuddhi with people, we need a completely different kind of atmosphere to maintain them. Their ways will be very different; they won't fit into the social structure. They will be of a completely different nature and energy. We usually don't encourage sadhana on Vishuddhi, because people become unnecessarily powerful. Power without the necessary balance can be self-destructive and also destructive to the world. Unless a person is at a certain level of accomplishment and balance, beyond certain aspects of life, we never put him on Vishuddhi sadhana.

So we didn't have anybody that we could use for Vishuddhi consecration and time was passing by. Because there was no other way in that short span of time, I used a yogi with a certain accomplishment, who was beyond his physical body. He was a disembodied being, looking for dissolution. This might sound unbelievable to you. It was late night on an *amavasya*[1] and over five hundred or six hundred people were witness to this process. Do you know that people use either lemons, eggs, coconuts or sesame balls as a medium to trap certain beings? We used a coconut in a certain way to trap this being and do what we had to do. He was being willingly trapped, not unwillingly. Once he realized how he was going to be used, he was more than willing. Once we set the coconut in a particular place, a little snake, about two feet long, crawled over there. Many times I picked it up and placed it somewhere else, but in a little while, it was back again. It wanted to be there. Snakes always get drawn to that kind of energy. So, we actually trapped this yogi, made him into pure energy and put him in the Vishuddhi chakra. He became a part of the Dhyanalinga. Even now, that's how the Vishuddhi is vibrating in the Dhyanalinga. That night, when that situation happened, people who were there didn't know what hit them; it was a very powerful experience.

Seeker: Sadhguru, is it okay to trap somebody like that?

Sadhguru: Hebbar, you are asking is it okay? As long as something is serving the purpose of liberating people, everything is okay with me. Just about anything is okay with me. I'm not somebody who is coming from some value structure, or ethics, or morals. What I'm saying may sound dangerous to you,

---

1 *amavasya* : the new moon.

but anybody who is on the path, this is how they are. Only good people, who are claiming to be spiritual, peddling solace in the world, only such people will say, "This is not okay; that's not okay".

For example, to make one man attain, Krishna is setting the price of ten thousand people's lives. In the Mahabharatha war, Arjuna asks Krishna, "What will I do killing all these people? Whether I become a king or a realized being, what's the point?" Krishna says, "It is okay. If you slaughter ten thousand people and if one man can attain, it is still worthwhile." That's the value he sets; the value it holds in terms of true life. If one person can realize, whatever price you pay in terms of life is not a problem; it is still worthwhile, because this is going to be forever. That fool whom you might have saved by not killing him in the war is going to just live for another thirty or forty years and die as an ignorant person; but once somebody transcends his physical limitations and functions out of his Realization, that person's work is eternal.

Even if you destroy the planet, break it into pieces, you still can't destroy this process or his work. This I can say about the Dhyanalinga also. Someday, if this planet falls apart, still the energy won't be destroyed. The Dhyanalinga is not in the stone; it's an energy form, and you cannot destroy it. If the planet disappears, still that form will be there, forever and ever. It is so. So the work of people who function beyond the physical is always eternal. If you work with your body, whatever you do, it can be wiped out tomorrow. If you work with your mind, the life span of your work is a little more. If you work with your prana, it's much more, but still that will also die, but if you work with that dimension which is beyond the physical, it's forever. To me, Gautama, the Buddha, or Patanjali[1] are not two thousand five hundred years ago, or five thousand years ago. As far as I am concerned, they are now, here, because for me they are always available, or at least their work is always available. I never read any scriptures written in their names, but everything that they did is just right here.

Seeker: So how do you trap a being, first of all, Sadhguru?

Sadhguru: Hebbar, just how we trapped you, just like that! (Laughs). What's my problem whether you have a body or you don't have one?

---

1 Patanjali: considered the father of yogic sciences.

Seeker: It does make a difference, Sadhguru, doesn't it?

Sadhguru: Not really.

Seeker: Master, just by attracting him to your energies…

Sadhguru: Yeah! See, what's my problem if you don't have a body? I don't even have to feed you. Life would be so much simpler (laughs).

Seeker: Does that mean, Sadhguru, that he doesn't have any choice? Now, if he's trapped in the Dhyanalinga, is there any possible evolution for him or is he just there…

Sadhguru: There's no 'he' anymore.

Seeker: What would you like to call him then, Sadhguru?

Sadhguru: There's no 'he' anymore. See, you need to understand this. When you do any sadhana, proper sadhana, you're moving away from your physical identification. First thing is, 'he' or 'she' comes from gender identification. You're identified with your body, your reproductive organs; that's why you are a 'he' or 'she'. Isn't it? As you do sadhana, you're not only moving away from your gender, you're also moving away from everything that you call as 'individual'. Now, when I say 'individual', it doesn't mean the way you think, "I am universal; I am God; I am this or that." That's not the point. You thinking, "I am universal," is very individual. In the West, this has become a huge fad now. Everybody claiming that I am an embodiment of God, I am Cosmic energy – it has become a huge madness in the new-age groups. So that doesn't take you anywhere away from your individuality. You're just trying to decorate your individuality with whatever words come to you: Cosmic, God, Son of God, Divine, Unbounded, whatever you call it. All these things are decorations to your individuality. In no way has your individuality disappeared even a little bit. In fact, with decoration, it enhances itself. That's all that happens, but by your very sadhana, your individual nature slowly recedes.

When you ask, "Is he trapped?" there's no 'he' as such. There was a 'he' when we caught him, but when we put him there, when the Vishuddhi was consecrated, there was no 'he' anymore. It's like somebody was making a pot, a mud pot. The pot was done, but not burnt yet. I took it and again made it into mud, and then again made a Linga out of it. That's how it is. You're thinking in terms of, "Oh! That person, is he trapped there? What will happen to him? What about his evolution?" There is no 'him' anymore. I just made him into the Dhyanalinga. It's just that we used this energy which was going around like a fool, as an individual. I destroyed his individuality and merged him into the Dhyanalinga. So there is no 'him' really, but that's how far language can go. Whichever way I say it, it says the same thing.

Seeker: So Master, can you say he's dissolved?

Sadhguru: Not dissolved. We established it as a particular quality, and merged it into the Dhyanalinga. Dissolution means no quality. This still has a quality. It's the quality of the Vishuddhi. The man was already powerful in the Vishuddhi, so we made use of him. We could have done it without him also. See, I could have just taken this tree, worked on it for a long time and made it into powerful Vishuddhi. It's possible, but it is an elaborate thing to do. This man was already evolved into the Vishuddhi. It was much simpler to work with him.

Seeker: So the idea of dissolution for this being doesn't arise, Sadhguru? There will be no dissolution?

Sadhguru: That doesn't arise for the whole Dhyanalinga, not just for the Vishuddhi alone. For the whole Dhyanalinga there is no dissolution. In a way, Shiva himself is trapped, if you want to look at it like that, but that's not how it is. If a form was bound by karmic substance as your form is, slowly as karma wears off, dissolution would have happened, but the Linga form is not held together by the karmic substance, so there is no possibility of dissolution. For the whole Dhyanalinga, there's no dissolution. See, I am telling you, even if the creation disappears, still it won't go. It has been made like that. The karmic substance has been taken away and another system has been used to create the energy form and establish it. Only when there's a karmic substance, you can pull the plug on the karma and it dissolves. Now, karma has been taken away, or there's no karma for it and still it has a form, so it can't dissolve. The question of dissolution doesn't arise. Not just for Vishuddhi; it is so for all the seven chakras.

Seeker: Master, this being, the disembodied being, had a karmic structure, right? Was it taken away?

Sadhguru: It was taken, not taken away. There's a difference. It was taken, not broken. If the karmic structure is broken, it will dissolve. See, he still had other chakras. Right now, let's say you're here. The most powerful chakra in you is Vishuddhi. Seventy percent of your life revolves around your Vishuddhi, but another thirty percent is still there, functioning in the remaining six chakras. Only because of that, you still hold a form. Just with Vishuddhi, you cannot hold a form. So now, we convert the remaining thirty percent also into Vishuddhi. Everything becomes Vishuddhi, and the little karma that's holding it together is taken, not broken.

Seeker: It has to go somewhere, right Sadhguru?

Sadhguru: It has to go somewhere.

Seeker: You took it on yourself and dissolved it, Master?

Sadhguru: Where else to take it? Shall I put it on you? Where else to take it? When it's taken, we just take it. It is not necessarily dissolved immediately; the process of life will work it out.

Seeker: Sadhguru, for Vishuddhi, you used this disembodied being, but what about the other chakras? Did you use somebody else's energy?

Sadhguru: This needs to be understood. The spiritual body doesn't really have chakras. Your own spiritual body, the etheric body, doesn't really have chakras. It is only the energy body, the pranic body that has chakras in it. So, the Cosmic energy that descends in the form of the Linga, which was made possible with this triangle formation, was just drawn down. That doesn't have chakras. That doesn't have anything, but it has to be held through the chakras. The chakras are created by prana. When we were locking the chakras, that was the time when they were created with the energy taken from the people who were consecrating it. So this is like a little bit of pranic body minus the normal karmic material. The only karma it has is that of the three nadis of three different energy systems which are bound together.

That bondage is the karma. There is no other karma in it. So the chakras exist only in the pranic body. If the pranic body is not there, the spiritual body cannot tie itself. When it can't hold a form, it just dissolves. So what you are calling as a chakra in the Dhyanalinga is pranic; the rest is just the etheric body. That's why he's so vibrant, because what holds him is just seven points. The rest is all... just absolute vibrancy. With you, what holds you down is not just seven points; it is a million different points.

Seeker: Sadhguru, has anything ever been written about the science of creating a Dhyanalinga?

Sadhguru: Nowhere really, except it finds mention in just one sentence in the Rig Veda, where it says that the Dhyanalinga will be successfully created only by a *grihastha*[1] yogi. Any number of yogis have attempted this, but it didn't happen.

Seeker: All this knowledge that you have about the science of making a Dhyanalinga is just because your Guru touched your forehead with his staff?

Sadhguru: Yes, it had come through that staff. People who were involved and witness to the Dhyanalinga consecration could clearly see that it involved very complex processes; and I am not a spiritually educated person. I have never been to anybody to study anything, but people who saw me then clearly knew that I was crystal clear about what I was doing, absolutely clear. Not the kind of clarity that comes from thought, but the kind of clarity that comes from an inner knowing. Whenever the need to know any dimension of life presented itself, at that moment, the answers were always there within me. Life has always been like that for me.

---

1 *grihastha*: a householder.

Seeker: Sadhguru, if one is under the negative influence of the occult, would the Dhyanalinga be of help?

Sadhguru: Many of you may not have not noticed this, but there are the Vanashree[1] and Patanjali shrines at the entrance of the temple. They are in the space of a fifteen-degree angle from the Dhyanalinga. That's why they are located at that point. Otherwise, architecturally, I would have liked to locate them much closer. Generally, people who are possessed by some spirits or who are impacted by the occult and such problems are asked to sit either in a forward fifteen degree angle or a rear side fifteen degree angle, depending upon the type of problem that they have.

That space has been especially created like that so that people can make use of it. Whether you're aware of it or not, the negative use of energy like black magic and others is there. The fifteen-degree angle is where the doorway is. Whether you know it or not, everyone who enters just drops the negative influences they are carrying. There have been thousands who have dropped such influences. That's why people who have been to the temple find that suddenly life has changed for them. This is because the negative impacts on their life have dropped. When we say 'negative impacts', it's not necessarily in terms of somebody doing something negative to you. In so many ways, you could have just taken in some negativity. See, it's not necessary that somebody should poison this fruit. The fruit might have some natural poison in it, which enters my body when I eat it. Similarly, the negative aspects of life can enter you in so many ways. It is not necessary that somebody is sitting there and plotting against you. So the entrance of the temple, the first fifteen-degree angle, is created for this purpose, and before people seek anything else, these things are just taken care of. They just have to walk in that space, about sixty or seventy feet, and that by itself takes care of these negativities.

Usually in Shiva temples, they create a separate occult temple where a Bhairava[2], Bhoothnath[3] or some other fierce form of Shiva or Shakthi is consecrated. You have to go there first; only then you go to Shiva. The idea is, if you have such negativities, you get them cleared, and only then you go on to

---

1 Vanashree: lit. the deity of the Forest, name of the feminine deity in the form of a tree at the Dhyanalinga temple.

2 Bhairava: a fierce form of Shiva.

3 Bhoothnath: master of five elements – another form of Shiva.

experience a highly positive energy. Here, the very way the temple structure is – and the very way people walk into the temple – is a complete process, so we have not established a separate occult temple; but I could establish a separate occult temple one or two years before I leave. We have created a small space for that in the outer parikrama. It's more as a safeguard to ensure that people don't misuse the Dhyanalinga temple in the future.

When we went on the karma yatra, somebody took me to a Shiva temple - a very powerful and beautiful place, totally abandoned, next to the river Mahanadi. It is a totally uninhabited area, but some king had built this wonderful temple there. All kinds of people who do negative work just come and camp in the temple for many months. Nobody dares to go near them, because these people are so fierce; they have an enormous presence about them. Very negative, but a very powerful presence they have about themselves. So they landed up and they used the temple in whichever way they wanted. They would do animal sacrifices, and all sorts of things. They're just trying to use this positive energy to acquire powers and things like that. They totally distorted the temple with their misuse. So, when the temple trustees knew that I was coming, they approached me and said, "There is nobody to correct this temple. You must come." Then I spent the day there, sort of, setting the temple right.

Seeker: Are you saying Sadhguru, the presence of the occult temple will…?

Sadhguru: Will take care of that. They can't misuse the energies of the main temple. That's why when they build very powerful temples they also build an occult temple on the outer periphery which can be used by people who want to practice that art. They don't want the main temple to be used. This occult temple will be of a different nature, but they won't use it because they can easily set up an occult temple of their own. Consecrating an occult temple is of a totally different nature. Those who are well versed in those arts can easily do that, but putting the Dhyanalinga together is beyond them. The idea is to ensure that Dhyanalinga is not ever used for negative purposes, but at the same time not denying the occult, allowing a possibility for that also.

Seeker: Master, would the occult temple be a place that everybody could visit? Would it be beneficial to go to that place?

Sadhguru: Yes, it will be beneficial. See, for certain types of diseases and for a few other influences, generally there will be a certain temple outside the main temple. At times, even animal sacrifices are allowed there. There are many such temples. We could take you to such temples. Do you want to go?

Seeker: (Shocked) And see animal sacrifice, Sadhguru!?

Sadhguru: When you sacrifice an animal, there is a sudden release of energy. That's what you're causing with death; and the people who perform these sacrifices know how to use that. It's a very negative art, but it is there. What, Peter? Why are you shaking your head and looking so shocked? Don't you wage wars?

Seeker: Me? If I had a choice? No! No!

Sadhguru: (Laughs).

Seeker: Sadhguru, can the energies of the Dhyanalinga get distorted over a period of time?

Sadhguru: The Dhyanalinga won't get distorted because the consecration is of a different nature altogether. See, many temples, unfortunately, are receding because of improper maintenance. Receding energy causes damage to human life. Lingas which have been consecrated with mantras need constant rejuvenation. They are energized, but they are constantly dissipating. They have always told you, if you have a stone idol in your house, every day pooja must happen. If an idol gets damaged, or if you don't take care of it, the energy will start receding. If you keep idols with receding energies in your house, it will start sucking people in and it will cause harm to you. It's not good to be around such energies. In the tradition, they have always told you that even if a little bit of damage occurs to the idol, you should throw it into a river or a well, because receding energies are not good for people.

The uniqueness of the Dhyanalinga is that the energies have been taken to a certain peak and locked properly. It doesn't need any maintenance. For five thousand years, if you don't take care of it, it will still remain the same. It doesn't need any pooja. It doesn't need any *abhisheka.*[1] It doesn't need any mantras. It doesn't need any kind of recharging processes. It's a perennial source of energy. It will always remain so. There is no question of the Dhyanalinga becoming a receding energy or a distorted energy. It's just that we don't want it to be misused. Especially when occult people find a place like this, which can't recede or be distorted, they may come and invade the place. Suppose there's a strong occult cult growing somewhere, the first thing they will know is that there's a place like this. They all know about the Dhyanalinga by now. That's for sure, no question about it. You go to any occult person, he will know.

See, this incident occurred when we were nearing the completion of the Dhyanalinga consecration, when Vijji was still with us. Bharathi met a saint called Venkanna Babu. He was a totally uneducated man. When he saw them, the first thing he said was, "What your Guru is doing is too incredible. It is happening wonderfully, but it won't happen as easily as you think. It will take its toll." Nobody had ever told him about the Dhyanalinga; he just knew. Just a week after that, Vijji left her body. All those who are deeply into occult, all those cats will know the existence of the Dhyanalinga. They don't have to hear about it through somebody. It will always be their intention to use a place like that in some way. It makes their sadhana so much easier. They will know exactly how to make use of it.

Seeker: Sadhguru, what's the difference between a *Jyotir Linga*[2] and the Dhyanalinga?

Sadhguru: The Dhyanalinga is purely for meditative purposes. There are other benefits, but that's not the reason why it has been created. See, what are the benefits that you're normally seeking? Well-being, health, prosperity, all these aspects are just for survival, isn't it? What I say is, if it is survival, take care of it to the extent your brains allow. If you're seeking something else, only then you talk about the Divine.

1 *abhisheka* : sprinkling or pouring of water, milk, etc.
2 Jyotir Linga : a Linga of fire or light.

The survival part, just use your limbs and brains and do it; that's enough. You don't have to use God for your survival. That's too much survival; you're too focused on your survival. Jyotir Lingas were created more for general well-being than for anything else. I had wanted to go to Ujjain, which has one of the Jyotir Lingas, for a long time; that was a place my Guru had visited. I went there. This temple has been destroyed twice by the Muslim invaders; the inner temple is totally gone. Somebody saved the Linga by putting it underground, otherwise the invaders would have broken that too. An ordinary modern temple stands in place of the old one, which was destroyed.

I entered the temple. It almost dislodged me from my body. The place is so powerful. I didn't expect it at all. I became sick right there, started running a high temperature. It took me three days to recover. The place just knocked me off; you would not believe it. I became completely loose, almost like I was leaving the body. People with me got really scared. They had seen me in very extreme states, but there are states where the safety limits are crossed, and here it was very much so. It was so powerful; just the temple was unbelievable. For my kind of body, with certain parts of my energy body in complete disarray after the consecration process, I would need a certain preparation to enter such spaces. My energies are always trying to jump the body; they are on the edge. I don't go to the Dhyanalinga too often when I am at the yoga center. I don't want to go there because it's not a very good thing for me. The Dhyanalinga has all the seven chakras, so it is not like the Ujjain temple. Though the Dhyanalinga is more balanced, it still pulls me out. I would like to go there every day, but I don't. Once in a while I go and even then I never meditate in the Dhyanalinga temple. I just look around.

Seeker: You said there is one Dhyanalinga in Bhopal which came close to completion. Why wasn't it completed, Sadhguru?

Sadhguru: Just a little over a thousand years ago, an attempt to create a Dhyanalinga came close to completion and failed in Bhojpur, somewhere about twenty-five or thirty kilometers from Bhopal. A large part of the temple work was completed and then abandoned. Even the consecration work, ninety percent of it was completed. This particular yogi, an accomplished person, prepared fourteen people, seven men and seven women, to represent the Ida and Pingala. He worked with them for many years and brought them to a certain level of energy. He had the support of a king who built a beautiful temple as an ornament for the Dhyanalinga. It is still incomplete, a half-built temple, very beautifully structured. The local story is, it seems that they started the final stage of the consecration in the evening. They had to complete it before the morning, but when the rooster crowed in the early morning, the process was still not completed and they stopped the work; that's how it goes. They did this work in the year 992 and the instructions they gave still hold today. It is so, in Bhojpur, even today, pooja is not done for this Linga. People simply offer flowers and coconuts. The coconuts are not broken inside the temple. There's no lamp either. It's a huge Linga, almost the same proportion as the Dhyanalinga, except that the gowripeeta is bigger there, it's more than eighteen feet. They built the temple halfway and started consecrating the Linga. As the consecration neared completion, one of the women who was involved in the consecration process left her body. The temptation to leave the body is so much, because here, you have an opportunity where your contact with the body is so minimal; with little effort, you can leave it. It's absolute dissolution.

Suppose you're driving on the highway, let us say from Coimbatore to Bombay. You drive, maybe over thirty hours; Bombay city limits start approaching. Now, at the outskirts of the city is where most of the accidents happen because, "Oh! At last we're there!" Something in you slackens. When you were driving on the highway, you wanted to reach the destination, so you were going with a certain sense of awareness. Now that you're nearing, "Oh! We're here!" slackens something in you. That's the time, due to lack of alertness, most of the accidents happen on the highways. Similarly, for the Bhopal Linga too, ninety percent of the work was done. It was a saga of many years of work; people were euphoric, and this temptation of wanting to leave the body was so high. You have come to a certain mastery within yourself, where you're able to keep a minimal contact with the body and be there steadily. Just a little more and you could flip the body off.

Years of work were now coming to completion. One of the women involved in the consecration process left the body, and the process ran into trouble. Then the yogi decided to play both the roles of being a man and a woman using his Ida and Pingala, which is an enormous stress on the system. He played this role and he would have completed the process, because what was left was very little. At that time certain violence - some invasion - happened, and his left foot was chopped off. Once his left foot was gone, his Ida didn't function any more; only the Pingala could work. He couldn't play this double role and the whole process got stuck again. Then, making certain adjustments, they decided that the *yogi* and another woman would just shed their bodies, merge into the Linga and complete the consecration. So they trained another *yogi* to lock the energies the moment it was fully energized.

These are the two different aspects involved in the consecration. One thing is to take it to the peak of energy. Another thing is to lock it. If you don't lock it, it will dissipate. Now, these two people merged into it. The Linga was fully energized, but the other *yogi* could not lock it on time. One thing was, the situation was so overwhelming. Your Guru, your Master, your life and breath, dropped his body. You were sitting there watching. You were supposed to do these things properly. It was too overwhelming; he couldn't do it. Immediately, the Linga cracked vertically through; a three to four inch crack appeared. Those of you who have been there have seen that the crack is plastered with cement. The whole project was abandoned. It was ninety-five percent done, but is a painful form. Two people gave their lives. They had done so much work on it, but it had not been fulfilled. It's very powerful, but very tragic. The Linga just remains like that, very powerful, but slightly distorted. The energy is not receding. If it had been consecrated with mantras, it would have receded by now. A thousand years is a lot of time, but it hasn't receded. The Linga stayed there, incomplete, broken.

If you go there, if you're sensitive, if you just sit there, you will see, tears of pain will simply come into your eyes. Not of joy. A certain pain will come into you, because the Linga got distorted, the energy got distorted, but since it was so well established, almost to completion, it's not totally dead. It is still alive. If it dies totally it will just become stone, but right now it is alive, but in a distorted state. As we were nearing the temple by car, some eight or nine kilometers away, I had unbearable pain written on my face. People had to hold me; like that I had become. I knew I was close to the temple and somewhere, something was wrong. When we reached there, I couldn't get out of the car; I was in that condition, totally finished, so much pain, unbearable pain in my spine. My left foot was also totally cold, as if it had been put in cold water, but the other foot was perfectly normal. It took some time for me to make it all right. When I went there, my body couldn't take it. If you're sensitive, it affects your body and at the same time, it is tremendous – very, very powerful. It will just twist you inside; it's a very tragic Linga.

That was some experience, a very powerful experience. For all of us who went there, there was tremendous pain in the spine, as if it had been crushed. Bharathi almost left the body, became almost out of hand. Somehow, we put her back together.

We were aware that these things could happen to us also. I had always planned my life in such a way that the moment the Dhyanalinga was done, I would leave the body. That's how it was always planned. That's one of the main reasons why nobody has heard of me in this country, because I never planned to propagate myself. I always planned to leave after the Dhyanalinga was complete.

Seeker: Does it mean, Sadhguru, that everytime you go to some place you relive everything that happened there?

Sadhguru: If it's worth knowing, yes.

Seeker: Sadhguru, you said that the energy in the Bhopal Linga is distorted. So people who go and sit there, isn't their energy affected or distorted in some way?

Sadhguru: How many people really go to sit and meditate? Distorted doesn't mean everything about it has gone bad. As I said, when Bharathi sat, it immediately became a very spiritual process for her. The Linga is still active, but so many aspects of it have gone out of shape because the locking didn't happen properly. Other parts of it are intact. So it's not all about the distortion, but definitely that may cause a little pain. If Tina goes there, she will cause a flood! (Laughs).

Seeker: You say that ninety-five percent of the consecration process was completed. What about the energy there; is it locked? Can nothing be done about it, Sadhguru?

Sadhguru: Yes, mostly. It got distorted because it was not properly locked. Something can be done, but it is too much work. Who is going to go there and do it? Where are the people to do it? You have to prepare people to stay there and do whatever is needed.

Seeker: But wouldn't it have been easier - I don't know, Sadhguru, I am just asking - to continue this one instead of starting a whole new Dhyanalinga from the beginning?

Sadhguru: It would have been more difficult than creating a new one and who would allow you to do it? It is owned by the archaeological society. Why would they allow you to do anything? We wanted to spend the night there, but they wouldn't allow us.

Seeker: What do you mean by distorted, Sadhguru?

Sadhguru: See, it is just like this: in a certain structure, some reinforcement is needed to give it a proper shape. Suppose the reinforcement is not proper at one point; the structure will start getting distorted.

Seeker: Does this mean, Sadhguru, that the people who are in the sphere of that Linga will experience distorted energy in terms of their emotions and mental well-being?

Sadhguru: Yes. When Bharathi went and sat there, she didn't realize what was happening to her. She just thought she had sat there for two or three minutes, but actually she was there for over forty-five minutes. I became very concerned that she could leave her body. Her energy became like a proper channel. If I had just left her there, that day she would have left. All the people there gathered around us and I started knocking on her *Ajna*[1] and doing many things to pull her back. Because of the situation, it was not possible to do anything more subtle. It took almost forty-five minutes to bring her back. When she sat there, she didn't realize what was happening. The situation started to build up. That moment for her was just like when she was sitting for the Dhyanalinga consecration process. So if people who are in a certain state of openness sit there, they might get pulled out. For her it was working well, as a Linga should, but for me it was painful. Once I pulled her back, it became very painful for her also. It wasn't pain in the usual sense. It was like a distortion.

---

1 *Ajna* : lit. command center. Located between the eyebrows, it is also known as the 'third eye'.

Seeker: Sadhguru, when we were traveling with you on the train on the way to the Himalayas, as we went through Bhopal, you recreated the energy of the Bhopal Linga in the train compartment. This seemed to be too incredible, because you said that it took you three lifetimes to create the Dhyanalinga at Isha…

Sadhguru: We did create the energy of the Linga in the railway compartment. See, if we want to create a new Dhyanalinga now, I can do it in an hour, but it won't last; the energy will dissipate. With the support of a form or without it, I can create one now, but within a few hours the energy will dissipate. Usually, people who use Lingas for occult purposes create one every time they need it. If they want to do some kind of process they create one, and it just lasts for an hour or two. That's enough for them. They just use it at that moment and it is over; and again when they need it, they will create another one. But creating the Dhyanalinga, which is going to last forever, has taken lifetimes of effort.

When we were in Bhopal, the Linga was probably ten to twelve kilometers away. The energies of the Bhopal Linga were created to last forever. So me recreating it in a railway compartment seems crazy. How can I say it? I am always doing everything possible to make people understand and realize that the highest dimension of life is also the simplest. You can approach it either with great seriousness or with utmost playfulness. Every human being can walk on the street like a Dhyanalinga, with all his seven chakras vibrant and at their peak. We should see a day like this in the world, where lots of people are like this. That would be wonderful (laughs). The question is not about what gods or rituals you're into; the question is just about how fluid you have become. From being a solid persona you need to become very fluid and malleable.

Being playful is always misunderstood as being loose, or not paying enough attention, but you can never play any game unless your attention is one hundred percent. Playfulness has come not because you're not involved, but because you're not serious about the game. This morning someone asked me, "If I am not identified with what I am doing, can I really give myself?" Only if you're playful can you really give yourself. People always understand that to be playful means you're not being involved, you are lax. You cannot be lax in a game; if you're playing, you have to be absolutely involved; otherwise, you will never know what a game is. If for a moment there's no involvement, the game is lost. So this energy could be recreated anywhere at any moment. The whole struggle was to create it in a particular way so that it will be everlasting. Creating a Linga could be done right now in the railroad compartment, but to make this energy everlasting takes something else.

Seeker: Similarly, can another yogi somewhere else create the energy structure of our Dhyanalinga for his disciples and make them experience it, Master?

Sadhguru: Definitely. If there are people of that caliber, they definitely can. There is no question about it. A few people who had never been to the Dhyanalinga, or even heard of it, have spoken very authoritatively about it. This is because these people know what it is and are able to see it the way it is. To create it for a few hours – there should be many who can do it, but to make it an eternal possibility is a huge challenge.

Seeker: Sadhguru, what is the difference, if any, between you and the Dhyanalinga?

Sadhguru: There's no difference. It's just that I still have the problems of eating and sleeping. He doesn't. Otherwise, there's no difference, except that I can walk; he can't (laughs). Now, what you're referring to as the Dhyanalinga is the highest possible subtle body. It is at its peak vibration with all the seven chakras intact. It was consecrated by creating a certain vortex, which drew in enormous amounts of energy. Another difference is that I took three lifetimes to become like this; he managed it in three years. That's a big difference. The etheric body, or the subtle body, was constructed using enormous amounts of energy. If we had made it any more intense, it couldn't have retained a form; it was in that level of intensity. This was the peak of intensity that you could hold within the dimensions of a form. The Dhyanalinga is the highest possible being sitting there all the time, stable, steady, always the same way because he has no problems of a mental body, karmic body or physical body. He is always the same because he's just a subtle body.

In theory, it is possible to slowly construct a human physical body for the Dhyanalinga, and to create a being like that – somebody who will walk – if we're willing to work towards this. In theory, it is possible, but to get all the ingredients and all the forces together is an enormous job. Once we create a physical body, to sustain himself in such peak energies, he would have to do so many things. Above all, once you have a physical body, people's ability to experience what's beyond that will decrease, because once you see a person, you start judging – seeing what's right and wrong about him, what appeals to you or doesn't. All these judgments will take away your ability to experience that being. That's the huge difference. To create the subtle body itself took enormous amounts of work. If we want to create grosser dimensions of the body, we can create a very beautiful human being without him being born through a womb, because the subtle body is properly established. It would be like having Shiva back, alive, walking, but it wouldn't serve any purpose and would involve too much. It's very difficult to tell you logically or sensibly what this is all about.

This reminds me: when Vivekananda was a highly energetic and intense young boy, he was very skeptical and full of questions. He wanted to investigate everything. He had won many awards in debates and was always looking for more debates with whomever he met. When he met Ramakrishna he asked him, "You're always talking about God. What is the proof that there is God?" He was expecting some great explanation, which he obviously had the logic to break down, and he would defeat him. Ramakrishna said, "I am the proof." Vivekananda didn't expect this answer. He was expecting some explanation as to how there's a creation and a creator. So when Ramakrishna said, "I am the proof," he didn't know what to say. He sat there, bewildered. Ramakrishna thought this fellow's snooty logic was making him stupid. Vivekananda had enormous intensity, but he was missing the whole point. So Ramakrishna just took his foot and placed it on Vivekananda's chest. He lost all of his logic, and tears started flowing. Tears and Vivekananda were impossible. Logical people cannot shed a tear unless they're touched in their innermost depth. Tears just started flowing and then he said, "I'm very sorry I even asked you such a question."

Now, if you think logically, it seems impossible that there is no difference between the Dhyanalinga and me. Even if you have experienced the Dhyanalinga in some way for a moment, it still sounds absolutely egoistic for me to say this; but really, there's no difference. If you don't like it, I can't help it. Slowly you will see, as the days pass, I won't be interested in keeping up any façade for anybody's sake. We have done enough of that in order to bring about the necessary goodwill and understanding into people so that they could become receptive enough. We don't have to continue doing that for a lifetime. Those who are too logical and whose ability to live life is very much on the surface may fall off. I don't want them to fall off, but they may, because I am too blunt. It's all right. This is how it is.

When you go to the Dhyanalinga, just sit there – you don't have to believe or disbelieve anything. It's as if a good dinner is being served in front of you. You're not overly hungry nor do you dislike the food. Simply sit there, not trying to grab it. Just be willing, open, not making any judgments about the food in front of you. You must sit in front of the Dhyanalinga like that, not doing anything, but not putting your foot into the food either. Sit there with a certain willingness and openness; then you will see that this is not just a symbol. The Dhyanalinga is not just a stone standing there anymore. You will see it is like a living being in every way.

Somebody who doesn't have a physical, mental or karmic body, but only has a subtle body – spiritual or etheric body – can only touch you on that level. If we teach you Hatha Yoga, kriyas, or if we change your mental attitude through the programs, and you practice for some time, then you give it up, you will see, you will go back to square one. But once you're touched at the level of your etheric body, you can't get rid of it. Whether you live or die, it still goes with you. This is what initiation means. It's not just a bundle of instructions. The idea is to touch you on the level of your etheric body so that it can never be taken away, no matter what kind of life you live, or how ignorantly you live. The seed can't die; that's how it is put across. That's what an initiation means.

When you sit in front of a living Guru, you have many problems, judgments, likes and dislikes, because invariably you end up looking at his personality. People have left their Gurus for all kinds of frivolous things. This happened with J. Krishnamurti, a realized being and very wonderful man. There was a certain lady who was very close to him and deeply involved with his work. She was always around him and traveled to many places with him. Once when he was in Amsterdam, Holland, he went into a shop to buy a tie for himself. He was so meticulous about choosing a tie, because he was very conscious about everything and also what he wore. He could throw the tie away if he wanted to, but when he wears it, he wants it to be in a certain way. So he went into the shop and spent nearly four hours picking out one tie. He pulled out every tie in the shop, looked at it, put it on, and then said, "No." It took him four hours to select just one tie. This woman watched and watched and watched, and as minutes passed, in her mind his enlightenment receded. She thought a man who could be so concerned about what kind of tie he wears couldn't be Enlightened, and she left him. Many such stupid things are done because of your judgments.

People have left their Gurus for even more frivolous things. This is simply because, in your day-to-day life, you are deeply caught up with your own physical and mental bodies. What has happened within you on deeper dimensions is not in your moment-to-moment awareness. Certain moments you know this is the deepest thing that has happened to you in your life. The rest of the time your mind will argue and prove to you that it's not so. With Dhyanalinga, you don't have these problems because it doesn't carry a physical or mental body. If you experience him once, every time you sit, you will look up to him reverentially. If he had a physical body, one moment you would be looking up to him reverentially, the next moment you would be judging him and condemning him for something. It's bound to happen. So he has come with extra advantages.

Seeker: Sadhguru, why are there no rituals in the Dhyanalinga temple?

Sadhguru: Traditionally, rituals were made by understanding certain processes in the existence. They were created so that the place of ritual gathers a certain amount of energy, a certain amount of prana for people to benefit from. There are various types of rituals performed for different benefits that one can derive. There is a science to it. If it is performed properly – keeping the basic norms in the ritual and the performer, how he is and how competent he is – certain energy fields can be created, but these rituals would be meaningless in the space of Dhyanalinga, where the intensity of the energy is so dominant.

The presence of Dhyanalinga is very powerful in the form of energy. Performing any ritual would be absolutely meaningless in that kind of space, because Dhyanalinga has gone through *prana prathishta*. It is in the highest level of intensity that any form can be. If you intensify the energy beyond this, it's bound to become formless. When this level of intensity and this kind of energy is present, performing a ritual would be meaningless because rituals are of those dimensions which create a certain type of energy.

Dhyanalinga is manifested with all the seven chakras in place. The seven chakras represent the seven dimensions of life. It is a complete system of energy. Dhyanalinga is a complete system of energy that one can make use of on many levels of life. In a space like this, rituals would be of no significance and out of place.

Seeker: Sadhguru, then what do I do in the temple if I can't do pooja? For me, a temple and pooja go together. I will be lost in the temple without all this.

Sadhguru: Balu, I thought you were already lost! Now, maybe to find yourself you have to go sit there without your pooja business. As I already mentioned, when a person is in a state of offering, when he is becoming an offering, he's most receptive. All yogic practices were created in such a way that the practices are performed as an offering to the Guru. To get the best out of the temple, one should approach it the same way one does his yogic practices, by offering himself. When we impart yoga, the practices are always taught in such a way that they're more than just practices. They are more an offering to the Guru. This is a device, a way that makes you open and receptive. It is based on this that in our tradition, bowing down and other kinds of processes have been created. For example, if you take the first practice that most practitioners of yoga are doing in the morning, surya namaskar, the sun salutation, is not only a form of exercise and a way of balancing your system; it is also a way of offering yourself. It's a kind of worship using your whole body, and in the process of offering yourself, you become most receptive to whatever the early morning sun has to offer you, to whatever the day has to offer you. The best can be imbibed into you by making your whole system into an offering.

Definitely, the best way to go into a temple is to go with a sense of offering; not of offering something, not of offering something in return for something else, just making yourself into an offering. It would definitely help for a person to balance his system before he enters the temple. Right now, the bhramhacharis who are there can assist people who wish to go through a process of balancing their system in doing a few minutes of *nadi shuddhi* [1] before they enter the temple. The system then becomes more receptive for what's available there.

1 *nadi shuddhi* : referring to purification of the nadis through a certain yogic practice.

Being in the sphere of the Dhyanalinga, being in such an intense field of energy, is not a time for one to make requests. Whatever you may want, whatever you may seek from your mind is only a limited possibility. What's possible in this sphere is much bigger than what you could ever think of. So, if you trust that the Divine is of a higher intelligence than you, it's better to just make yourself an offering and allow the Divine to function through you, rather than you deciding what should happen. That's the reason why we're saying it's not a place of prayer. It's not a place for you to request, it's not a place for you to suggest, it's not the place for you to in any way direct the course of what should happen to you. Just allow it to happen to you; just allow the higher intelligence to function through your system.

Seeker: Okay Sadhguru, after listening to you my poojas seem to be disappearing into thin air, but only when people are satisfied on the material plane they can seek spirituality. And you also said this many times…

Sadhguru: Yes, Balu, we have to cater to your kind, too (laughs). Personally, I never catered to material well-being, blessing, this and that. Though the Dhyanalinga is consecrated mainly for spiritual well-being, it also has the other dimensions of life in it if you want to make use of it. The spiritual aspect is available every day, but other aspects are available on different days. For people who are seeking material well-being, Monday is the day. It's my hope that the days that are allotted for spiritual well-being will be crowded, but I fear that the day for material well-being may become overcrowded (laughs). I never wanted to cater to that, but right now people have a need. If they don't fulfill it, they will not grow. Only if it is fulfilled will they look for something else; otherwise they can't leave it. We can't force them to leave this need. Force will never work. Somehow, they have to come to a certain level of awareness, understanding or fulfillment. The Dhyanalinga is created so that it caters to everything in different ways. It's a very powerful situation. The Dhyanalinga will radiate different qualities on different days of the week by which one can derive various benefits.

Seeker: Sadhguru, I know that you might make fun of me for asking, but can you tell us more?

Sadhguru: To make you find yourself I am willing to do anything. Mondays are very important for the Shiva bhakthas, and they generally fast on that day. It is considered most conducive for people who want to make a spiritual beginning; it is the root of all growth and it brings awareness of the Divine in you. Earth being the *tathwa*[1] of this day, it stirs the spiritual energies in the most fundamental way and helps one transcend the limitations of food and sleep. It helps in fertility, childbirth and cleansing of the *doshas*[2] in the body and mind. It can release one from financial and emotional insecurity, and remove the fear of death. It firmly establishes one within the body and also in the world outside.

Water being the tathwa on Tuesdays gives you the fluidity to create your life the way you want it. It's helpful for those seeking purification. This is also supportive for procreation, imagination, intuition, mental stability and conjugal relationships. What Balu, you seem very excited; are we going to see you with Malathi on Tuesdays? (Laughs). And you can send your brood of three on Wednesdays; it's very beneficial for the health and well-being of children below four years of age. It creates a zest for life and aids in material well-being and general health, with fire being the tathwa. It also nurtures selflessness and self-confidence, and brings physical balance with a deep understanding of the body.

On Thursday, air being the tathwa, freedom becomes the way. It's an important day to seek the Divine. A meeting and a balance of the higher and lower is achieved. On this day, love and devotion, radiance and innocence are the way, and it's a very good day to shed karmic bondage.

Friday, space being the tathwa, will assist you to seek limitlessness and freedom. It is highly purifying for anyone suffering from any kind of poison or negative energies, curses or bad vibrations. It can improve memory, concentration, patience, self-confidence and synchronicity with nature. Your dependence on food and water can be reduced. We should be asking Raja to be here every Friday (laughs).

Balu: Looks like I have to be here for the whole week, Sadhguru!

Sadhguru: Wait, it is not over yet! Saturday is the *Mahatathwa*, beyond all duality. It can help you go beyond the five elements. The qualities of that day are peace and wisdom, and it's a very important day

1 *tathwa* : element, as in the five elements.

2 *doshas* : defect or blemish. Specifically refers to defects in the physical, mental or energy bodies.

for those seeking Realization. It leads to knowledge and enlightenment. You can become in tune with the Cosmic laws and become one with everything. Sunday is a celebration of life beyond all senses. It's the best day to receive the Guru's Grace, and it aids in breaking the illusion of the individual self.

Seeker: Sadhguru, are you saying I can receive the Guru's Grace by sitting in the temple?

Sadhguru: When you say Dhyanalinga, it is the highest manifestation of the Divine. It is like a living person, with all the seven chakras manifesting themselves at their peak. It is alive. It is not on the physical plane; it is on the level of the etheric body or the spiritual body. There's a whole body of a person in a very subtle way. It's definitely like a Guru, maybe not a physical Guru who speaks to you, but still a Guru. A Guru is not there to speak to you or to guide you on the physical level. Your relationships in the world are physical, mental or emotional, but the relationship with your Guru is such that he touches you in those dimensions where others cannot. Dhyanalinga definitely touches you in these dimensions, so it is definitely your Guru.

For you to make use of it as your Guru, a simple way is just to gaze at the Dhyanalinga for a few minutes and then sit with eyes closed, not trying to visualize, not trying to imagine, not trying to bring it back into your memory – that will happen by itself. We want to imprint the form of the Dhyanalinga within yourself, into your energy system, because it's not a physical form, it's an energy form. The stone Linga that you see was only used as scaffolding to create the energy form. It is the energy form that imprints itself on your system. It functions from within. Once you allow this to happen, it's always with you, guiding you, making things happen to you on deeper dimensions within you. See, you're also made of the same stuff, but in you it is dormant, almost absent. It is unable to find that level of intensity, because you are too stuck with your karmic substances – your physical, your mental and your pranic bodies. If you raise your pitch, you can also become like that, as intense and beautiful. So it definitely functions as your Guru, and for one who is into any spiritual sadhana, it's extremely useful. You can clearly experience this.

Seeker: I experienced *nadha aradhana* in the Dhyanalinga temple, which has been the most beautiful and moving experience of my life. Sadhguru, what is the importance of the offering of sounds?

Sadhguru: You should perceive this properly. In a sense, nadha aradhana is not doing anything in particular. The offering of sounds is not doing anything in terms of energy. The reason why it was brought in was because the energy of the Dhyanalinga can become so enormously powerful that people may feel too overwhelmed by it. So we started making sounds to ease it – not to increase it, but to ease it. If there was a huge movement of people coming to the temple, that would be handled by itself. Right now, on certain days we have about ten or fifteen thousand people, but on other days just a few hundred people. So many times of the day, and especially during the night, there's nobody moving around in the temple; it is still. In the stillness, the energy of the Dhyanalinga becomes overwhelming. When it is so overwhelming, when any situation is overwhelming, a natural reaction of a human being would be to close up. This is because humans spend their whole lives being concerned about their survival. If they enter a situation which is overwhelming, their defence mechanism just closes them up. They create a cocoon of protection that doesn't allow the external to enter. When people come to the Dhyanalinga, they tend to close themselves instead of opening themselves, because it's too overwhelming. So now we're just doing a nadha, or a sound. To listen to the sound, you open yourself. The moment you open yourself, the energies begin to work; it's just a trick. Every moment could be like that, but most people don't have that receptivity. If I just sit here, you won't be receptive to me. So I am talking; now you become receptive to me, but actually I can do more things to you when I'm not speaking than when I'm speaking, because the most significant aspect of my life is when I am not doing anything. The most significant aspect of me is when I am really not doing anything; that's when I am explosive.

Seeker: What do you mean by 'not doing anything', Sadhguru?

Sadhguru: There's a clear misunderstanding with people that if you do yoga, ultimately you won't do anything but just sit. If you're able to sit and not do anything, it doesn't mean you can't handle the other aspects of life. The main thing with non-doing is that even if you work twenty-four hours a day, you don't feel like you have done anything, okay? This is because you're not identified with your actions. You're just doing action as it's needed.

Seeker: Sadhguru, do I have to believe in Shiva to sit in the Dhyanalinga temple? Why the Shivalinga form?

Sadhguru: By creating the Dhyanalinga, we wanted to create a space where it is so intense that you don't need any belief system. You don't have to believe in Shiva, Rama,[1] or anything; simply come and sit there. If you're receptive, something else begins to happen to you. A new energy penetrates you. You can't help it. You don't need any belief. You just need to be open; that's all. Let's say a non-believer drives a car. Will it go? This is what you're asking, or if a non-believer sits here, will this light still make him see? The question is of that nature. It doesn't matter whether you're a believer or a non-believer. The moment you turn on the light, it is there for everybody. Believers don't get any extra light.

The Dhyanalinga becomes necessary when people in the society are slowly moving to a higher level of awareness. When people are not intense, pooja will do. To create a pooja Linga it doesn't take anything because the Linga is not important; even a stick or a stone will do. You can worship anything as a Linga, because what's there in the Linga is not important. For a bhaktha what's there is not the point; only his feeling is important. With the Dhyanalinga, it's not so. Even when you don't have any feeling, if you simply sit, it starts touching you in a different way. The whole science is about what you call as Shiva. You must understand this: the word 'Shiva' means 'that which is not', okay? Why we use Shiva and not some other form of God is because the other forms seem to be good people, and you can easily get attached to them. We use Shiva because it's very difficult to get attached to him. In Tamil Nadu, you have been told that you shouldn't keep Shiva's form in your house. He is the *Maheshwara*, but he has no space in your home; why? Maheshwara means he is beyond all gods; but then why does he have

1 Rama: the hero of the epic Ramayana, believed to be an incarnation of Lord Vishnu.

no space in your house? If he's there, his very form is such that all your attachments will get destroyed, and you don't want that. You have made big investments in your attachments, and even though they have brought you very painful dividends, you still can't throw them away.

These investments may melt away without you knowing what's happening. That's why they told you to banish Shiva from your house. Shiva means 'that which is not'. Everything that is there is nature, or creation, isn't it? Because you're stuck with the creation, problems have come. If you want to communicate with the Creator, you should go after that which is not there. Do you understand? So the Dhyanalinga is almost like trapping Shiva and keeping him fixed there. He doesn't come down easily. He demands his own price, in his own way. It's a very deep science. People who have come from the Himalayan trip can tell you about some places where, if you're open to it, the energy will take you over. When a place is charged with that kind of energy, spiritual growth becomes easy. Sadhana becomes very simple. If you have to pick up that much energy within your system by practices, it would take a very long time, but in the right kind of atmosphere, you can very easily generate the necessary energy.

Seeker: In the Indian culture, the Linga is referred to as a phallic symbol. In the same breath we also say that this is the highest manifestation of the Divine. Master, how do you explain this seeming contradiction?

Sadhguru: As I have already mentioned before, the first form, the primordial energy form, is in the shape of a Linga. The final form before dissolution is also a Linga. Now, in the Indian culture, this has been looked at in many ways. In India, Shiva is rarely represented with a face. He's mostly represented as a Linga. A Linga is a combination of the feminine and the masculine. Shiva is also seen as the destroyer. In no other culture can we find people worshipping the destroyer. To worship the source of destruction comes from a deep understanding. Not only that, only a culture with a very deep understanding of life would dare to symbolize Shiva, their God, their Mahadeva, in a form which could be seen as a phallus and still worship it. This Linga and *yoni,*[1] this symbolism is once again something that no other culture could have ever thought of. When the masculine and the feminine meet at the lowest level, it is known as sex.

---

1 *yoni*: feminine aspect of the Linga.

When the same masculine and feminine meet at the highest level, it signifies the union of Shiva and Shakthi. In this conjunction, *Shiva* is *rupa*, or form; Shakthi is Shoonya, or nothingness. Shiva is Purusha; *Shakthi* is *Prakrithi*, the undifferentiated force of nature. The Linga as the manifestation of the Shiva-Shakthi principle demonstrates the persistence of all pairs of opposites, and nothing can exist in this universe without its opposite or contrast.

Sex is based in the lowest chakra. When you talk about God, when you talk about Divinity, it is supposed to be the highest. Here, in India, the highest in life is represented by the lowest symbolism. When your energies are being dissipated on the level of Muladhara, then your energies are on the sexual level. This same energy, if it moves to the pinnacle, the Sahasrar, it becomes Enlightenment, becomes Realization; the same energy has taken the gross to the Divine. The whole process of evolution is just to make the same energies meet at the highest point instead of the lowest. Shiva is the meeting of this masculine and feminine at the Sahasrar. There's a snake wrapped around his neck with the hood open; that's a symbol which shows that the *Kundalini*[1] has reached the Sahasrar. The Shakthi has a tremendous urge to go and meet Shiva. He won't come down, so she has to go up and meet him. So those people who don't take the trouble of going up and meeting him will dissipate their energies at the Muladhara level, in the form of sex.

Seeker: At times, you have said that energy knows no discretion; it has no limit. Is it so for the Dhyanalinga too, Sadhguru?

Sadhguru: Energy has no discretion in the sense that you can make it function in many ways. Energy as such doesn't have discretion. This is why human nature has always been considered to be sacred, because it has a conscious discretion. With energy, we can create a certain fixed discretion; we can establish it in certain ways. For example, let us say you plant a neem seed in the earth. The seed

1 *Kundalini* : Cosmic energy which is depicted as a snake coiled at the base of the spine.

and the earth both have a discretion that it must grow only into a neem tree and bear only neem fruit. They have that much fixed discretion. If you're hungry and you want a mango, the neem tree can't produce one because it doesn't have that kind of discretion. Even if it has feelings towards you, it still can't have that discretion, because energy functions that way.

This is the reason why we have held human nature as the highest possibility. Human nature has conscious discretion. Everywhere else, energy just functions with a certain type of discretion, a fixed discretion. Similarly, the Dhyanalinga is also a very powerful energy and has an established sense of discretion, but no conscious discretion. If somebody comes with a particular desire, a particular need within him, depending upon how his energy is, accordingly the Dhyanalinga functions. Suppose there's a man who is longing for spiritual well-being, but today he's caught up in his present situation of life, and he desires to get more money. Now Dhyanalinga will only address that energy longing in him. What his basic energy is longing for, it will address only that. It won't address this moment's thought. It will only address that energy in the way it is longing. Suppose his longing is very deep about the material aspects of life, then Dhyanalinga will address that. This addressing is not conscious on the part of the Dhyanalinga. It's just a fixed discretion. This is how energy functions everywhere. This is why God has been described as *Nirguna* energy because he has no particular attributes of his own. He doesn't have conscious discretion. Energy is formless; that which creates is formless.

Seeker: I am still not clear, Sadhguru. If energy knows no discretion, how would it be if a person stands in front of the Dhyanalinga with a deep longing? Will the Dhyanalinga satisfy this longing, whatever it may be? Suppose there's a murderer standing there with a deep desire to murder somebody. What happens then? And suppose a drug addict or a sex maniac wants these things to happen more and more. How does this energy emanating from the Dhyanalinga function?

Sadhguru: As I have already said, you may believe many things about yourself as to who you are, but fundamentally you are a certain amount of life energy functioning in a certain way, with certain longings, certain limitations and a certain direction. The ultimate direction is common for everybody, but the immediate directions are many. What you call as 'myself' is just a certain amount of energy functioning in a certain way. So what we refer to as the Dhyanalinga is a certain energy form. It is just that it's a subtler, more intense or a higher level of energy manifestation, but this energy can only respond to whatever your energy situation is. If your energy situation is moving towards sickness, then it will move you towards health. If your energy situation is longing for something very deeply, then it will move to fulfill that.

On the level of your mind, if you're thinking about something, that thought is not addressed by the Dhyanalinga. That's why we're always saying, don't go there asking for something. Just sit there. Simply sit there without asking for anything or trying to do anything. If you simply sit there, whatever your deepest longing is – even if you're unconscious of that longing – that's what will be quenched and only that will bring peace and well-being to you. On the surface, what you long for today and find tomorrow is quite meaningless. There are deeper longings within you that have sprung from your karmic nature, of which you may not be aware. These are what the Dhyanalinga addresses. It does not address this moment's thought because it may not mean anything to you tomorrow. When I repeatedly said that Dhyanalinga is for your spiritual growth, what it means is that every human being, whatever the desire he nurtures within him, is only seeking expansion – unlimited expansion, the infinite. The Dhyanalinga addresses that. Energy is only functioning as energy; it only responds to the other energy situation. It doesn't know other dimensions or conscious discretion. Because of the multi-dimensional quality of the Dhyanalinga, an established discretion has been set.

Seeker: So the possibility is always there, Sadhguru, that the person whose very energies have become such that they're seeking material benefits will be satisfied. So the same can be true for these types of people – murderers, drug addicts, sex maniacs – if the longing is very strong. If the energy has no discretion then how does it function?

Sadhguru: Devi (laughs), you know very well that in India there are various kinds of deities. When people want to go to war, they invoke their gods and they believe their gods are with them, supporting them in killing and finding victory. Now, the gods are not responding to their killing. They're just responding to the deep longing of non-fulfillment within them. This empowers them in a certain way. How they use this is their discretion. Every kind of energy can be abused, and you can't even call it misuse.

The same electricity that is being used to light this place is also being used in the electric chair to kill someone. So it's not the question of electricity being good, bad, or supporting evil. That's not the point. Energy is just energy. Similarly, the Dhyanalinga addresses the deepest longing within you. Most of the time your deepest core isn't to kill. The deepest sphere of your energy is to seek fulfillment. Right now, you may believe that by getting this much money you may be fulfilled or by killing this person you may be fulfilled, but fundamentally the deepest aspect of your energy is seeking fulfillment. If somebody who's thinking, "If I kill my neighbor, I will be fulfilled," sits in the temple, when the energy of the Dhyanalinga functions within him, and brings real fulfillment, the person may lose the incentive to kill somebody. Only because somebody is so unfulfilled and believes that by killing he will become fulfilled, he wants to do that, but if he attains fulfillment just sitting in the Dhyanalinga, the need to take that action will go away in his life.

Seeker: Just now Sadhguru, you said that the warriors going to battle asked the gods to empower them and they were empowered. At that moment, at the deepest of their core, this is what they asked for and they got it. So in the same way, can it happen in the Dhyanalinga, too? Because the same way as electricity gives you light, it can also put you to death, so isn't the same true with the Dhyanalinga also?

Sadhguru: I said they *believe* their gods are with them and they fight the war. The war was won by those who fought the war intelligently, with valor and with other capabilities that were required. It's a huge psychological boost for them to believe that the gods are fighting with them, and it still is the major way it's being used today. Getting a psychological boost by believing that a god is with you will help you initially, but that's not going to affect the result of the war. The result of the war is not decided by whether your god is with you or not. It's decided by the way you fight and what happens there. The same goes for every action that we do.

When we say Dhyanalinga empowers you; when somebody wants to kill, there's such a deep sense of non-fulfillment that he believes that only by killing can he get fulfillment. If that unfulfilled state is taken away from him, the compulsion to kill may also be taken away. It's not that if a murderer comes to the Dhyanalinga, he won't commit a murder. That's not the point. At the same time, if he comes here, would the Dhyanalinga give him special powers to murder? No! It is the deep sense of non-fulfillment in him that will be definitely addressed. When it is addressed, there's a possibility that he may not get into such actions.

Seeker: This mud-and-brick structure, the dome, so earthy and yet so out-of-this-world, which houses the Dhyanalinga, I am wonder-struck by this as much as I am wonder-struck by you! So what is the recipe of these two, Sadhguru?

Sadhguru: Nathalie! You're asking for the recipe. The recipe of the dome I will give you, but mine I wish and hope that you would be able to grasp and digest! Architecturally, the temple is an engineering marvel. The elliptical dome that we built to house the Dhyanalinga is seventy-six feet in diameter and thirty-three feet high. No steel, no cement and no concrete were used; just brick and mud mortar stabilized with lime, sand, alum and herbal additives. It's the only structure like this on the planet right now. The simple technology used in this is that all the bricks are trying to fall down at the same time, but the way the dome is made, they can never fall. The nature of the design ensures a life of at least five thousand years for the dome. The Dhyanalinga has seven copper rings representing the seven chakras, and towers to a height of thirteen feet, nine inches. It's partially encased within the gowripeeta in the form of a seven-coiled snake. It's kept constantly wet to enable everyone to easily receive the energies emanating from it.

In terms of energy, in a way, the Dhyanalinga is a mixture, a concoction of pure awareness and madness, the peak of that, the highest mixture, a cocktail. In the future, if one day some realized beings who are very sensitive come to that place and access the Dhyanalinga the way it really is, they will go crazy with laughter. Because that is how it is created. It is so dead serious on one level, it is so ridiculous on the other level. It is pure awareness on one level and sheer madness on another. It was built like that, slowly. It is life-sustaining in one way. It is life-taking in another way. If people can really access the way the Dhyanalinga has been created, if they can really see it, they will just go crazy with laughter; but it's also the Dhyanalinga which doesn't allow me to go too crazy. Because I have taken this work upon myself, I have curtailed myself in many ways, learned all the tricks of the society, and played the normal game. Otherwise, they wouldn't have allowed the Dhyanalinga to happen.

This is a bond for me. This is my Guru's dream. Because I took it upon myself, it kept me going. If this wasn't there, you wouldn't have seen the same person. He would have been very different. It would have been very hard to digest him. That is how he would have been. Now he's very sane and straight; he knows all the ways, he knows all the tricks.

Afterword

When we embarked on the mission of compiling these monumental pages of intense interaction with Sadhguru, it was not without an element of mischief. Over the years, we had seen many people approach Sadhguru with questions. Questions of any and every kind: some casual and curious, some intense, profound, and burning; some cynical and skeptic, some mischievous and malicious. Yet, each received fittingly…

What inspired us most was the oft- repeated scene where multitudes came with their lives and inner energies knotted up and left with their faces and lives lit-up by just one sathsang. Then there were those who were stunned and stupefied, and kept coming back again and again, until a point arrived where they had no need to ask to know. All in all, it was always an intense process that witnessed the flowering of many, even those unwary questioners.

Sadhguru has often said he never answers the question, but always the questioner. His answers are never meant to edify the asker, but to unblock his inner energies so as to dissolve the question. With these pages we hoped to let loose a whirlwind upon the world that would suck, twist and turn people in large numbers in a tempestuous process of the Self.

To our surprise, at a Book reading Sathsang at the Yoga Center, shortly after the release of the first edition of this book, Sadhguru, who had concluded the earlier book *Encounter the Enlightened* by saying "The gloriousness of the written word is but the excreta of the deluded mind...", revealed that the mystical aspects of the current book were not just in the contents alone but in the form as well, making it a potent and formidable concoction. The written word herein was hence carefully crafted to function as a yantra, offering the reader keys to deeper dimensions of life.

In Sadhguru's own words:

> *When you labor through 500 pages of word, we want to provide you certain keys- keys to the Existence, opening a certain dimension of life which is not in normal access to people. If you are open to it, it will do things. But if we talk about it, then people try to use it in certain ways and it won't work.*
>
> *The only book where every part of it is a key is the* Yoga Sutras. *Every part of it – that's dangerous. That's very dangerous. That's why Pathanajali took enormous care in using the language in a particular way. His mastery of language is not just scholarly; his mastery of the language is something that is not normally considered human. Because of that kind of mastery over language, he dared to write the sutras in such a way that every part of it is like a yantra.*

Logically, they don't mean much, but experientially if you imbibe it, if you receive it, then it's an explosive possibility. There is a yantra involved in it. If you allow it, it is another big dimension opening up within you.

You don't have to read it; you don't have to know the language. You can do Braille on Yoga Sutras. *Even if you don't know Sanskrit language, you just touch it with your fingers; it will still do things to you. Some parts of Mystic's Musings – I won 't tell you which ones – are made like that, just to intrigue.*

Those parts, which need not necessarily emotionally and intellectually mean something to you, but when you read them, set forth a certain experience in you.

Probably a spoken book like this, a book that was spoken and not written – like Mystic's Musings – that too in English language, has never happened before. The language has never been used in this context. I don't think so. I have not seen any.

Hence, it our sincere hope that these musings from an unfathomable mystic transport you, in many ways, into the overwhelming sacred space of a Guru.

Isha Foundation

Isha Foundation is a non-religious, not-for-profit, public service organization, founded by Sadhguru which addresses all aspects of human well-being. From its powerful yoga programs for inner transformation to its inspiring projects for society and environment, Isha activities are designed to create an inclusive culture that is the basis for global harmony and progress. This approach has gained worldwide recognition and reflects in Isha Foundation's Special Consultative Status with the Economic and Social Council (ECOSOC) of the United Nations.

Supported by hundreds and thousands of active and dedicated volunteers in over 150 centers worldwide, the Foundation's activities serve as a thriving model for human empowerment and community revitalization throughout the world.

Isha Yoga Center

Isha Yoga Center, founded under the aegis of Isha Foundation, is located on 150 acres of lush land at the foothills of the Velliangiri Mountains that are part of a reserve forest with abundant wildlife. Created as a powerful *sthana* (a center for inner growth), this popular destination attracts people from all parts of the world. It is unique in its offering of all aspects of yoga - *gnana* (knowledge), *karma* (action), *kriya* (energy), and *bhakthi* (devotion) and revives the *Guru-shishya* paramapara (the traditional method of knowledge transfer from Master to disciple).

The Center houses the architecturally distinctive Spanda Hall and Garden, a 64,000 sq ft meditation hall and program facility that is the venue of many residential programs. Also located at the Center are the Dhyanalinga Yogic Temple, Theerthakund, Isha Rejuvenation Center, Isha Home School and Vanaprastha for families. Isha Yoga Center provides a supportive environment for people to shift to healthier lifestyles, improve their relationships, seek a higher level of self-fulfillment, and realize their full potential.

Dhyanalinga Yogic Temple

The Dhyanalinga is a powerful and unique energy form created by Sadhguru from the essence of yogic sciences. It is the first of its kind to be completed in over 2,000 years. The Dhyanalinga Yogic Temple is a meditative space that does not ascribe to any particular faith or belief system nor does it require any ritual, prayer, or worship.

Within this architectural marvel, a pillarless dome structure, the vibrational energies of the Dhyanalinga allow even those unaware of meditation to experience a deep state of meditativeness, revealing the essential nature of life.

Every week, thousands of people converge at this unique meditation center to seek out inner peace and silence. Focal point of Isha Yoga Center, the Dhyanalinga is rapidly gaining in its global reputation as being one of the most sought out places for meditation.

Isha Yoga Programs

Isha Yoga programs allow individuals to take tangible steps towards their inner growth. These programs are designed by Sadhguru as a rare opportunity for self-discovery under the guidance of a Realized Master.

An array of programs are conducted regularly by the Foundation worldwide. These programs establish optimal health and vitality, enhanced mental calm and clarity, and instill a deep sense of joy. They can be easily integrated into one's everyday life and embrace the human effort to reach inner awareness.

Action for Rural Rejuvenation

A long-time vision of Sadhguru, Action for Rural Rejuvenation (ARR) is a pioneering social outreach program. ARR aims at providing comprehensive and ongoing rural rehabilitation services, such as free medical relief, yoga programs, nature awareness programs, and community games to the heart of the rural communities of India, creating an opportunity for villagers, including women and children, to take responsibility for their own lives, and restore and reach their ultimate well-being. So far ARR has helped over 1.7 million people in more than 3,500 villages of South India (as at 07/2007).

Isha Vidhya

Isha Vidhya, an Isha Education Initiative, is committed to raise the level of education and literacy in rural India and help disadvantaged children realize their full potential. The project seeks to ensure quality education for children in rural areas in order to create equal opportunities for all to participate in and benefit from India's economic growth.

With English computer-based education, complemented by innovative methods for overall development and blossoming of each individual, Isha Vidhya Schools empower rural children to meet future challenges. Sadhguru's intention and goal is to start 206 English "Computer Friendly" Matriculation Schools within the next five to seven years, at least one in each taluk of Tamil Nadu. The schools are expected to benefit over 500,000 students when fully functional.

Project GreenHands

An inspiring ecological initiative of Isha Foundation, Project GreenHands seeks to prevent and reverse environmental degradation and enable sustainable living. The project aims to create 10% additional green cover in the state of Tamil Nadu in southern India. Drawing extensively on people's participation, 114 million trees will be planted state-wide by the year 2010.

As a first step, a mass tree planting marathon was held on 17 October 2006. It resulted in 852,587 saplings being planted in 6284 locations across 27 districts in the state, by over 256,289 volunteers in just one day, setting a Guinness World Record.

Isha Rejuvenation

Surrounded by thick forests, at the tranquil foothills of the Velliangiri Mountains, Isha Rejuvenation helps individuals to experience inner peace and the joy of a healthy body. It offers a unique and powerful combination of programs, scientifically designed by Sadhguru, to bring vibrancy and proper balance to one's life energies. The programs contain a synthesis of allopathic, ayurvedic and siddha treatments, and complementary therapies, along with the sublime wisdom of ancient Indian sciences and spirituality.

All the proceeds of Isha Rejuvenation contribute towards providing free health care to rural villagers, under the Action for Rural Rejuvenation initiative.

Isha Home School

Isha Home School aims at providing quality education in a challenging and stimulating home-like environment, designed specifically for the inner blossoming and the well-rounded development of the child.

With its prominent international faculty and Sadhguru's personal involvement in the curriculum, Isha Home School kindles the innate urge within a child to learn and know. Focus is given to inculcating life values and living skills whilst maintaining the rigor of academic excellence as per national and international standards. It does not propagate any particular religion, philosophy or ideology, but rather encourages the child to seek a deeper experience and inner understanding of the fundamentals of life.

Isha Business

Isha Business is a venture that aims to bring a touch of Isha into the homes and environment of the community, and ultimately enrich people's lives. This opportunity is made available through its numerous products and services, from architectural designs, construction, interior design, furniture design and manufacturing, landscape design, handicrafts and soft furnishings, to designer outfits from Isha Raiment.

All profits from this venture are used to serve the rural people of India, through Isha Foundation's Action for Rural Rejuvenation initiative.

How To Get To Isha Yoga Center

Isha Yoga Center is located 30 km west of Coimbatore, at the foothills of Velliangiri Mountains which are part of the Nilgiris Biosphere. Coimbatore, a major industrial city in South India, is well connected by air, rail and road. All major national airlines operate regular flights into Coimbatore from Chennai, Delhi, Mumbai and Bangalore. Train services are available from all the major cities in India. Regular bus and taxi services are also available from Coimbatore to Isha Yoga Center.

Visitors should contact Isha Yoga Center for availability and reservation of accommodation well in advance of arrival to the center, as they are generally fully booked.

abhisheka	Sprinkling or pouring of water, milk etc. Often used in religious, yogic or ceremonial contexts, particularly in tantric rituals. A ritual of empowerment also used to denote initiation in general.
adi	The first or fetal; primordial or embryonic, the beginning.
agnihotri yagna	Vedic ritual using the elemet of fire.
ajna chakra	Lit. command wheel. The sixth of seven major energy centers of the human body. Physically, located between the eyebrows, it is also known as the 'third eye'. Derives its name from the fact that it is an able receiver of the Guru. Hence, it is also called 'Guru-chakra'.
akka	Lit. sister – a respectful way of addressing a woman, in the Tamil language. Here, it refers to a saint popularly known as Akka Mahadevi – a 12th century queen in Karnataka, who renounced everything to go in search of Shiva, her celestial husband. Akka is known for her spiritual couplets, which are revered even today as classic poetry.
amavasya	The new moon – the darkest night of the month. The planetary positions of the earth and moon have long been made use of by spiritual seekers in India to enhance their spiritual practices.
amma	Mother – a reverential way of addressing a woman.
amman temple	Refers to temples which have feminine deities, a place of worship of Kali or Shakthi. Often used in occult practices.
Anahatha chakra	The fourth chakra, known as the 'lotus of the heart' or the 'heart chakra', it has been recognized as a special locus of the sacred within the human body. Celebrated as the seat of the Divine, the center is related to emotion and love.
ananda	Bliss, unconditional joy.
Ananda Tirtha	Gautama's elder cousin, who eventually became a disciple
anandamaya kosha	The innermost body or the bliss body.
anatma	Lit. the soul-less one.
anga	A limb, or aspect of yoga.

anga mardhana	Mardhana' means to kill – 'anga mardhana' means killing of the limbs of the body – the means to experience bodiless-ness.
annamaya kosha	Food-formed sheath or the gross body (sthula sharira), made up of the five gross elements or *bhoothas* – earth, wind, water, fire, ether – which are resolved again into their initial states after death.
aradhana	Lit. adoration.
Ardhanarishwara	Another manifestation of Shiva, beyond duality, in the form of half man and half woman.
Arjuna	Hero of the great epic Mahabharatha, to whom Krishna imparted the Divine message of the Bhagavad Gita.
asana	Lit. seat. Generally referring to yogic postures, or postures that lead one's energies to liberation. One of the eight limbs of yoga.
ashram	Sacred dwelling of spiritual seekers under the guidance of a Guru, or spiritual Master.
Ashtanga Yoga	The eight limbs, or disciplines, of yoga: yama, niyama, asana, pranayama, pratyahara, dharana, dhyana, and samadhi, as described by sage Patanjali.
AshtavakraAssam	One with eight deformities. An ancient spiritual master par excellence.
Atharva Veda	Indian state in the northeast region of the country.
Atma	Last of the four Vedas, that expounds the technology of using physical energy to one's advantage. Individual spirit, the supreme soul or Bhrahman.
baba	Lit. father. Common term used to address any elder, especially in the religious communities.
Badrinath	A holy place in the Himalayas – the holiest of shrines for the Vaishnavaites (followers of Lord Vishnu). This temple was established by Adi Shankara, one of the foremost scholars of South India, around the ninth century A.D.
Bala Krishna	Lord Krishna, as a child.
bala yogi	Child yogi. Refers to someone who attains Enlightenment at an early age and usually does not retain the body for long thereafter.
Bhaghirathi	River Ganga at its origin, where it melts its way out of the 'ice cave' called Gomukh.
Bhairava	A fierce form of Shiva.

bhaktha	A devotee.
bhakthi	Devotion. Refers to the spiritual path of Self-Realization through love and devotion. Intense desire and will for union with one's chosen deity.
Bhava Spandana program	"Bhava" means sensation or feeling. "Spandana" means to resonate, or emphatic vibration. This four day high intensity residential program is offered as a part of Isha Yoga programs, to experience levels of consciousness that take one to an experience beyond the limitations of body and mind.
Bhojpur	A town in Madhya Pradesh, Central India.
bhootha	Ghoul or a ghost. Also refers to the five primary elements of nature - earth, wind, fire, water, and ether.
Bhoothnath	Master of the five elements – another form of Shiva.
Bhramha	The Creator in the classic trinity of Hinduism, the other two gods being Vishnu and Shiva.
bhramhachari	'Bhraman' means divine and 'charya' means path. One who is on the path of the Divine. Usually refers to one who has formally been initiated into monkhood through a certain energy process.
bhramhacharini	A female bhramhachari.
bhramhacharya	The path of the divine. A life of celibacy and studentship on the path of spirituality moving towards the highest modifications of the senses. The first of four stages of life as per the *Varnashrama Dharma.*
Bhramhin	Member of the priestly Hindu caste, which is the highest in the Indian caste system.
bodhi tree	The sacred tree under which Buddha attained enlightenment.
Buddha	One who is above buddhi (intellect). Generally used to refer to Gautama the Buddha.
buddhi	Faculty of discrimination, analysis, logical and rational thought; the intellect.
budubuduku	A traditional gypsy soothsayer in Karnataka.
Chakra	Lit. wheel. Here, it refers to the seven junctions of nadis in the pranic body. Though seven major chakras are associated with the human body, there are a total of 114 chakras, of which two are outside the body. Each chakra has a distinct color, form, sound and quality associated with it.
Chakreshwara	One who has attained mastery over all the chakras.
Chamundi Hills	A famous pilgrimage center on the outskirts of Mysore, India, which was patronized by the Maharajas of Mysore. Also the place where Sadhguru had a deep experience of the Self at the age of twenty-five.

Coimbatore	A major industrial city in Tamil Nadu, a South Indian state.
Cudappah	A small town in the state of Andhra Pradesh, India.
deva	A generic term used to describe a class of celestial beings. Also referred to as God in Hindu mythology.
devi	Goddess, the feminine aspect of the Divine.
dhamma	Spiritual path set forth by Gautama, the Buddha.
dharana	Maintaining mental focus. One of the eight limbs of yoga.
dharma vada	Theological debate.
Dronacharya	The royal tutor of the Pandavas and Kauravas, princes of the Indian epic Mahabharatha.
dhyana	Meditative state. One of the eight limbs of yoga.
Dhyanalinga	A powerful energy form consecrated by Sadhguru exclusively for the purpose of meditation, at Isha Yoga Center.
dosha	Defect or blemish. Specifically refers to defects in the physical, mental or energy bodies.
Dostoevsky	A well known Russian author and philosopher who lived in the nineteenth century.
Dussehra	A traditional Indian festival of color, dance and music that lasts nine days, culminating in the celebration of the victory of good over evil. The celebration of this festival in Mysore attracts thousands of people from all over the country.
Essenes	Ancient Jewish sect of ascetics and mystics which existed from the second century B.C. to the second century A.D. A secret school of mysticism which is known to have aided Jesus during his life.
Forest Flower	Quarterly newsletter published by Isha Foundation.
gandharva	A class of celestial beings who are usually gifted with extraordinary talents such as music and dance.
Gandhi	Refers to Mahatma (great soul) Gandhi, an Indian nationalist leader, considered the father of the freedom movement. His peaceful, non-violent methods of protest were revolutionary, and brought an element of spirituality into public life.
Ganga	A major Indian River. Originating in the Himalayan glaciers, it is held extremely sacred. The legend says that it is a heavenly downpour routed through the locks of Shiva. Water from this river is carried to all parts of the country for religious rituals, including those of birth and death. It is also customary to cremate the dead on the banks of the river Ganga or immerse the bodies in the river itself.

Gangotri	Place of origin of the river Ganga in the Himalayas.
Gita	Lit. song. Refers to the *Bhagavad Gita*, one of the most sacred teachings of the Hindus. This central episode of the epic *Mahabharatha* is a dialogue between Lord Krishna and his chief disciple Arjuna, on the battlefields of the Kurukshetra. Krishna imparts to the warrior-prince Arjuna his knowledge on yoga, asceticism, dharma and the manifold spiritual path.
gnana	Knowledge, perception, discrimination. One of the four kinds of yogas.
Goa	An Indian state on the western coast known for its pristine beaches.
Gomukh	Lit. cow-face. A place in the upper Himalayas, the location where the glacier forms the river Ganga. The glaciatic form has melted in such a way that it resembles the face of a cow.
Goraknath	A great spiritual master who was one of the disciples of Matsyendranath. He is believed to have lived sometime between 900 and 1225 A.D.
gowripeeta	The base or the feminine portion of a linga.
grihastha	A householder, the second of the four stages of life as per the *Varnashrama* classification of the stages of life.
guna	Lit. quality or attribute. Refers to the three qualities of mind: tamas (inertia), rajas (activity) and sattwa (purity).
guru	Lit. dispeller of darkness. A spiritual Master; a Realized being who guides spiritual seekers towards liberation.
Guru pooja	Invoking the Grace of the Guru.
Hatha Yoga	Physical form of yoga involving different bodily postures and practices. Used as both a purificatory and preparatory step for meditation and higher dimensions of spiritual experience.
Himachal Pradesh	A North Indian State in the Himalayan region.
Himalayas	Lit. the abode of ice and snow. Range of mountains in the north of India which plays an important part in Indian history, mythology, art and spirituality.
Ida	One of the major pranic channels in the body. Located on the left side of the body, is feminine (intuitive) in nature.
Indra	The chief or the king of the Gods in Indian mythology.
Isha	Formless Divine energy. Also the name chosen by Sadhguru for the Foundation created to offer the ultimate spiritual possibility to all mankind.

Isha Yoga program	Refers to the foundation level program offered all over the world by Isha Yoga Center, wherein Yoga is experienced as a living science. Sadhguru's provocative questions compel one to look deeper within oneself and bring the necessary awareness to find experiential answers about life itself.
Ishwara	The supreme Lord. Another name of Shiva.
jala	Water, one of the five elements of nature.
Janaka	An ancient Indian King and an enlightened disciple of Sage Ashtavakra, Janaka was known for his extraordinary wisdom.
Jyotir Linga	Lingas of special importance to the Shaivaites. There are twelve Jyotir Lingas in India which are a part of the mandatory pilgrimage of any Shiva devotee.
Kaivalya	Aloneness, oneness or absolute. A state of ultimate oneness. Patanjali used the name Kaivalya to describe the goal and fulfillment of Yoga, the state of complete detachment from transmigration. Virtually synonymous with mukthi, Kaivalya is the highest condition, resulting in liberation.
Kaivalya padha	The fourth and final part of Patanjali's *Yoga Sutra*, dealing with absolution.
kaka pranayama	Kriya involving a sound like a bird call, which makes one less available to gravity. Taught in Isha Yoga programs.
Kali	A powerful goddess; a form of Shakthi in a fierce aspect. She signifies annihilation through which the seed of life emerges. She inspires terror and love at the same time.
Kanti Sarovar	A serene lake in the Himalayas, considered to be the abode of Shiva.
kapala-bhati	Lit. skull-brightening. A certain powerful yoga kriya which is taught in Isha Yoga basic programs.
karma	Refers to the volition with which one performs action. Karma is the mechanism by which relative existence maintains itself. Referring to past action, the cause of all bondage. That which binds one to the body and creates tendencies that rule one's life. Law of cause and effect.
karma kanda	The region of karma.
karma yoga	The path of selfless service.
Karthikeya	Another name for the second, six-faced son of Shiva. He has six faces.
kaya	Body or sheath.
kechari mudra	Mudra consisting of turning the tongue backwards so that the 'nectar' flowing down from the Sahasrar, after the rise of Kundalini, is arrested.

Kedar	Short for Kedarnath - a pilgrimage place in the Himalayas.
khanda	Region.
Kaanphat	Lit. torn ear. A spiritual sect in Northern India, who are so called because of their tradition of piercing their ears.
kosha	Lit. sheath, vessel, layer.
Krishna	Divine incarnation of Lord Vishnu, historically over 3500 years ago, Krishna is one of the most popular gods of the Hindu pantheon. A Yadava prince and the central character of the epic *Mahabharatha*, His discourse to his chief disciple Arjuna in the form of the *Bhagavad Gita* is the most sacred of Hindu scriptures.
Krishnamurti, Jiddu	Twentieth century spiritual Master of great repute.
kriya	Lit. act, rite. Refers to a certain class of yogic practices. Inward action as opposed to karma, or external action.
krodha	Anger, aversion.
Kukkarahalli	A beautiful lake at the Mysore university that has been an inspiration for many poets and writers.
Kumara Parvat	A mountain peak in the Western Ghats - a powerful spiritual destination. Samadhi of Subramanya the six faced yogi, son of Shiva.
kumbha	An earthen pot. Storage or fullness.
Kumbha Mela	A major spiritual and religious festival on the banks of river Ganga. During this time millions of spiritual aspirants converge on the banks of the river Ganga and take a ceremonial dip. A nexus of cosmic energy every twelve years, celebrated at Allahabad and other places in India by a gathering of sages and mystics.
kumbhaka	Breath retention during yogic practice, especially in the practice of pranayama.
kumkum	Vermilion or red powder made of turmeric and lime worn by the Hindus at the point of the third eye on the forehead.
Kundalini	Lit. serpent power. Cosmic energy which is depicted as a snake coiled at the base of the spine (Muladhara chakra) and that eventually, through the practice of yoga, rises up the Sushumna nadi. As it rises, the Kundalini awakens each successive chakra, until it reaches the Sahasrar. The manifested Kundalini becomes Kula, the all-transcending light of consciousness.
laddu	A popular Indian sweet, in the form of lemon-sized balls.

lakh	One hundred thousand in the Indian number system.
Linga	Lit. the first form; the primordial form. An energy form consecrated for worship, generally associated with Lord Shiva.
maha	An adjective or prefix meaning great, mighty, powerful, lofty, noble.
Mahabharatha	One of India's great national epics, which revolves around the conflict between two royal families, the Pandavas and Kauravas, in the great battle of Kurukshetra, approximately 1424 B.C. The plot illustrates simple truths and ethical principles.
Mahadeva	Great God, a common epithet for Shiva.
Mahanadi	Great goddess, a common epithet for Parvathi, the consort of Shiva.
Mahadevi	A major Indian river flowing through central India, known for its devastating floods.
Mahaparinibbana	Buddhist term for Mahasamadhi, or Nirvana, the complete dissolution of the Self, the ultimate goal of spiritual seekers.
Maharaj	Lit. great king, a respectful form of address for an Indian monarch or spiritual leader.
Maharishi	Great seer, a title of respect for an adept *yogi*.
Mahasamadhi	Complete dissolution of the Self also known as Nirvana, and Mahaparinibbana in other spiritual traditions. The dropping of the physical body in full awareness.
Mahashivarathri	An important festival in India, celebrated on the night before the new moon in the month of Magha, or February-March, each year. On this night spiritual seekers observe an all-night vigil filled with chanting and meditation, keeping their spines upright to support the upsurge of spiritual energy. At Isha, this night is colorfully celebrated in the presence of Sadhguru, drawing thousands of meditators from all over the world.
mahatma	Lit. great soul. Title of respect given to people held in high esteem, especially saints.
Maheshwara	The Great Lord, another name of Shiva, the destroyer in the classic triad of Hinduism, the other two gods being Bhramha and Vishnu.
Mahishasura Mardhana	The killing of a certain asura or demon in Indian mythology.
mala	Garland or necklace.
mandala	Refers to a region, an area within the body or the cosmos. Also represents consecrated space and is thought to be the body of one's chosen deity. The mandala is used to worship that deity and, through

complex visualization practices, to become one with it. Also refers to the physiognomic cycle, a time period of forty days, the natural period of many physiological processes in the body.

Manipuraka chakra	The third chakra, located a little below the navel. It provides the whole body with the vital energy needed for survival.
mantra	A sound, syllable, word or phrase endowed with special power. Mantras are most effective on the path of liberation when given by the preceptor through initiation.
mantric	Of mantra; one who is an adept in the use of mantras.
Matsyendranath	Lit. Lord of the Fish. A yogi of celestial proportions who lived around the tenth century A.D. The Guru of Goraknath, he is believed to have been an incarnation of Shiva himself.
maya	Delusion, the veil of illusion which conceals one's true nature, or conceals reality. It is used in contrast with the absolute reality.
mela	A large, colorful festival.
Mirabai	A Rajput princess of the medieval period who, intoxicated by her devotion for Lord Krishna, spent most of her life as a wandering saint, singing praises of the Lord. A poetess and mystic, her life story and bhajans are extremely popular even today.
Mizoram	An Indian state in the north-eastern region.
mukthi	Release, liberation, final absolution of the Self from the chain of death and rebirth. The highest goal of all spiritual seekers.
muladhara chakra	The first chakra, the psychoenergetic chakra located at the perineum. Source of the central channel (Sushumna-nadi) of the life force.
nadha	Sound, tone, vibration, music.
nadi	Channel through which the life force, or prana, flows in the energy body. There are 72,000 nadis interconnecting the chakras. The three main nadis are named Ida, Pingala, and Sushumna.
naga	Lit. serpent. Symbol of the Kundalini coiled at the base of the spine; one of the secondary types of life forces (prana).
Naga Babas	People belonging to a certain spiritual sect in North India, who are known to wander naked in the Himalayas with just vibhuthi smeared on the body, even during the coldest winter seasons.
naga dosha	Condition in which a diembodied snake possesses a human being.

Namaskar Traditional salutation which acknowledges the divinity within a person.

naraka Equivalent to the Western term Hell. Nether world.

Naren Childhood name of Swami Vivekananda.

Nari Woman.

neem A common deciduous evergreen tree (Azadirachta indica) which grows in India, known for its extremely bitter leaves, fruits and flowers. Used extensively for its innumerable medicinal qualities, neem is sometimes called 'the village pharmacy'. Over 100 pharmacologically active substances have been identified in this plant.

nethi Lit. 'not this'. A way of cleansing oneself of illusions or wrong identities.

Nilgiri Lit. blue peaks. Refers to a certain hilly district located north of Coimbatore, known for its rich wildlife.

Nirguna Devoid of any quality, untainted and beyond duality.

Nirmana-kaya A created body. Adept yogis are known to have created and possessed physical bodies for themselves to fulfill certain special purposes.

Nischala Unshakeable, unwavering.

Nishkarma Karmically unaffected by one's actions.

Nityananda, Swami A reclusive South Indian yogi and an extraordinary mystic who lived in the twentieth century and spent the later part of his life near Mumbai in Maharashtra. The Guru of many disciples, including Swami Muktananda.

ojas Subtle energy.

Orissa An Indian state on the East coast.

Palani A South Indian town that is famous for its Murugan (son of Shiva) temple.

pancha bhootha The five primary elements of nature - earth, wind, fire, water, and ether.

Paramahamsa Lit. supreme swan. An honorific term applied to an adept who enjoys liberation or Enlightenment.

parikrama Outer periphery of a temple.

Parvathi One of the many names for the Universal Mother, and consort of Shiva.

Patanjali Lit. one who fell (pat) into the palm (anjali). Refers to an ancient spiritual Master of extraordinary understanding, considered the father of yogic sciences. Believed to be an incarnation of Ananta, or Shesha, the thousand-headed ruler of the serpent race, Patanjali is best known for his work Yoga Sutras. The Yoga Sutras have been disclosed in a manner that cannot be understood by a superficial perusal of the text. Rather, it has been attributed the quality of being an encrypted code intended for the spiritual Masters who have the necessary understanding to properly impart the veiled practices.

peyi-pishachi A phrase used to denote ghosts and spirits.

Pindari A community of bandits.

Pingala One of the major pranic channels of the body. Located on the right side of the body, it is masculine in nature

Pongal A South Indian delicacy made of boiled rice, gram and pepper corns. Also, a very popular Tamil festival. It marks the change in the tilt in the Earth's axis of rotation.

Pooja Worship, a Vedic ritual for the invocation of Divine energy and Grace.

Prakrithi The feminine aspect of life. Refers to Nature or Creation.

prana Fundamental life force; vital energy.

pranamayakosha The energy sheath or body.

pranayama A powerful yogic practice that uses certain breathing techniques to generate and direct the flow of prana in the human body.

pranic Of prana.

prarabdha The karma allotted for this lifetime.

prasada Blessed food.

Prathishta Process of consecration or energizing an object with Divine energies. These processes are mainly of two kinds - *mantra prathishta*, through chanting of appropriate mantras and performing of rituals and *prana prathishta*, through a direct process involving the consecrator's own prana shakthi - life energies.

pratibha Lit. luster. One who has the needed qualities for initiation or Enlightenment.

pretha A kind of ghost or spirit.

pungai tree Pongamia pinnata. A tropical medicinal tree native to India, known for its shade giving and oxygen generating capabilities. The oil of the pongam seeds is traditionally used in oil lamps.

purana Mythological texts.

purusha	The masculine aspect of life. Also refers to man.
Raigarh	A town in the Central Indian state of Madhya Pradesh.
Rajasthan	Indian State in the western region, known for its desert terrain.
Rama	The hero of the epic Ramayana, believed to be an incarnation of Lord Vishnu.
Ramakrishna Paramahamsa	A mid-nineteenth century spiritual Master who lived mostly in Calcutta. A devotee of Goddess Kali, he frequently went into ecstatic states of samadhi. One of his best-known disciples is Swami Vivekananda, who established and propagated the Ramakrishna Order, which has a world wide following today.
Ramana Maharshi	Early twentieth century spiritual Master who lived in the hills of Tiruvanamalai near Chennai, in South India. His teachings revolve around self-inquiry. He is believed to have enlightened not only humans, but also a cow and a crow.
Ramanashram	An ashram located in Tiruvanamalai, established by Ramana Maharshi.
Rameshwaram	A sacred coastal town in South India, the closest point in India to the neighboring country, Sri Lanka. Figures in the epic Ramayana, where Rama built a bridge from India to Sri Lanka to enable his army to cross the ocean.
rasa	Lit. juice, the essence.
rudhraksha	Sacred beads. Seeds of a tree (glaeocarpus ganitrus Roxb) found mostly in the Himalayan region. According to the legend, a tear from Lord Shiva fell to Earth and from it grew the Rudhraksha tree. Known to have many medicinal and transcendental qualities, a rudhraksha mala is one of the few possessions of an Indian spiritual seeker.
sadhaka	A spiritual seeker who has undertaken spiritual disciplines, usually under the guidance of a master.
sadhana	Spiritual practices which are used as a means to realization.
Sadhananda	Lit. the one forever in bliss. One of the names of Shiva.
sadhguru	A spiritual teacher who is Enlightened, or has Realized the Self, whose knowledge or realization comes from within rather than from any teachings learned outside.
sadhu	An accomplished spiritual seeker. Sadhus usually have no fixed abode and travel from one place to another, most often living on alms. There are countless sadhus on the roads, byways, mountains, riverbanks and caves of India who, by their very existence, have a profound effect on the consciousness of the world.

Sahasrar chakra	Lit. thousand-spoked wheel. The seventh and highest chakra of the human system corresponding to the crown of the head.
sakshi	Lit. witness, a common way of describing the Self. Witness consciousness.
samadhi	Deep state of equanimity; one of the eight limbs of yoga. Greatly celebrated in the lore, experience of samadhi is immensely therapeutic and deeply transformative in nature.
Sambalpur	A small town in the state of Orissa, India.
samsara	The world, the existence, the domain of karma, protracted delusion of the mind. The cycle of birth, death, and rebirth.
samskara	Ritual, in the general sense. Denotes rites such as the birth ceremony, tonsure, marriage, cremation, etc. In yoga, it stands for the indelible imprints in the subconscious left behind by our daily experiences.
Samyama	A confluence of the states of dharana, dhyana and samadhi. Here, it refers to the eight-day meditation program conducted by Sadhguru, where one is transported into explosive states of meditativeness. This program is an opportunity to shed lifetimes of karma and experience deep states of meditativeness and samadhi.
sanchita karma	The total accumulated karma of a person.
Sangamitra	The daughter of the great king Ashoka and a disciple of Buddha.
sankalpa	Resolve.
Sanskrit	An ancient Indian language specially designed to suit expressions and transmission of the spiritual experience.
sanyas	On the path of spirituality, the fourth of the four stages of life as per the *Varnashrama Dharma*. The spontaneous withdrawal from the world in search of Self Realization.
sanyasi	An ascetic, a renunciate. One who has irrevocably renounced worldly possessions and relationships to seek Divine awakening, Self Realization.
sathsang	Lit. in the company of Truth; a congregation of seekers.
shaiva	Lit. of Shiva; worshipper of Shiva.
Shakthi	Lit. power. Divine consort of Shiva. The Creation is envisioned as a play of Shiva and Shakthi which symbolizes the duality of existence, or the Yin and Yang.
shakti moola	Energy source.

Shambho	Another name for Shiva, which denotes his loving nature.
Shankara	Lit. the benevolent; one of the many names of Shiva. Also refers to Adi Shankaracharya, the celebrated ninth century teacher of Advaita Vedanta and the founder of neo-monastic orders. In his life of thirty-two years, he traveled several times throughout India and was responsible for the renaissance of the Hindu tradition.
Shankaran Pillai	Refers to the hero in many of Sadhguru's jokes and anecdotes. He is usually a frail man whose idiocies are typical of the common man.
Shanmugha	Lit. six faced; one of the sons of Shiva.
Sharada Devi	Wife of Shri Ramakrishna Paramahamsa.
shavasana	Lit. corpse posture. One of the over six hundred asanas in the classical yogic tradition. Practiced intermittently between other asanas, it is known for its rejuvenating effect on the system.
shishya	Lit. pupil or disciple. One who has submitted himself to a teacher or a Guru.
Shiva	Lit. that which is not. The Great Lord; the Destroyer in the trinity.
Shiva linga	Symbol of Shiva traditionally used in worship.
Shivayogi	A name borne by Sadhguru in one of his previous lifetimes.
Shoonya	Lit. emptiness. An effortless process of conscious non-doing, Shoonya meditation is an extremely powerful and unique form of meditation taught by Sadhguru in a live form in the Isha Yoga programs.
Shrimath	Short for Shrimath, a respectful title for a man.
shuddhi	Lit. purification A basic component of spiritual life.
shudra	Member of the fourth and lowest Hindu caste, that of menial laborers.
siddha	One who has attained perfection or mastery over a certain mystical aspect of life.
siddhi	Power; paranormal or supernormal accomplishment.
smaran	Remembrance, usually, of the Divine. One of the aspects of bhakthi yoga.
spandana	To resonate; empathic vibration.
Subramanya	Son of Shiva. Also refers to Kukke Subramanya, a town at the Foothills of Kumara Parvat, in the coastal region of Karnataka state.
Suka	A well known sage of the yogic lore.

sukha pranayama	A yogic practice of balancing the prana in the Ida and the Pingala nadis.
Surya	The sun.
Sushumna	The central channel in the energy body which conducts the Kundalini, or spiritual force.
Swadisthana chakra	Lit. abode of the self, the second of the seven chakras of the human body. Situated just above the genitalia.
swami	He who knows or is master of himself. A respectful title for a Hindu monk, usually a sanyasi, an initiate dedicated wholly to spiritual life.
tantra	The science of using mantra, the sound, and yantra, the form. Refers to an esoteric Indian spiritual tradition.
tantric	Of Tantra; a practitioner of Tantra.
Tapovan	A place above Gomukh, on the banks of Gangotri, the glaciatic origin of the river Ganga.
tathwa	Element, as in the five elements; principle or philosophy.
Thai Poosam	An important festival held on the day of pushya nakshatra of the Tamil month of Thai (near the full moon day of January-February). Celebrated with great intensity and fervor, it is a day on which many South Indian sages have chosen to leave their body.
thali	A large dinner plate.
Thiruvanaikaval	A town near Trichy in South India.
turya	Beyond the three states of waking, dreaming, and sleeping. A transcendental state of awareness and bliss.
Ujjain	The capital of the ancient kingdom of Magadh and one of the seven sacred Hindu cities. Also a great center of learning and scholarly pursuits. Located in present day Madhya Pradesh.
Upanishads	Sacred texts in the Hindu culture.
vada	A popular south Indian savory made of ground lentils and deep fried.
vaidhya	Traditional doctor; also refers to traditional system of medicine.
vajrasana	Lit. diamond posture. One of the dynamic yogic postures, through which the practitioner imbibes the hardness and the brilliance of a diamond.
Vajreshwari	A place in the state of Maharashtra.

Vanashree	Lit. the deity of the Forest. Name of the feminine deity in the form of a tree at the Dhyanalinga temple.
vasana	Tendencies or desire; subliminal trait left behind in the mind by action and desire.
Veda	Refers to the oldest portion of the Hindu scriptures.
Vedanta	Lit. end of perceivable knowledge; the philosophy or teachings of the Vedas.
vibhuthi	Sacred, consecrated ash. Applied to different parts of the body, makes one more sensitive to subtle life forces. Application to the upper chakras activates the chakras and makes them more receptive. Some sects of Shaivites also smear vibhuthi all over the body to sensitize the system and ward off cold.
Vishuddhi	One of the seven chakras, is the center of power and vision. Located at the pit of the throat.
vishwa rupa darshana	An experience of the vastness of the existence. Also, a rare Cosmic Vision of the Master granted by the Master to the deserving disciple.
Vivekananda	The best known of the disciples of Ramakrishna Paramahamsa, Vivekananda is often considered as a role model for Indian youth.
Vyasa	An ancient sage with legendary powers of vision, one who documented the epic *Mahabharatha*.
yagna	Sacrifice, one of the main pillars of the Vedic ritual system.
yaksha	Celestial disembodied beings who are believed to inhabit secluded places.
Yama	The Lord of Death, the ruler of the nether world. Riding a buffalo, his vehicle, a visit from Yama means the time of death for a person has come. Also refers to the first limb of Yoga, used along with the second limb, niyama, to codify the 'do's and don'ts' of Yoga.
yatra	Travel, journey, pilgrimage.
yogini	A female practitioner of Yoga.
yoni	Lit. the source, origin. Refers to the female genitalia.

Index